OFFICE 2016
Simplified®

WITHDRAWN

by Elaine Marmel

isual

OFFICE 2016 SIMPLIFIED®

Published by
John Wiley & Sons, Inc.
10475 Crosspoint Boulevard
Indianapolis, IN 46256

www.wiley.com

Published simultaneously in Canada

Wiley publishes in a variety of print and electronic formats and by print-on-demand. Some material included with standard print versions of this book may not be included in e-books or in print-on-demand. If this book refers to media such as a CD or DVD that is not included in the version you purchased, you may download this material at http://booksupport.wiley.com. For more information about Wiley products, visit www.wiley.com.

Library of Congress Control Number: 2015950484

ISBN: 978-1-119-07474-8 (pbk); ISBN: 978-1-119-07475-5 (ebk); ISBN: 978-1-119-07494-6 (ebk)

Manufactured in the United States of America

10 9 8 7 6 5 4 3 2 1

Trademark Acknowledgments

Contact Us

For general information on our other products and services, please contact our Customer Care Department within the U.S. at 877-762-2974, outside the U.S. at 317-572-3993, or fax 317-572-4002.

For technical support, please visit www.wiley.com/techsupport.

Media Credits

Border Collie image: Photo by Paul Englefield/CC-BY-SA. Pages 28, 35, 362.

Boxer image: Photo by Donn Dobkin, Just a Moment Photography, from M. Book/CC-BY-SA. Pages 38-39.

Eagle image: www.public-domain-image.com/free_images/fauna-animals/birds/eagle-birds-images/bald-eagle-pictures. Pages 60, 62-63, 114-115.

Golden Retriever image: Photo by Donn Dobkin, Just a Moment Photography, from M. Book/CC-BY-SA. Pages 356-357.

National Archives video: www.archives.gov/press/press-releases/2012/nr12-67.html. Page 93.

Sales

Contact Wiley
at (877) 762-2974 or
fax (317) 572-4002.

Credits

Acquisitions Editor
Aaron Black

Project Editor
Sarah Hellert

Technical Editor
Vince Averello

Copy Editor
Scott Tullis

Production Editor
Barath Kumar Rajasekaran

Manager, Content Development & Assembly
Mary Beth Wakefield

Vice President, Professional Technology Strategy
Barry Pruett

About the Author

Elaine Marmel is President of Marmel Enterprises, LLC, an organization that specializes in technical writing and software training. Elaine has an MBA from Cornell University and worked on projects to build financial management systems for New York City and Washington, D.C., and train more than 600 employees to use these systems. This experience provided the foundation for Marmel Enterprises, LLC to help small businesses manage the project of implementing a computerized accounting system.

Elaine spends most of her time writing; she has authored and co-authored more than 90 books about Microsoft Excel, Microsoft Word, Microsoft Project, QuickBooks, Peachtree, Quicken for Windows, Quicken for DOS, Microsoft Word for the Mac, Microsoft Windows, 1-2-3 for Windows, and Lotus Notes. From 1994 to 2006, she also was the contributing editor to monthly publications *Inside Peachtree* and *Inside QuickBooks*.

Elaine left her native Chicago for the warmer climes of Arizona (by way of Cincinnati, OH; Jerusalem, Israel; Ithaca, NY; Washington, D.C., and Tampa, FL), where she basks in the sun with her PC, her cross-stitch projects, and her dog Jack.

Author's Acknowledgments

Because a book is not just the work of the author, I'd like to acknowledge and thank all the folks who made this book possible. Thanks to Aaron Black for the opportunity to write this book. Thank you, Donna Baker, for doing a great job to make sure that I "told no lies." Thank you, Scott Tullis, for making sure I was understandable and grammatically correct — it's always a pleasure to work with you. And, thank you, Sarah Hellert, for managing all the players and manuscript elements involved in this book; that's a big job, and you're up to the task.

How to Use This Book

Who This Book Is For

This book is for the reader who has never used this particular technology or software application. It is also for readers who want to expand their knowledge.

The Conventions in This Book

❶ Steps

This book uses a step-by-step format to guide you easily through each task. Numbered steps are actions you must do; bulleted steps clarify a point, step, or optional feature; and indented steps give you the result.

❷ Notes

Notes give additional information — special conditions that may occur during an operation, a situation that you want to avoid, or a cross reference to a related area of the book.

❸ Icons and Buttons

Icons and buttons show you exactly what you need to click to perform a step.

❹ Simplify It

These tips offer additional information, including warnings and shortcuts.

❺ Bold

Bold type shows command names, options, and text or numbers you must type.

❻ Italics

Italic type introduces and defines a new term.

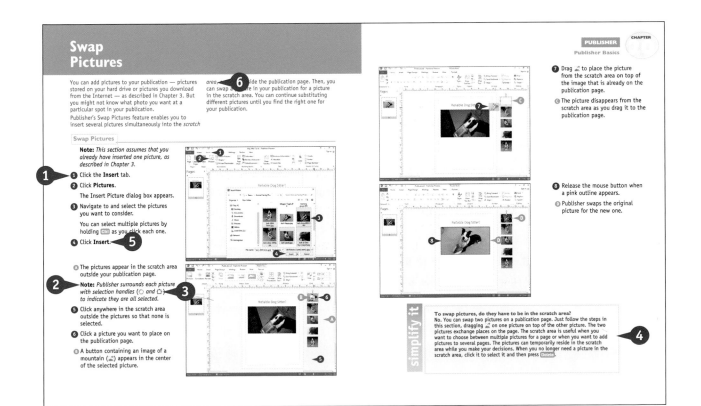

Table of Contents

OFFICE FEATURES

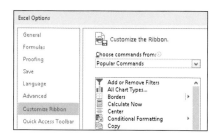

CHAPTER 5

Adding Text

CHAPTER 6

Formatting Text

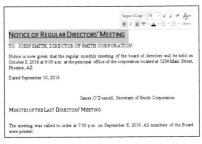

CHAPTER 7

Adding Extra Touches

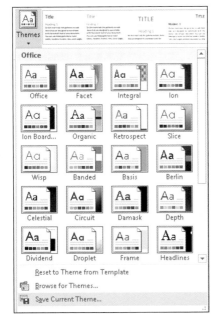

Table of Contents

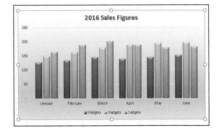

Table of Contents

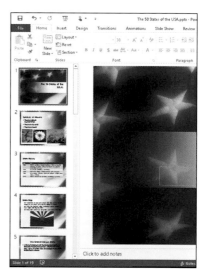

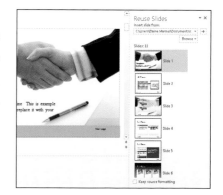

Database Basics

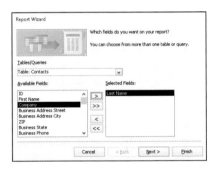

Adding, Finding, and Querying Data

Table of Contents

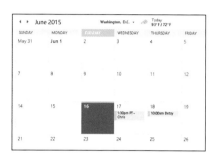
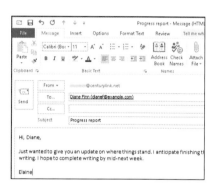

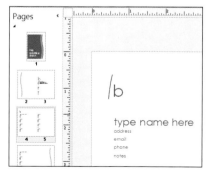

Fine-Tuning a Publication

ONENOTE

Taking Notes with OneNote

Organizing and Sharing Notes

PART I

Office Features

The Office 2016 applications share a common look and feel. You can find many of the same features in each program, such as the Ribbon, Quick Access Toolbar, program window controls, and the File tab. Many of the tasks you perform, such as creating and working with files, share the same processes and features throughout the Office suite.

Even the techniques you use to work with graphic elements, such as moving and resizing them, do not change from one Office application to the next. In this part, you learn how to navigate the common Office features and basic tasks.

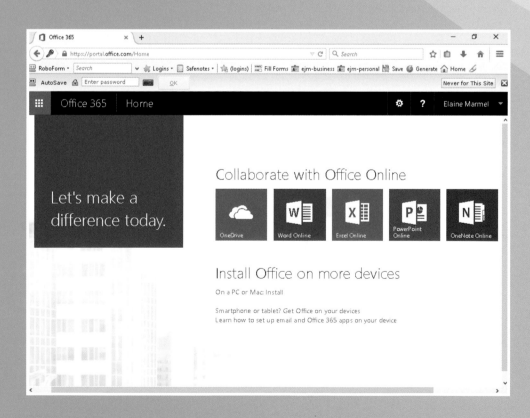

Start and Exit Office Applications

Office 2016 runs on a 1-gigahertz (GHz) or faster x86- or x64-bit processor with 1 or 2 gigabytes of RAM, based on your processor speed. Your system must be running Windows 7, Windows 8, Windows 10, Windows Server 2008 R2, or Windows Server 2012.

This section uses Access to demonstrate how to open a program from Windows 10. Once an Office program opens, its Start screen appears, helping you to find a document you recently worked on or to start a new document. For other ways to open or start a new document, see Chapter 2.

Start and Exit Office Applications

1 Click in the search box.

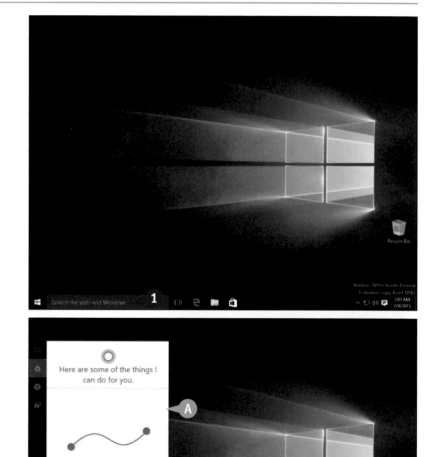

A The message box introducing Cortana appears.

Note: *Cortana is the Windows 10 search assistant. Click **Learn more** to read about Cortana.*

② Start typing the name of the program; for this example, type **Access**.

Ⓑ A list of choices appears that match the letters you typed.

③ Click the choice matching the program you want to open.

The program opens and displays its Start screen, which helps you open new or existing documents; see Chapter 2 for other ways to open documents.

Ⓒ You can use this panel to open an existing document.

Ⓓ You can use this area to start a new document.

Ⓔ This area indicates whether you have signed in to your Office 365 subscription.

Note: *See Chapter 4 for details about signing in to Office 365.*

Ⓕ To exit from the program, click the **Close** button (✕).

Note: *If you do not see the **Close** button (✕), slide the mouse (⇖) into the upper right corner of the screen until it appears.*

Can I create a shortcut to open an Office application?
You can, but pinning the program to the Windows taskbar or Start menu is easier. Follow Steps **1** and **2** in this section. Then, right-click the program name in the list. From the menu that appears, click **Pin to taskbar** or **Pin to Start**. Windows 10 pins the program to the Windows taskbar or the Start menu. To open the program, click the program's button on the taskbar or Start menu. Programs pinned to the Start menu appear on the right side of the menu as tiles.

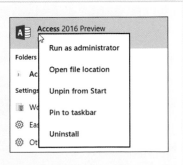

Navigate the Program Windows

All Office programs share a common appearance and many of the same features, and when you learn your way around one Office program, you can easily use the same skills to navigate the others. These common features include scroll bars, a Ribbon, and a Quick Access Toolbar (QAT). The Ribbon contains commands that Microsoft Office determines that you use most often, and the QAT contains frequently used commands; you can customize both elements.

A Title Bar

Displays the name of the open file and the Office program.

B Quick Access Toolbar

Displays quick-access buttons to commonly used commands such as Save, Undo, and Redo.

C Ribbon

Displays groups of related commands in tabs. Each tab offers buttons for performing common tasks.

D Program Window Controls

These buttons enable you to control the appearance of the program window. You can minimize the Ribbon, and you can minimize, maximize, restore, or close the program window.

E Office 365 Indicator

If you see your name, you are signed in to your Office 365 subscription. You can click your name to display a menu that enables you to manage your Microsoft account settings or switch to a different Microsoft account. If you are not signed in, this area shows a Sign in link. See Chapter 4 for details about signing in to Office Online.

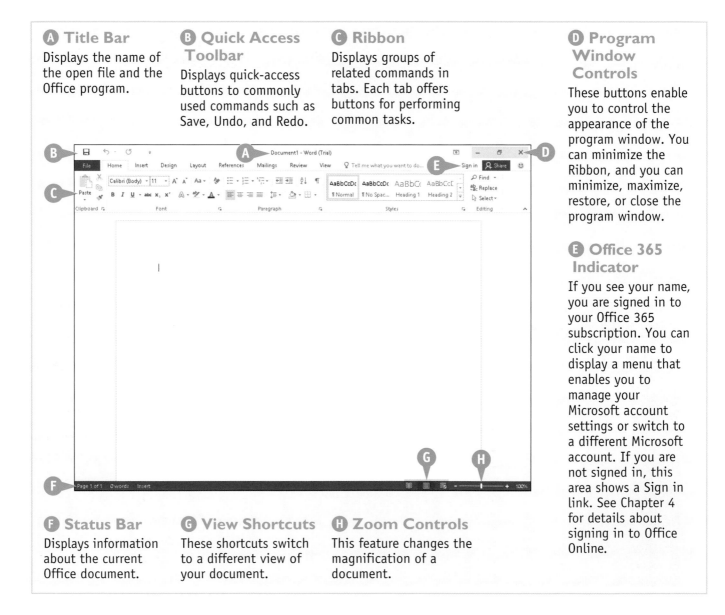

F Status Bar

Displays information about the current Office document.

G View Shortcuts

These shortcuts switch to a different view of your document.

H Zoom Controls

This feature changes the magnification of a document.

Work with Backstage View

You can click the File tab to display Backstage view. In Backstage view, you find a list of actions that you can use to open, save, print, remove sensitive information, and distribute documents as well as set Word program behavior options. You can also use Backstage to manage the places on your computer hard drive or in your network that you use to store documents, and to manage your Office 365 account.

Work with Backstage View

1 Click the **File** tab to display Backstage view.

Ⓐ Commonly used file and program management commands appear here.

Ⓑ Buttons you can click appear here.

Ⓒ Information related to the button you click appears here. Each time you click a button, the information shown to the right changes.

Note: *The New, Close, and Options commands do not display buttons or information, but take other actions.*

2 Click the **Back** button (◉) to return to the open document.

Change the Color Scheme

You can use Office themes and background patterns to change the appearance of the program screen. Themes control the color scheme the program uses, and background patterns can add interest to the screen while you work. Color schemes can improve your ability to clearly see the screen, but be aware that background patterns might be distracting.

Office themes are available even if you are not signed in to Office 365, but to use background patterns, you must sign in to Office 365. For details on how to sign in and out of Office 365, see Chapter 4.

Change the Color Scheme

Note: *Make sure you are signed in to Office 365. See Chapter 4 for details.*

1 Click **File** to open Backstage view.

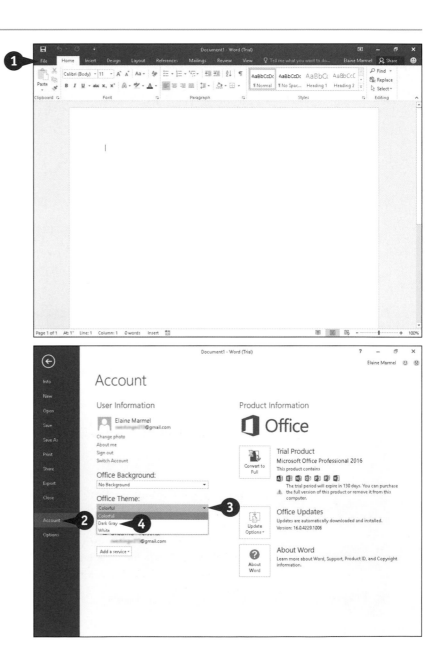

2 Click **Account**.

3 Click the **Office Theme** ▼.

4 Click an Office theme.

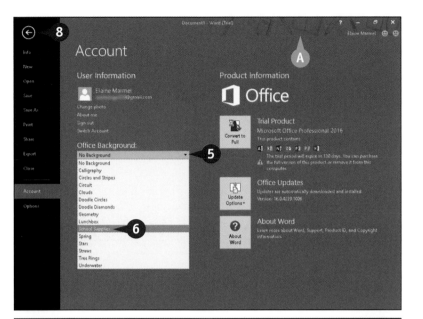

The colors of your program change.

Note: *Some theme changes are more subtle than others.*

5 Click the **Office Background** ▾.

6 Point the mouse (⇖) at a choice in the menu to highlight that choice.

Ⓐ A background pattern appears at the top of the window. The pattern remains as you work on documents.

7 Click the pattern you want to use or click **No Background**.

8 Click the **Back** button (⬅) to return to your document.

The Office theme and background you selected appear.

Ⓑ The background appears in the title bar and the tabs of the Ribbon.

---

simplify it

What happens if I select an Office background and then sign out of Office 365?
The background no longer appears in the program, but will reappear when you next sign in to Office 365. Similarly, theme changes you make while signed in to Office 365 might disappear when you sign out of Office 365. With themes, however, you do not need to be signed in to Office 365 to make a selection. Just complete Steps **1** to **4**.

Find a Ribbon Command

When you need to take an action that you do not take on a regular basis, you can make use of Office 2016's new feature, the Tell Me What You Want To Do feature. The Tell Me What You Want To Do search feature helps you find commands on the Ribbon.

You can still use the Ribbon directly, as described in the next section, "Work with the Ribbon." The Tell Me What You Want To Do search feature is most useful when you are not sure where on the Ribbon to find the command you need.

Find a Ribbon Command

1. Open a document in an Office program.

   Note: *See Chapter 2 for details on opening an Office document.*

2. Click here.

Ⓐ A list of commonly requested actions appears.

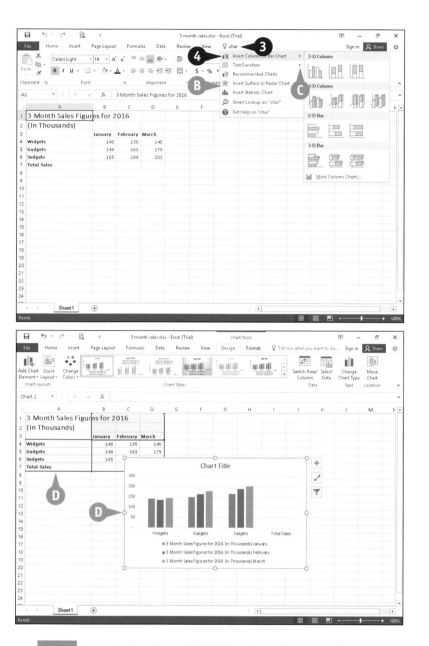

③ Type a brief description of the action you want to take.

Ⓑ The program lists possible commands you can use to complete your task.

④ Click a command to use it.

Ⓒ Commands with arrows (▶) display additional commands.

Ⓓ The program performs the action you selected; in this example, Excel charts the worksheet data.

Will I need to type a description of the action I want to take if it is the same action I have previously taken?
No. The Tell Me What You Want To Do search box remembers your previous searches and displays them on the menu that appears when you perform Step **2**.

If I no longer want my previous searches to appear, can I clear them from the list?
No. The Tell Me What You Want To Do feature retains your searches in the Recently Used section of the menu that appears when you click in the search box.

Work with the Ribbon

In addition to letting an Office program help you find a command, you can select commands using the Ribbon. Each Ribbon tab contains groups of related command buttons. Each button performs a common task. Some tabs appear only when needed. For example, if you select a table, the Ribbon displays the Table Tools tab.

In all Office programs, you can customize the Ribbon to support the way you work. For example, you can create your own Ribbon tab that contains the buttons you use most often; that way, you can avoid switching tabs to use a particular command.

Work with the Ribbon

Using the Ribbon

1 Click the tab containing the command you want to use.

2 Click the command.

Ⓐ Buttons with arrows (▾) display additional commands.

Ⓑ You can click the dialog box launcher (🔽) to display a dialog box of additional settings.

Create a Ribbon Tab

1 Click the **File** tab.

2 Click **Options** to display the Options dialog box.

3 Click **Customize Ribbon**.

4 Click the tab you want to appear to the left of the new tab.

5 Click **New Tab**.

Ⓒ Word creates a new tab and a new group on that tab. To reposition the tab, click it and click the arrows.

6 Click **New Tab (Custom)**.

7 Click **Rename** to display the Rename dialog box.

8 Type a name for your tab and click **OK**.

9 Click **New Group (Custom)** and repeat Steps **7** and **8** to rename the group.

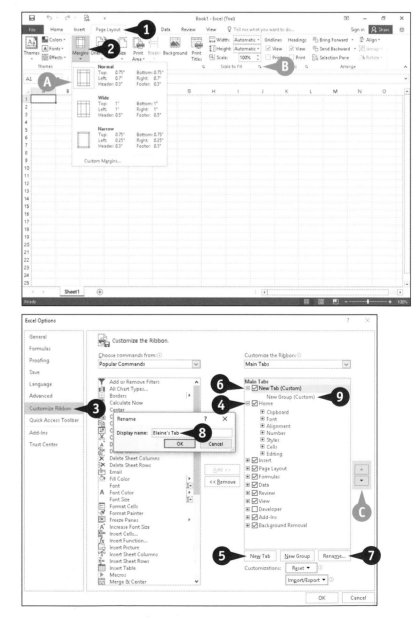

Add Buttons

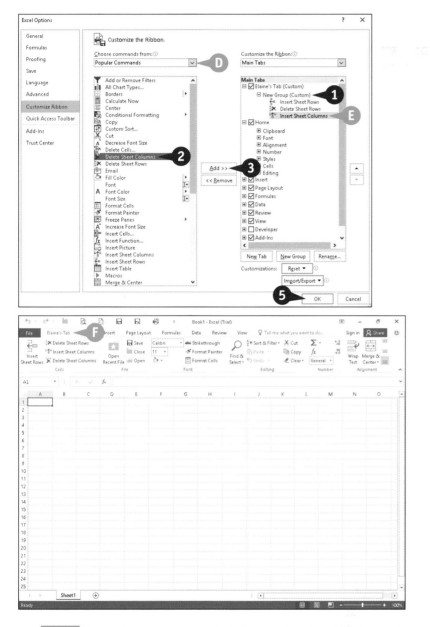

1 Click the group on the tab you created.

2 Click a command.

D If the command you want does not appear in the list, you can click the **Choose commands from** ⌄ and select **All Commands**.

3 Click **Add**.

E The command appears below the group you created.

4 Repeat Steps **2** and **3** for each button you want to add to the group.

5 Click **OK**.

F The new tab appears on the Ribbon. If you positioned your tab as the first tab, it will appear each time you open the program.

<table>
<tr><td style="vertical-align:top">**simplify it**</td><td>

How do I assign keyboard shortcuts to the buttons I add to my group?
Each Office program assigns keyboard shortcuts for you, based on the keys already assigned to commands appearing on the tab where you placed your group. You can place the same button on two different tabs, and if you do, the program assigns different keyboard shortcuts to that button on each tab.

</td><td>

What can I do if I decide that I do not want a custom tab on the Ribbon?
Reopen the program's Options dialog box and deselect the check box beside the tab you created (☑ changes to ☐). Click **OK**.

</td></tr>
</table>

Customize the Quick Access Toolbar

The Quick Access Toolbar, or QAT, is located in the top left corner of the program window above the File and Home tabs. It offers quick access to the frequently used Save, Undo, and Redo commands. If you want, you can customize this toolbar to include other commands you use often, such as the Quick Print, Print Preview, or any other command.

You can also reposition the QAT so that it appears below the Ribbon rather than above it; and, if you change your mind, you can put the QAT back above the Ribbon.

① Click the **More** button (⯆).

Ⓐ You can click any of the common commands to add them to the toolbar.

Ⓑ You can click **Show below the Ribbon** if you want to display the toolbar below the Ribbon.

② Click **More Commands**.

The Options dialog box appears.

③ Click the **Choose commands from** ⯆.

④ Click a command group.

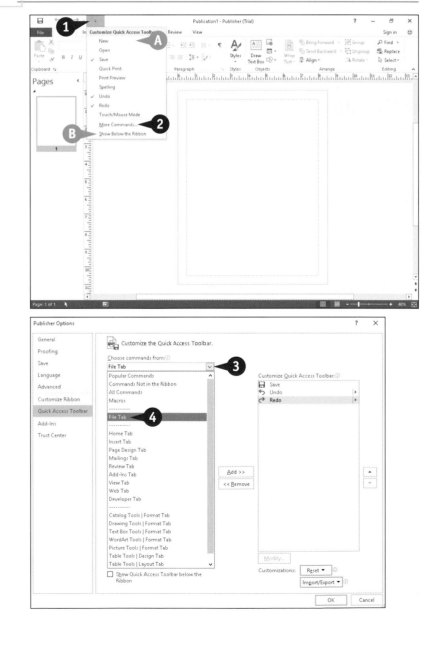

14

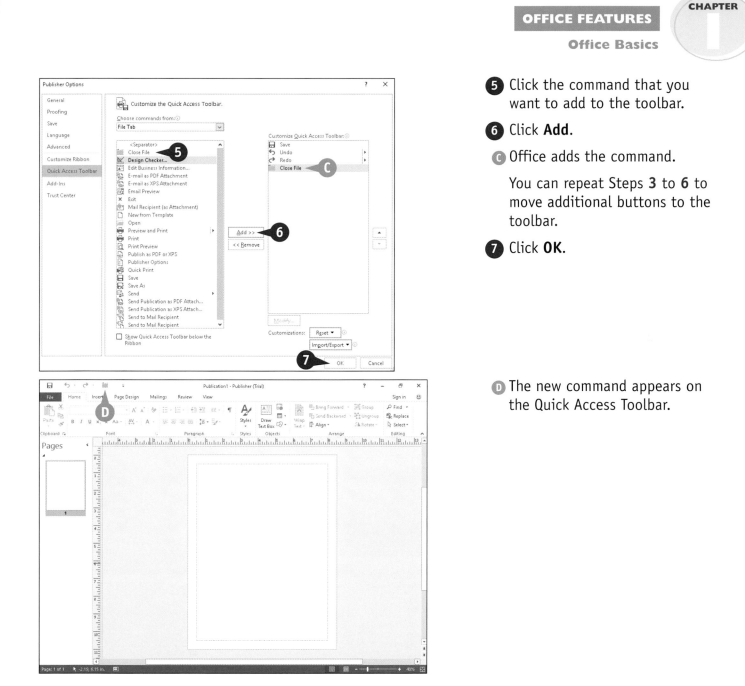

5 Click the command that you want to add to the toolbar.

6 Click **Add**.

C Office adds the command.

You can repeat Steps **3** to **6** to move additional buttons to the toolbar.

7 Click **OK**.

D The new command appears on the Quick Access Toolbar.

How do I remove a button from the Quick Access Toolbar?

To remove a command, reopen the program's Options dialog box by following the steps in this section, click the command name in the list on the right, click the **Remove** button, and click **OK**. The button no longer appears on the toolbar.

Are there other ways to customize the Quick Access Toolbar?

Yes. You can add commands to the toolbar directly from the Ribbon. Simply click the tab containing the command that you want to add, right-click the command, and then click **Add to Quick Access Toolbar**. The command appears immediately as a button on the toolbar.

Using an Office Program on a Tablet PC

Using Office 2016 on a tablet offers a different experience than using the programs on a computer with a keyboard and mouse. This section shows you how to open an Office program on a touch device and how to switch between Touch and Mouse modes.

Office enhancements for tablets are limited primarily to enlarging buttons on the Quick Access Toolbar and the Ribbon to make selecting commands easier. For a friendlier touch experience, consider using universal Office apps for various mobile devices, which, although not as powerful as Office 2016, were written specifically for touch devices. You can share documents across platforms.

Using an Office Program on a Tablet PC

Start a Program

Note: *This section uses PowerPoint to demonstrate gestures.*

1 Tap the Windows **Start** button (⊞).

Ⓐ The Windows 10 Start menu displays Most Used programs on the left.

Ⓑ Program tiles appear on the right side.

Ⓒ If the program you want to open appears in the Most Used list, you can tap it to open it. Or you can scroll through the program tiles on the right to find and tap the program you want to open.

2 Tap **All apps**.

Ⓓ An alphabetical list of programs installed on your computer appears.

3 Scroll through the list and tap the Office program you want to start.

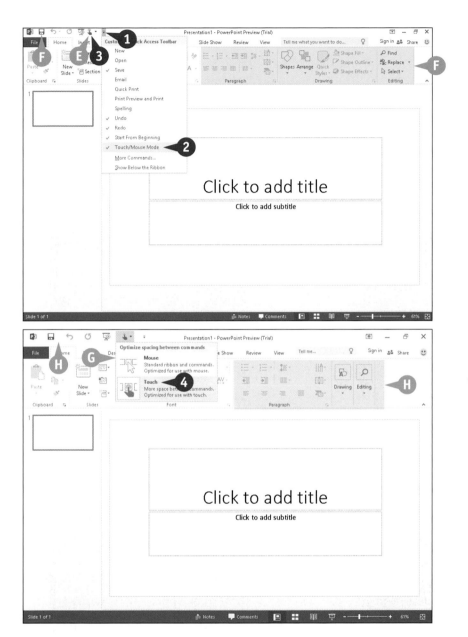

Using Touch/Mouse Mode

1 Tap the **More** button (◄).

2 Tap **Touch/Mouse Mode**.

E PowerPoint adds the Touch/Mouse Mode button to the Quick Access Toolbar.

Note: *By default, each Office program displays the screen in Mouse mode.*

F In Mouse mode, buttons on the Quick Access Toolbar and the Ribbon are smaller.

3 Tap **Touch/Mouse Mode** on the Quick Access Toolbar.

G A drop-down menu appears.

4 Tap **Touch**.

H The Office program enlarges the size of buttons on the Quick Access Toolbar and the Ribbon, grouping Ribbon buttons as needed.

simplify it

Are there any other features in Office 2016 programs that make the programs easier to use on touch devices?

Yes, Word's Read Mode contains buttons (◄ and ►) on the left and right sides of the screen (**A**) that you can tap to change pages. See Chapter 8 for details on switching to Read Mode. For a more touch-friendly experience, consider using Office on an iPad or Android device.

are so much obliged to the honorable gen-
ed it success. In this particular of salaries to
from a persuasion that it is right, and from
and their judgment may possibly change
the contrary, great advantages.

and avarice—the love of power and the
d in view of the same object, they have, in
the same time, be a place of profit, and
ish government so tempestuous. The
distracting its councils, hurrying it som
f peace.

A ►

Create a New File

When you open an Office program (except Outlook and OneNote), the program's Start screen greets you; see Chapter 1 for details. If Word, Excel, PowerPoint, Access, or Publisher is already open and you want to create a new document, workbook, presentation, database, or publication, you create a new file using

Backstage view. When you do, you have the option of creating a blank file or basing the file on a template. Outlook opens by default to the Inbox, and OneNote opens to an explanatory page in a OneNote file that you use. See Part VI for details on Outlook and Part VIII for details on OneNote.

Create a New File

Create a New Word, Excel, PowerPoint, Access, or Publisher File

1 Click the **File** tab.

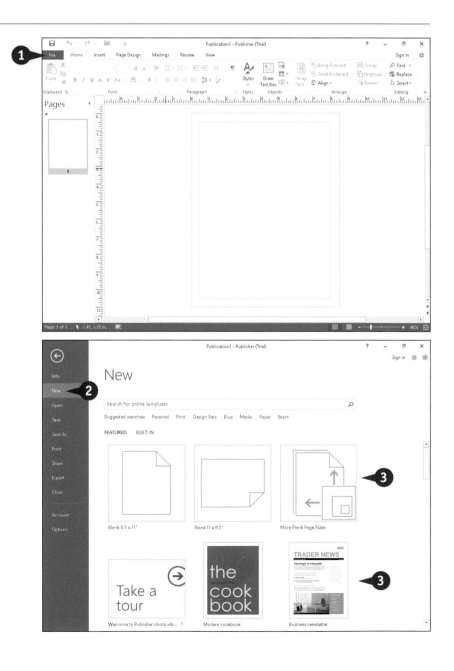

2 Click **New**.

The New screen appears.

3 Click the type of file that you want to create.

If you click a template, a preview appears; if you like what you see, click **Create** and the new file opens.

Note: *A template contains predefined settings that serve as the foundation for your document, saving you the effort of manually creating the settings.*

If you click a blank document, no preview appears; instead, a new blank document appears.

Create a New Outlook Item

Note: *Outlook by default hides Ribbon buttons and displays only tabs. To view the buttons, click any tab.*

Ⓐ You can use the Navigation bar at the bottom of the Outlook window to switch between the types of items Outlook supports: email message, calendar item, contact, or task.

① Click **Home**.

② Click **New Items**.

Ⓑ A list of available types of Outlook items appears.

③ Click the appropriate type of item you want to create. For example, to create an email message, click **E-mail Message**. To create a Calendar item, click **Appointment** or **Meeting**, and so on.

Ⓒ The new item, an appointment in this example, opens.

---

simplify it

The other programs display Ribbon buttons by default, but Outlook does not. Can I make Outlook always display Ribbon buttons?
Yes. At the upper right edge of the program title bar, click the **Ribbon Display Options** button (⊞) (Ⓐ) and, from the menu that appears, click **Show Tabs and Commands** (Ⓑ). You can hide Ribbon buttons in any Office program using the same technique.

Ⓐ ⊞ — ⬚ ×

Auto-hide Ribbon
Hide the Ribbon. Click at the top of the application to show it.

Show Tabs
Show Ribbon tabs only. Click a tab to show the commands.

Show Tabs and Commands — Ⓑ
Show Ribbon tabs and commands all the time.

Save
a File

You save files you create in Office programs so that you can use them at another time. When you save a file, you can give it a unique filename and store it in the folder or drive of your choice.

After you save a document for the first time, you can click the **Save** button (🖫) on the Quick Access

Toolbar (QAT) to save it again. The first time you save a document, the program prompts you for a document name. Subsequent times, when you use the Save button (🖫) on the QAT, the program saves the document using its original name without prompting you.

Save a File

Ⓐ Before you save a document, the program displays a generic name in the title bar.

① Click the **File** tab.

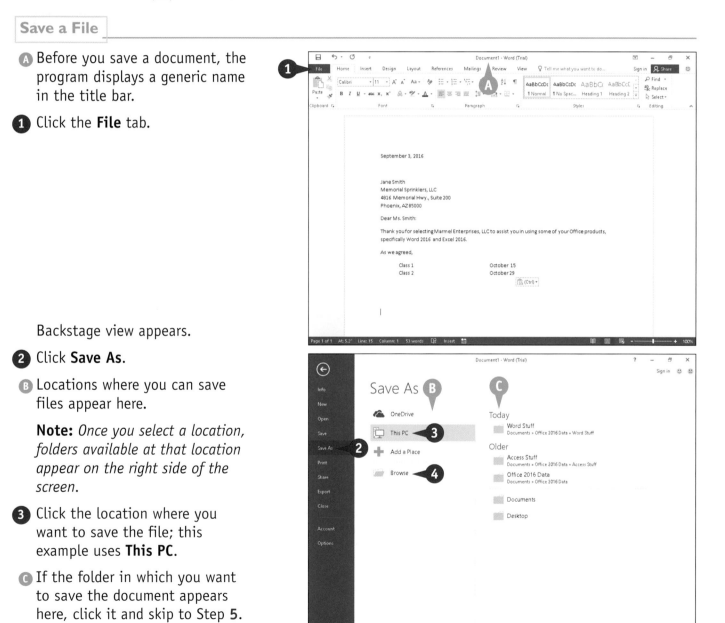

Backstage view appears.

② Click **Save As**.

Ⓑ Locations where you can save files appear here.

Note: *Once you select a location, folders available at that location appear on the right side of the screen.*

③ Click the location where you want to save the file; this example uses **This PC**.

Ⓒ If the folder in which you want to save the document appears here, click it and skip to Step **5**.

④ Click **Browse**.

The Save As dialog box appears.

5 Type a name for the document.

D You can click in the folder list to select a location on your computer in which to save the document.

E You can click **New folder** to create a new folder in which to store the document.

6 Click **Save**.

F Word saves the document and displays the name you supplied in the title bar.

G For subsequent saves, you can click the **Save** button (🖫) on the Quick Access Toolbar to quickly save the file.

---

simplify it

Can I save a file using a different file type?
Yes. Each Office program saves to a default file type. For example, a Word document uses the DOCX file format and Excel uses the XLSX file format. If you want to save the file in a format compatible with previous versions of Office, you must save it in the appropriate format, such as Word 97-2003 Document for previous versions of Word. To save a file in a different format, click the **Save as type** 🔽 in the Save As dialog box and choose the desired format from the list that appears.

Open a File

You can open documents that you have saved previously to continue adding data or to edit existing data. If you are not sure where you saved a file, you can use the Open dialog box's Search function to locate it.

In Word 2016, you can open and edit PDF files. Because Word optimizes PDF files to enable you to edit text, editing a PDF file in Word works best if you used Word to create the original PDF file. If you used a different program to create the PDF file, the result might not look exactly like the original PDF.

Open a File

① Click the **File** tab.

Backstage view appears.

② Click **Open**.

Ⓐ By default, the Office program displays recently opened documents. If you see the file you want to open, you can click it to open it and skip the rest of these steps.

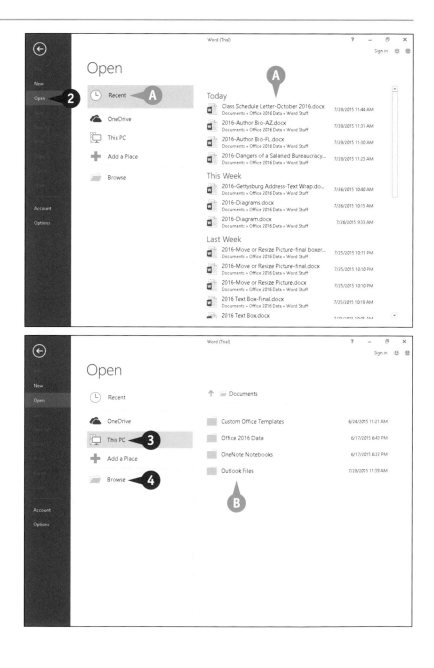

③ Click the place where you believe the document is stored. This example uses **This PC**.

Ⓑ If the folder containing the document appears here, click it and skip to Step **6**.

④ Click **Browse**.

The Open dialog box appears.

C If you chose the wrong place, you can search for the file by typing part of the filename or content here.

5 Click in the folder list to navigate to the folder containing the document you want to open.

6 Click the document you want to open.

7 Click **Open**.

The file opens in the program window.

D To close a file, click the **Close** button (✕) in the upper right corner. If you have not saved the file, the program prompts you to save it.

Are there any tricks to searching for a file?
Yes. To search most effectively for a file, start by following Steps **1** to **5** to locate and open the folder in which you believe the file was saved. Then, type the file's name in the search box. Files containing the search term in either the filename or as part of the file's content appear highlighted in the bottom of the Open dialog box. Word also displays files containing a close match.

Print
a File

If a printer is connected to your computer, you can print your Office files. For example, you might distribute printouts of a file as handouts in a meeting.

When you print a file, you have two options: You can send a file directly to the printer using the default settings, or you can open the Office application's

Print screen to change these settings. For example, you might opt to print just a portion of the file, print using a different printer, print multiple copies of a file, collate the printouts, and so on. (Printer settings vary slightly among Office programs.)

Print a File

1 Click the **File** tab.

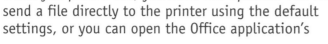

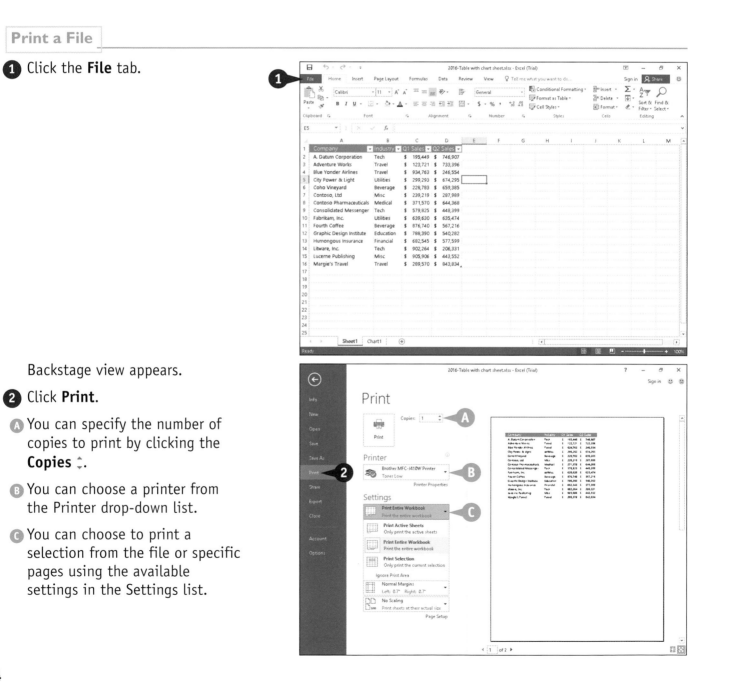

Backstage view appears.

2 Click **Print**.

Ⓐ You can specify the number of copies to print by clicking the **Copies ‡**.

Ⓑ You can choose a printer from the Printer drop-down list.

Ⓒ You can choose to print a selection from the file or specific pages using the available settings in the Settings list.

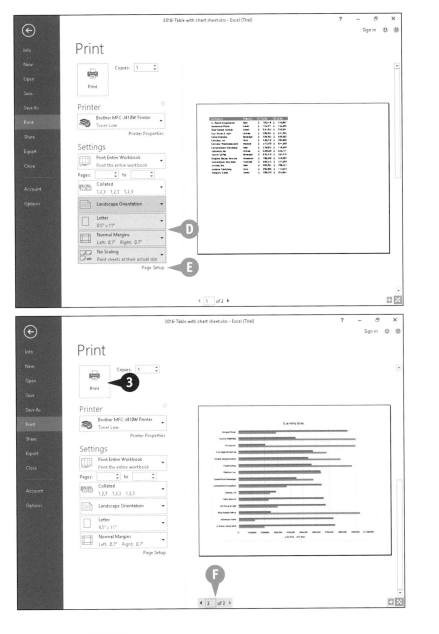

D You can select additional print options under Settings. For example, you can choose from various paper sizes and to print in landscape or portrait orientation.

E If you do not see the setting you want to change, click **Page Setup** to view additional settings.

F You can page through a preview of your printed file by clicking these arrows (◀ and ▶).

3 Click **Print**.

The Office program sends the file to the printer for printing.

How do I print using default settings?
If you do not need to change any of your default print settings, you can simply click the **Quick Print** button (🖨) on the Quick Access Toolbar (QAT). If the Quick Print button does not appear on your QAT, you can add it. To do so, click the **More** button (▼) to the right of the QAT and click **Quick Print** in the list of commands that appears. You can also add a **Print Preview and Print** button (🔍) to the QAT; clicking that button opens the Print screen from Backstage view.

Email
a File

You can share a file with others via email. For example, suppose that you have a colleague who must present a project for approval at an upcoming meeting. Your colleague approaches you, asking for guidance concerning what to discuss. You put together a skeleton PowerPoint presentation and you want to email it to your colleague.

Although you could create a new email message with an attachment, you can send a file from the program you used to create the file, as described here. Note that, to open a file, recipients must have the appropriate software on their computer.

Email a File

1 With the document you want to share via email open, click the **File** tab.

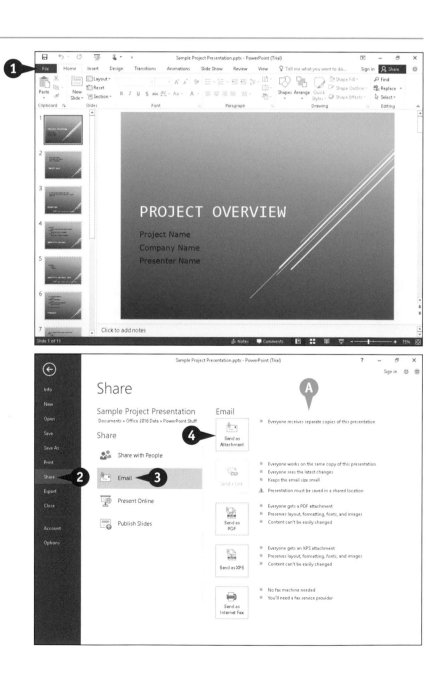

Backstage view appears.

2 Click **Share**.

3 Click **Email**.

A Options for emailing the file appear here.

4 Click **Send as Attachment**.

Note: *If you are sending a file that you do not want anyone to edit, click **Send as PDF** or **Send as XPS**.*

Office launches an Outlook new message window.

B The name of your file appears in the window's Subject line.

C The file is attached to the message.

5 Type the message recipient's email address in the **To** box.

6 Type your text in the body of the message.

7 Click **Send**.

Office places the message in your email program's outbox.

simplify it

What if my recipient does not have the necessary software to open the file?

You can send the file in PDF or XPS format, which maintains the appearance of your file, but the file cannot easily be changed — meaning your recipient cannot edit the file. Alternatively, you can suggest that the recipient download an Office program viewer; a viewer can, for example, help an Office 2007 user open an Office 2016 file. To find a view, go to Microsoft.com and search for the appropriate program viewer. Finally, you can suggest that the recipient use the appropriate Office web app, available in OneDrive; see Chapter 4.

Select Data

You can select data in your file to perform different tasks, such as deleting it, changing its font or alignment, applying a border around it, or copying and pasting it. Selected data appears highlighted.

Depending on the program you are using, Office offers several different techniques for selecting data.

For example, in Word, PowerPoint, Outlook, and Publisher, you can select a single character, a word, a sentence, a paragraph, or all the data in the file. In Excel and Access tables, you typically select cells. In OneNote, use the technique appropriate to the type of data you want to select.

Select Data

Select Data in Word, PowerPoint, or Publisher

Note: *You can use this technique to select characters, words, sentences, and paragraphs.*

1 Click to one side of the word or character that you want to select.

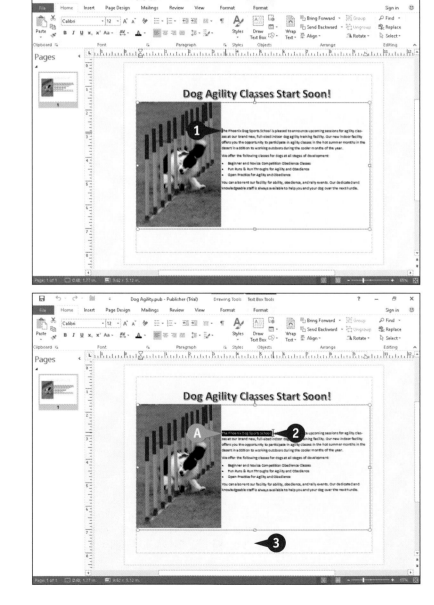

2 Drag the mouse (⇱) across the text that you want to select.

A The program highlights the characters to indicate that they are selected.

3 To cancel a selection, click anywhere outside the text or press any arrow key on your keyboard.

Select Cells in Excel or Access

1 Click the cell representing the upper left corner of the cells you want to select.

2 Drag the cell pointer across the cells you want to select.

B The program highlights the characters to indicate that they are selected.

3 To cancel a selection, click anywhere outside the text or press any arrow key on your keyboard.

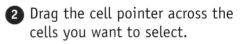

How can I use my keyboard to select text?
To select text or cells to the left or right of the insertion point or cell pointer, press Ctrl + Shift + ← or Ctrl + Shift + →. To select a paragraph or cells above or below the insertion point or cell pointer, press Ctrl + Shift + ↑ or Ctrl + Shift + ↓. To select all text or cells from the insertion point or cell pointer location onward, press Ctrl + Shift + End. To select all the text or cells above the insertion point or cell pointer location, press Ctrl + Shift + Home. To select all the text or cells containing data in the file, press Ctrl + A.

Cut, Copy, and Paste Data

You can use the Cut, Copy, and Paste commands to move or copy data. For example, you might cut or copy text or a picture from a Word document and paste it elsewhere in the same Word document, in another Word document, or in a PowerPoint slide or a Publisher file.

When you cut data, it is removed from its original location; when you copy data, the program duplicates the selected data, leaving it in its original location. You can move or copy data using two methods: drag-and-drop or buttons on the Ribbon. This section demonstrates drag-and-drop using Word, and Ribbon buttons using Excel.

Cut, Copy, and Paste Data

Cut or Copy in Word, PowerPoint, Publisher, or Outlook

1 Select the data that you want to cut or copy. This example cuts text.

2 Click and drag the data to a new location.

A As you drag, ▷ changes to ▷.

To copy the data, you can press and hold `Ctrl` as you drag, and ▷ changes to ▷.

B A bold insertion point marks where the text will appear as you drag.

3 Release the mouse to drop the data in place.

C The data appears in the new location.

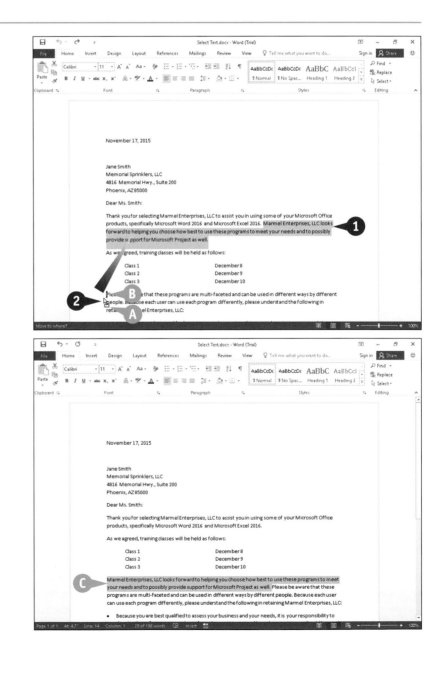

Cut or Copy in Excel or Access

1 Select the cell(s) that you want to cut or copy. This example copies a formula.

2 Click the **Home** tab.

3 Click the **Cut** button (✂) to move data or the **Copy** button (📋) to copy data.

Note: *You can also press* Ctrl + X *to cut data or* Ctrl + C *to copy data.*

The outline around the selected cell(s) changes to an animated dashed box and the data is stored in the Windows Clipboard.

4 Select the cells where you want the cut or copied data to appear.

Note: *You can also open another file into which you can paste the data.*

5 On the Home tab, click **Paste**. Alternatively, to preview how the text will look before you paste it, click ⯆ below the Paste button and position your mouse (⬚) over each button that appears.

Note: *You can also press* Ctrl + V *to paste data.*

D The data appears in the new location.

<table>
<tr><td rowspan="2">simplify it</td><td>**When I paste cut or copied data, an icon appears. What is it?**
The Paste Options button (📋 (Ctrl) ▾) displays Paste-formatting choices when you click it; the options that appear depend on the program you are using and the location where you want to paste. You also can ignore the Paste Options button (📋 (Ctrl) ▾); eventually, it disappears.</td><td>**Can I cut or copy multiple selections?**
Yes, you can, using the Office Clipboard, which holds up to 24 items that you can paste in any order you choose. To display the Office Clipboard, click the dialog box launcher (⯗) in the Clipboard group on the Ribbon's Home tab. Then select and cut or copy.</td></tr>
</table>

Arrange Windows

You can simultaneously view multiple files. For example, you might view two versions of a Word document side by side to compare their contents or view two Excel workbooks to compare data. If the files you want to compare are particularly long, you can enable the Synchronous Scrolling option to scroll both files at the same time.

In addition to viewing multiple files simultaneously, you can split the window of one long file into scrollable panes to view different portions of it. For example, you might split a document to compare how portions of it are formatted.

Arrange Windows

View Multiple Files

1 Open two or more files.

2 Click the **View** tab.

3 Click **View Side by Side**.

Ⓐ Both files appear on-screen side by side.

Ⓑ To scroll both files at the same time, you can click **Window** and then click **Synchronous Scrolling**.

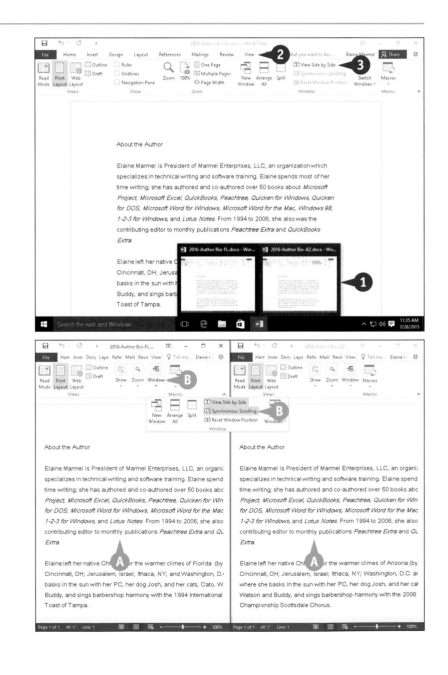

C You can click the **Maximize** button (☐) to restore a window to its full size.

D You can click the **Close** button (✖) to close a file.

Split a Window

1 To split the window displaying a single file into scrollable panes, click the **View** tab.

2 Click **Split**.

E Horizontal and vertical bars appear.

3 Drag the bar up, down, right, or left to resize the panes, and click to set the bar in place when the panes are the desired size.

To return the page to a full document, click **Split** again.

What does the Switch Windows button do?
If you have two or more files open, click **Switch Windows** to view a list of all open files in the current Office program. You can then choose a file in the list to view it.

Can I display two Excel files one on top of the other?
Yes. Click the **View** tab and then click **Arrange All**. The Arrange Windows dialog box opens, and you can select how you want to display multiple files: horizontally, vertically, tiled (where each window appears in a square pane), or cascaded (where windows appear one behind another).

Insert a Picture

You can illustrate your Office files with images that you store on your computer. For example, if you have a photo or graphic file that relates to your Excel data, you can insert it onto the worksheet. If you have a photo or graphic file that relates to the subject matter in your document, you can insert it into the document to help the reader understand your subject. After you insert a picture, you can resize, move, or modify the graphic in a variety of ways, as described in the section "Understanding Graphics Modification Techniques," later in this chapter.

Insert a Picture

1 Click in your document where you want to add a picture.

Note: *You can move the image to a different location after inserting it onto the page. See the section "Resize and Move Objects."*

2 Click the **Insert** tab.

3 Click **Pictures**.

The Insert Picture dialog box appears.

Ⓐ The folder you are viewing appears here.

Note: *Image files come in a variety of formats, including GIF, JPEG, and PNG.*

Ⓑ To browse for a particular file type, you can click ⌄ and choose a file format.

Ⓒ You can click in the folder list to navigate to commonly used locations where pictures may be stored.

4 Navigate to the folder containing the picture you want to add to your document.

5 Click the picture you want to add.

6 Click **Insert**.

D The picture appears in your document, selected and surrounded by handles (○ and ☐).

E Picture Tools appear on the Ribbon; you can use these tools to format pictures.

F You can drag ○ to rotate the picture (○ changes to ⟳).

G You can click **Wrap Text** to control text flow around the picture.

To remove a picture that you no longer want, you can click the picture and press Delete.

If I am sharing my file with others, can I compress the pictures to save space?
Yes. To compress an image, click the image, click the **Format** tab on the Ribbon, and click the **Compress Pictures** button (🖻) in the Adjust group. In the Compress Pictures dialog box, fine-tune settings as needed and click **Compress**.

I made changes to my picture, but I do not like the effect. How do I return the picture to the original settings?
You can click the **Reset Picture** button (🖻 ▾), located in the Adjust group on the Format tab, to restore a picture to its original state but not its original size.

Insert an Online Picture

In addition to pictures stored on your computer's hard drive, you can add interest to your Office files by inserting a picture or clip art image from an online source into a Word, Excel, PowerPoint, Publisher, Outlook, or OneNote document. Be careful when choosing online pictures and make sure that they fall into the public domain or that you have written permission to use the picture.

Office 2016 programs use Bing.com to search for images, and a Bing search displays images licensed by Creative Commons, a nonprofit organization that helps individuals license their works.

Insert an Online Picture

Note: *If you are working in Word or Excel, switch to Print Layout view.*

1. Click in your document where you want to add a picture.

   Note: *You can move the graphic to a different location after you insert it. See the section "Resize and Move Objects," later in this chapter.*

2. Click the **Insert** tab.

3. Click **Online Pictures**.

   Note: *In some Office programs, Online Pictures does not appear directly on the Insert tab. In this case, click **Illustrations**.*

   The Insert Pictures window appears.

   Note: *If you sign in using a Microsoft account, you also can search Facebook, Flickr, and your OneDrive space.*

4. Click in the search box and type a description of the kind of image you want.

5. Click the **Search** button (🔍).

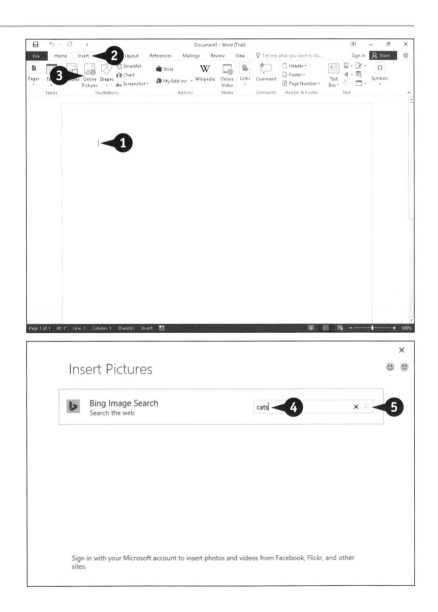

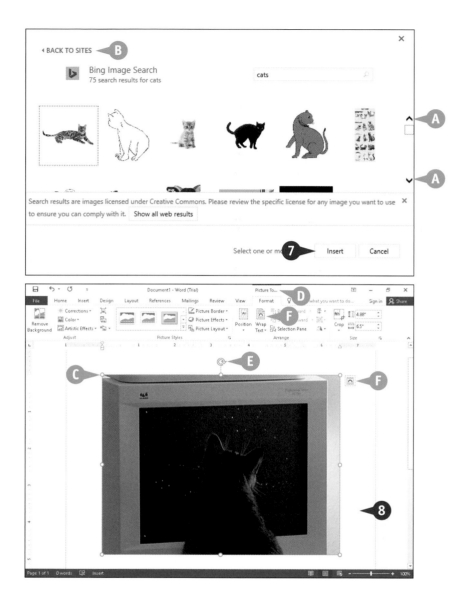

The results of your search appear.

Ⓐ You can click the arrows (∧ and ∨) to navigate through the search results.

Ⓑ You can click **Back to Sites** to return to the Insert Picture window and search for a different image.

❻ Click the picture you want to add to your document.

❼ Click **Insert**.

Ⓒ The picture appears in your document, selected and surrounded by handles (○).

Ⓓ Picture Tools appear on the Ribbon; you can use these tools to format the picture.

Ⓔ You can drag ⟳ to rotate the picture.

Ⓕ You can click Wrap Text or the **Layout options** button (⊠) to control text flow around the picture.

❽ When you finish working with your online picture, click anywhere else in the work area.

Why must I make sure that the image I choose falls into the public domain?
Privately owned images are often available for use only if you agree to pay a fee and/or get the owner's permission to use the image. You can use a public domain image without paying a royalty and/or obtaining the owner's permission to use the image.

How does Creative Commons work?
At creativecommons.org, you find links to license or search for images at several places, such as Flickr or Google Images. Search results do not guarantee an image is licensed by Creative Commons. You need to click an image to examine its licensing information.

Resize and Move Objects

Pictures and other types of images are also called *graphic objects*. If a graphic object is not positioned where you want it or if it is too large or too small, you can move or resize it. When you select a graphic object, handles appear on each side of the graphic object; you can use these handles to resize it. Alignment guides — green lines — appear as you move a graphic object to help you determine where to place it. Once you have picked the spot for the graphic, the alignment guides disappear.

Resize and Move Objects

Move a Graphic

1 Click a graphic object.

A Handles (○) surround the graphic.

Note: *In Publisher, ⬜ and ○ surround the graphic.*

2 Position the mouse over a graphic object or the edge of a text box (I⁼ or I changes to ⬧).

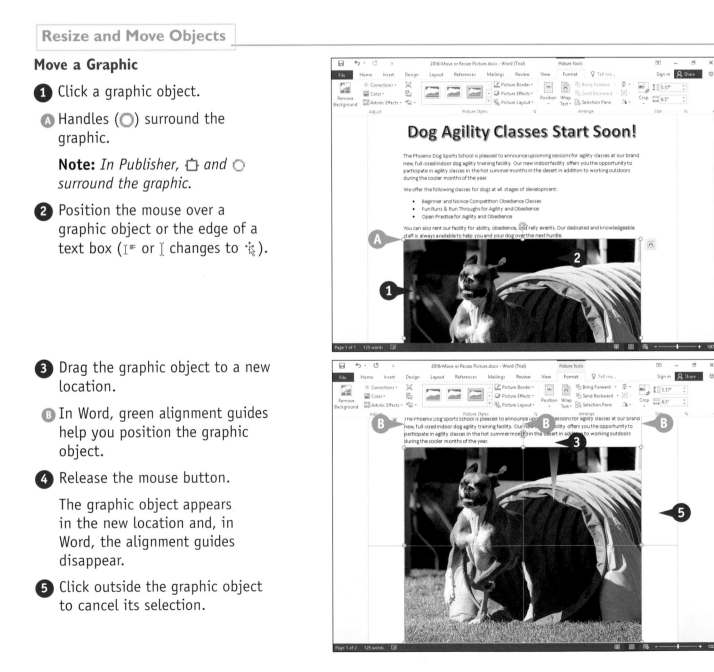

3 Drag the graphic object to a new location.

B In Word, green alignment guides help you position the graphic object.

4 Release the mouse button.

The graphic object appears in the new location and, in Word, the alignment guides disappear.

5 Click outside the graphic object to cancel its selection.

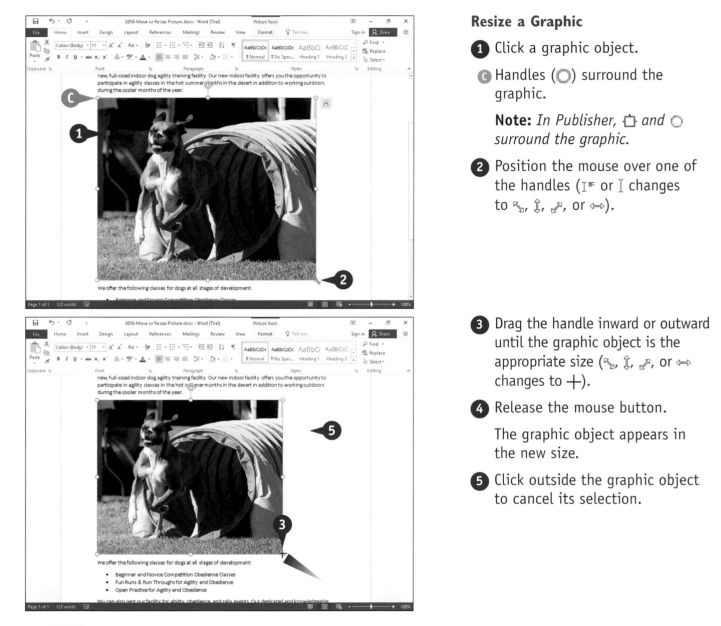

Resize a Graphic

1 Click a graphic object.

C Handles (○) surround the graphic.

Note: *In Publisher, ⬚ and ○ surround the graphic.*

2 Position the mouse over one of the handles (⫶ or ⌶ changes to ⬉, ⬍, ⬈, or ⬌).

3 Drag the handle inward or outward until the graphic object is the appropriate size (⬉, ⬍, ⬈, or ⬌ changes to ✛).

4 Release the mouse button.

The graphic object appears in the new size.

5 Click outside the graphic object to cancel its selection.

Can I control how text wraps around an object?
Yes, if you insert the object into a Word or Publisher file. Click the object, click **Wrap Text** in the Format tab, and choose a wrap style.

Does it matter which handle I use to resize a graphic?
Yes. If you click and drag any of the corner handles, you maintain the proportion of the graphic as you resize it. The handles on the sides, top, or bottom of the graphic resize only the width or the height of the graphic, causing your graphic to look distorted.

Understanding Graphics Modification Techniques

In addition to inserting, moving, and resizing pictures as described in this chapter, you can insert and modify other types of graphic objects — shapes, screenshots, SmartArt, WordArt, and charts — in all Office programs except Access. The available graphic objects vary from program to program; the specific types of available graphic objects appear on the Insert tab of the program. You insert these objects using basically the same techniques you use to insert pictures.

You can modify an object's appearance using a variety of Ribbon buttons that appear on a Tools tab specific to the type of graphic object you select.

Crop a Picture

You can use the Crop tool to create a better fit, to omit a portion of the image, or to focus the viewer on an important area of the image. You can crop a picture, screenshot, or clip art image. When you crop an object, you remove vertical and/or horizontal edges from the object. The Crop tool is located on the Format tab on the Ribbon, which appears when you click the object you want to crop.

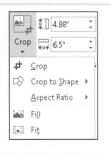

Rotate or Flip a Graphic

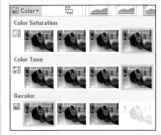

After you insert an object such as a piece of clip art or a photo from your hard drive into a Word document, you may find that the object appears upside down or inverted. Fortunately, Word makes it easy to flip or rotate an object. For example, you might flip a clip art image to face another direction, or rotate an arrow object to point elsewhere on the page. Or, for dramatic effect, you can rotate or flip pictures, clip art images, and some shapes. Keep in mind that you cannot rotate text boxes.

Correct Images

You can change the brightness and contrast of a picture, clip art, or a screenshot to improve its appearance, and you can sharpen or soften an image. Suppose, for example, the image object you have inserted in your Word, Excel, or PowerPoint file is slightly blurry, or lacks contrast. You find the image-correction tools on the Picture Tools Format tab on the Ribbon, which appears when you click to select the object to which you want to apply the effect.

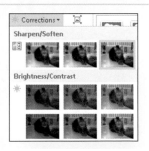

Make Color Adjustments

You can adjust the color of a picture, screenshot, or clip art image by increasing or decreasing color saturation or color tone. You can also recolor a picture, screenshot, or clip art image to create an interesting effect.

Color saturation controls the amount of red and green in a photo, whereas color tone controls the amount of blue and yellow.

Remove the Background of an Image

You can remove the background of a picture, screenshot, or clip art image. For example, suppose that you inserted a screenshot of an Excel chart in a Word document; the screenshot would, by default, include the Excel Ribbon. You can use the Remove Background tool in the Adjust group on the Picture Tools Format tab to remove the Excel Ribbon and focus the reader's attention on the chart.

Add an Effect

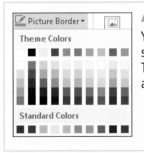

You can use tools to assign unique and interesting special effects to objects. For example, you can apply a shadow effect, create a mirrored reflection, apply a glow effect, soften the object's edges, make a bevel effect, or generate a 3-D rotation effect. You can find these tools on the Format tab of the Ribbon, which appears when you click to select the object to which you want to apply the effect. (Note that the Picture Effects tool is not available in Publisher.)

Apply a Style to a Graphic

You can apply a predefined style to a shape, text box, WordArt graphic, picture, or clip art image. Styles contain predefined colors and effects and help you quickly add interest to a graphic. Applying a style removes other effects you may have applied, such as shadow or bevel effects. Sample styles appear on the Picture Tools Format or Drawing Tools Format tab when you click the **More** button ($\overline{\overline{\vee}}$) in the Picture Styles or Shape Styles group.

Add a Picture Border or Drawing Outline

You can add a border to a picture, shape, text box, WordArt graphic, clip art image, or screenshot. Using the Picture Border or Shape Outline tool, which appears on the Picture Tools Format or Drawing Tools Format tab, you can control the thickness of the border, set a style for the border — a solid or dashed line — and change the color of the border.

Apply Artistic Effects

You can apply artistic effects to pictures, screenshots, and clip art to liven them up. For example, you can make an image appear as though it was rendered in marker, pencil, chalk, or paint. Other artistic effects might remind you of mosaics, film grain, or glass. You find the Artistic Effects button on the Picture Tools Format tab, which appears when you click to select the object to which you want to apply the effect.

Office and the Cloud

Today, people are on the go but often want to take work with them to do while sitting in the waiting room of their doctor's office, at the airport, or in a hotel room. Using Office 2016, you can work from anywhere using almost any device available because, among other reasons, it works with SharePoint and OneDrive, Microsoft's cloud space. From OneDrive, you can log in to cloud space and, using Office web apps — essentially, tools with which you are already familiar — get to work.

You also can download Office universal apps for various platforms. You can share documents across platforms.

Sign In to the Cloud

Signing in to Office Online or to your Office 365 subscription connects your Office programs to the world beyond your computer. Office Online offers free access to the online, limited-edition versions of the Office programs that you can use on any computer. Purchasing an Office 365 subscription gives you access to full versions of the Office desktop programs and the online versions of the products. Signing in gives you access to online pictures and clip art stored at Office.com and enables Office to synchronize files between your computer, OneDrive, and SharePoint

Elaine Marmel

Elaine@marmelenterprises.onmicrosoft.com

About me

Account settings

Switch account

OneDrive and Office 2016

OneDrive is a cloud storage service from Microsoft that you can use with Office 2016; 15GB are free, and you can rent additional space. Office 2016 saves all documents by default to your OneDrive space so that your documents are always available to you.

Using Office Web Apps

You can open and edit Word, Excel, OneNote, and PowerPoint documents from your OneDrive using Office web apps, which are scaled-down editions of Office programs that you can use to easily review documents and make minor changes.

Collaborate with Office Online

OneDrive   Word Online   Excel Online   PowerPoint Online

Take Your Personal Settings with You Everywhere

Office 2016 keeps track of personal settings like your recently used files and color theme and makes them available from any computer just by signing in to Office. Word and PowerPoint also remember the paragraph and slide you were viewing when you closed a document, and they display that location when you open the document on another machine, making it easy for you to get back to work when you move from one work location to another.

Your Documents Are Always Up-to-Date

Office 2016 saves your Office documents by default in the OneDrive folder you find in File Explorer. As you work, Office synchronizes files with changes to your OneDrive in the background. And, the technology does not slow down your work environment because Office uploads only changes, not entire documents, saving bandwidth and battery life as you work from wireless devices.

Name	Date modified	Type
Documents	5/11/2015 2:51 AM	File folder
Music	5/11/2015 2:51 AM	File folder
Pictures	5/11/2015 2:51 AM	File folder
Public	5/11/2015 2:51 AM	File folder
.lock	5/11/2015 2:51 AM	LOCK File

OneDrive

Share Your Documents from Anywhere

Share

Invite people

Get a link

Shared with

Anyone with this edit link

Everyone
Can only view

You can share your documents both from within an Office program and from your OneDrive. And, from either location, you can email a document to recipients you choose, post a document to a social media site, or create a link to a document that you can provide to users so that they can view the document in a browser. You can also use Microsoft's free online presentation service to present Word and PowerPoint documents online.

Take Advantage of the Office Store

The Office Store contains add-in applications that work with Office programs. For example, Microsoft Word and Excel come with a dictionary you use to look up words but you also can use an add-on dictionary for Word or Excel that you can download from the Microsoft Store. Click **Store** to open your browser to the Store web page.

Office 2016 on Demand

Office 2016 comes in "traditional" editions, where you buy the program; you can install any traditional edition on one machine. Office 2016 also comes in "subscription" editions; essentially, you pay an annual rental fee to use the software on five PCs or Macs.

Subscription editions include the Office on Demand feature; subscribers can run temporary instances of Word, Excel, PowerPoint, Access, Publisher, Visio, and Project on computers where they normally would not be able to install software. To keep the process fast, only parts of the application actually download as needed, and it runs locally. When a program closes, it uninstalls itself.

Subscribers must be online and logged in to validate their right to use Office on Demand.

Sign In to Office 365

You can use Office Online or your Office 365 subscription to work from anywhere. While signed in from any device, you can use one of the free Office web apps. Office roams some of your personal settings such as your Recent Documents list so that you always have access to them. Desktop product users typically sign in using an Office 365 subscription, as described in this section and, for the most part, throughout the book.

When you work offline, Office creates, saves, and opens your files from the local OneDrive folder. Whenever you reconnect, Office automatically uploads your changes to the cloud.

Sign In to Office 365

 Open an Office program.

The program's Start screen appears.

 Click the Sign In link.

Note: *If you are viewing a document, click the Sign In link in the upper right corner of the screen.*

The Sign In window appears.

③ Type the Microsoft account email address associated with your Office 365 subscription.

④ Click **Next**.

⑤ Type your password.

Ⓐ If you have trouble signing in, you can click this link to reset your password.

⑥ Click **Sign in**.

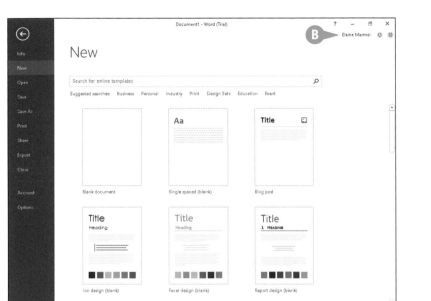

B This area indicates that you have signed in to Office 365.

Note: *Office Online offers free access to the online, limited-edition versions of the Office programs that you can use on any computer. Office 365 is a subscription you purchase to use full versions of the Office programs; Office 365 includes both the desktop and the online versions of the products.*

simplify it

How do I sign out of Office 365?
In any Office program, follow these steps:

1 Click the **File** tab.

2 Click **Account**.

Note: *In Outlook, click* ***Office Account.***

3 Click **Sign out.**

A The Remove Account dialog box appears, warning you that continuing removes all customizations and synchronization might stop.

Note: *In most cases, it is perfectly safe to click* ***Yes***. *If you are unsure, check with your system administrator.*

4 Click **Yes.**

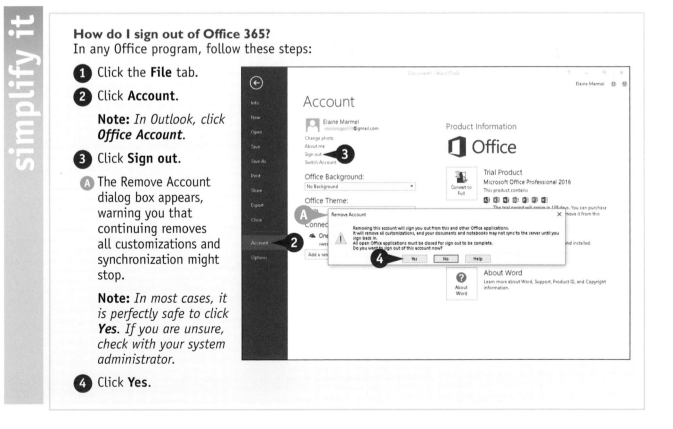

Share a Document from Office

You can easily share documents using Office 365. You can share an Office document by posting it using a social network, posting to a blog, or sending a document as an email attachment. You can also take advantage of a free online presentation service Microsoft offers and share your document by presenting it online. Or, as shown in this section, you can send a link to your OneDrive — as part of Office 2016, you receive free cloud space at OneDrive — where the recipient can view and even work on only the shared document. When you finish, you can stop sharing the document.

Share a Document from Office

Share a Document

Note: *You must be signed in to Office 365 and the document you want to share must be stored in the cloud. See the Simplify It tip for details.*

1. With the document you want to share on-screen, click **Share**.

The Share pane appears.

2. In the **Invite People** box, type email addresses of people with whom you want to share.

Note: *If you enter multiple addresses, Office separates them with a semicolon (;).*

3. Click ▼ and specify whether these people can edit or simply view the document.

Ⓐ You can type a personal message to include with the invitation.

4. Click **Share**.

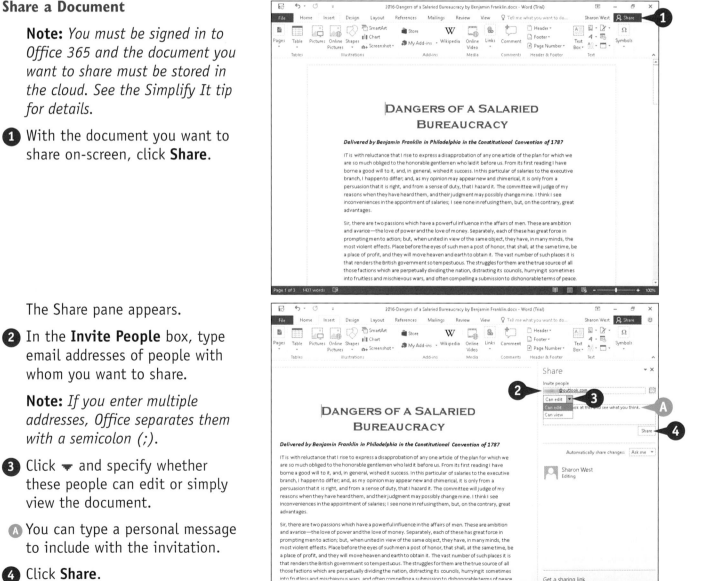

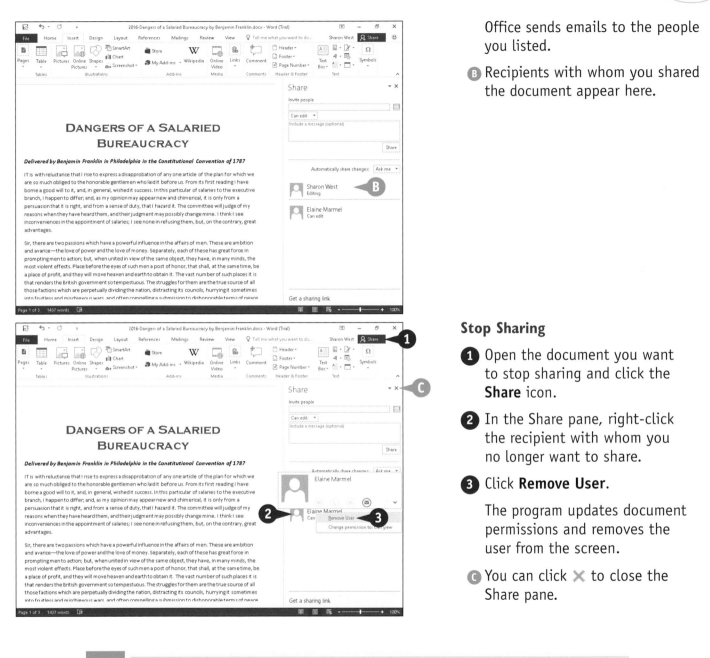

Office sends emails to the people you listed.

Ⓑ Recipients with whom you shared the document appear here.

Stop Sharing

❶ Open the document you want to stop sharing and click the **Share** icon.

❷ In the Share pane, right-click the recipient with whom you no longer want to share.

❸ Click **Remove User**.

The program updates document permissions and removes the user from the screen.

Ⓒ You can click ✕ to close the Share pane.

simplify it

Why do I see a screen indicating I must save my document before sharing it?
If you have not previously saved your document to your OneDrive space, the Office program prompts you to do so before starting the Share process. Click the **Save to Cloud** button that appears. The program displays the Save As pane in Backstage view; click your OneDrive and then click a folder in the Recent Folders list or click **Browse** to navigate to the OneDrive folder where you want to place the document.

Download Apps from the Office Store

You can use the Office Store to download add-on applications (or, apps) for Word, PowerPoint, or Excel. For example, the dictionary you use to look up words in Microsoft Word 2016 does not automatically install when you install the program. But, when you need an add-on, you can download it from the Office Store.

In addition to add-on apps you have used in the past, the Office Store also contains apps created by developers outside of Microsoft — apps that work with Word, Excel, and PowerPoint. The developer can choose to charge for an app or make it available for free.

Download Apps from the Office Store

1 Click the **Insert** tab.

2 Click **My Add-ins**.

The Office Add-ins dialog box appears, displaying the My Apps tab.

3 Click the **Store** tab to search for new apps.

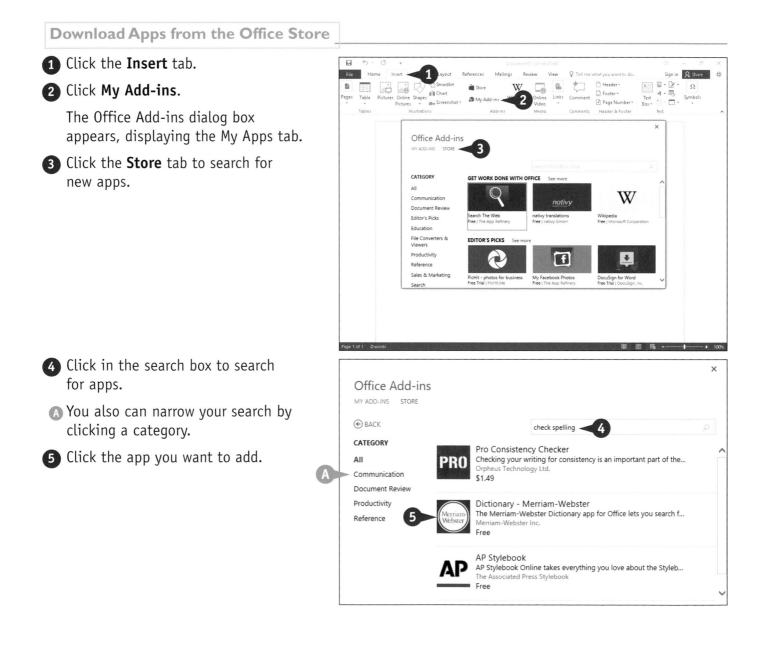

4 Click in the search box to search for apps.

A You also can narrow your search by clicking a category.

5 Click the app you want to add.

The details for the app appear.

Note: *This section adds the Merriam-Webster Dictionary app to Word (and Excel) as an example.*

6 Click **Trust It**.

The app loads.

B For the Merriam-Webster Dictionary app, a pane opens on the right side of the Word screen, enabling you to type a word to look up.

What should I do for add-ins for other Office 2016 programs?
OneNote and Publisher use the Add-Ins pane of the Options dialog box, as they did in earlier editions of Office, to manage add-ins. For dictionary lookups, these programs use the same Review tab that appears in earlier editions of Office. In Outlook, pop out a reply or a forward message window and the Review tab becomes visible. Access manages its add-ins using the Add-In Manager, available from the Database Tools tab.

Sign In to OneDrive

You can use your OneDrive and Office 2016 programs to work from any location in the world on any trusted device. OneDrive offers you online storage from Microsoft. With Office 2016, you automatically receive a small amount of storage space for free, and you can rent additional storage space for a nominal fee.

You use a browser and a Microsoft Account to sign in to OneDrive. Once you have signed in to OneDrive, you can use Office web apps to open and edit documents. Office 2016 technology synchronizes documents stored in your OneDrive with documents stored on trusted devices.

Sign In to OneDrive

1 Open your browser.

2 In the address bar, type **onedrive.com** and press `Enter`.

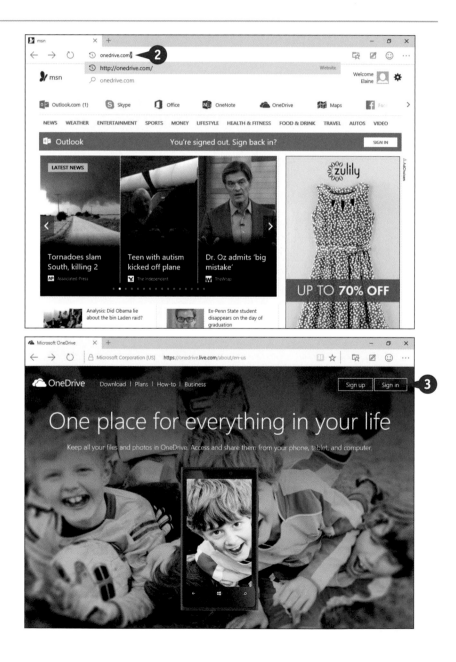

You are redirected to the OneDrive Home page.

3 Click **Sign in**.

4 A banner appears where you type your email address and click **Next**.

Ⓐ The full sign-in page appears, populated with your email address.

➎ Type your Microsoft Account password.

➏ Click **Sign in**.

Your OneDrive space appears.

How do I sign out of OneDrive?
Click your name (Ⓐ) and then click **Sign out** (Ⓑ).

Using an Online App in OneDrive

From OneDrive, you can use Office web apps to open and edit Office documents with the same basic editing tools you use in the Office program.

Although you cannot create or use macros, you can use these editing tools to perform basic functions in each Office program. For example, in the Word online app shown in this section, you can apply character and paragraph formatting, such as bold or italics, and you can align text. You can change margins, edit headers and footers, and insert a table or a picture stored on the local drive.

Using an Online App in OneDrive

Open the Document

1 Sign in to OneDrive at https://onedrive.com.

2 Open the folder containing the document you want to view.

3 Click the document.

The document appears in the web app for viewing only.

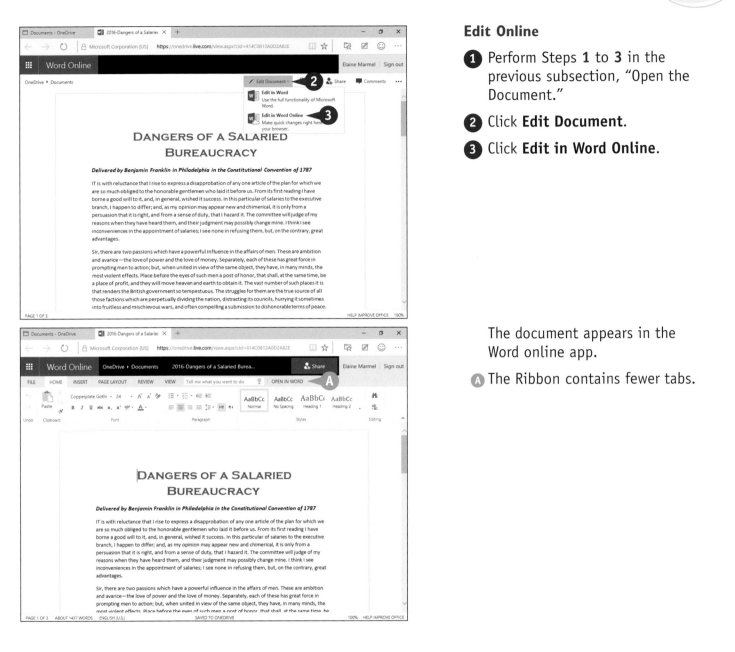

Edit Online

1 Perform Steps **1** to **3** in the previous subsection, "Open the Document."

2 Click **Edit Document**.

3 Click **Edit in Word Online**.

The document appears in the Word online app.

A The Ribbon contains fewer tabs.

How do I save my work in an online app?
The answer depends on the online app. OneNote automatically saves changes as you work. In the Word, Excel, and PowerPoint online apps, you save new documents by clicking the **File** tab and then clicking **Save As**; subsequently, the online app uses the name you originally supply. See the next section, "Using an Office Program from OneDrive," for information on using Publisher and Access while you are on the go.

How do I close a document I opened in the cloud?
Each online app opens in its own browser tab. Close the browser tab.

Using an Office Program from OneDrive

You can use Office 2016 to work from anywhere. For example, suppose you work on a document stored in your OneDrive space and discover that you need tools not available in the online app. If Office 2016 is installed on the computer, you can use OneDrive tools to open the file in the appropriate Office program.

If Office 2016 is *not* installed on the computer *but* you have a subscription to Office 2016, OneDrive can open the Office program you need. In just a few seconds, OneDrive installs it on the computer you currently use. When you close the program, OneDrive uninstalls it.

Using an Office Program from OneDrive

1 Open a document and edit it using an online app.

Note: *See the previous section, "Using an Online App in OneDrive," for details.*

Note: *This section uses an Excel workbook as an example.*

2 Click **Open In Excel**.

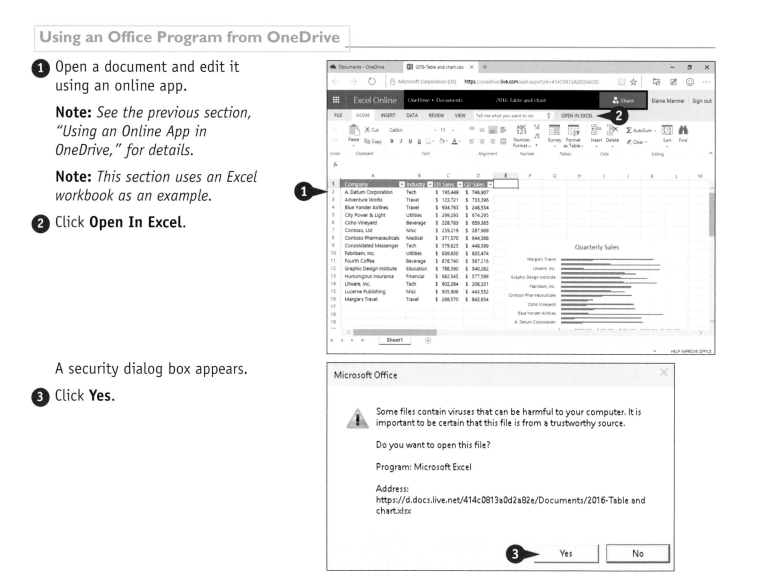

A security dialog box appears.

3 Click **Yes**.

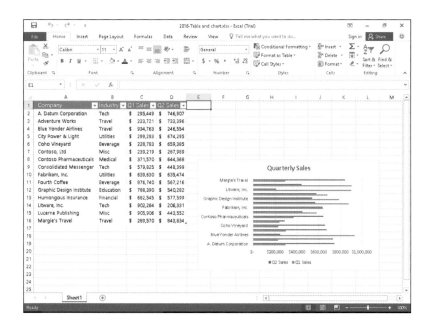

The file opens in the appropriate Office program.

Note: *As long as the file is open in the Office desktop application, you cannot edit it using the web app, but you can view it.*

simplify it

How can I tell that changes I have made are saved to my OneDrive space?
When you save your document in the Office program, watch the status bar in the program. A message (Ⓐ) appears, telling you that your changes are being uploaded to your OneDrive space.

Upload a Document to OneDrive

You can upload any document from your computer to your OneDrive at any time. By default, Office 2016 saves all documents to the OneDrive folder on your computer and then, in the background, synchronizes the contents of the OneDrive folder with your OneDrive.

But suppose that you sign out of Office 365 and choose to save documents locally on your computer. If you then find that you need a document in your OneDrive space to edit while you travel, you can place a document into your OneDrive folder on your computer and then upload it from your OneDrive space.

Upload a Document to OneDrive

1 Sign in to OneDrive using your browser.

Note: *See the section "Sign In to OneDrive" for details.*

2 Click to display the folder where you want to place the document.

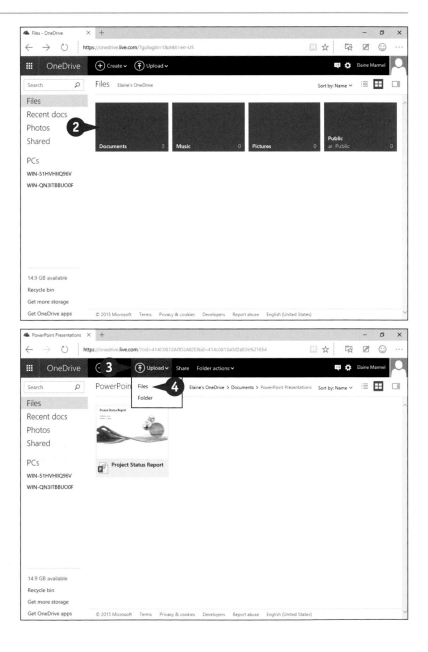

3 Click **Upload**.

4 Click **Files**.

The Open dialog box appears.

5 Navigate to the folder containing the file you want to upload.

6 Click the file.

7 Click **Open**.

A The file appears in your OneDrive space.

How do I create a folder in my OneDrive space so that I can organize my documents by type?

Navigate to the OneDrive folder where you want to place the new folder. Then, click **Create** (**A**) and, from the menu that appears, click **Folder**. Supply a name for the folder and click **Create**.

Share a Document Using OneDrive

You can use the OneDrive app to share a document stored on your OneDrive. Suppose that you finish the work on a document from your OneDrive space and you are ready for others to review it. You do not need to use the Office program installed on your local computer to invite others to review the document; you can use commands available in OneDrive.

OneDrive offers three ways to share a document: You can send the document by email, share it using a social media service of your choice, or send a link to the document on your OneDrive.

Share a Document Using OneDrive

Open a Document to Share

1 In OneDrive, open the document you want to share.

2 Click **Share**.

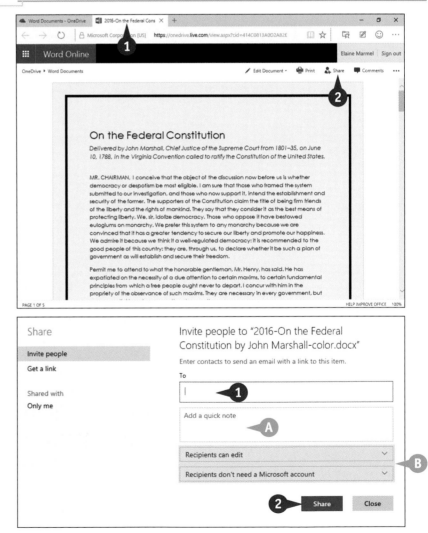

The Share dialog box appears.

Note: *Follow the steps in one of the following subsections to share the document.*

Share via Email

1 Fill in the email address of the person(s) with whom you want to share the document.

A You can include a personal message here.

B Use these list boxes to control how recipients can edit.

2 Click **Share**.

Email messages are sent to the recipients you supplied, providing a link to the document.

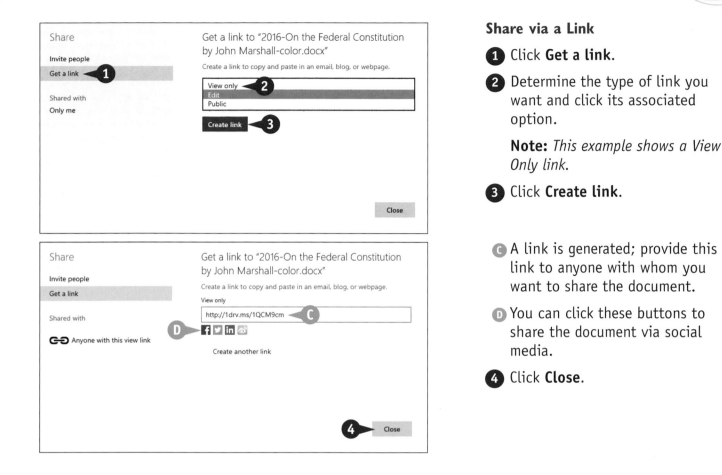

Share via a Link

1 Click **Get a link**.

2 Determine the type of link you want and click its associated option.

Note: *This example shows a View Only link.*

3 Click **Create link**.

C A link is generated; provide this link to anyone with whom you want to share the document.

D You can click these buttons to share the document via social media.

4 Click **Close**.

simplify it

How do I stop sharing a document?
Open the document and click **Share**. A window like this one appears. Click an entry in the Shared With list (**A**). Then, click **Remove link** (**B**). Repeat this process for each link you want to remove.

PART II

Word

You can use Word to tackle any project involving text, such as correspondence, reports, and more. Word's versatile formatting features enable you to easily enhance your text documents and add elements such as tables or headers and footers or to create numbered and bulleted lists. And, if you share documents with others, you can use Word's reviewing tools to monitor changes made as a document progresses from original to final form. In this part, you learn how to build and format Word documents and tap into Word's tools to review and proofread your documents.

Change Word's Views

You can control how you view your Word document in several ways. For example, you can use the Zoom feature to control the magnification of your document with either the Zoom slider or the Zoom buttons. You can even zoom an image separately from your document.

You can also choose from five different views: Print Layout, which displays margins, headers, and footers;

Outline, which shows the document's outline levels; Web Layout, which displays a web page preview of your document; Read Mode, which optimizes your document for easier reading; and Draft, which omits certain elements such as headers and footers.

Change Word's Views

Using the Zoom Tool

1 Drag the **Zoom** slider on the Zoom bar.

A You can also click a magnification button to zoom in or out.

B You can click the percentage to display the Zoom dialog box and precisely control zooming.

C Word magnifies the document, and the degree of magnification appears here.

Switch Layout Views

1 Click the **View** tab on the Ribbon.

2 Click a layout view button.

Word displays a new view of the document.

In this example, Read Mode view helps you focus on reading a document. See Chapter 8 for details on Read Mode.

D You can also switch views using the View buttons at the bottom of the program window.

---

simplify it

How can I zoom an image?
While in Read Mode view, double-click an image. Word enlarges the image and displays a zoom magnifying glass (🔍) in the upper right corner of the image. When you click 🔍 again, the image enlarges to fill your screen. You can click the zoom demagnifying glass (🔍) to return to the first zoom level, or you can press Esc or click anywhere outside the image to return to Read Mode. See Chapter 8 for more on Read Mode.

Type and Edit Text

You can use Word to quickly type and edit text for a letter, memo, or report. By default, Word is set to Insert mode; when you start typing, any existing text moves over to accommodate the new text. If you have set up Word to toggle between Insert mode and Overtype mode, you can press Insert to switch to Overtype mode. In Overtype mode, the new text overwrites the existing text.

Word makes typing easy; you do not need to worry about when to start a new line within a paragraph, and you can easily start new paragraphs and delete text.

Type and Edit Text

Type Text

1 Start typing your text.

A At the end of a line, Word automatically starts a new line, wrapping text to the next line for you.

B The insertion point marks your location in the document and moves to the right as you type. Text you type appears to the left of the insertion point.

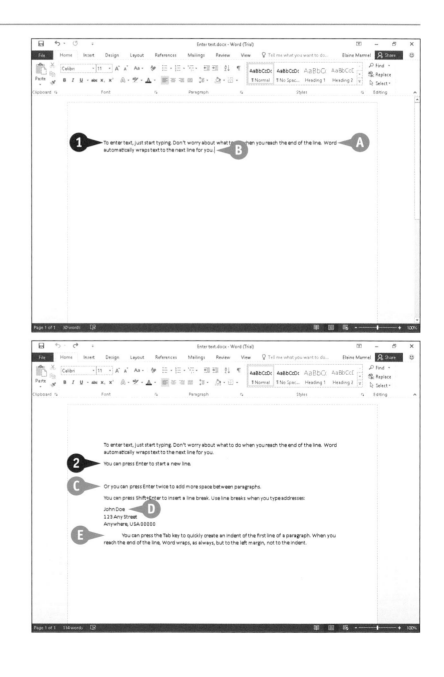

2 Press Enter to start a new paragraph.

C You can press Enter twice to add an extra space between paragraphs.

D You can press Shift + Enter to insert a line break and start a new line when your text does not fill the line. You often use line breaks when typing addresses.

E You can press Tab to quickly indent the first line of text in a paragraph.

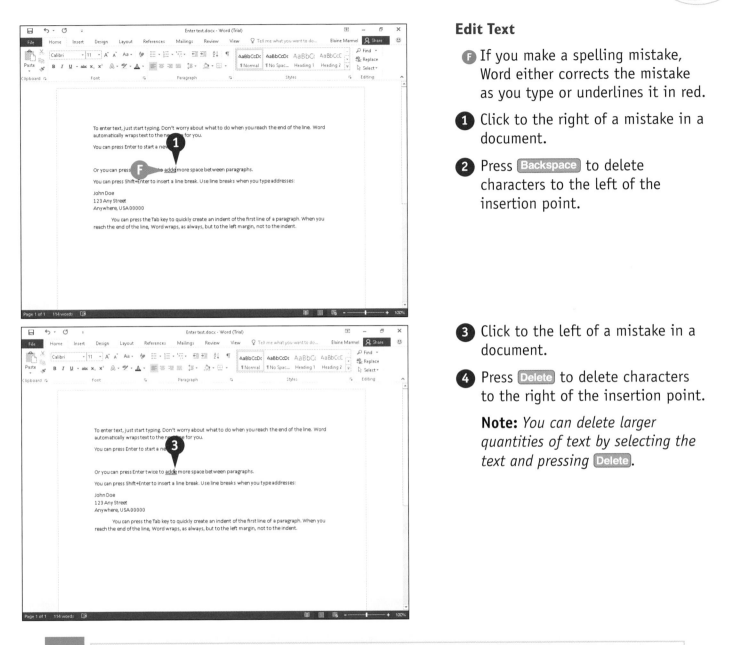

Edit Text

F If you make a spelling mistake, Word either corrects the mistake as you type or underlines it in red.

1 Click to the right of a mistake in a document.

2 Press `Backspace` to delete characters to the left of the insertion point.

3 Click to the left of a mistake in a document.

4 Press `Delete` to delete characters to the right of the insertion point.

Note: *You can delete larger quantities of text by selecting the text and pressing* `Delete`.

---

simplify it

What is the difference between the Insert and Overtype modes?
By default, Word is set to Insert mode so that, when you click to place the insertion point and start typing, any existing text moves to the right to accommodate new text. In Overtype mode, new text overwrites existing text. To toggle between these modes, enable `Insert` and then press it. To enable `Insert`, click the **File** tab, click **Options**, and click **Advanced** in the window that appears. Under Editing Options, select **Use the Insert key to control Overtype mode** (☐ changes to ☑) and then click **OK**.

Insert Quick Parts

Suppose you repeatedly type the same text in your documents — for example, your company name. You can add this text to the Quick Part Gallery in Word; then, the next time you need to add the text to a document, you can select it from the gallery instead of retyping it.

In addition to creating your own Quick Parts for use in your documents, you can use any of the wide variety of preset phrases included with Word. You access these preset Quick Parts from the Building Blocks Organizer window. (See the first Simplify It tip for more information.)

Insert Quick Parts

Create a Quick Parts Entry

1. Type the text that you want to store, including all formatting that should appear each time you insert the entry.

2. Select the text you typed.

3. Click the **Insert** tab.

4. Click the **Quick Parts** button (⊞ ·).

5. Click **Save Selection to Quick Part Gallery**.

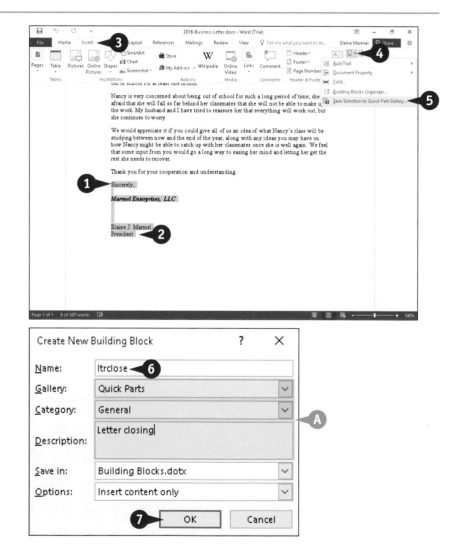

The Create New Building Block dialog box appears.

6. Type a name that you want to use as a shortcut for the entry.

Ⓐ You can also assign a gallery, a category, and a description for the entry.

7. Click **OK**.

Word stores the entry in the Quick Part Gallery.

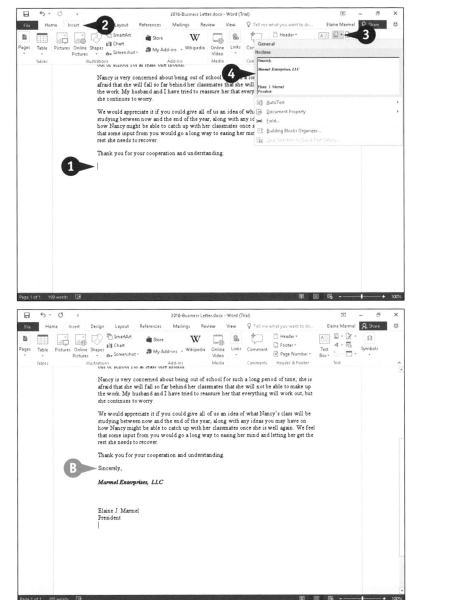

Insert a Quick Part Entry

1 Click in the text where you want to insert a Quick Part.

2 Click the **Insert** tab.

3 Click the **Quick Parts** button (📄 ▾).

All building blocks you define as Quick Parts appear in the Quick Part Gallery.

4 Click the entry that you want to insert.

B Word inserts the entry into the document.

How do I insert a preset Quick Part?
Click the **Insert** tab on the Ribbon, click the **Quick Parts** button (📄 ▾), and click **Building Blocks Organizer** to open the Building Blocks Organizer. Locate the Quick Part you want to insert (they are organized into galleries and categories), click it, and click **Insert**.

How do I remove a Quick Parts entry?
To remove a Quick Parts entry from the Building Blocks Organizer, open the Organizer (see the preceding Simplify It tip for help), locate and select the entry you want to remove, click **Delete**, and click **Yes** in the dialog box that appears.

Insert Symbols

From time to time, you might need to insert a mathematical symbol or special character into your Word document. From the Symbol Gallery, you can insert many common symbols, including mathematical and Greek symbols, architectural symbols, and more.

If you do not find the symbol you need in the Symbol Gallery, you can use the Symbol dialog box. The Symbol dialog box displays a list of recently used symbols as well as hundreds of symbols in a variety of fonts. You can also use the Symbol dialog box to insert special characters.

Insert Symbols

1 Click the location in the document where you want the symbol to appear.

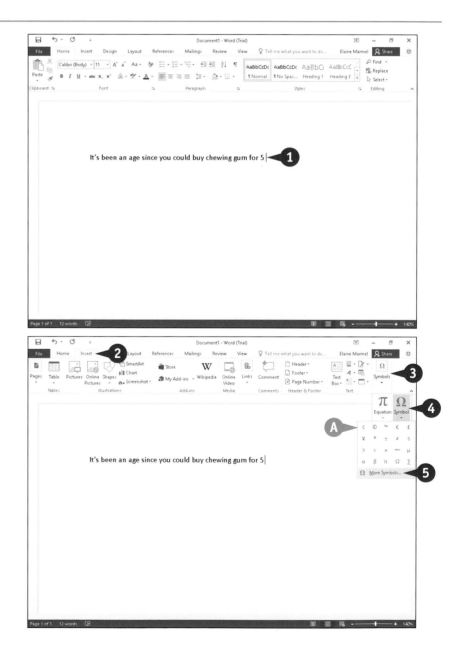

2 Click the **Insert** tab.

3 Click **Symbols**.

4 Click **Symbol**.

Ⓐ A gallery of commonly used symbols appears. If the symbol you need appears in the gallery, you can click it and skip the rest of these steps.

5 Click **More Symbols**.

The Symbol dialog box appears.

6 Click ∨ to select the symbol's font.

The available symbols change to match the font you selected.

B You can click ⋀ and ⋁ to scroll through available symbols.

7 Click a symbol.

8 Click **Insert**.

C The symbol appears at the current insertion point location in the document.

Note: *You can control the size of the symbol the same way you control the size of text; see Chapter 6 for details on sizing text.*

The dialog box remains open so that you can add more symbols to your document.

9 When finished, click **Close**.

How do I add a special character?
To add a special character, open the Symbol dialog box and click the **Special Characters** tab. Locate and click the character you want to add, and then click **Insert**. Click **Close** to close the dialog box.

	Character:	Shortcut key:
—	Em Dash	Alt+ Ctrl+ Num -
–	En Dash	Ctrl+ Num -
-	Nonbreaking Hyphen	Ctrl+ Shift+ _
¬	Optional Hyphen	Ctrl+-
	Em Space	
	En Space	
	1/4 Em Space	
°	Nonbreaking Space	Ctrl+ Shift+ Space
©	Copyright	Alt+ Ctrl+ C
®	Registered	Alt+ Ctrl+ R
™	Trademark	Alt+ Ctrl+ T
§	Section	
¶	Paragraph	
...	Ellipsis	Alt+ Ctrl+ ,
'	Single Opening Quote	Ctrl+ ` `
'	Single Closing Quote	Ctrl+ ' '
"	Double Opening Quote	Ctrl+ ` "
"	Double Closing Quote	Ctrl+ ' "

Create a Blog Post

If you keep an online blog, you can use Word to create a document to post on it and take advantage of the many proofing and formatting tools available in Word. You can then post the blog entry directly from Word.

To post your blog entry, you must first set up Word to communicate with the Internet server that hosts your online blog; the first time you post a blog entry from Word, the program prompts you to register your blog account. Click Register Now, choose your blog provider in the dialog box that appears, and follow the on-screen prompts.

Create a Blog Post

Note: *You must be connected to the Internet to complete this section.*

1 Open Word or, if Word is already open, click the **File** tab.

2 Click **New**.

3 Click **Blog post**.

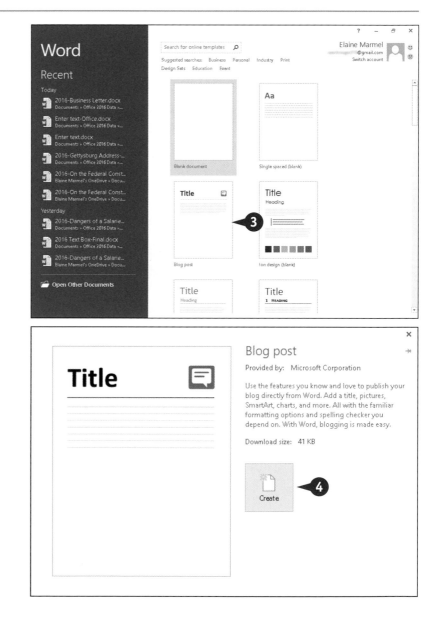

Word displays details about the Blog post template.

4 Click **Create**.

Word opens the blog post document.

Note: *The first time you use the blog feature, Word prompts you to register your blog account. Click **Register Now**, choose your blog provider in the dialog box that appears, and follow the on-screen prompts.*

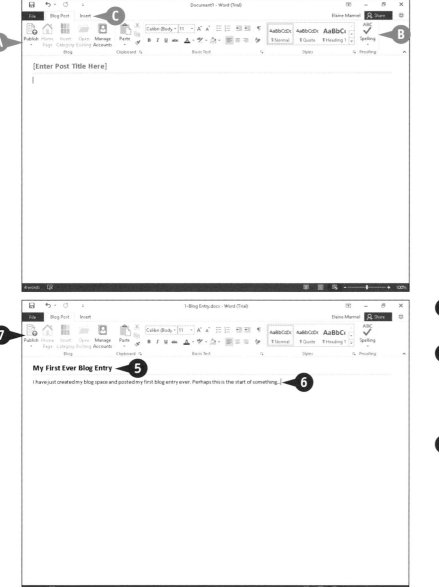

A You can use the buttons in the Blog group to manage blog entries. For example, you can click **Manage Accounts** to set up blog accounts.

B You can use the tools in the other Ribbon groups to format text as you type.

C You can use the buttons on the Insert tab to incorporate tables, pictures, clip art, shapes, graphics, screenshots, WordArt, symbols, and hyperlinks in a blog entry.

5 Click here and type a title for your blog entry.

6 Click here and type your entry.

Note: *You can save your blog entry on your hard drive the same way you save any document.*

7 Click **Publish**.

Word connects to the Internet, prompts you for your blog username and password, and posts your entry.

A message appears above the blog entry title, identifying when the entry was posted.

simplify it

Can I edit my blog accounts from within Word?
Yes. Click the **Manage Accounts** button on the Blog Post tab when viewing a blog page in Word to open the Blog Accounts dialog box. Here, you can edit an existing account, add a new account, or delete an account that you no longer use.

Can I post entries as drafts to review them before making them visible to the public?
Yes. Click ▼ on the bottom of the **Publish** button and click **Publish as Draft**. When you are ready to let the public view your entry, open it in Word and click **Publish**.

Change the Font, Size, and Color

By default, when you type text in a Word document, the program uses an 11-point Calibri font. You can change font — also called the *typeface* — text size, and color to alter the appearance of text in a document. For example, you might change the font, size, and color of your document's title text to emphasize it. In addition, you can use Word's basic formatting commands — Bold, Italic, Underline, Strikethrough, Subscript, and Superscript — to quickly add formatting to your text. And, you can change the font that Word applies by default for the body of a document.

Change the Font, Size, and Color

Change the Font

1 Select the text that you want to format.

A If you drag to select, the Mini toolbar appears faded in the background, and you can use it by moving the mouse (↖) toward the Mini toolbar.

2 To use the Ribbon, click the **Home** tab.

3 Click the **Font** ⯆ to display the font.

Note: *Word displays a sample of the selected text in any font at which you point the mouse (↖).*

4 Click the font you want to use.

B Word assigns the font to the selected text.

5 Click anywhere outside the selection to continue working.

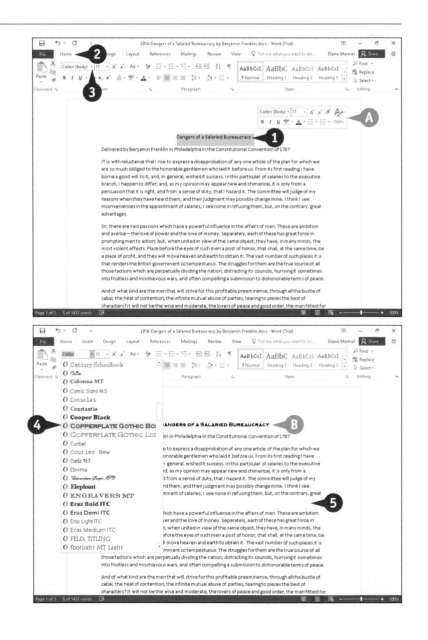

Change the Size

1 Select the text that you want to format.

C If you drag to select, the Mini toolbar appears faded in the background, and you can use it by moving the mouse (↖) toward the Mini toolbar.

2 To use the Ribbon, click the **Home** tab.

3 Click the **Font Size** ▼.

Note: *Word displays a sample of the selected text in any font size at which you point the mouse (↖).*

4 Click a size.

D Word changes the size of the selected text.

This example applies a 24-point font size to the text.

Note: *You also can change the font size using the **Increase Font Size** and **Decrease Font Size** buttons (A⁺ and A˅) on the Home tab. Word increases or decreases the font size with each click of the button.*

5 Click anywhere outside the selection to continue working.

---

simplify it

How do I apply formatting to my text?
To apply formatting to your text, select the text you want to format, click the **Home** tab, and click the **Bold** (**B**), **Italic** (*I*), **Underline** (U), **Strikethrough** (abc), **Subscript** (x₂), or **Superscript** (x²) button.

What is the toolbar that appears when I select text?
When you select text, the Mini toolbar appears, giving you quick access to common formatting commands. You can also right-click selected text to display the toolbar. To use any of the tools on the toolbar, simply click the desired tool; otherwise, continue working, and the toolbar disappears.

continued

Change the Font, Size, and Color *(continued)*

Changing the text color can go a long way toward emphasizing it on the page. For example, if you are creating an invitation, you might make the description of the event a different color to stand out from the other details. Likewise, if you are creating a report for work, you might make the title of the report a different color from the information contained in the report, or even color-code certain data in the report. Obviously, when selecting text colors, you should avoid choosing colors that make your text difficult to read.

Change the Color

1 Select the text that you want to format.

A If you drag to select, the Mini toolbar appears faded in the background, and you can use it by moving the mouse (⍦) toward the Mini toolbar.

2 To use the Ribbon, click the **Home** tab.

3 Click ▼ next to the **Font Color** button (**A** ▼) and point the mouse (⍦) at a color.

B Word displays a sample of the selected text.

4 Click a color.

Word assigns the color to the text.

This example applies a blue color to the text.

5 Click anywhere outside the selection to continue working.

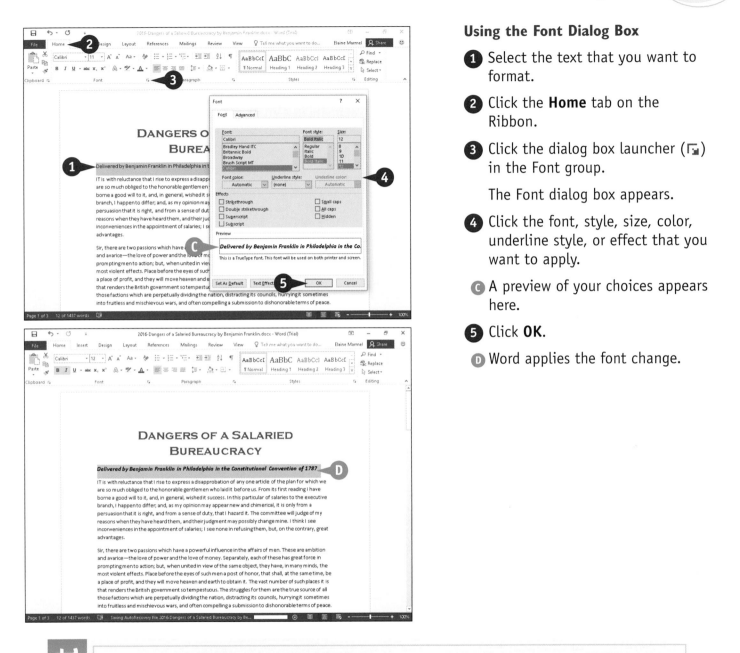

Using the Font Dialog Box

1 Select the text that you want to format.

2 Click the **Home** tab on the Ribbon.

3 Click the dialog box launcher (⌐) in the Font group.

The Font dialog box appears.

4 Click the font, style, size, color, underline style, or effect that you want to apply.

C A preview of your choices appears here.

5 Click **OK**.

D Word applies the font change.

Can I change the default font and size?
Yes. To change the default font and size, follow these steps: Display the Font dialog box. Click the font and font size that you want to set as defaults. Click the **Set As Default** button. A new dialog box appears. Specify whether the change should apply to this document only or to all documents created with the current template. Click **OK**, and click **OK** again to close the Font dialog box. The next time you create a new document, Word applies the default font and size that you specified.

Align
Text

You can use Word's alignment commands to change how text and objects are positioned horizontally on a page. By default, Word left-aligns text and objects. You can also choose to center text and objects on a page (using the Center command), align text and objects to the right side of the page (using the Right Align command), or justify text and objects so that they line up at both the left and right margins of the page (using the Justify command). You can change the alignment of all the text and objects in your document or change the alignment of individual paragraphs and objects.

Align Text

1 Click anywhere in the paragraph that you want to align or select the paragraphs and objects that you want to align.

2 Click the **Home** tab.

3 Click an alignment button.

The **Align Left** button (≡) aligns text with the left margin, the **Center** button (≡) centers text between the left and right margins, the **Align Right** button (≡) aligns text with the right margin, and the **Justify** button (≡) aligns text between the left and right margins.

Word aligns the text.

This example centers the text on the document page.

Ⓐ This text is aligned with the left margin.

Ⓑ This text is centered between both margins.

Ⓒ This text is aligned with the right margin.

Ⓓ This text is justified between both margins.

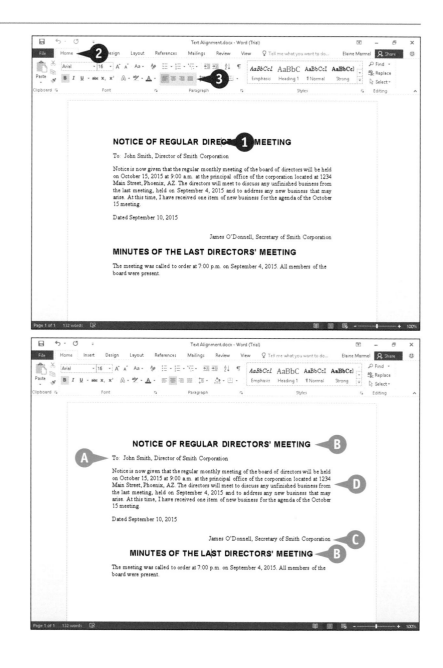

Set Line Spacing

You can adjust the amount of spacing that appears between lines of text in your paragraphs. For example, you might set 1.5 spacing to make paragraphs easier to read. By default, Word assigns 1.08 spacing for all new documents.

You can also control how much space appears before and after each paragraph in your document. You

might opt to single-space the text within a paragraph, but to add space before and after the paragraph to set it apart from the paragraphs that precede and follow it.

Set Line Spacing

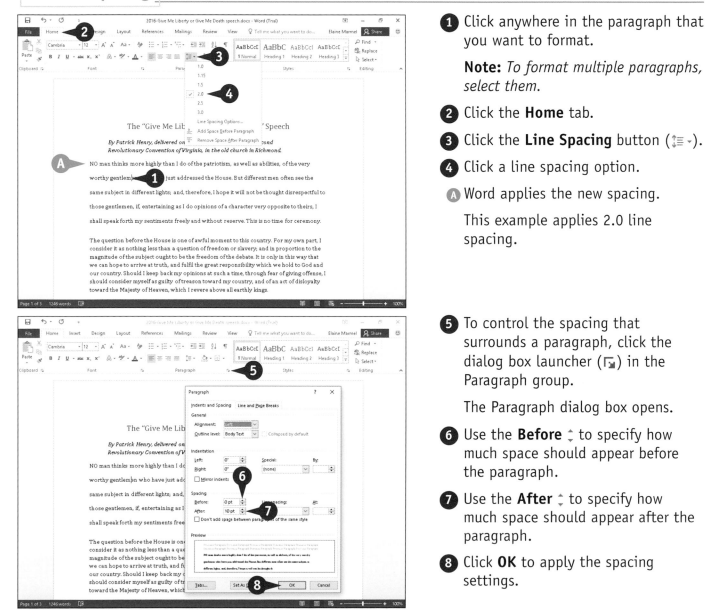

1. Click anywhere in the paragraph that you want to format.

   Note: *To format multiple paragraphs, select them.*

2. Click the **Home** tab.

3. Click the **Line Spacing** button (⬍≡ ▾).

4. Click a line spacing option.

   Ⓐ Word applies the new spacing.

   This example applies 2.0 line spacing.

5. To control the spacing that surrounds a paragraph, click the dialog box launcher (⬓) in the Paragraph group.

   The Paragraph dialog box opens.

6. Use the **Before** ⬍ to specify how much space should appear before the paragraph.

7. Use the **After** ⬍ to specify how much space should appear after the paragraph.

8. Click **OK** to apply the spacing settings.

Indent
Text

You can use indents as a way to control the horizontal positioning of text in a document. Indents are simply margins that affect individual lines or paragraphs. You might use an indent to distinguish a particular paragraph on a page — for example, a long quote.

You can indent paragraphs in your document from the left and right margins. You also can indent only the first line of a paragraph or all lines *except* the first line of the paragraph. You can set indents using buttons on the Ribbon, the Paragraph dialog box, and the Word ruler.

Indent Text

Set Quick Indents

1 Click anywhere in the paragraph you want to indent.

2 Click the **Home** tab on the Ribbon.

3 Click an indent button.

A You can click the **Decrease Indent** button (≣) to decrease the indentation.

B You can click the **Increase Indent** button (≣) to increase the indentation.

C Word applies the indent change.

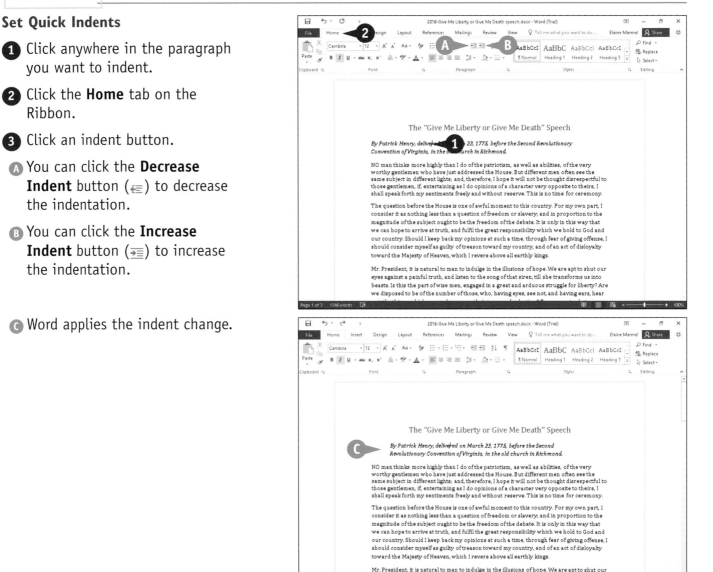

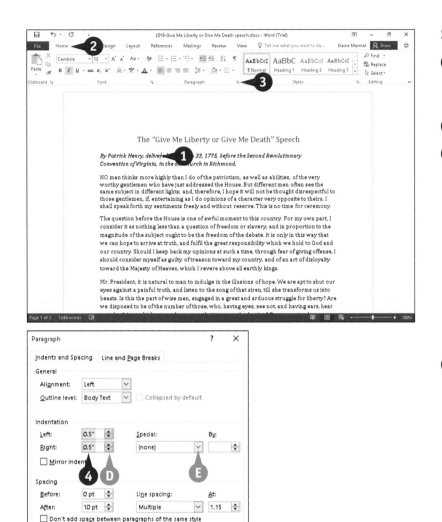

Set Precise Indents

1 Click anywhere in the paragraph you want to indent or select the text you want to indent.

2 Click the **Home** tab on the Ribbon.

3 Click the dialog box launcher (⌐⌐) in the Paragraph group.

The Paragraph dialog box appears.

4 Type a specific indentation in the **Left** or **Right** indent box.

D You can also click a spin arrow (⌃⌄) to set an indent measurement.

E To set a specific kind of indent, you can click the **Special** ⌄ and then click an indent.

F The Preview area shows a sample of the indent.

5 Click **OK**.

Word applies the indent to the text.

How do I set indents using the Word ruler?

The ruler contains markers for changing the left indent, right indent, first-line indent, and hanging indent. Click the **View** tab and select **Ruler** (☐ changes to ☑) to display the ruler. On the left side of the ruler, drag the **Left Indent** button (☐) to indent all lines from the left margin, drag the **Hanging Indent** button (△) to create a hanging indent, or drag the **First Line Indent** button (▽) to indent the first line only. On the right side of the ruler, drag the **Right Indent** button (△) to indent all lines from the right margin.

Set Tabs

You can use tabs to create vertically aligned columns of text in your Word document. To insert a tab, simply press Tab on your keyboard; the insertion point moves to the next tab stop on the page.

By default, Word creates tab stops every 0.5 inch across the page and left-aligns the text on each tab stop. You can set your own tab stops using the ruler or the Tabs dialog box. You can also use the Tabs dialog box to change the tab alignment and specify an exact measurement between tab stops.

Set Tabs

Set Quick Tabs

1 Click the **View** tab.

2 Select **Ruler** (☐ changes to ☑) to display the ruler.

3 Click here until the type of tab marker that you want to set appears.

ㄴ sets a left-aligned tab.

⊥ sets a center-aligned tab.

⌐ sets a right-aligned tab.

⊥: sets a decimal tab.

❙ sets a bar tab (displays a vertical bar at the tab location).

4 Select the lines to which you want to add the tab.

5 Click the ruler at the tab location you want.

On each selected line, Word adds a tab at the location you clicked.

6 Click at the end of the text after which you want to add a tab.

7 Press Tab.

8 Type the text that should appear in the next column.

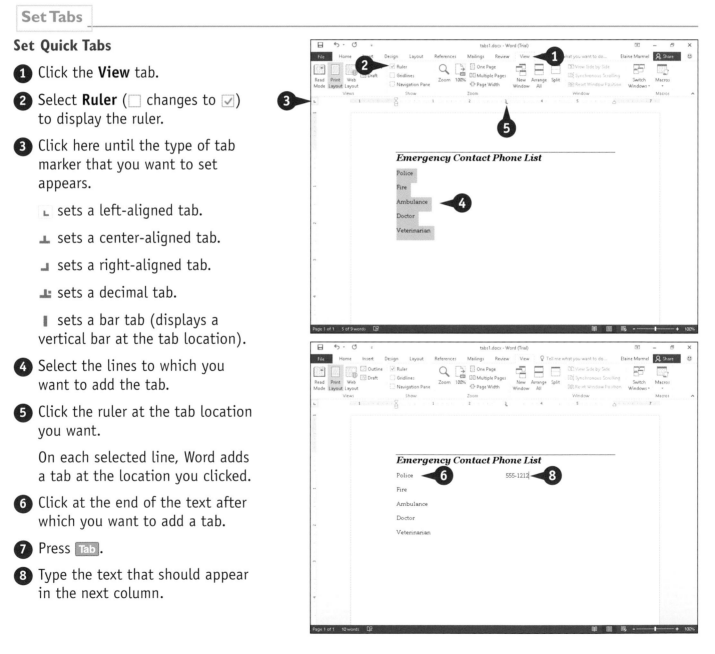

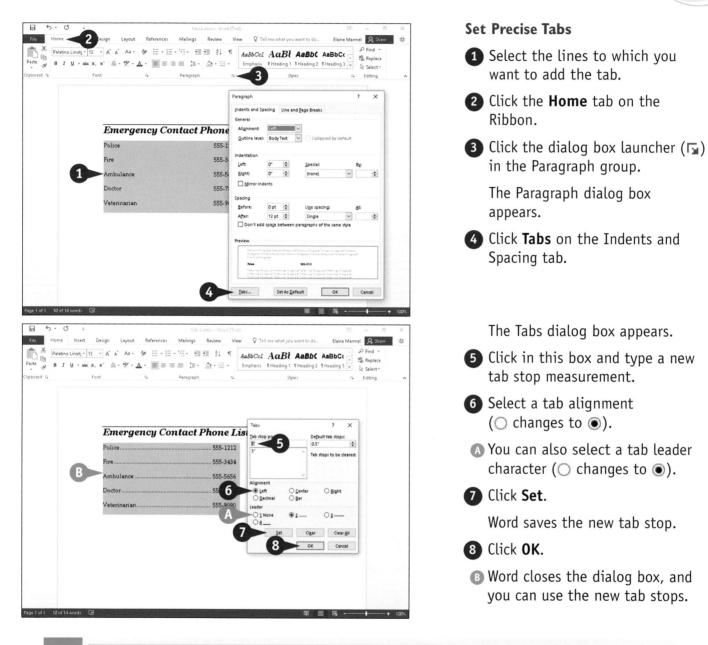

Set Precise Tabs

1 Select the lines to which you want to add the tab.

2 Click the **Home** tab on the Ribbon.

3 Click the dialog box launcher (⌐₅) in the Paragraph group.

The Paragraph dialog box appears.

4 Click **Tabs** on the Indents and Spacing tab.

The Tabs dialog box appears.

5 Click in this box and type a new tab stop measurement.

6 Select a tab alignment (○ changes to ◉).

Ⓐ You can also select a tab leader character (○ changes to ◉).

7 Click **Set**.

Word saves the new tab stop.

8 Click **OK**.

Ⓑ Word closes the dialog box, and you can use the new tab stops.

Can I remove tab stops that I no longer need?
Yes. To remove a tab stop from the ruler, drag the tab stop off the ruler. To remove a tab stop in the Tabs dialog box, select it and then click **Clear**. To clear every tab stop that you saved in the Tabs dialog box, click **Clear All**.

What are leader tabs?
You can use leader tabs to separate tab columns with dots, dashes, or lines. Leader tabs help readers follow the information across tab columns. You can set leader tabs using the Tabs dialog box, as shown in this section.

Set Margins

By default, Word assigns a 1-inch margin all the way around the page in every new document that you create. However, you can change these margin settings. For example, you can set wider margins to fit less text on a page, or set smaller margins to fit more text on a page. You can apply your changes to the current document only, or make them the new default setting, to be applied to all new Word documents you create. When you adjust margins, Word sets the margins from the position of the insertion point to the end of the document.

Set Margins

Set Margins Using Layout Tools

1 Click anywhere in the document or section where you want to change margins.

2 Click the **Layout** tab on the Ribbon.

3 Click **Margins**.

The Margins Gallery appears.

4 Click a margin setting.

A Word applies the new setting.

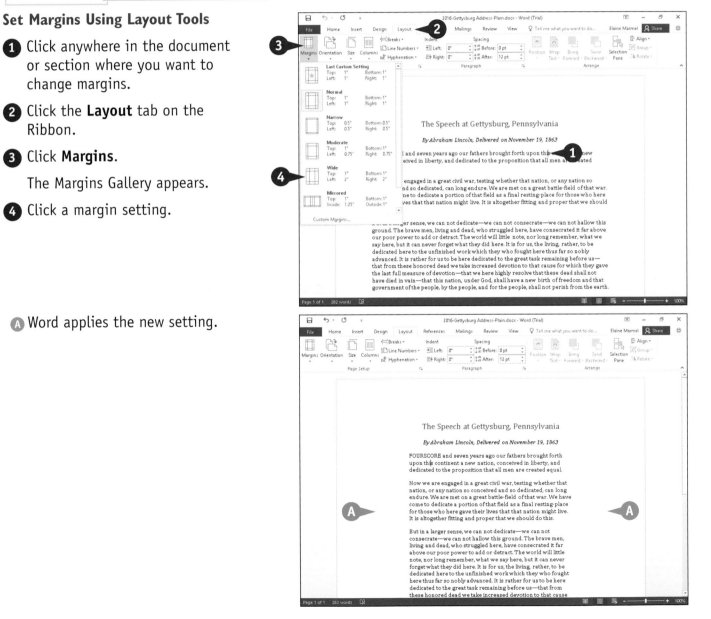

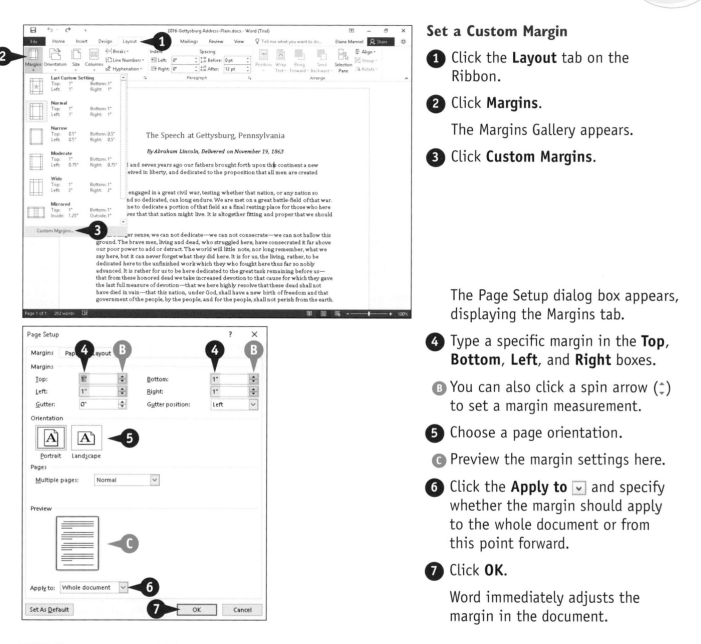

Set a Custom Margin

1 Click the **Layout** tab on the Ribbon.

2 Click **Margins**.

The Margins Gallery appears.

3 Click **Custom Margins**.

The Page Setup dialog box appears, displaying the Margins tab.

4 Type a specific margin in the **Top**, **Bottom**, **Left**, and **Right** boxes.

B You can also click a spin arrow (⬍) to set a margin measurement.

5 Choose a page orientation.

C Preview the margin settings here.

6 Click the **Apply to** ⬇ and specify whether the margin should apply to the whole document or from this point forward.

7 Click **OK**.

Word immediately adjusts the margin in the document.

simplify it

How do I set new default margins?
Make the desired changes to the Margins tab of the Page Setup dialog box, and click **Set As Default** before clicking **OK**. Click **Yes** in the dialog box that appears, asking if you want to change the default settings for every new document.

Why is my printer ignoring my margin settings?
In most cases, printers have a minimum margin setting of 0.25 inch. If you set your margins smaller than your printer's minimum margin setting, you place text in an unprintable area. Check your printer documentation for more information.

Create Lists

You can draw attention to lists of information by using bullets or numbers. Bulleted and numbered lists can help you present your information in an organized way. A bulleted list adds dots or other similar symbols in front of each list item, whereas a numbered list adds sequential numbers or letters in front of each list item. As a general rule, use bullets when the items in your list do not follow any particular order, and use numbers when the items in your list follow a particular order.

You can create a list as you type it or after you have typed list elements.

Create Lists

Create a List as You Type

1 Type **1.** to create a numbered list or ***** to create a bulleted list.

2 Press `Spacebar` or `Tab`.

A Word automatically formats the entry as a list item and displays the AutoCorrect Options button () so that you can undo or stop automatic numbering.

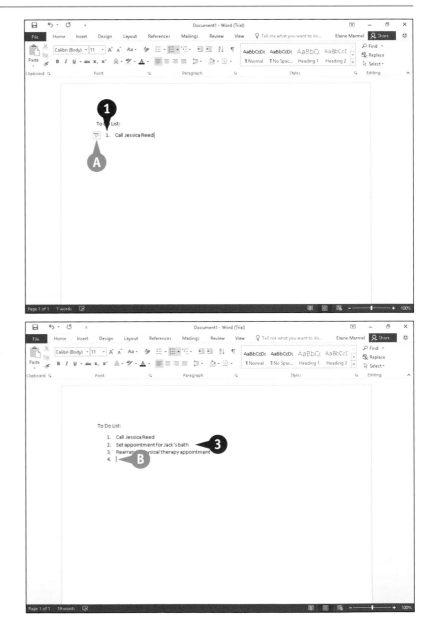

3 Type a list item.

4 Press `Enter` to prepare to type another list item.

B Word automatically adds a bullet or number for the next item.

5 Repeat Steps **3** and **4** for each list item.

To stop entering items in the list, press `Enter` twice.

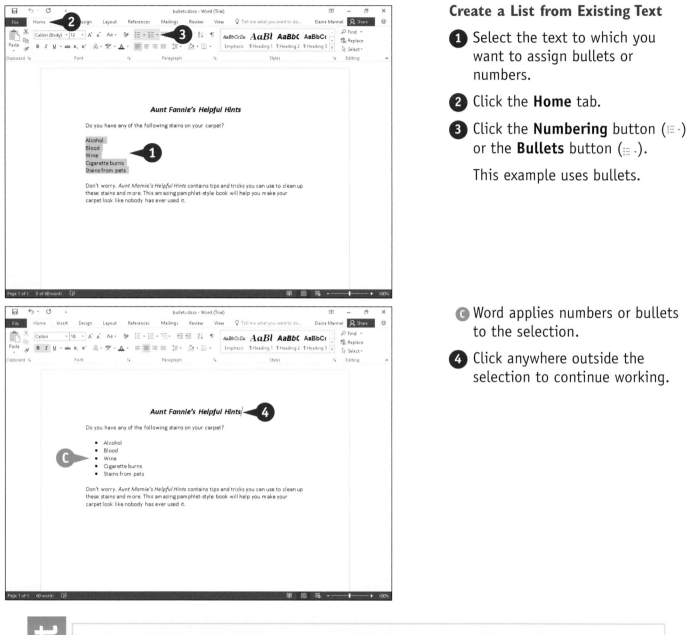

Create a List from Existing Text

1 Select the text to which you want to assign bullets or numbers.

2 Click the **Home** tab.

3 Click the **Numbering** button (≔ ▾) or the **Bullets** button (≔ ▾).

This example uses bullets.

C Word applies numbers or bullets to the selection.

4 Click anywhere outside the selection to continue working.

Can I create a bulleted or numbered list with more than one level, like the type of list you use when creating an outline?

Yes. Click the **Multilevel List** button (⊞⊟). Click a format (**A**) from the menu that appears and then type your list. You can press Enter to enter a new list item at the same list level. Each time you press Tab, Word indents a level in the list. Each time you press Shift + Tab, Word outdents a level in the list.

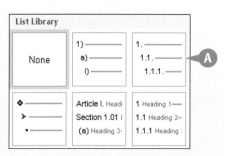

Copy
Formatting

Suppose you have applied a variety of formatting options to a paragraph to create a certain look — for example, you changed the font, the size, the color, and the alignment. If you want to re-create the same look elsewhere in the document, you do not have to repeat the same steps as when you applied the original formatting, again changing the font, size, color, and alignment. Instead, you can use the Format Painter feature to "paint" the formatting to the other text in one swift action. With the Format Painter feature, copying formatting is as easy as clicking a button.

Copy Formatting

① Select the text containing the formatting that you want to copy.

Ⓐ If you drag to select, the Mini toolbar appears in the background, and you can use it by moving the mouse (⌖) toward the Mini toolbar.

② To use the Ribbon, click the **Home** tab.

③ Click the **Format Painter** button (⏹).

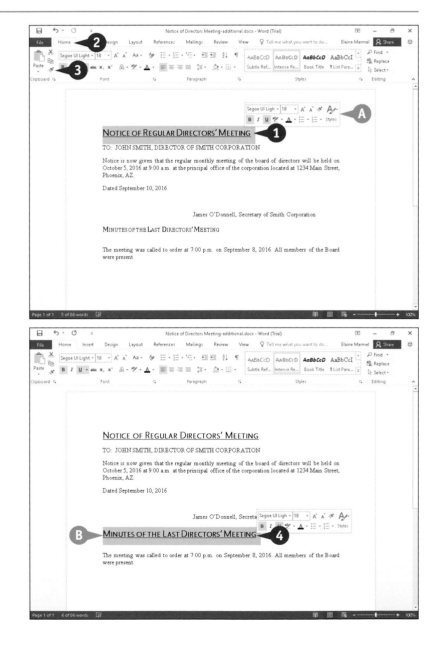

The mouse (⌖) changes to ⏹I when you move the mouse over your document.

④ Click and drag over the text to which you want to apply the same formatting.

Ⓑ Word copies the formatting from the original text to the new text.

To copy the same formatting multiple times, you can double-click the **Format Painter** button (⏹).

You can press Esc to cancel the Format Painter feature at any time.

Clear Formatting

Sometimes, you may find that you have applied too much formatting to your text, making it difficult to read. Or perhaps you simply applied the wrong formatting to your text. In that case, instead of undoing all your formatting changes manually, you can use the Clear Formatting command to remove any formatting you have applied to the document text. When you apply the Clear Formatting command, Word removes all formatting applied to the text and restores the default settings.

Clear Formatting

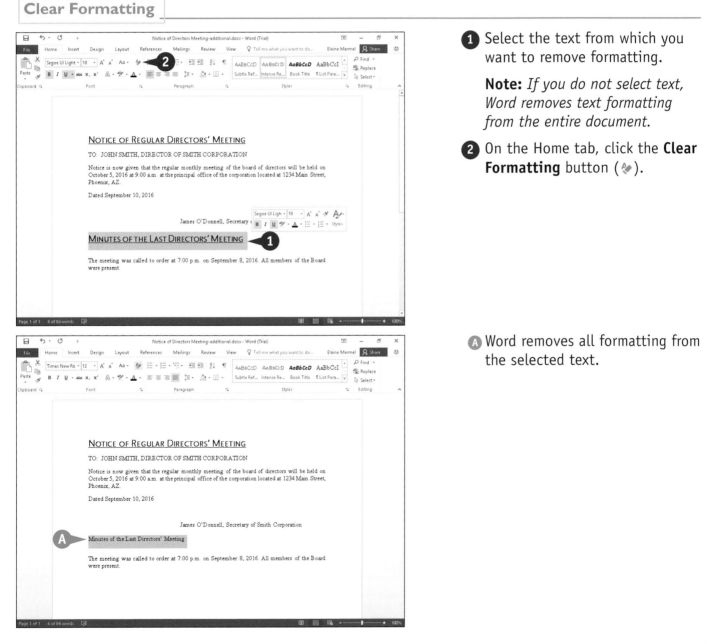

1 Select the text from which you want to remove formatting.

Note: *If you do not select text, Word removes text formatting from the entire document.*

2 On the Home tab, click the **Clear Formatting** button ( ).

A Word removes all formatting from the selected text.

Format with Styles

Suppose you are writing a corporate report that requires specific formatting for every heading. Instead of assigning multiple formatting settings over and over again, you can create a style with the required formatting settings and apply it whenever you need it. A *style* is a set of text-formatting characteristics. These characteristics might include the text font, size, color, alignment, spacing, and more.

In addition to creating your own styles for use in your documents, you can apply any of the preset styles that Word supplies. These include styles for headings, normal text, quotes, and more.

Format with Styles

Create a New Quick Style

1 Format the text as desired and then select the text.

2 Click the **Home** tab on the Ribbon.

3 Click the **More** button (⟱) in the Styles group.

4 Click **Create a Style**.

The Create New Style from Formatting dialog box appears.

5 Type a name for the style.

6 Click **OK**.

Word adds the style to the list of Quick Styles.

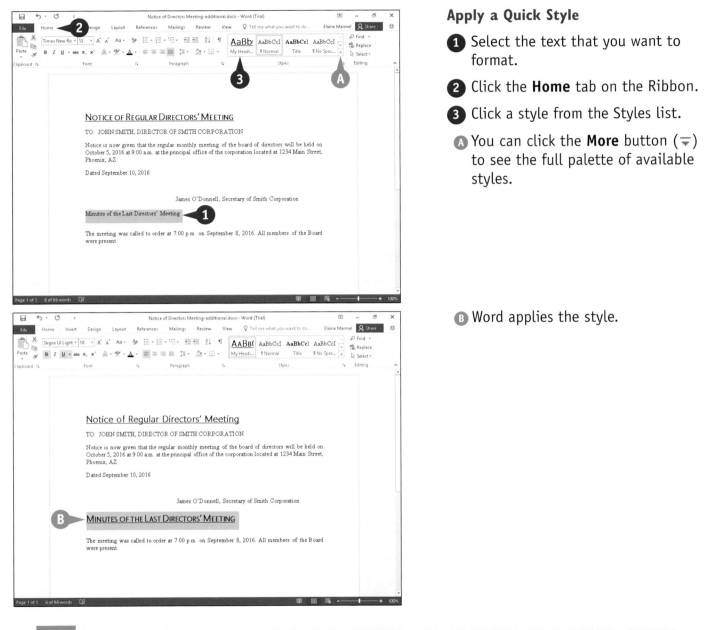

Apply a Quick Style

1 Select the text that you want to format.

2 Click the **Home** tab on the Ribbon.

3 Click a style from the Styles list.

A You can click the **More** button (⩣) to see the full palette of available styles.

B Word applies the style.

How do I remove a style that I no longer need?
From the Home tab, display the full Quick Styles palette, right-click the style that you want to remove, and click the **Remove from Style Gallery** command. Word immediately removes the style from the Quick Styles list.

How do I customize an existing style?
On the Home tab, in the Styles Gallery, right-click the style and click **Modify** to display the Modify Style dialog box. Click the type of change that you want to make. For example, to switch fonts, click the **Fonts** option and then select another font.

Using a Template

A *template* is a special file that stores styles and other Word formatting tools. When you create a Word document using a template, the styles and tools in that template become available for you to use with that document. Word comes with several templates preinstalled, and you can also create your own.

Pre-existing templates come typically with boilerplate text you can use as a model for your document. Simply select the boilerplate text and replace it with your own text. To add more text to the document, use the styles in the Styles Gallery, applying them to headings and important text.

Using a Template

1 From any document, click **File**.

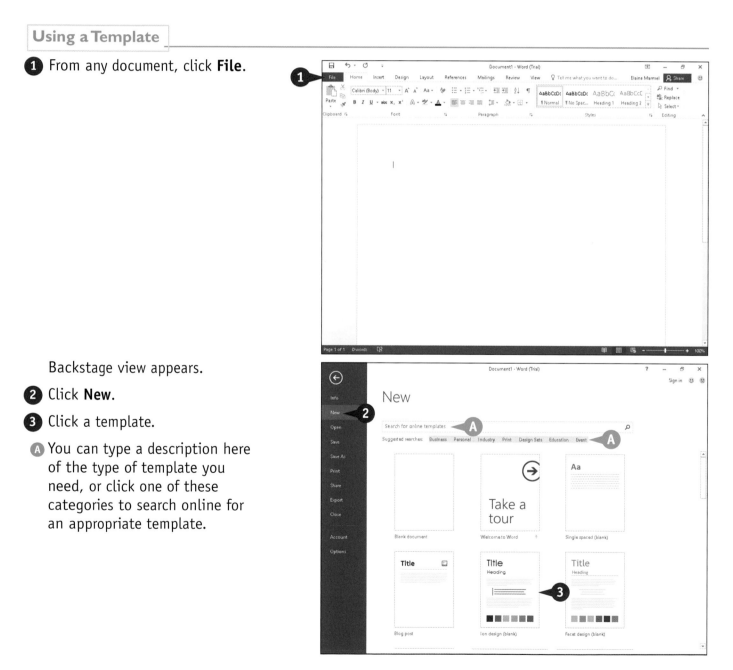

Backstage view appears.

2 Click **New**.

3 Click a template.

Ⓐ You can type a description here of the type of template you need, or click one of these categories to search online for an appropriate template.

Title

Heading
To take advantage of this template's design, use the Styles gallery on the Home tab. You can format your headings by using heading styles, or highlight important text using other styles, like Emphasis and Intense Quote. These styles come in formatted to look great and work together to help communicate your ideas.

Go ahead and get started.

Ion design (blank)

Provided by: Microsoft Corporation

A simple starting document featuring the Ion design. It has a clean look with a touch of personality that's perfect for any document. This template is great for when you want to start from blank but don't want the default look. To take advantage of this design, simply format headings and other text using the Styles gallery on the Home tab.

Download size: 38 KB

Create

④

Word displays a window like this one that describes the template you selected.

④ Click **Create**.

A document containing the template's styles appears.

Ⓑ You can replace boilerplate text with your own text.

Ⓒ You can use styles in the Styles Gallery to continue formatting the document.

Note: *See the previous section, "Format with Styles," for details on using and creating styles.*

How can I create my own templates?
The easiest way to create a template is to base it on an existing Word document that uses styles. Open the document on which you want to base your template, click the **File** tab, and click **Save As**. Select a place and click a folder, or click **Browse**. The Save As dialog box opens; locate and select the folder in which you want to save the template, type a name for it in the **File Name** box, click the **Save as type** ⌄, and choose **Word Template**. Click **Save** and Word saves the template in the folder you chose.

Insert an Online Video

You can insert a video available on the Internet into a Word document. After you have inserted the video, you can play it directly from the Word document.

You can insert videos you find using Bing Search or videos available on YouTube, or you can insert a video

embed code — an HTML code that uses the `src` attribute to define the video file you want to embed. Most videos posted on the Internet are public domain, but, if you are unsure, do some research to determine whether you can use the video freely.

Insert an Online Video

① Click where you want the video to appear.

② Click the **Insert** tab.

③ Click **Online Video**.

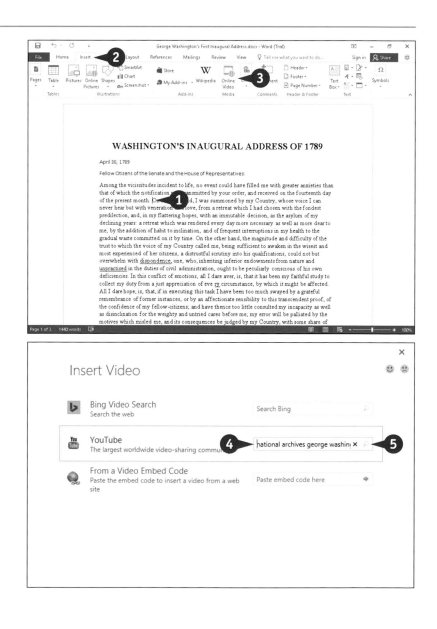

The Insert Video window appears.

④ In one of the search boxes, type a description of the video you want to insert.

Note: *This example searches YouTube.*

⑤ Click the **Search** button (🔍).

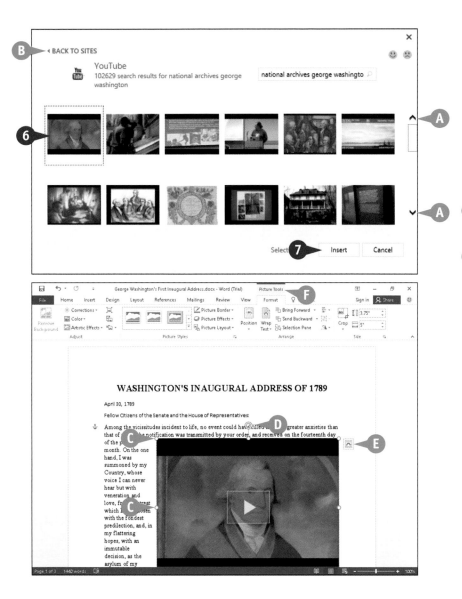

The results of your search appear.

Ⓐ You can click the arrows (∧ and ∨) to navigate through the search results.

Ⓑ You can click **Back to Sites** to return to the Insert Video window and search for a different video.

6 Click the video you want to add to your document.

7 Click **Insert**.

Ⓒ The video appears in your document, selected and surrounded by handles (○).

Ⓓ You can drag ⟳ to rotate the video.

Ⓔ The Layout Options button (▣) controls text flow around the video; see the section "Insert an Online Picture" in Chapter 3 for more information.

Ⓕ Picture Tools appear on the Ribbon; you can use these tools to format the video.

How do I play an inserted video?
From Print Layout view or Read Mode view, click the video **Play** button (▶). The video appears in its own window, the document appears behind a shaded, translucent background, and the Play button appears black. Click anywhere on the video — not just on the Play button — to start the video; as you slide the mouse (🖑) over the video, the Play button changes to red. To stop the video and return to the document, click anywhere outside the video on the shaded translucent background of the document window or press Esc.

Assign a Theme

A *theme* is a predesigned set of styles, color schemes, fonts, and other visual attributes. Applying a theme to a document is a quick way to add polish to it. And, because themes are shared among the Office programs, you can use the same theme in your Word document that you have applied to worksheets in Excel or slides in PowerPoint.

Note that the effect of applying a theme is more obvious if you have assigned styles such as headings to your document. The effects of themes are even more pronounced when you assign a background color to a page.

Assign a Theme

Apply a Theme

1 Click the **Design** tab.

2 Click the **Themes** button.

3 Click a theme.

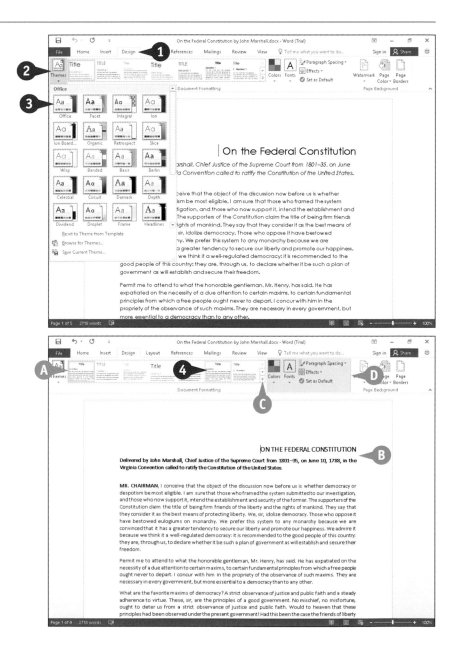

Although nothing seems to happen, Word applies the theme to the current document.

4 To see the effects of a theme, slide your mouse (⇧) across the styles in the Style Sets palette.

Ⓐ The leftmost entry in the Style Sets palette represents the currently applied style set.

Ⓑ Word displays the changes a style set will make to your document; click a style set to select it.

Ⓒ You can click the **More** button (⥥) to display additional style sets.

Ⓓ You can use these tools to change the formatting of the theme's colors, fonts, paragraph spacing (⩦), and effects (⬤).

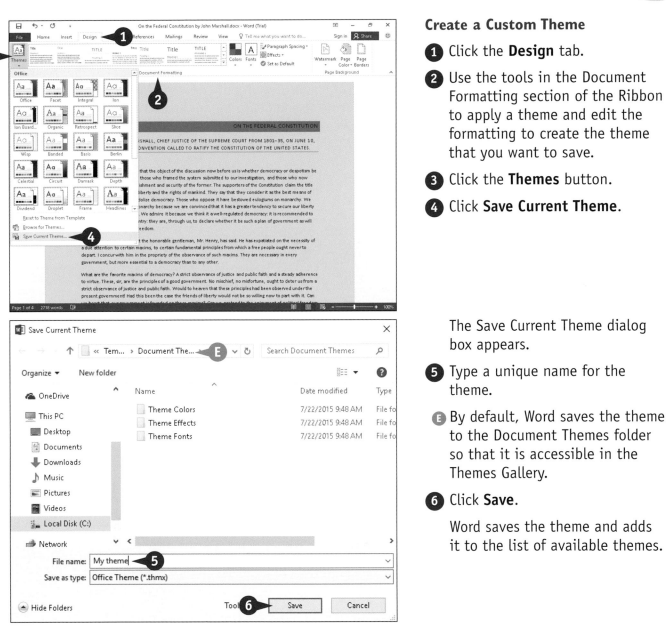

Create a Custom Theme

1. Click the **Design** tab.

2. Use the tools in the Document Formatting section of the Ribbon to apply a theme and edit the formatting to create the theme that you want to save.

3. Click the **Themes** button.

4. Click **Save Current Theme**.

The Save Current Theme dialog box appears.

5. Type a unique name for the theme.

E. By default, Word saves the theme to the Document Themes folder so that it is accessible in the Themes Gallery.

6. Click **Save**.

Word saves the theme and adds it to the list of available themes.

---

simplify it

How did you make the page blue?

To apply a page color, click the **Design** tab on the Ribbon, click the **Page Color** button in the Page Background group, and click a color in the palette; Word applies the color you selected to the background of the page. Although you can apply a background color to the pages of your document, be aware that Word does not save page colors as part of themes. Remember that themes are most effective in helping you establish a set of predefined styles available in a document. For help applying a style, see the section "Format with Styles" in Chapter 6.

Add
Borders

You can apply borders around your text to add emphasis or make the document aesthetically appealing. You can add borders around a single paragraph, multiple paragraphs, or each page in the document. (Be aware that you should not add too many effects, such as borders, to your document because it will become difficult to read.)

Word comes with several predesigned borders, which you can apply to your document. Alternatively, you can create your own custom borders — for example, making each border line a different color or thickness. Another option is to apply shading to your text to set it apart.

Add Borders

Add a Paragraph Border

1 Select the text to which you want to add a border.

2 Click the **Home** tab on the Ribbon.

3 Click the **Borders** button (⊞ ▾).

4 Click a border.

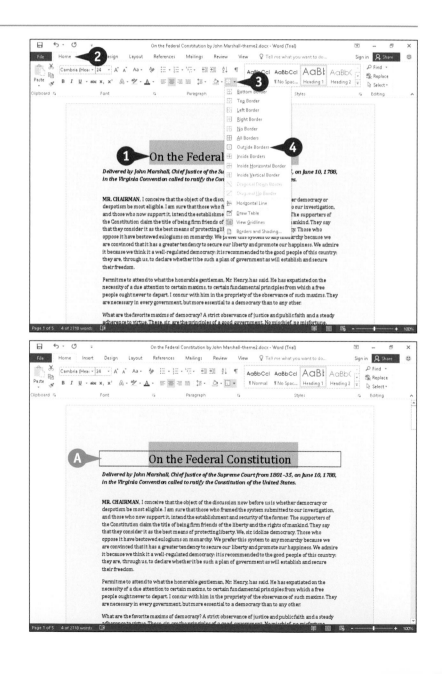

A Word applies the border to the text.

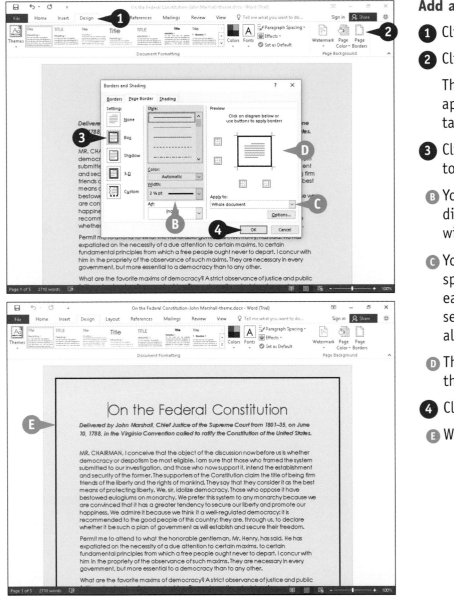

Add a Page Border

1 Click the **Design** tab.

2 Click the **Page Borders** button.

The Borders and Shading dialog box appears, and displays the Page Border tab.

3 Click the type of border that you want to add.

B You can use these settings to select a different border line style, color, and width.

C You can click the **Apply to** to specify whether to apply the border to each page of your entire document, a section, the first page of a section, or all pages of a section except the first.

D The Preview area displays a sample of the selections.

4 Click **OK**.

E Word applies the page border.

---

simplify it

How do I add shading to my text?
To add shading behind a block of text, select the text, click the **Home** tab on the Ribbon, click the **Shading** button (🖌) in the Paragraph group, and click a color.

How do I create a custom border?
Select the text to which you want to add a border, open the **Borders and Shading** dialog box, click the **Borders** tab, and choose **Custom**. Choose the settings to apply to the first line of the border; then click in the **Preview** area where you want the line to appear. Repeat for each line you want to add, and then click **OK**.

Create Columns

You can create columns in Word to present your text in a format similar to a newspaper or magazine. For example, if you are creating a brochure or newsletter, you can use columns to make text flow from one block to the next.

If you simply want to create a document with two or three columns, you can use one of Word's preset columns. Alternatively, you can create custom columns, choosing the number of columns you want to create in your document, indicating the width of each column, specifying whether a line should appear between them, and more.

Create Columns

Create Quick Columns

1 Select the text that you want to place into columns.

Note: *If you want to apply columns to all text in your document, skip Step 1.*

2 Click the **Layout** tab.

3 Click the **Columns** button.

4 Click the number of columns that you want to assign.

 Word displays the selected text, or your document if you skipped Step **1**, in the number of columns that you specified.

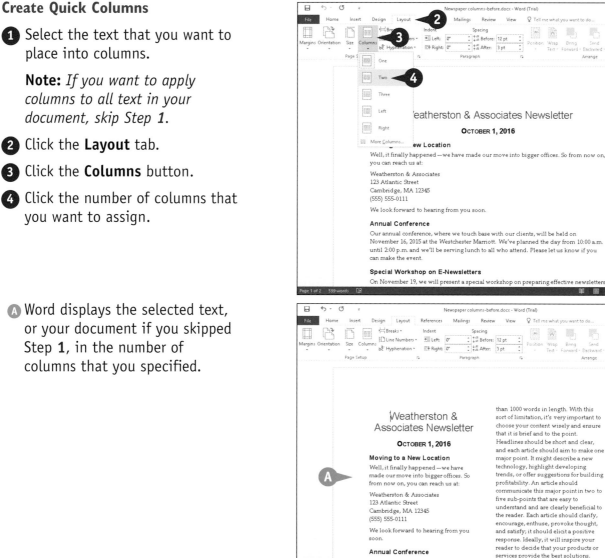

98

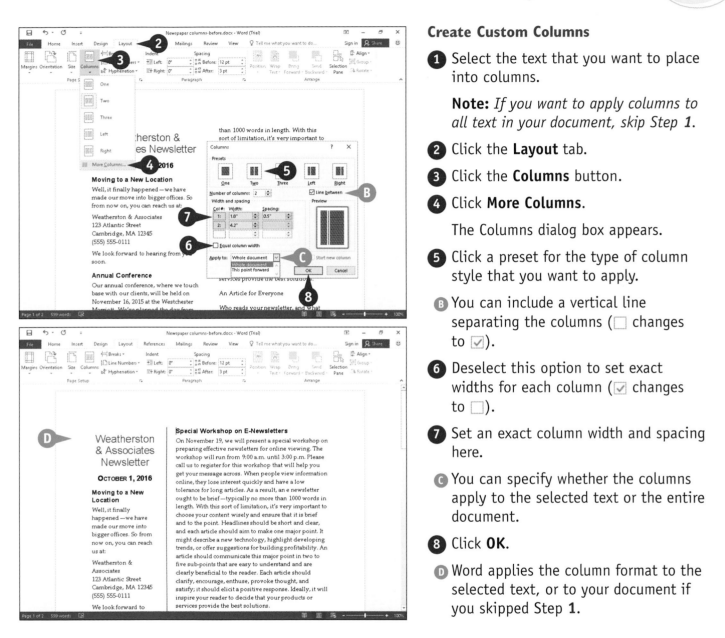

Create Custom Columns

1 Select the text that you want to place into columns.

Note: *If you want to apply columns to all text in your document, skip Step 1.*

2 Click the **Layout** tab.

3 Click the **Columns** button.

4 Click **More Columns**.

The Columns dialog box appears.

5 Click a preset for the type of column style that you want to apply.

B You can include a vertical line separating the columns (☐ changes to ☑).

6 Deselect this option to set exact widths for each column (☑ changes to ☐).

7 Set an exact column width and spacing here.

C You can specify whether the columns apply to the selected text or the entire document.

8 Click **OK**.

D Word applies the column format to the selected text, or to your document if you skipped Step **1**.

simplify it

How do I wrap column text around a picture or other object?
Click the picture or other object that you want to wrap, click the **Format** tab, click the **Wrap Text** button, and then click the type of wrapping that you want to apply.

Can I create a break within a column?
Yes. To add a column break, click where you want the break to occur and then press Ctrl + Shift + Enter . To remove a break, select it and press Delete . To return to a one-column format, click the **Columns** button on the Layout tab, and then select the single-column format.

Insert a Table

You can use tables to present data in an organized fashion. For example, you might add a table to your document to display a list of items or a roster of classes. Tables contain columns and rows, which intersect to form cells. You can insert all types of data in cells, including text and graphics.

To enter text in a cell, click in the cell and then type your data. As you type, Word wraps the text to fit in the cell. Press `Tab` to move from one cell to another. You can select table cells, rows, and columns to perform editing tasks and apply formatting.

Insert a Table

Insert a Table

1. Click in the document where you want to insert a table.

2. Click the **Insert** tab.

3. Click the **Table** button.

Ⓐ Word displays a table grid.

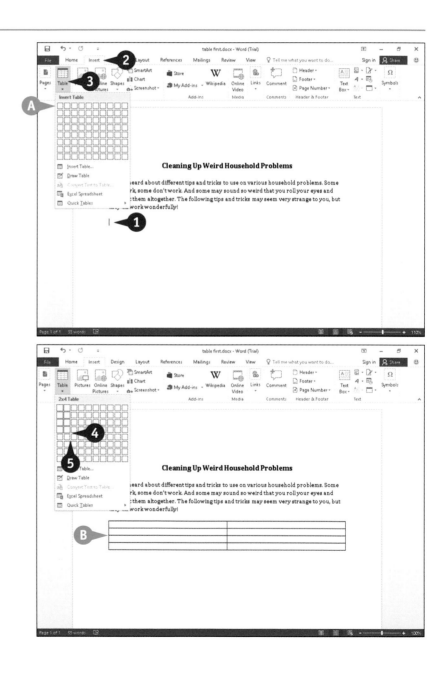

4. Slide the mouse (⇖) across the squares that represent the number of rows and columns you want in your table.

Ⓑ Word previews the table as you drag over cells.

5. Click the square representing the lower right corner of your table.

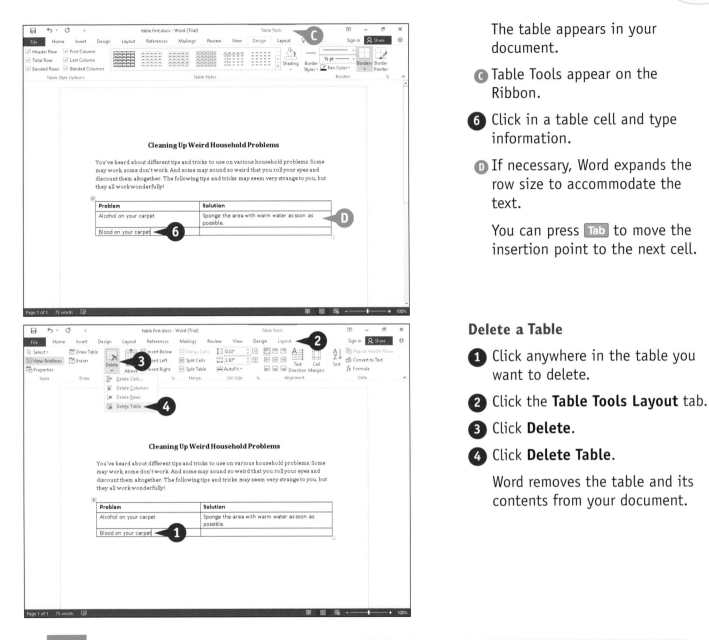

The table appears in your document.

C Table Tools appear on the Ribbon.

6 Click in a table cell and type information.

D If necessary, Word expands the row size to accommodate the text.

You can press `Tab` to move the insertion point to the next cell.

Delete a Table

1 Click anywhere in the table you want to delete.

2 Click the **Table Tools Layout** tab.

3 Click **Delete**.

4 Click **Delete Table**.

Word removes the table and its contents from your document.

simplify it

Can I add rows to a table?
Yes. To add a row to the bottom of the table, place the insertion point in the last cell and press `Tab`. To add a row anywhere else, use the buttons in the Rows & Columns section of the Layout tab.

What, exactly, is a table cell?
A *cell* refers to the intersection of a row and column in a table. In spreadsheet programs, columns are named with letters, rows with numbers, and cells using the column letter and row number. For example, the cell at the intersection of Column A and Row 2 is called A2.

Apply Table Styles

When you click in a table you have added to your document, two new tabs appear on the Ribbon: Design and Layout. You can use the table styles found in the Design tab to add instant formatting to your Word tables. Word offers numerous predefined table styles, each with its own unique set of formatting characteristics, including shading, color, borders, and fonts.

The Design tab also includes settings for creating custom borders and applying custom shading. You can also use check boxes in the Table Style Options group to add a header row, emphasize the table's first column, and more.

Apply Table Styles

1 Click anywhere in the table that you want to format.

2 Click the **Table Tools Design** tab on the Ribbon.

3 Click a style from the Table Styles list.

Note: *You can click the **More** button (⩔) in the lower right corner of the Table Styles Gallery to display the entire palette of available styles.*

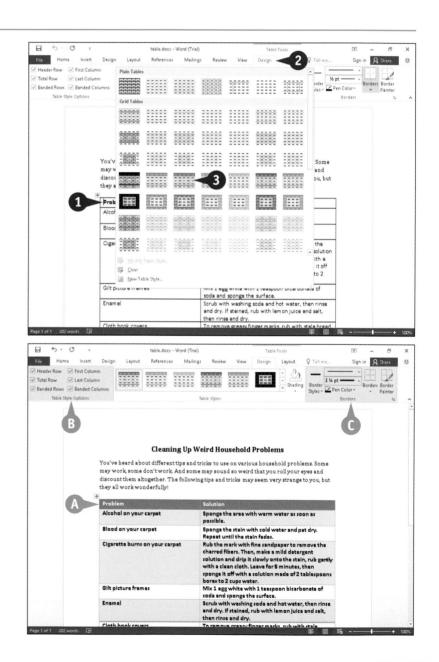

Ⓐ Word applies the style.

Ⓑ You can toggle table parts on or off using the Table Style Options check boxes.

Ⓒ You can click these options to change the shading and borders.

Insert Table Rows or Columns

You can easily insert rows or columns into a table after you create it. You can insert rows at the beginning, the end, or in the middle of the table, and you can insert columns at either edge of the table or in the middle of the table.

If you applied a table style to your table, Word adjusts the appearance of the table to maintain the table style when you add a row or column to the table.

Insert Table Rows or Columns

1 Click in the row next to the row where you want to add a new row.

Note: *To add a column, click in the column next to the column where you want to add a new column.*

2 Click the **Table Tools Layout** tab.

3 Click **Insert Above** or **Insert Below**.

Note: *To add a column, click* **Insert Left** *or* **Insert Right**.

A Word inserts the new row (or column) at the location you specified and selects the new row (or column).

Note: *This section inserts a row above another in the middle of a table.*

B Word adjusts any table style you applied.

Note: *To quickly add a row to the bottom of your table, click in the cell at the end of the last cell in the table and press* Tab.

Add Headers and Footers

If you want to include text at the top or bottom of every page, such as the title of your document, your name, or the date, you can use headers and footers. Header text appears at the top of the page above the margin; footer text appears at the bottom of the page below the margin.

To view header or footer text, you must display the document in Print Layout view. To switch to this view, click the View tab and click the Print Layout button. Then double-click the top or bottom of the page, respectively, to view the header or footer.

Add Headers and Footers

1 Click the **Insert** tab.

2 Click the **Header** button to add a header, or click the **Footer** button to add a footer.

This example adds a footer.

A The header or footer Gallery appears.

3 Click a header or footer style.

Word adds the header or footer.

B The text in your document appears dimmed.

C The insertion point appears in the Footer area.

D Header & Footer Tools appear on the Ribbon.

E Some footers contain information prompts.

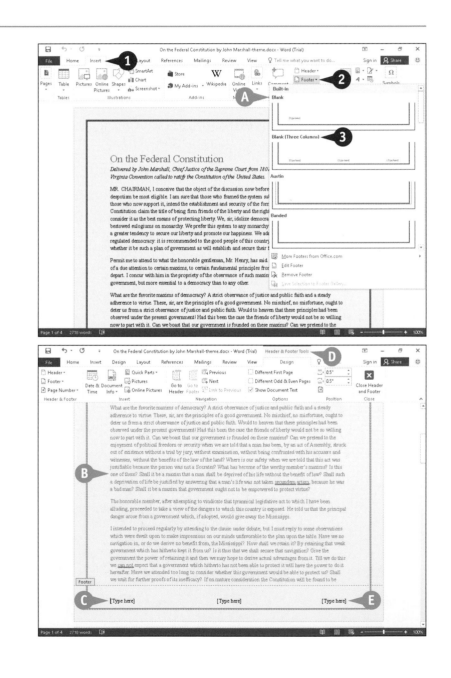

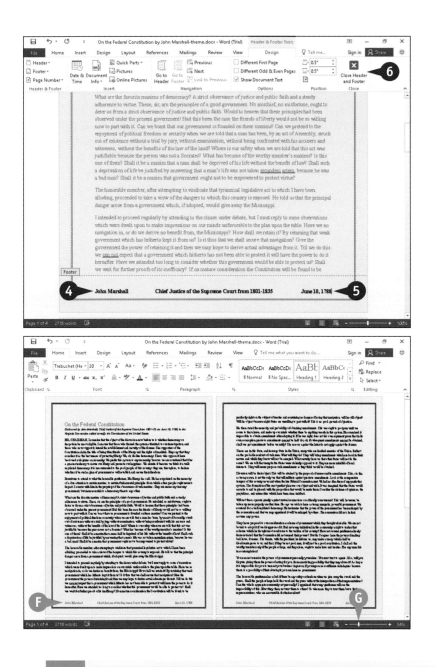

④ Click or select an information prompt.

⑤ Type footer information.

⑥ Click **Close Header and Footer**.

Ⓕ Word closes the Header & Footer Tools tab and displays the header or footer on the document page.

Ⓖ You can zoom out to view the header or footer on multiple pages of your document.

Note: *To edit a header or footer, click the **Insert** tab on the Ribbon, click the **Header** or **Footer** button, and click **Edit Header** or **Edit Footer** to redisplay the Header & Footer Tools tab.*

simplify it

Can I omit the header or footer from the first page?
Yes. Click the **Insert** tab, click the **Header** or **Footer** button, and click **Edit Header** or **Edit Footer**. Next, select **Different First Page** (☐ changes to ☑) in the Options group. If you want to remove the header or footer for odd or even pages, select **Different Odd & Even Pages** (☐ changes to ☑).

How do I remove a header or footer?
Click the **Insert** tab, click the **Header** or **Footer** button, and click **Remove Header** or **Remove Footer**. Word removes the header or footer from your document.

Insert Footnotes and Endnotes

You can include footnotes or endnotes in your document to identify sources or references to other materials or to add explanatory information. When you add a footnote or endnote, a small numeral or other character appears alongside the associated text, with the actual footnote or endnote appearing at the bottom of a page or the end of the document, respectively.

When you insert footnotes or endnotes in a document, Word automatically numbers them for you. As you add, delete, and move text in your document, any associated footnotes or endnotes are likewise added, deleted, or moved, as well as renumbered.

Insert Footnotes and Endnotes

Insert a Footnote

1 Click where you want to insert the footnote reference.

2 Click the **References** tab.

3 Click **Insert Footnote**.

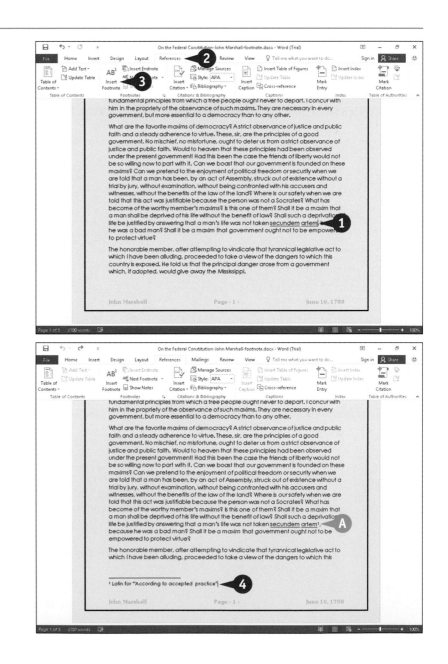

A Word displays the footnote number in the body of the document and in the note at the bottom of the current page.

4 Type the footnote text.

You can double-click the footnote number or press Shift + F5 to return the insertion point to the place in your document where you inserted the footnote.

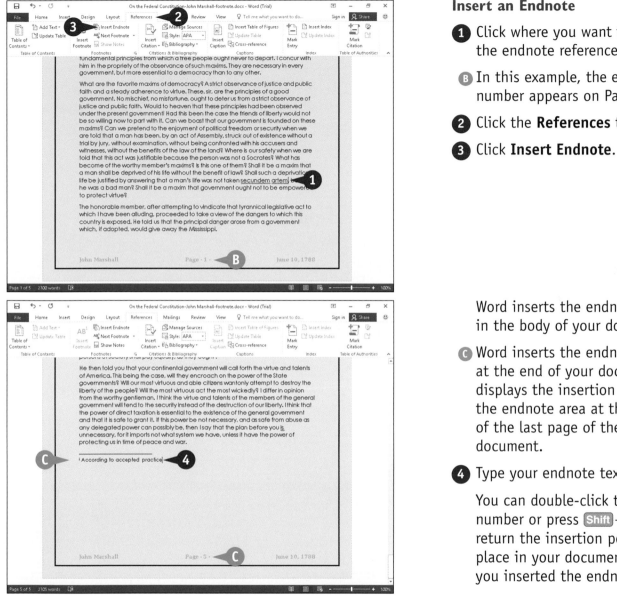

Insert an Endnote

① Click where you want to insert the endnote reference.

Ⓑ In this example, the endnote number appears on Page 1.

② Click the **References** tab.

③ Click **Insert Endnote**.

Word inserts the endnote number in the body of your document.

Ⓒ Word inserts the endnote number at the end of your document and displays the insertion point in the endnote area at the bottom of the last page of the document.

④ Type your endnote text.

You can double-click the endnote number or press Shift + F5 to return the insertion point to the place in your document where you inserted the endnote.

How can I change the starting number for footnotes or endnotes in my document?

If you need to change the starting footnote or endnote number in your document — for example, if you are working on a new chapter, but you want the numbering to continue from the previous one — click the **References** tab and click the dialog box launcher (⌐) in the Footnotes group. The Footnote and Endnote dialog box appears; click in the **Start at** box and type a number or use the spin arrow (⬍) to set a new number. Click **Apply** to apply the changes to the document.

Insert Page Numbers and Page Breaks

You can add page numbers to make your documents more manageable. For example, adding page numbers to longer documents can help you keep the pages in order after printing. You can add page numbers to the top or bottom of a page or in the page margins or at the current location of the insertion point.

Adding page breaks can help you control where text appears. For example, add a page break at the end of one chapter to ensure that the next chapter starts on its own page. You can insert page breaks using the Ribbon or your keyboard.

Insert Page Numbers and Page Breaks

Insert Page Numbers

1 Click the **Insert** tab.

2 Click Page Number.

Page number placement options appear.

3 Click a placement option.

A gallery of page number alignment and formatting options appears.

4 Click an option.

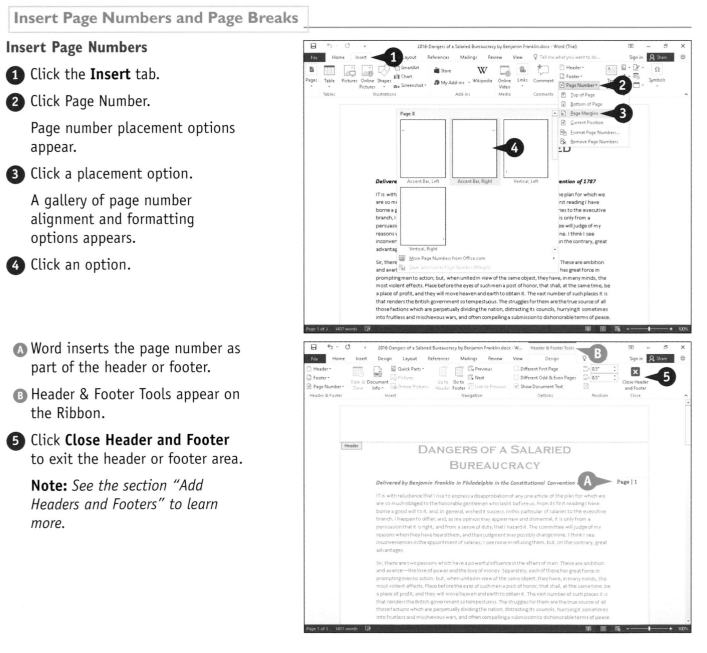

A Word inserts the page number as part of the header or footer.

B Header & Footer Tools appear on the Ribbon.

5 Click **Close Header and Footer** to exit the header or footer area.

Note: *See the section "Add Headers and Footers" to learn more.*

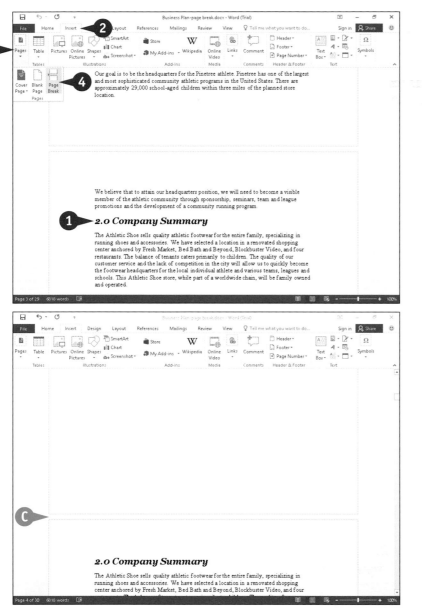

Insert Page Breaks

1 Click in the document where you want to insert a page break.

2 Click the **Insert** tab.

3 Click **Pages**.

4 Click **Page Break**.

C Word inserts a page break and moves all text after the page break onto a new page.

Is there a faster way to insert a page break?
Yes. You can use keyboard shortcuts to quickly insert a page break as you type in your document. You can insert a page break by pressing Ctrl + Enter. You can also insert a line break by pressing Shift + Enter.

Can I change the page number style?
Yes. Click the **Page Number** button on the Insert tab, and then click **Format Page Numbers**. The Page Number Format dialog box appears. You can change the number style to Roman numerals, alphabetical, and more. You can also include chapter numbers with your page numbers.

Generate a Table of Contents

You can use Word to generate a table of contents (TOC) for your document that automatically updates as you change your document. Word generates a TOC by searching for text that you format using one of Word's predefined heading styles — Heading 1, Heading 2, and Heading 3. It then copies this text

and pastes it into the TOC. You can select from Word's gallery of TOC styles to establish the TOC's look and feel.

You can create a TOC at any time, continue working, and update the TOC automatically with new information whenever you want.

Generate a Table of Contents

Style Text as Headings

① Click anywhere in the line that you want to style as a heading.

② Click the **Home** tab.

③ In the Styles group, click the style you want to apply.

Ⓐ If you do not see the style you want to apply, click the **More** button (▼) and choose the desired style from the Quick Style Gallery.

Ⓑ If the style you want to apply does not appear in the Quick Style Gallery, click the dialog box launcher (▣) and choose the desired style from the Styles pane, as shown here.

Ⓒ Word applies the style you chose to the selected text.

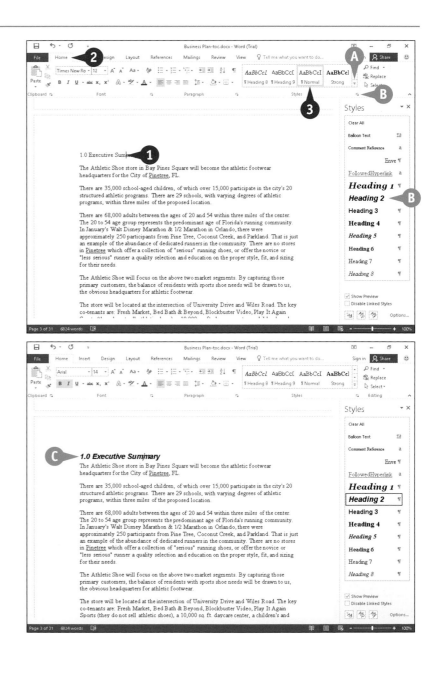

Generate a Table of Contents

1 Click the location in your document where you want to insert a TOC.

2 Click the **References** tab.

3 Click **Table of Contents**.

4 From the gallery that appears, click the TOC style you want to use.

Ⓓ Word generates a TOC.

Note: *To delete a TOC, click the **Table of Contents** button and choose **Remove Table of Contents**.*

Note: *If you edit your document, you can update your TOC to reflect the changes by clicking the **Update Table** button in the References tab's Table of Contents group; then specify whether to update page numbers only or the entire table, including heading names and levels.*

---

simplify it

Can I include additional heading styles, such as Heading 4, in the table of contents?
Yes. Complete Steps **2** to **4** in the subsection "Generate a Table of Contents," selecting **Custom Table of Contents** in Step **4** to display the Table of Contents dialog box. Click the **Show levels** ⬍ (**Ⓐ**) to change the number of heading styles included in the TOC. Click **OK**. Word prompts you to replace the current TOC. Click **Yes** to update the TOC.

General		
For**m**ats:	From template	⌄
Show **l**evels:	4	⬍ ◀ Ⓐ

111

Create a Bibliography

You can use Word to generate a bibliography for your document, formatting the entries using the style of your choice: APA, The Chicago Manual of Style, GB7714, GOST – Name Sort, GOST – Title Sort, Harvard – Anglia, IEEE, ISO 690 – First Element and Date, ISO 690 – Numerical Reference, and so on.

For Word to determine what entries should appear in the bibliography, you must cite sources in your document as you work. Word then collects the information from these citations to generate the bibliography. (Note that when you add a source to a document, Word saves it for use in subsequent documents.)

Create a Bibliography

Add a Citation

1. Click at the end of the sentence or phrase that contains information you want to cite.

2. Click the **References** tab.

3. Click **Insert Citation**.

4. Click **Add New Source**.

   The Create Source dialog box opens.

5. Click the **Type of Source** and select the type of source you want to cite (here, **Journal Article**).

   The fields in the Create Source dialog box change depending on the source you select.

6. Enter the requested information.

7. Click **OK**.

   Ⓐ Word adds a citation to your document, and adds the source to the Insert Citation menu.

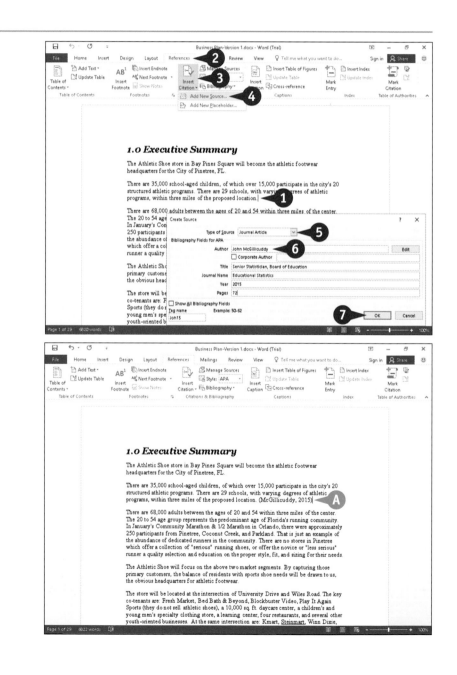

Generate the Bibliography

1 Click the location where the bibliography should appear (typically at the end of the document).

2 Click the **References** tab.

3 Click the **Bibliography** button.

4 Click one of the predesigned bibliography gallery options.

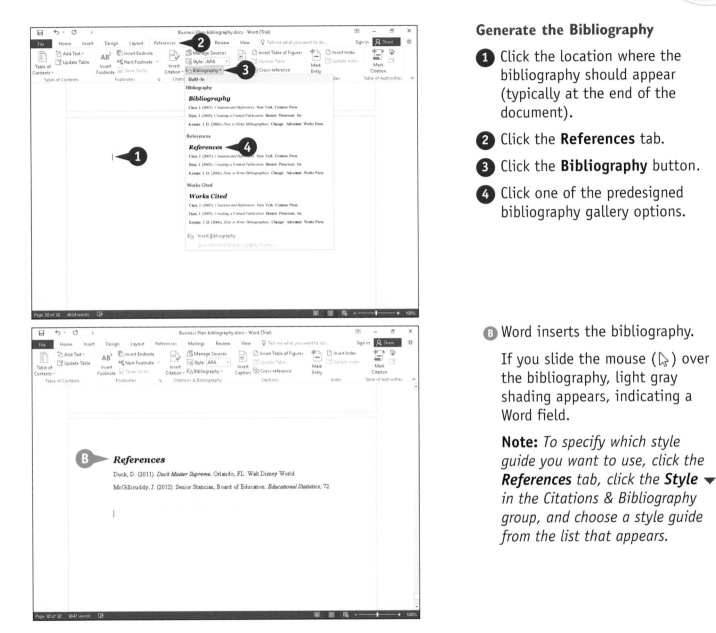

B Word inserts the bibliography.

If you slide the mouse (⌖) over the bibliography, light gray shading appears, indicating a Word field.

Note: *To specify which style guide you want to use, click the* ***References*** *tab, click the* ***Style*** ▼ *in the Citations & Bibliography group, and choose a style guide from the list that appears.*

What can I do if I do not have all the information I need about a citation?
If you want to add a citation to your document but you are missing some of the required information, you can create a placeholder. To do so, click the **References** tab, click **Insert Citation**, and choose **Add New Placeholder**. The Placeholder Name dialog box opens; type a name for the placeholder. Later, add citation information by clicking the **Manage Sources** button in the **References** tab to open the Manage Sources dialog box, clicking the placeholder under Current List, clicking **Edit**, and entering the necessary information.

Work in Read Mode View

Read Mode view optimizes your document for easier reading and helps minimize eye strain when you read the document on-screen. This view removes most toolbars, and supports mouse, keyboard, and tablet motions. While you work in Read Mode view, you can look up words in the dictionary, search the Internet for a word or phrase, highlight important text, and insert comments in documents you are reviewing. If you are viewing a long document in Read Mode view, you can also use the Navigation pane to move around the document. For details on using the Navigation pane, see the section "Scan Document Content."

Work in Read Mode View

Highlight Important Text

1 Click 📖 to display the document in Read Mode view.

2 Select the words you want to highlight and right-click.

3 From the menu that appears, click **Highlight**.

4 Click a highlight color.

A Word highlights the selected text in the color you chose.

5 Click anywhere outside the highlight to see its full effect and continue working.

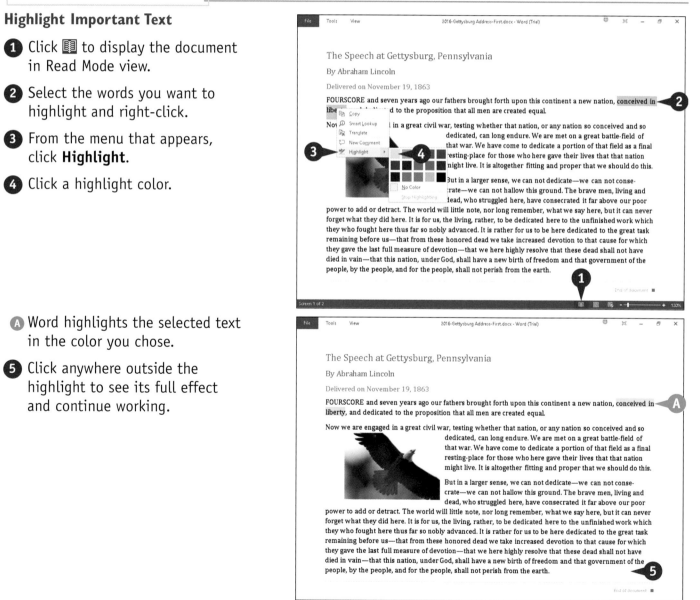

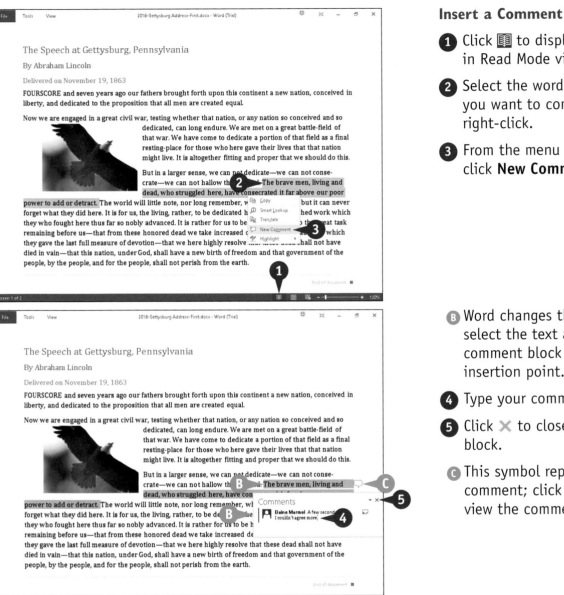

Insert a Comment

1 Click 📖 to display the document in Read Mode view.

2 Select the words about which you want to comment, and right-click.

3 From the menu that appears, click **New Comment**.

Ⓑ Word changes the color used to select the text and displays a comment block containing the insertion point.

4 Type your comment.

5 Click ✖ to close the comment block.

Ⓒ This symbol represents your comment; click it at any time to view the comment.

What are some of the different views available in Read Mode?
To display all comments in the document, click **View** and then click **Show Comments**. To view your document as if it were printed on paper, click **View** and then click **Layout**. From the menu that appears, click **Paper Layout**.

Can I change the column width?
Yes. Click **View** and then click **Column Width**. From the menu that appears, choose **Narrow** or **Wide**; click **Default** to return to the original column view. Note that on a standard monitor, Default and Wide look the same; Wide takes effect on widescreen monitors.

Find and Replace Text

Suppose you want to edit a paragraph in your document that contains a specific word or phrase. You can use Word's Find tool to search for the word or phrase instead of scrolling through your document to locate that paragraph.

In addition, you can use the Replace tool to replace instances of a word or phrase with other text. For

example, suppose you complete a long report, only to discover that you have misspelled the name of a product you are reviewing; you can use the Replace tool to locate and correct the misspellings.

Find and Replace Text

Find Text

1. Click at the beginning of your document.

2. Click the **Home** tab.

3. Click **Find**.

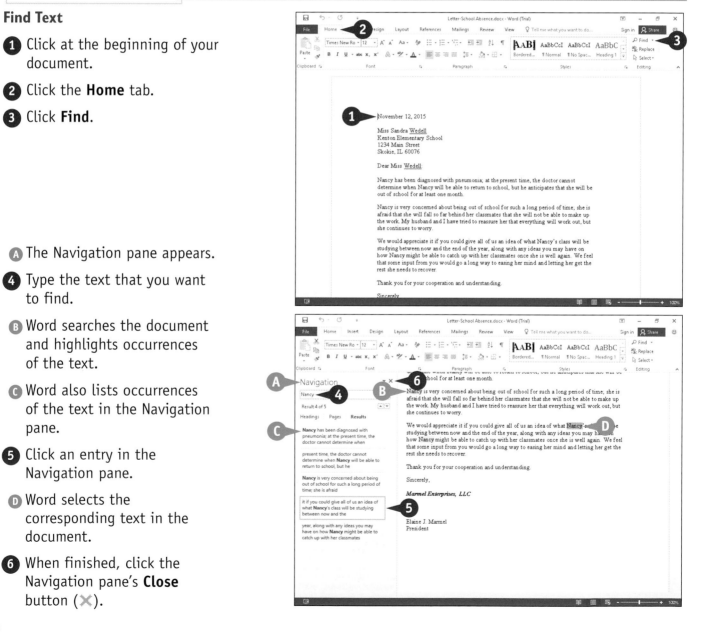

A. The Navigation pane appears.

4. Type the text that you want to find.

B. Word searches the document and highlights occurrences of the text.

C. Word also lists occurrences of the text in the Navigation pane.

5. Click an entry in the Navigation pane.

D. Word selects the corresponding text in the document.

6. When finished, click the Navigation pane's **Close** button (✕).

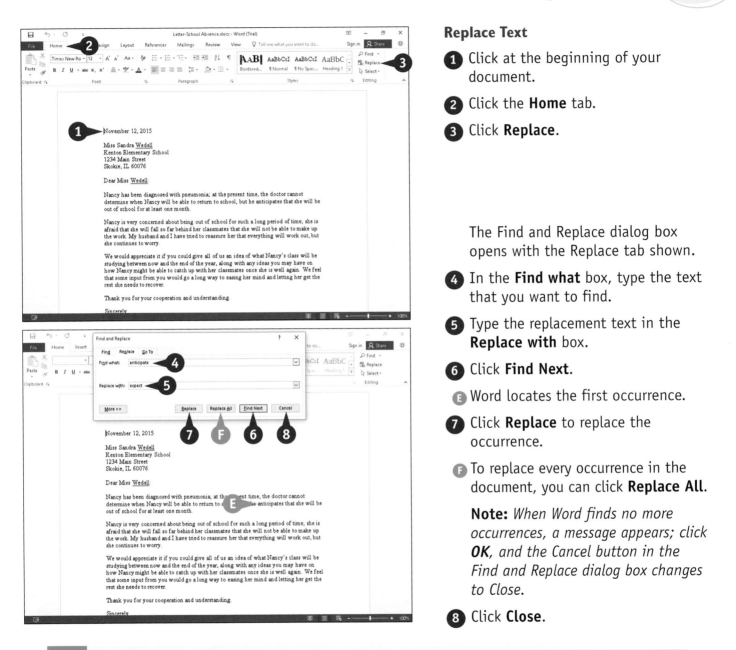

Replace Text

1 Click at the beginning of your document.

2 Click the **Home** tab.

3 Click **Replace**.

The Find and Replace dialog box opens with the Replace tab shown.

4 In the **Find what** box, type the text that you want to find.

5 Type the replacement text in the **Replace with** box.

6 Click **Find Next**.

E Word locates the first occurrence.

7 Click **Replace** to replace the occurrence.

F To replace every occurrence in the document, you can click **Replace All**.

Note: *When Word finds no more occurrences, a message appears; click OK, and the Cancel button in the Find and Replace dialog box changes to Close.*

8 Click **Close**.

---

simplify it

Where can I find detailed search options?
Click **More** in the Find and Replace dialog box to reveal additional search options. For example, you can search for matching text case, whole words, and more. You can also search for specific formatting or special characters by clicking **Format** and **Special**.

How can I search for and delete text?
Start by typing the text you want to delete in the **Find what** box; then leave the **Replace with** box empty. When you search and click **Replace**, Word looks for the text and replaces it with nothing, effectively deleting the text for which you searched.

Scan Document Content

If you are working with a very long document, using the scroll bar on the right side of the screen or the Page Up and Page Down keys on your keyboard to locate a particular page in that document can be time consuming. To rectify this, you can use the Navigation pane to navigate through a document.

This pane can display all the headings in your document or a thumbnail image of each page in your document. You can then click a heading or a thumbnail image in the Navigation pane to view the corresponding page.

Scan Document Content

Navigate Using Headings

Note: *To navigate using headings, your document must contain text styled with Heading styles. See Chapter 6 for details on styles.*

1 Click the **View** tab.

2 Select **Navigation Pane** (☐ changes to ☑).

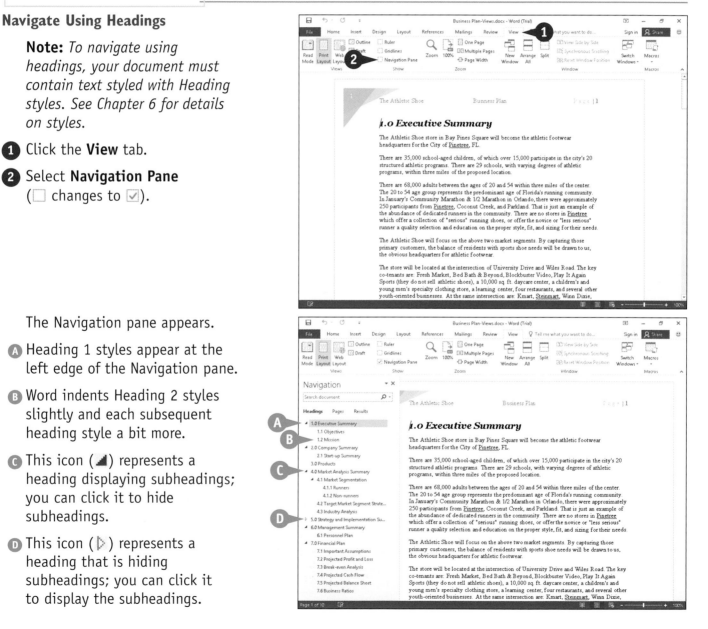

The Navigation pane appears.

Ⓐ Heading 1 styles appear at the left edge of the Navigation pane.

Ⓑ Word indents Heading 2 styles slightly and each subsequent heading style a bit more.

Ⓒ This icon (◢) represents a heading displaying subheadings; you can click it to hide subheadings.

Ⓓ This icon (▷) represents a heading that is hiding subheadings; you can click it to display the subheadings.

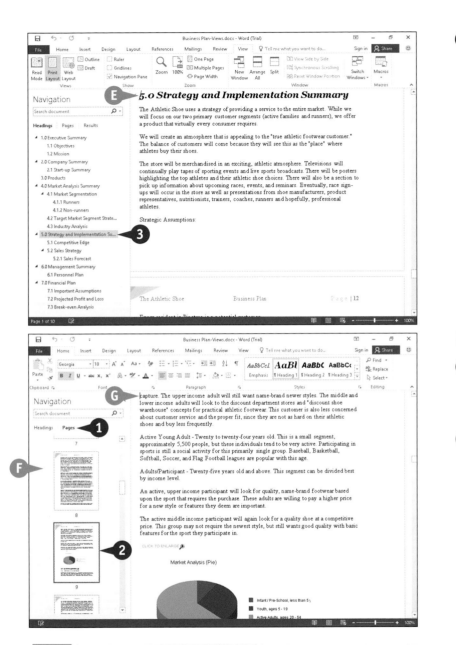

3 Click any heading in the Navigation pane to select it.

E Word moves the insertion point to this heading in your document.

Navigate by Page

1 Click **Pages**.

F Word displays each page in your document as a thumbnail.

2 Click a thumbnail.

Note: *Word surrounds a selected thumbnail with a heavy blue border.*

G Word selects that page in the Navigation pane and moves the insertion point to the top of that page.

What can I do with the Search Document box?
You can use the Search Document box to find text in your document; see the "Find Text" subsection of the section "Find and Replace Text" for details on using this box and on other ways you can search for information in your document.

Can I control the headings that appear?
Yes. While viewing headings, right-click any heading in the Navigation pane. From the menu that appears, point at **Show Heading Levels** and, from the submenu that appears, click the heading level you want to display (for example, **Show Heading 1**, **Show Heading 2**, and so on up to **Show Heading 9**).

Check Spelling and Grammar

Word automatically checks for spelling and grammar errors. Misspellings appear underlined with a red wavy line, and grammar errors are underlined with a blue wavy line. If you prefer, you can turn off Word's automatic Spelling and Grammar checking features.

Alternatively, you can review your entire document for spelling and grammatical errors all at one time. To use Word's Spelling and Grammar checking feature, you must install a dictionary; see Chapter 4 for details on installing apps for Word.

Check Spelling and Grammar

Correct a Mistake

1 When you encounter a spelling or grammar problem, right-click the underlined text.

A A menu appears, showing possible corrections. Click one, if applicable.

B To ignore the error, click **Ignore All**.

C To make Word stop flagging a word as misspelled, click **Add to Dictionary**.

Run the Spell-Checker

1 Click at the beginning of your document.

Note: *To check only a section of your document, select the section first.*

2 Click the **Review** tab.

3 Click **Spelling & Grammar**.

D Word selects the first mistake and displays either the Spelling or the Grammar pane.

E The spelling or grammar mistake appears here.

F Suggestions to correct the error appear here.

G Definitions of the highlighted suggestion appear here.

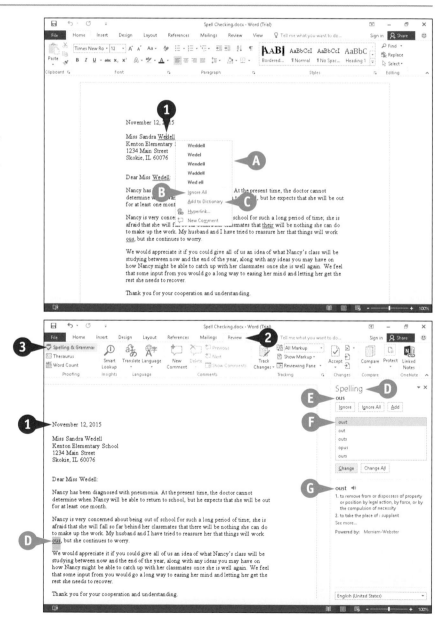

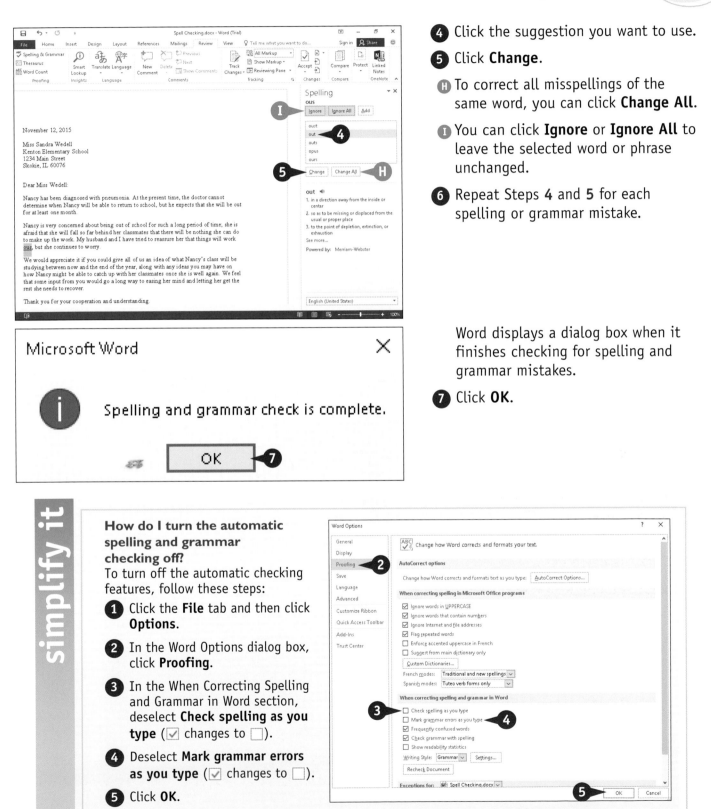

4 Click the suggestion you want to use.

5 Click **Change**.

Ⓗ To correct all misspellings of the same word, you can click **Change All**.

Ⓘ You can click **Ignore** or **Ignore All** to leave the selected word or phrase unchanged.

6 Repeat Steps **4** and **5** for each spelling or grammar mistake.

Word displays a dialog box when it finishes checking for spelling and grammar mistakes.

7 Click **OK**.

simplify it

How do I turn the automatic spelling and grammar checking off?

To turn off the automatic checking features, follow these steps:

1 Click the **File** tab and then click **Options**.

2 In the Word Options dialog box, click **Proofing**.

3 In the When Correcting Spelling and Grammar in Word section, deselect **Check spelling as you type** (☑ changes to ☐).

4 Deselect **Mark grammar errors as you type** (☑ changes to ☐).

5 Click **OK**.

Work with AutoCorrect

As you may have noticed, Word automatically corrects your text as you type. It does this using its AutoCorrect feature, which works from a preset list of misspellings.

To speed up your text-entry tasks, you can add your own problem words — ones you commonly misspell — to the list. The next time you mistype the word,

AutoCorrect fixes your mistake for you. If you find that AutoCorrect consistently changes a word that is correct as is, you can remove that word from the AutoCorrect list. If you would prefer that AutoCorrect not make any changes to your text as you type, you can disable the feature.

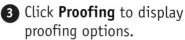

Work with AutoCorrect

1 Click the **File** tab.

Backstage view appears.

2 Click **Options**.

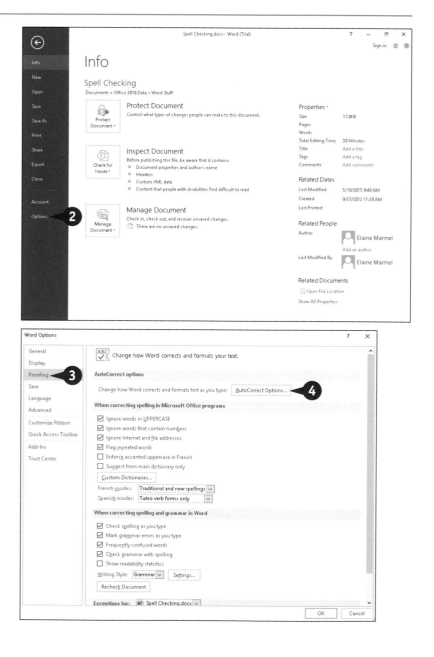

The Word Options dialog box appears.

3 Click **Proofing** to display proofing options.

4 Click **AutoCorrect Options**.

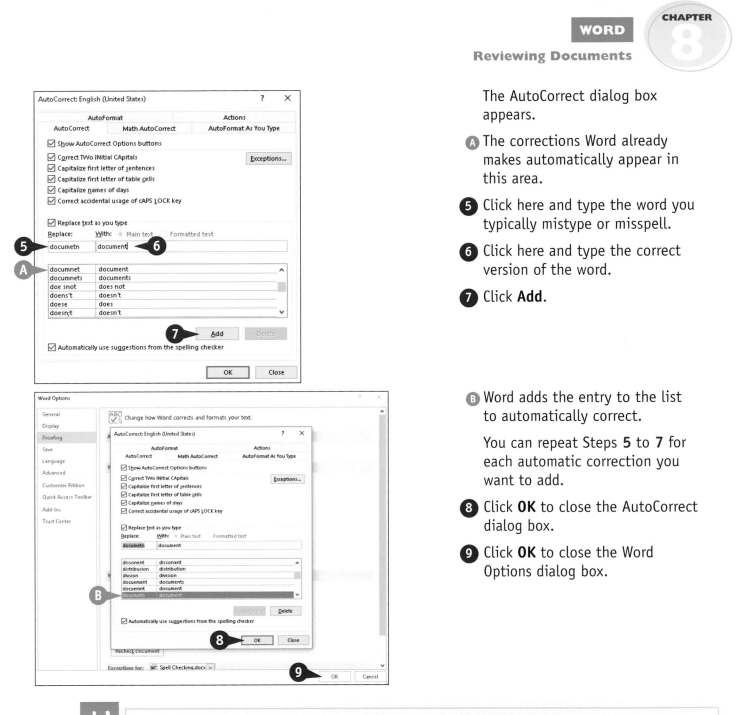

The AutoCorrect dialog box appears.

Ⓐ The corrections Word already makes automatically appear in this area.

5 Click here and type the word you typically mistype or misspell.

6 Click here and type the correct version of the word.

7 Click **Add**.

Ⓑ Word adds the entry to the list to automatically correct.

You can repeat Steps **5** to **7** for each automatic correction you want to add.

8 Click **OK** to close the AutoCorrect dialog box.

9 Click **OK** to close the Word Options dialog box.

simplify it

How does the automatic correction work?
As you type, if you mistype or misspell a word stored as an AutoCorrect entry, Word corrects the entry when you press Spacebar, Tab, or Enter.

What should I do if Word automatically replaces an entry that I do not want replaced?
Position the insertion point at the beginning of the AutoCorrected word and click the **AutoCorrect Options** button (📄). From the list that appears, click **Change back to**. To make Word permanently stop correcting an entry, follow Steps **1** to **4**, click the stored AutoCorrect entry in the list, and then click **Delete**.

Using Word's Thesaurus and Dictionary

If you are having trouble finding just the right word or phrase, you can use Word's thesaurus. The thesaurus can help you find a synonym — a word with a similar meaning — for the word you originally chose, as well as an antonym, which is a word with an opposite meaning.

You also can, through the Smart Lookup feature, use Bing to explore the web using a word in your document. Bing returns a variety of entries found on the web and can provide you with a definition of the word using the Oxford University Press Dictionaries.

Using Word's Thesaurus and Dictionary

Using Word's Thesaurus

1. Click anywhere in the word for which you want to find a substitute or opposite.

   Note: *You can press* Shift + F7 *to display the Thesaurus pane.*

2. Click the **Review** tab.

3. Click **Thesaurus** (📖).

   The Thesaurus pane appears.

   A The word you selected appears here.

   B Each word with an arrow on its left and a part of speech on its right represents a major heading.

   Note: *You cannot substitute major headings for the word in your document.*

   C Each word listed below a major heading is a synonym or antonym for the major heading.

4. Point the mouse (⬚) at the word you want to use in your document and click the ▼ that appears.

5. Click **Insert**.

   Word replaces the word in your document with the one in the Thesaurus pane.

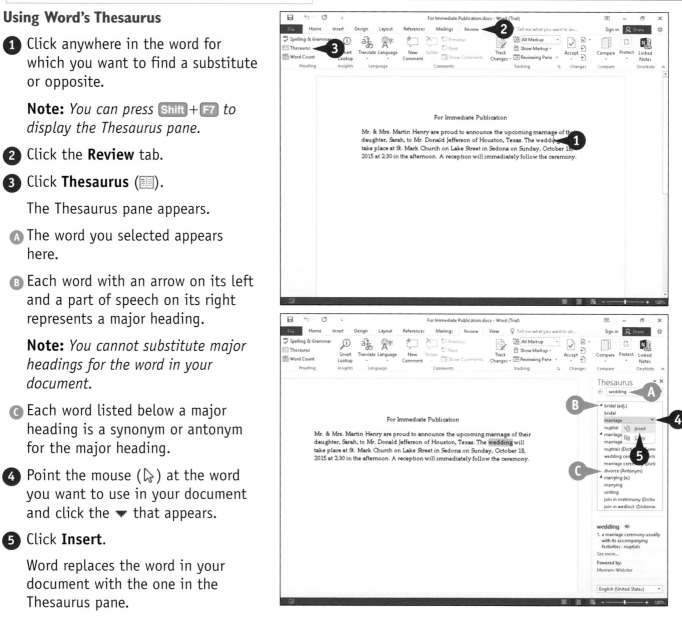

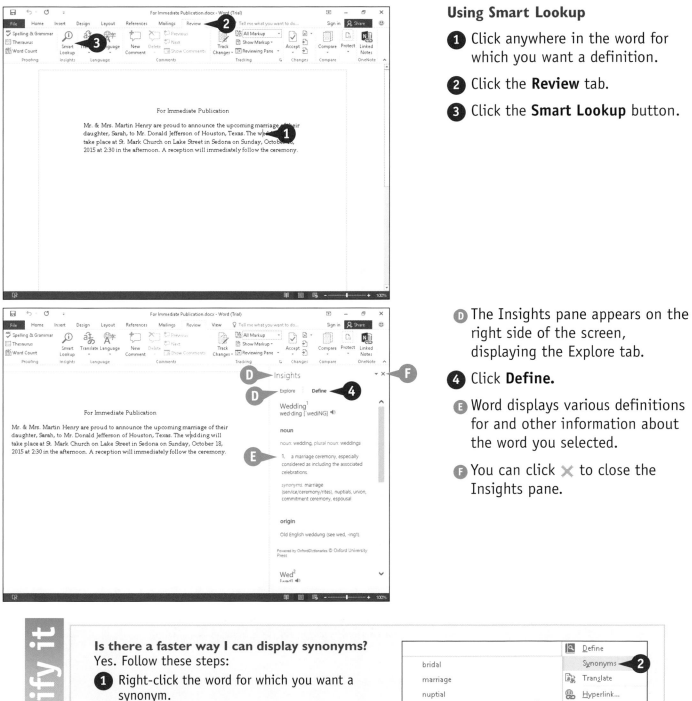

Using Smart Lookup

1 Click anywhere in the word for which you want a definition.

2 Click the **Review** tab.

3 Click the **Smart Lookup** button.

D The Insights pane appears on the right side of the screen, displaying the Explore tab.

4 Click **Define.**

E Word displays various definitions for and other information about the word you selected.

F You can click ✕ to close the Insights pane.

Is there a faster way I can display synonyms?
Yes. Follow these steps:

1 Right-click the word for which you want a synonym.

2 Click **Synonyms.**

3 To replace the word in your document, click a choice in the list that appears.

Translate Text

You can translate a word from one language to another using language dictionaries installed on your computer. If you are connected to the Internet, the Translation feature searches the dictionaries on your computer as well as online dictionaries.

Although the feature is capable of fairly complex translations, it may not grasp the tone or meaning of your text. You can choose Translate Document from the Translate drop-down menu to send the document over the Internet for translation, but be aware that Word sends documents as unencrypted HTML files. If security is an issue, do not choose this route; instead, consider hiring a professional translator.

Translate Text

Translate a Word or Phrase

1 Select a word or phrase to translate.

2 Click the **Review** tab.

3 Click **Translate**.

4 Click **Translate Selected Text**.

Note: *The first time you use this feature, a warning appears explaining that text will be sent over the Internet; click* **Yes**.

The Research task pane appears.

A The phrase you selected appears here.

B The current translation languages appear here.

C You can click ▼ to display available translation languages.

D The translation appears here.

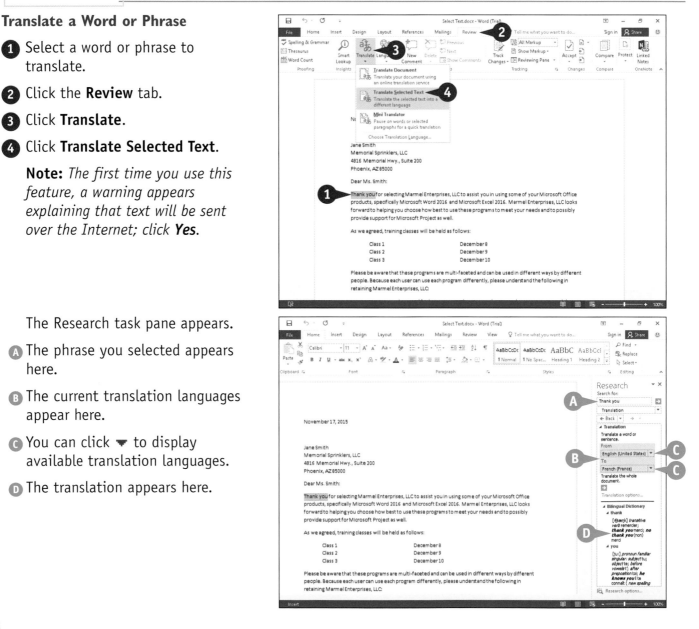

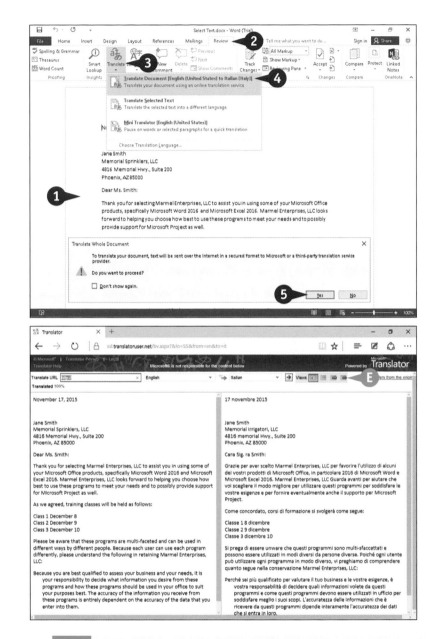

Translate a Document

1 Open the document you want to translate.

2 Click the **Review** tab.

3 Click **Translate**.

4 Click **Translate Document**.

Note: *If the Translation Language Options dialog box appears, select the translation language you want to use.*

The Translate Whole Document dialog box appears, notifying you that your document will be sent over the Internet for translation.

5 Click **Yes**.

Your browser opens, displaying the translated document.

E You can use these Views buttons to display the documents side by side as shown here.

---

simplify it

How do I choose a different language when translating the entire document?

Follow these steps: Click the **Review** tab. Click **Translate**. From the menu that appears, click **Choose Translation Language**. The Translation Language Options dialog box opens. Click the **Translate from** ☑ and the **Translate to** ☑ and choose languages (Ⓐ). Click **OK**.

Translation Language Options

a➔b Choose translation languages

Choose document translation languages

Ⓐ Translate from: English (United States)

Translate to: Italian (Italy)

Track and Review Document Changes

If you share your Word documents with others, you can use the program's Track Changes feature to identify the edits others have made, including formatting changes and text additions or deletions. The Track Changes feature uses different colors for each person's edits, so you can easily distinguish edits made by various people. By default, Word displays changes in Simple Markup view, which indicates, in the left margin, areas that have changes. This section demonstrates how to track and interpret changes.

When you review the document, you decide whether to accept or reject the changes.

Track and Review Document Changes

Turn On Tracking

1 Click the **Review** tab on the Ribbon.

2 Click **Track Changes** to start monitoring document changes.

3 Edit the document.

A A red vertical bar appears in the left margin area to indicate that changes were made to the corresponding line.

Note: *When you open a document containing tracked changes, Simple Markup is the default view.*

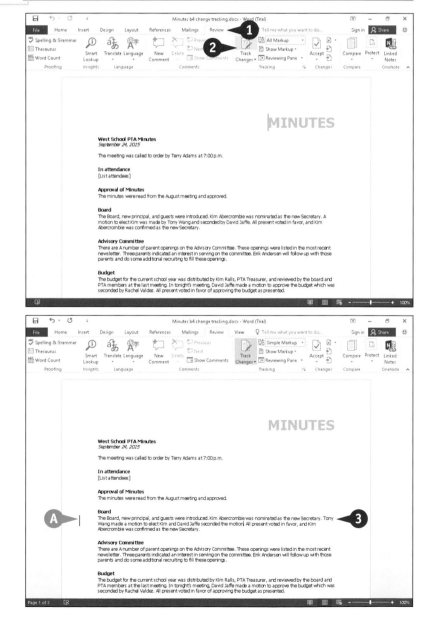

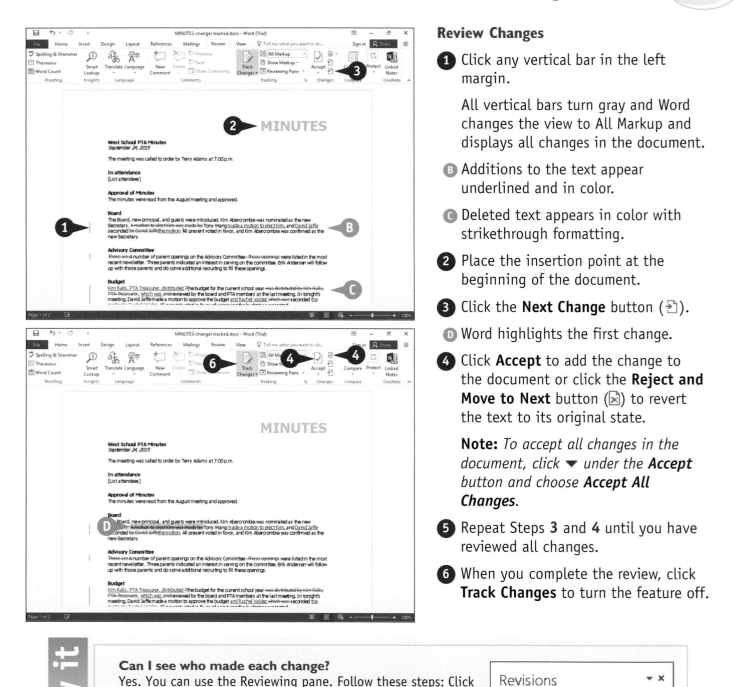

Review Changes

1 Click any vertical bar in the left margin.

All vertical bars turn gray and Word changes the view to All Markup and displays all changes in the document.

Ⓑ Additions to the text appear underlined and in color.

Ⓒ Deleted text appears in color with strikethrough formatting.

2 Place the insertion point at the beginning of the document.

3 Click the **Next Change** button (⊡).

Ⓓ Word highlights the first change.

4 Click **Accept** to add the change to the document or click the **Reject and Move to Next** button (⊡) to revert the text to its original state.

Note: *To accept all changes in the document, click ▼ under the **Accept** button and choose **Accept All Changes**.*

5 Repeat Steps **3** and **4** until you have reviewed all changes.

6 When you complete the review, click **Track Changes** to turn the feature off.

Can I see who made each change?
Yes. You can use the Reviewing pane. Follow these steps: Click the **Review** tab on the Ribbon, and then click **Reviewing Pane**. The Reviewing pane opens, summarizing the types of edits and showing each person's edits.

Revisions ▾ ✕

▲ 17 revisions ↻

Elaine J. Marmel Deleted
A motion to elect Kim was made by

Elaine J. Marmel Inserted
made a motion to elect Kim,

Elaine J. Marmel Inserted
David Jaffe

simplify it

Lock and Unlock Tracking

You can control who can turn tracking on and off using the Lock Tracking feature. This feature requires a password to turn off tracking. You no longer need to deal with the situation where you turn on tracking and send out a document for review, and when you get the document back, it contains no change markings because the reviewer turned the Track Changes feature off.

In the past, you needed to use the Compare Documents feature to determine how the reviewed document differed from the original. Now, you can lock tracking.

Lock and Unlock Tracking

Lock Tracked Changes

 In the document for which you want to lock tracked changes, click the **Review** tab.

② Click **Track Changes** to turn on tracking.

③ Click ▼ at the bottom of the **Track Changes** button.

④ Click **Lock Tracking**.

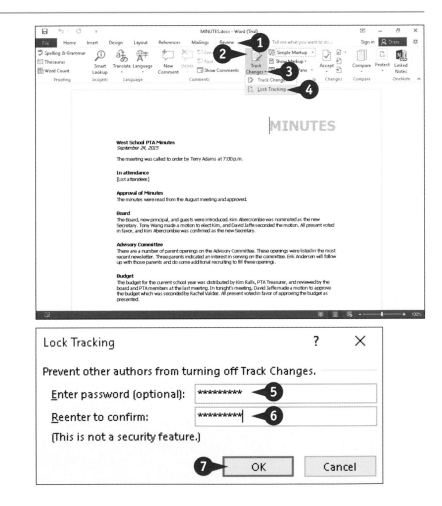

The Lock Tracking dialog box appears.

⑤ Type a password here.

⑥ Retype the password here.

⑦ Click **OK**.

Note: *Make sure you remember the password or you will not be able to turn off the Track Changes feature.*

Word saves the password and the Track Changes button appears gray and unavailable.

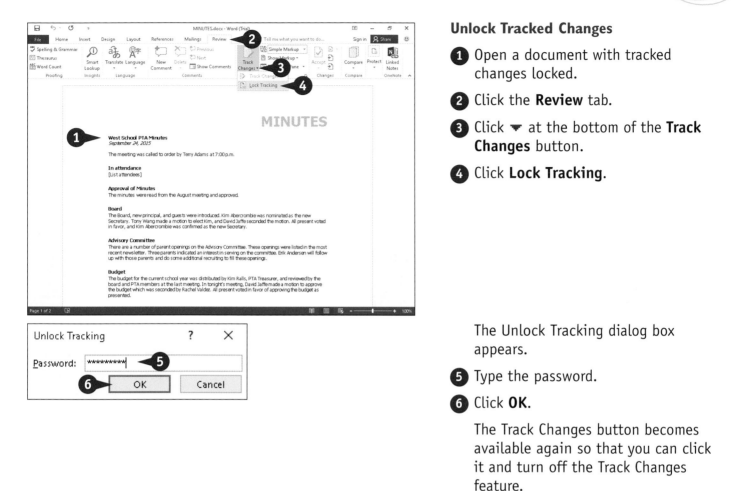

Unlock Tracked Changes

1. Open a document with tracked changes locked.

2. Click the **Review** tab.

3. Click ⯆ at the bottom of the **Track Changes** button.

4. Click **Lock Tracking**.

The Unlock Tracking dialog box appears.

5. Type the password.

6. Click **OK**.

The Track Changes button becomes available again so that you can click it and turn off the Track Changes feature.

simplify it

What happens if I supply the wrong password?
This message box appears. You can retry as many times as you want. If you cannot remember the password, you can create a new version that contains all revisions already accepted, which you can then compare to the original to identify changes. Press Ctrl + A to select the entire document. Then press Shift + ← to unselect just the last paragraph mark in the document. Then press Ctrl + C to copy the selection. Start a new blank document and press Ctrl + V to paste the selection.

Microsoft Word

! The password is incorrect.

Show Help >>

OK

Work with Comments

You can add comments to your documents. For example, when you share a document with other users, you can use comments to leave feedback about the text without typing directly in the document, and others can do the same.

To indicate that a comment was added, Word displays a balloon in the right margin near the commented text. When you review comments, they appear in a block. Your name appears in comments you add, and you can easily review, reply to, or delete a comment, or, instead of deleting the comment, you can indicate that you have addressed the comment.

Work with Comments

Add a Comment

1. Click or select the text about which you want to comment.

2. Click the **Review** tab.

3. Click **New Comment**.

A. A comment balloon and block appear, marking the location of the comment.

4. Type your comment.

5. Click anywhere outside the comment to continue working.

Review a Comment

1. While working in Simple Markup view, click a comment balloon.

B. Word highlights the text associated with the comment.

C. Word displays the Comments block and the text it contains.

Note: *To view all comments along the right side of the document, click* **Show Comments** *in the Comments group on the Review tab.*

2. Click anywhere outside the comment to hide the Comments block and its text.

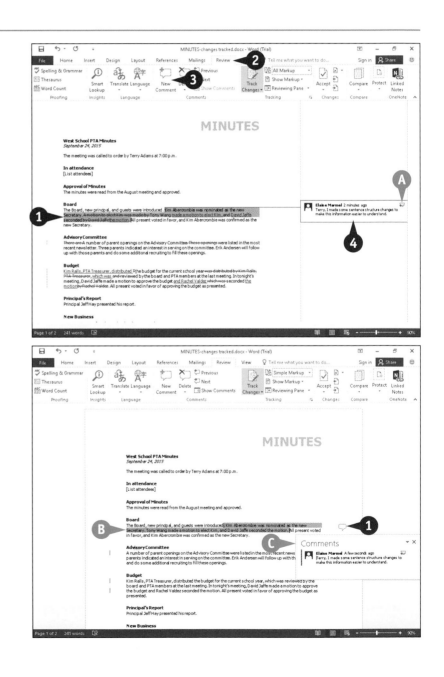

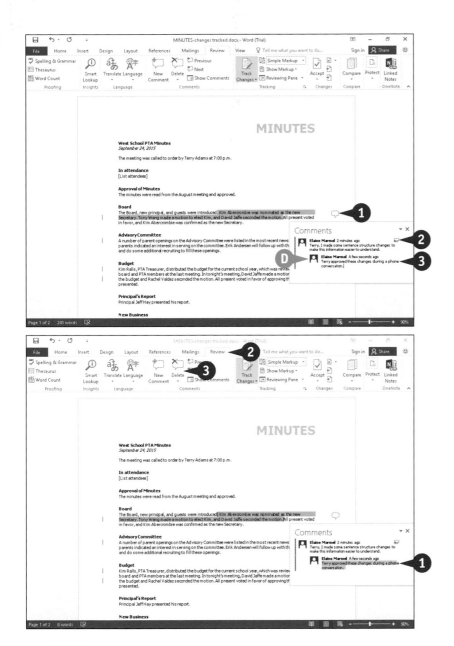

Reply to a Comment

1 While working in Simple Markup view, click a comment balloon to display its text.

2 Click the **Reply to Comment** button (🗨).

D Word starts a new comment, indented under the first comment.

3 Type your reply.

4 Click anywhere outside the comment to continue working.

Delete a Comment

1 Click the comment that you want to remove.

2 Click the **Review** tab.

3 Click **Delete**.

Note: *You can also right-click a comment and click **Delete Comment**. And, you can delete all comments in the document by clicking ▼ at the bottom of the **Delete** button and then clicking **Delete All Comments in Document**.*

Word deletes the comment.

simplify it

Can I indicate that I have addressed a comment without deleting it?
Yes, you can mark the comment as done. Right-click the text of the comment and choose **Mark Comment Done**. Word fades the comment text to light gray.

PART III

Excel

Excel is a powerful spreadsheet program. You can use Excel strictly as a program for manipulating numerical data, or you can use it as a database program to track and manage large quantities of data. For example, you can apply conditional formatting to a collection of data to determine the lowest and highest values in a list. You also can chart mathematical data and create tables, PivotTables, and PivotCharts of large quantities of data. In this part, you learn how to enter data into worksheets and tap into the power of Excel's formulas, functions, and charting capabilities to analyze data.

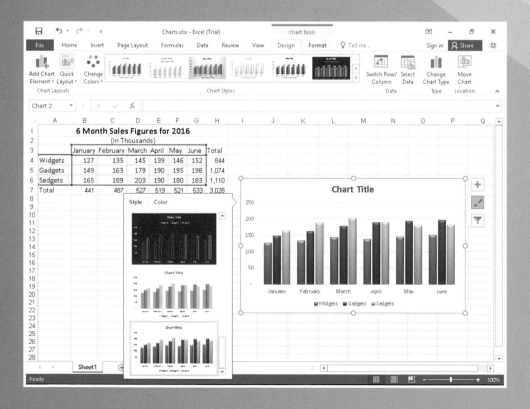

Enter Cell Data

You can enter data into any cell in an Excel worksheet. You can type data directly into the cell, or you can enter data using the Formula bar. Data can be text, such as row or column labels, or numbers, which are called *values*. Values also include formulas. Excel automatically left-aligns text data in a cell and right-aligns values.

Long text entries appear truncated if you type additional data into adjoining cells. Values too large to fit in a cell might be represented by a series of pound signs.

Enter Cell Data

Type into a Cell

1 Click the cell into which you want to enter data.

The cell you clicked is called the *active cell*.

2 Type your data.

A The data appears both in the cell and in the Formula bar.

B To store the data in the cell, press `Enter` or click the **Enter** button (✓).

Note: *If you press* `Enter`, *the cell pointer moves down one row. If you click the* ***Enter*** *button (✓), the cell pointer remains in the cell you clicked in Step* ***1***.

Type Data in the Formula Bar

1 Click the cell into which you want to enter data.

2 Click in the Formula bar.

3 Type your data.

C The data appears both in the Formula bar and in the cell.

4 Click the **Enter** button (✓) or press `Enter` to enter the data.

D To cancel an entry, you can click the **Cancel** button (✗) or press `Esc`.

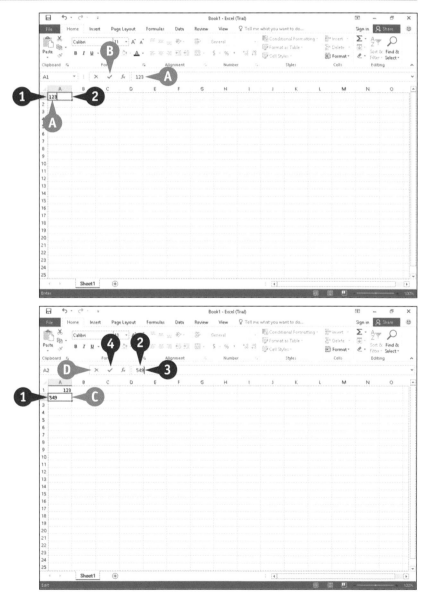

Select Cells

To edit data or perform mathematical or formatting operations on data in an Excel worksheet, you must first select the cell or cells that contain that data. For example, you might apply formatting to data in a single cell or to data in a group, or *range*, of cells.

Selecting a single cell is easy: You just click the cell. To select a range of cells, you can use your mouse or keyboard.

Select Cells

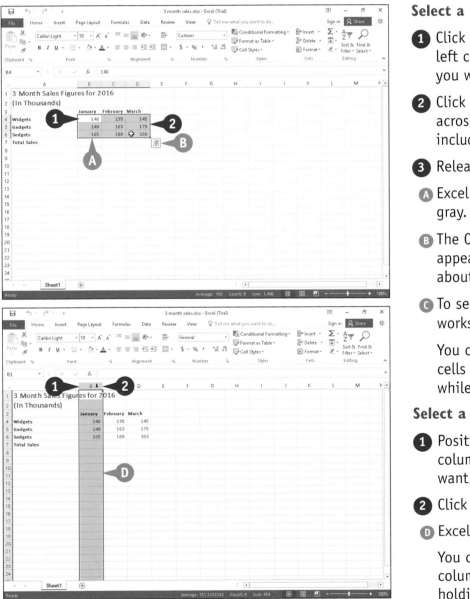

Select a Range of Cells

1 Click the cell representing the upper left corner of the range of cells that you want to select.

2 Click and drag down and to the right across the cells that you want to include in the range.

3 Release the mouse button.

A Excel highlights the selected cells in gray.

B The Quick Analysis button (📋) appears. See Chapter 10 for details about data analysis choices.

C To select all the cells in the worksheet, you can click here (◢).

You can select multiple noncontiguous cells by pressing and holding **Ctrl** while clicking cells.

Select a Column or Row

1 Position the mouse (⇩) over the column letter or row number that you want to select.

2 Click the column or row.

D Excel selects the entire column or row.

You can select multiple noncontiguous columns or rows by pressing and holding **Ctrl** while clicking column or row headings.

Faster Data Entry with AutoFill

You can use Excel's AutoFill feature to add a data series to your worksheet or to duplicate a single entry in your worksheet to expedite data entry. You can create number series and, using Excel's built-in lists of common entries, you can enter text series such as a list containing the days of the week or the months in the year. In addition, you can create your own custom data lists, as described in the Simplify It tip.

When you click a cell, a *fill handle* appears in the lower right corner of the cell; you use the fill handle to create a series.

Faster Data Entry with AutoFill

AutoFill a Text Series

1 Type the first entry in the text series.

2 Click and drag the cell's fill handle across or down the number of cells that you want to fill.

A ✥ changes to the Fill handle (**+**).

If you type an entry that Excel does not recognize as part of a list, AutoFill copies the selection to every cell that you drag over.

3 Release the mouse button.

B AutoFill fills in the text series and selects the series.

C The AutoFill Options button (⊞) may appear, offering additional options that you can assign to the data.

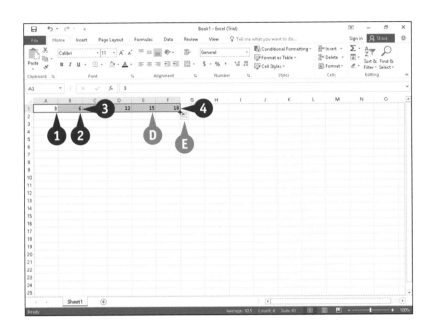

AutoFill a Number Series

1 Type the first entry in the number series.

2 In an adjacent cell, type the next entry in the number series.

3 Select both cells.

Note: *See the previous section, "Select Cells," to learn more.*

4 Click and drag the Fill handle across or down the number of cells that you want to fill.

⊕ changes to ✚.

5 Release the mouse button.

Ⓓ AutoFill fills in the number series and selects the series.

Ⓔ The AutoFill Options button (🖫) may appear, offering additional options that you can assign to the data.

simplify it

How do I create a custom list?

To add your own custom list to AutoFill's list library, first create the custom list in your worksheet cells. Then select the cells containing the list that you want to save. Click the **File** tab and then click **Options**. In the Options dialog box, click the **Advanced** tab. In the General section, click the **Edit Custom Lists** button. In the Custom Lists dialog box, click **Import**. Excel adds your list to the series of custom lists (Ⓐ). The entries in the list appear here (Ⓑ). Click **OK** to close the Custom Lists dialog box. Click **OK** again to close the Options dialog box.

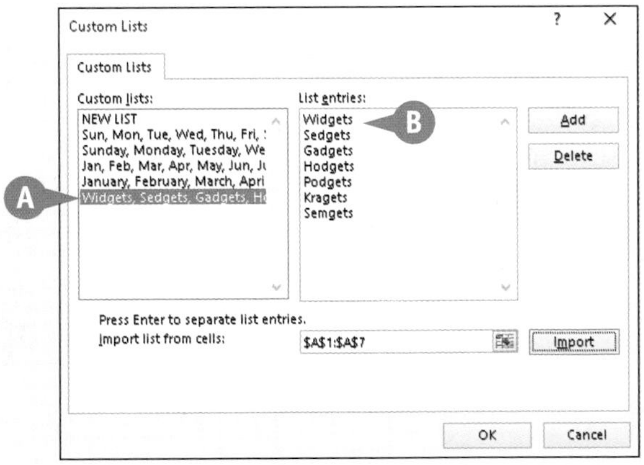

Custom Lists

Custom Lists

Custom lists:
NEW LIST
Sun, Mon, Tue, Wed, Thu, Fri, :
Sunday, Monday, Tuesday, We
Jan, Feb, Mar, Apr, May, Jun, Ju
January, February, March, Apri
Ⓐ Widgets, Sedgets, Gadgets, H

List entries:
Widgets Ⓑ
Sedgets
Gadgets
Hodgets
Podgets
Kragets
Semgets

Add
Delete

Press Enter to separate list entries.
Import list from cells: $A$1:$A$7   Import

OK   Cancel

Turn On Text Wrapping

By default, long lines of text appear on one line in an Excel table. If you type additional data into adjoining cells, long lines of text appear truncated, but they are not. If you select the cell and look at the Formula bar, you see all the text.

You can display all the text in a cell by resizing the column width (see the section "Resize Columns and Rows"). Or, you can wrap text within the cell so that some text appears on the next line. When you wrap text, Excel maintains column width and increases row height to accommodate the number of lines that wrap.

Turn On Text Wrapping

1 Click the cell in which you want to wrap text.

Note: *You can also apply text wrapping to multiple cells. See the section "Select Cells," earlier in this chapter, to learn how to select multiple cells for a task.*

2 Click the **Home** tab.

3 Click the **Wrap Text** button (📑).

A Excel wraps the text in the cell.

Note: *See the section "Resize Columns and Rows" to learn how to adjust cell depth and width to accommodate your data.*

You can center data across a range of selected cells in your worksheet. You can use Excel's Merge and Center command to quickly merge and center a title above multiple columns.

Click ▼ beside the Merge and Center button (⊞) for additional options. Merge Across merges each

selected row of cells into a larger cell. Merge Cells merges selected cells in multiple rows and columns into a single cell. Unmerge Cells splits a cell into multiple cells.

Center Data Across Columns

1 Select the cell containing the data that you want to center, along with the adjacent cells over which you want to center the data.

Note: *When you merge and center, Excel deletes any data in selected adjacent cells.*

2 Click the **Home** tab.

3 Click the **Merge and Center** button (⊞).

You can also click the **Merge and Center** ▼ to select from several merge options.

A Excel merges the cells and centers the data.

Adjust Cell Alignment

By default, Excel automatically aligns text to the left and numbers to the right of a cell. It also vertically aligns all data to sit at the bottom of the cell. If you want, however, you can change the horizontal and vertical alignment of data within cells — for example, you can center data vertically and horizontally within a cell to improve the appearance of your worksheet data.

In addition to controlling the alignment of data within a cell, you can also indent data and change its orientation in a cell.

Adjust Cell Alignment

Set Horizontal Alignment

1. Select the cells that you want to format.

2. Click the **Home** tab.

3. Click an alignment button:

   Click the **Align Left** button (≡) to align data to the left.

   Click the **Center** button (≡) to center-align the data.

   Click the **Align Right** button (≡) to align data to the right.

   Note: *To justify cell data, click the dialog box launcher (▣) in the Alignment group. In the Format Cells dialog box that appears, click the **Horizontal** ▼ and click **Justify**.*

   Excel applies the alignment to your cells.

A. This example centers the data horizontally.

Set Vertical Alignment

1 Select the cells that you want to format.

2 Click the **Home** tab.

3 Click an alignment button:

Click the **Top Align** button (≡) to align data to the top.

Click the **Middle Align** button (≡) to align data in the middle.

Click the **Bottom Align** button (≡) to align data to the bottom.

Excel applies the alignment to your cells.

B This example aligns the data to the middle of the cell.

---

simplify it

How do I indent cell data?
To indent data, click the **Increase Indent** button (⬚≡) on the Home tab. To decrease an indent, click the **Decrease Indent** button (⬚≡).

Can I change the orientation of data in a cell?
Yes. For example, you might angle column labels to make them easier to distinguish from one another. To do so, select the cells you want to change, click the **Home** tab, click ▼ next to the **Orientation** button (⬚ ▼), and click an orientation. Excel applies the orientation to the data in the selected cell or cells.

Change the Font and Size

You can change the font or the font size that you use for various cells in your worksheet. For example, you can make the worksheet title larger than the rest of the data, or you might resize the font for the entire worksheet to make the data easier to read. You can apply multiple formats to a cell — for example, you can change both the font and the font size of any given cell.

If you particularly like the result of applying a series of formatting options to a cell, you can copy the formatting and apply it to other cells in your worksheet.

Change the Font and Size

Change the Font

① Select the cell or range for which you want to change fonts.

② Click the **Home** tab.

③ Click the **Font** ▾.

You can use ▲ and ▾ to scroll through all the available fonts.

You can also begin typing a font name to choose a font.

④ Click a font.

Ⓐ Excel applies the font.

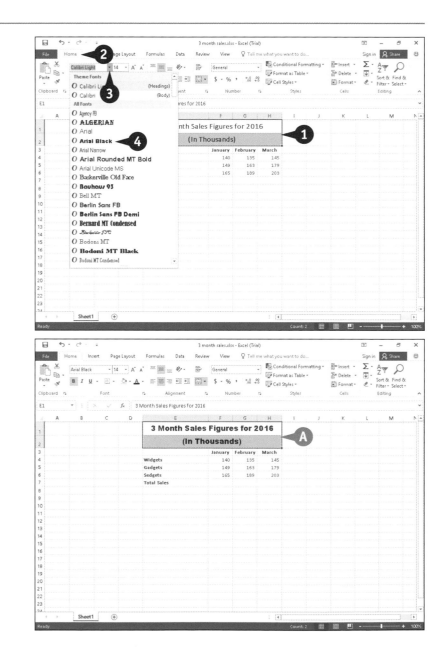

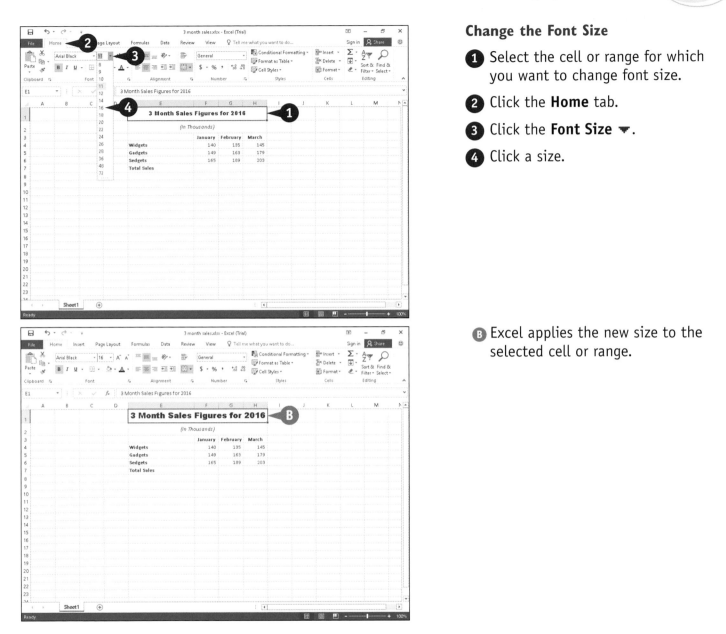

Change the Font Size

1 Select the cell or range for which you want to change font size.

2 Click the **Home** tab.

3 Click the **Font Size** ▼.

4 Click a size.

B Excel applies the new size to the selected cell or range.

Can I apply multiple formatting options at the same time?
Yes. The Format Cells dialog box enables you to apply a new font, size, or any other basic formatting options to selected data. To open it, click the **Home** tab and click the dialog box launcher (⌐) in the Font group.

How can I copy cell formatting?
Select the cell or range that contains the formatting you want to copy. Then, click the **Home** tab, and click the **Format Painter** button (✦) in the Clipboard group. Then click and drag over the cells to which you want to apply the formatting and release the mouse button to copy the formatting.

Change Number Formats

You can use number formatting to control the appearance of numerical data in your worksheet. For example, if you have a column of prices, you can format the data as numbers with dollar signs and decimal points. If prices listed are in a currency other than dollars, you can indicate that as well.

Excel offers several different number categories, or styles, to choose from. These include Currency styles, Accounting styles, Date styles, Time styles, Percentage styles, and more. You can apply number formatting to single cells, ranges, columns, rows, or an entire worksheet.

Change Number Formats

1. Select the cell, range, or data that you want to format.
2. Click the **Home** tab.
3. Click the **Number Format** ▼.
4. Click a number format.

Excel applies the number format to the data.

Ⓐ You can click the **Accounting Number Format** button ($ ▾) to quickly apply dollar signs to your data. Click the button's ▼ to specify a different currency symbol, such as Euro.

Ⓑ You can click the **Percent Style** button (%) to quickly apply percent signs to your data.

Ⓒ You can click the **Comma Style** button (▸) to quickly display commas in your number data.

Ⓓ You can click the dialog box launcher (⌐) in the Number group to open the Format Cells dialog box and display additional number-formatting options.

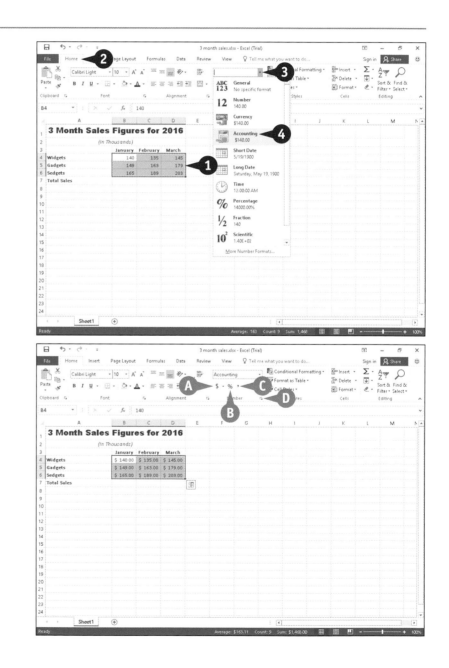

Increase or Decrease Decimals

You can control the number of decimal places that appear in numbers using the Increase Decimal and Decrease Decimal buttons. You may want to increase the number of decimal places shown in a cell if your worksheet contains data that must be precise to be accurate, as with worksheets containing scientific data. If the data in your worksheet is less precise or does not measure fractions of items, you might reduce the number of decimal places shown to two decimal places or no decimal places.

Increase or Decrease Decimals

1 Select the cell or range for which you want to adjust the number of decimal places displayed.

2 Click the **Home** tab.

3 Click a decimal button:

You can click the **Increase Decimal** button to increase the number of decimal places displayed.

You can click the **Decrease Decimal** button to decrease the number of decimal places displayed.

Excel adjusts the number of decimals that appear in the cell or cells.

A In this example, Excel adds a decimal place.

You can click the **Increase Decimal** button again to add another decimal.

Add Cell Borders and Shading

By default, Excel displays gridlines separating each cell to help you enter data, but the gridlines do not print (also by default). You can print gridlines or hide them from view.

Alternatively, you can add printable borders to selected worksheet cells to help define the contents or more clearly separate the data from surrounding cells. You can add borders to all four sides of a cell or to just one, two, or three sides. You also can apply shading to help set apart different data.

Add Cell Borders and Shading

Add Quick Borders

1 Select the cell or range around which you want to place a border.

2 Click the **Home** tab.

3 Click ▼ beside the **Borders** button (▦ ▾).

Note: *To apply the current border selection shown on the button, simply click the* **Borders** *button (▦ ▾).*

4 Click a border style.

A Excel assigns the borders to the cell or range.

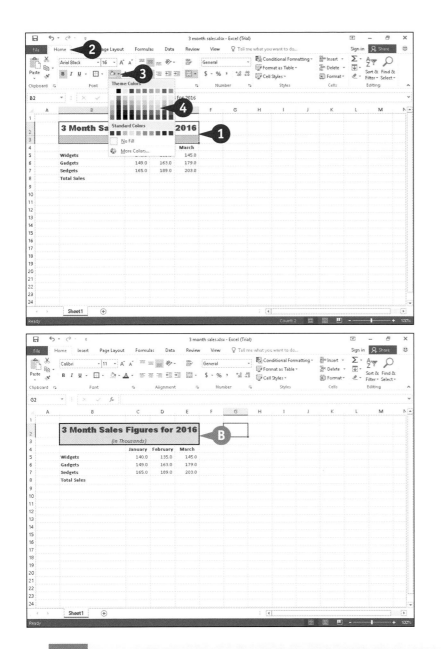

Add a Fill Color

1 Select the cells to which you want to apply a fill color.

2 Click the **Home** tab.

3 Click ▼ beside the **Fill Color** button (🪣 ▼).

4 Select a fill color.

Note: *Remember, if the color you select is too dark, your data can become difficult to read.*

B Excel applies the fill color to the selected cell or range.

Can I turn worksheet gridlines on and off?
Yes. Printing gridlines makes worksheet data easier to read on paper. On the other hand, you might want to turn off gridlines on-screen during a presentation. To control the appearance of gridlines, click the **Page Layout** tab. In the Sheet Options group, under Gridlines, deselect **View** to hide gridlines on-screen (☑ changes to ☐). Select **Print** (☐ changes to ☑) to print gridlines.

Format Data with Styles

You can apply preset formatting designs to your worksheet data using styles. You can apply cell styles to individual cells or ranges of cells, or table styles to a range of worksheet data. When you apply a table style, Excel converts the range into a table. Tables help you manage and analyze data independent of other data in the worksheet. For example, beside each column heading in a table, an AutoFilter ▼ appears that you can use to show only certain information in the table.

You can also apply a theme — a predesigned set of formatting attributes — to a worksheet. See the Simplify It tip for more details.

Format Data with Styles

Apply a Cell Style

1. Select the cell or range that you want to format.

2. Click the **Home** tab.

3. Click **Cell Styles**.

4. Click a style.

Ⓐ Excel applies the formatting to the selected cell or range.

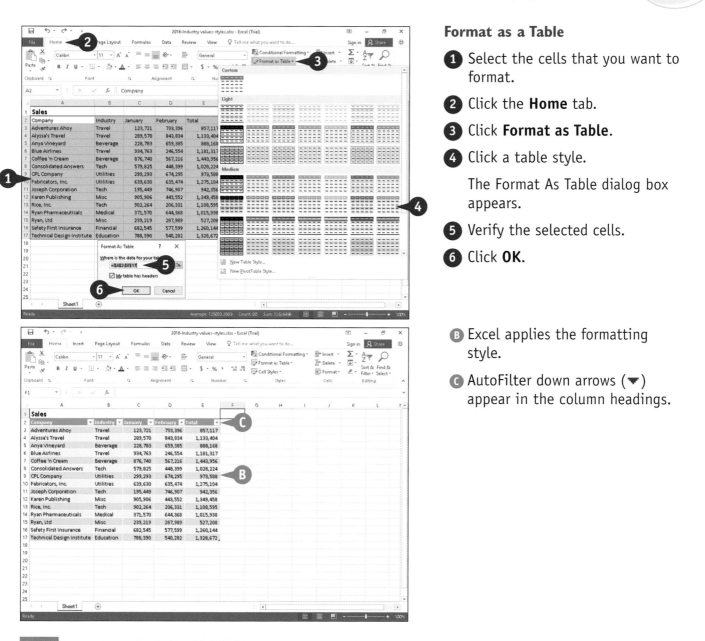

Format as a Table

1 Select the cells that you want to format.

2 Click the **Home** tab.

3 Click **Format as Table**.

4 Click a table style.

The Format As Table dialog box appears.

5 Verify the selected cells.

6 Click **OK**.

B Excel applies the formatting style.

C AutoFilter down arrows (▼) appear in the column headings.

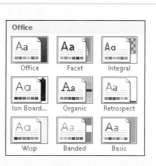

How do I apply a theme?
You can use themes to create a similar appearance among all the Office documents that you create. To apply a theme, click the **Page Layout** tab, click the **Themes** button, and select a theme from the list.

Apply Conditional Formatting

You can use Excel's Conditional Formatting tool to apply certain formatting attributes, such as bold text or a fill color, to a cell when the value of that cell meets a required condition. For example, if your worksheet tracks weekly sales, you might set up Excel's Conditional Formatting tool to alert you if a sales figure falls below what is required for you to break even.

In addition to using preset conditions, you can create your own. To help you distinguish the degree to which various cells meet your conditional rules, you can also use color scales and data bars.

Apply Conditional Formatting

Apply a Conditional Rule

1. Select the cell or range to which you want to apply conditional formatting.

2. Click the **Home** tab.

3. Click **Conditional Formatting**.

4. Click **Highlight Cells Rules** or **Top/Bottom Rules**.

   This example uses Top/Bottom Rules.

5. Click the type of rule that you want to create.

   A rule dialog box appears.

6. Specify the values that you want to assign for the condition.

7. Click **OK**.

   Ⓐ If the value of a selected cell meets the condition, Excel applies the conditional formatting.

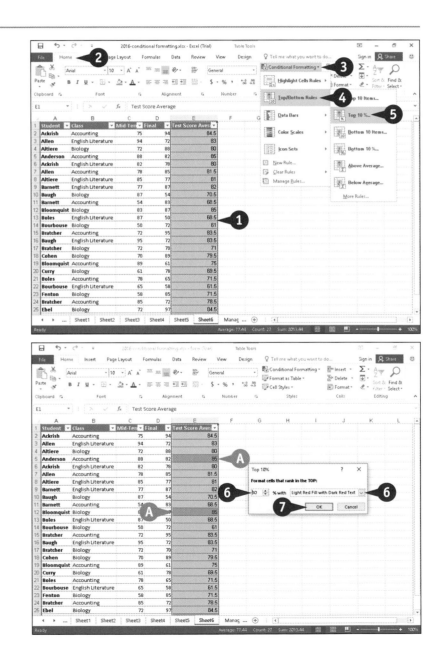

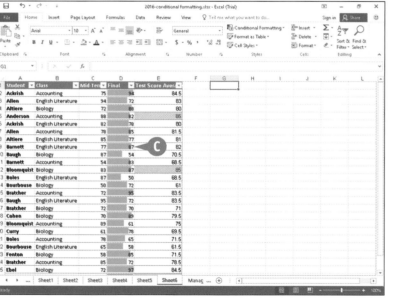

Apply Data Bars

1 Select the cell or range that contains the conditional formatting.

2 Click the **Home** tab.

3 Click **Conditional Formatting**.

4 Click **Data Bars**.

5 Click a data bar fill option.

B You can apply a color scale or an icon set instead by clicking **Color Scales** or **Icon Sets**.

C Excel applies the data bars to the selection. Longer data bars represent higher values in your selection.

---

simplify it

How do I create a new rule for conditional formatting?
Click the **Conditional Formatting** button on the Home tab and then click **New Rule** to open the New Formatting Rule dialog box. Here, you define the condition of the rule as well as what formatting you want to apply when the condition is met.

How do I remove conditional formatting from a cell?
Select the range that contains the formatting you want to remove, click the **Conditional Formatting** button on the Home tab, and then click **Manage Rules**. Next, click the rule you want to remove, click **Delete Rule**, and then click **OK**.

Add Columns and Rows

You can add columns and rows to your worksheets to include more data. For example, you may have typed product names in the rows of a worksheet that shows product sales over a period of time, but you did not include the region in which those products were sold. Now you find that you need to add region designations as row titles to segregate sales by region as well as by product.

You are not limited to inserting new columns and rows one at a time; if you want, you can insert multiple new columns and rows simultaneously.

Add Columns and Rows

Add a Column

1 Click the letter of the column that should appear to the right of the new column you want to insert.

2 Click the **Home** tab.

3 Click **Insert**.

You can also right-click a column heading and click **Insert**.

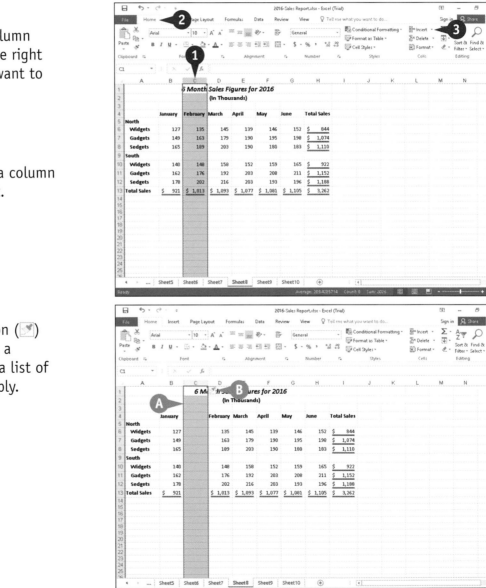

Ⓐ Excel adds a column.

Ⓑ The Insert Options button (🖋) appears when you insert a column; click it to view a list of options that you can apply.

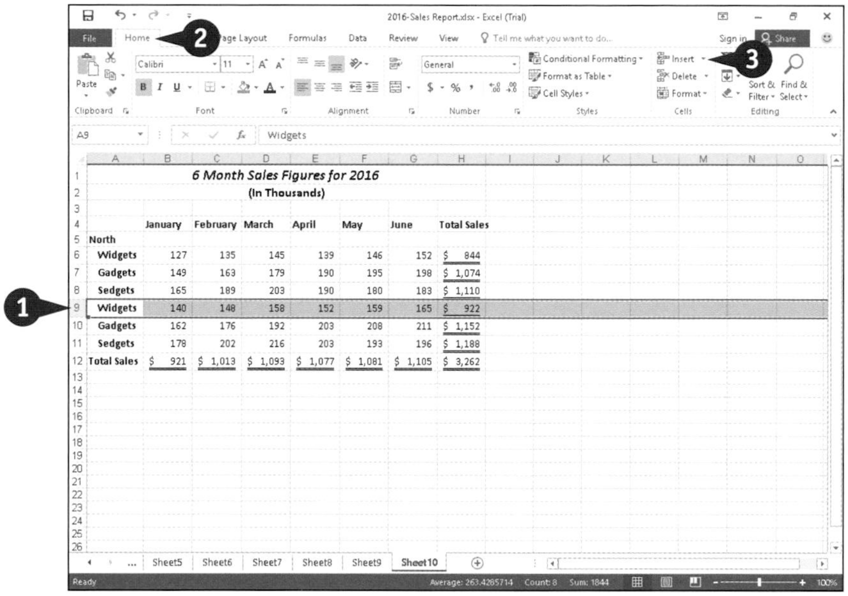

Add a Row

1 Click the number of the row that should appear below the new row you want to insert.

2 Click the **Home** tab.

3 Click **Insert**.

You can also right-click a row number and click **Insert**.

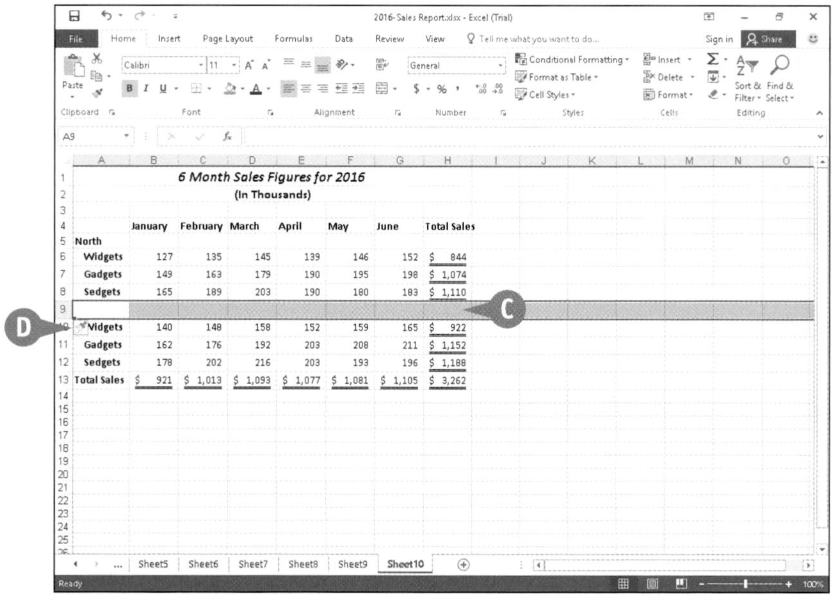

C Excel adds a row.

D The Insert Options button () appears, and you can click it to view a list of options that you can assign.

---

simplify it

How can I insert multiple columns and rows?
First, select two or more columns and rows in the worksheet; then activate the Insert command as described in this section. Excel adds the same number of new columns and rows as the number you originally selected.

What options appear when I click the Insert Options button?
For a new row, you can select **Format Same As Above**, **Format Same As Below**, or **Clear Formatting** (○ changes to ◉). For a new column, you can select **Format Same As Left**, **Format Same As Right**, or **Clear Formatting** (○ changes to ◉).

Resize Columns and Rows

Values that are too large to fit in a cell might appear as pound signs. Long lines of text appear on one line; if you type additional data into adjoining cells, long lines appear truncated, but they are not. If you select one of these cells and look at the Formula bar, you see the value or the text. To display long text in the worksheet, you can wrap it within the cell as described in the section "Turn On Text Wrapping," or you can resize the column. To display large values in the worksheet, you can resize the column. You can also resize rows.

Resize Columns and Rows

1 Position the mouse (◇) on the right edge of the column letter or the bottom edge of the row number that you want to resize.

The mouse (◇) changes to ↔ or ↕.

2 Click and drag the edge to the desired size.

A A solid line marks the new edge of the column or row as you drag, and Excel displays the new column width or row height.

3 Release the mouse button.

B Excel resizes the column or row and previously truncated values now appear.

C You can also select a column or row, click the **Format** button, and from the menu that appears, click **AutoFit Column Width** or **AutoFit Row Height** to resize the column or row to fit existing text.

Freeze Column and Row Titles On-Screen

When you work with a worksheet that contains more information than will fit on one screen, you can freeze one or more columns or rows to keep information in those columns and rows on-screen, regardless of where you place the cell pointer.

Freezing the top row or the leftmost column of your worksheet is very useful when the row or column contains headings or titles.

Freezing columns and rows only affects only on-screen work; it does not affect printing.

Freeze Column and Row Titles On-Screen

Note: *To freeze both a column and a row, click the cell to the right of the column and below the row that you want visible on-screen at all times.*

1 Click the **View** tab.

2 Click **Freeze Panes**.

3 Click a choice for freezing.

Freeze Panes freezes both a row of column headings and a column of row titles; otherwise, choose **Freeze Top Row** or **Freeze First Column**.

This example freezes the top row.

Excel freezes the areas you identified.

4 Press **Page down** or **Alt** + **Page down** to scroll down one screen or one screen to the right.

A The frozen columns or rows remain on-screen.

B The next page of rows or columns appears.

C To unlock the columns and rows, click **Freeze Panes** and then click **Unfreeze Panes**.

Name a Range

You can assign distinctive names to the cells and ranges of cells in a worksheet. A *range* is a rectangular group of cells; a range can also consist of a single cell. Assigning names to cells and ranges can help you more easily identify their contents. You can also use range names in formulas, which can help you decipher a formula. (Formulas are discussed later in this book.) Note that when it comes to naming ranges, you must follow some rules, as discussed in the Simplify It tip.

Name a Range

Assign a Range Name

1 Select the cells comprising the range that you want to name.

2 Click the **Formulas** tab.

3 Click **Define Name**.

The New Name dialog box opens.

Note: *Excel suggests a name using a label near the selected range. If you like the suggested name, skip Step 4.*

4 Type a name for the selected range in the **Name** field.

Ⓐ You can add a comment or note about the range here. For example, you might indicate what data the range contains.

5 Click **OK**.

Excel assigns the name to the cells.

Ⓑ When you select the range, its name appears in the Name box.

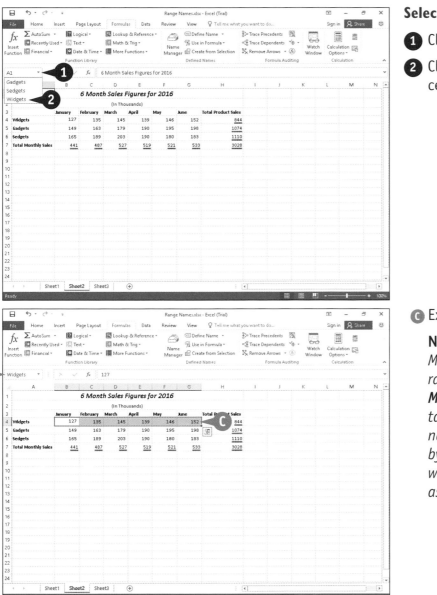

Select a Named Range

1 Click the **Name ▼**.

2 Click the name of the range of cells you want to select.

C Excel selects the cells in the range.

Note: *You can use the Name Manager to make changes to your range names. Click the **Name Manager** button on the Formulas tab. You can edit existing range names, change the cells referenced by a range, or remove ranges to which you no longer need names assigned in the worksheet.*

simplify it

What are the rules for naming ranges?

Each name can be no more than 255 characters and must be unique. You can use uppercase and lowercase letters in a range name, but Excel ignores case — sales and SALES are the same name. The first character must be a letter, an underscore (_), or a backslash (\). You cannot use spaces in a range name; instead, substitute the underscore or the dash. You cannot name a range using cell references such as A1 or $F$6, nor can you name a range using either the uppercase or lowercase forms of the letters C and R.

Clear or Delete Cells

You can clear the formatting applied to a cell, the contents of the cell, any comments you assigned to the cell, any hyperlink formatting in the cell, or all these elements. Clearing a cell is useful when you want to return the cell to its original state in Excel and you do not want to apply all of Excel's original formats manually.

You can also delete rows or columns of data. When you delete rows or columns, Excel adjusts the remaining cells in your worksheet, shifting them up or to the left to fill any gap in the worksheet structure.

Clear or Delete Cells

Clear Cells

1 Select the cell or range containing the data or formatting that you want to remove.

2 Click the **Home** tab.

3 Click the **Clear** button ( ).

4 Choose an option to identify what you want to clear.

This example clears formats.

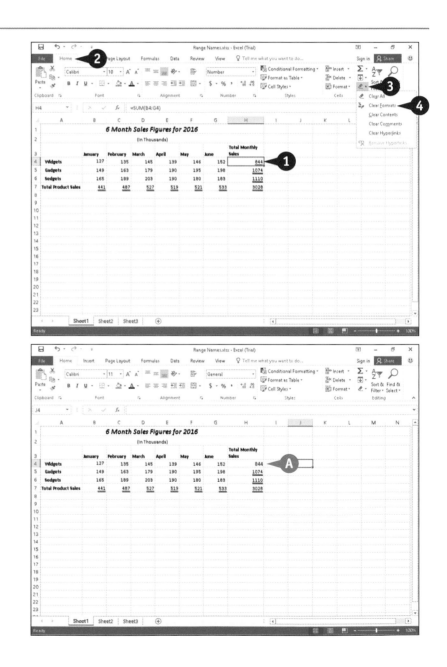

Ⓐ Excel clears the cell using the option you selected in Step **4**.

In this example, Excel clears the formatting but retains the cell data.

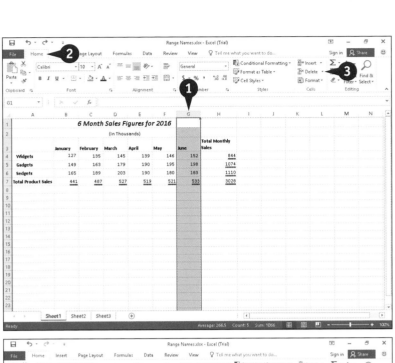

Delete Rows or Columns

① Click the number of the row or the letter of the column that you want to delete.

This example deletes a column.

② Click the **Home** tab.

③ Click **Delete**.

You can also right-click a row number or column heading and click **Delete**.

ⓑ Excel deletes the row or column and moves remaining data up or to the left to fill any gap in the worksheet structure.

simplify it

What is the difference between Clear Formats and Clear Contents?
Clear Formats removes just the formatting of a cell or range and leaves the contents of the cell or range. You retain the data and can reformat the cell or range; this command is most useful when you have applied several different formats and do not like the results. In a sense, Clear Formats lets you start over. Clear Contents, on the other hand, deletes the data in the cell but retains the cell's formatting. In this case, you can enter new data and it displays the same formatting as the data you cleared.

Split and Format a Column of Data

You can split a column of data into multiple columns. The Text to Columns feature is particularly useful when you open a list from another program. Typically, the information shows up on each row in one long string, but you want the information divided into columns.

After dividing the information, you can use the Flash Fill feature to format the data the way you want. With Flash Fill, you provide examples and, in most cases, Excel understands what you want and does the work. Note that you can use Flash Fill in regular Excel files as well as text files you import.

Split and Format a Column of Data

Convert Text to Columns

1 Open the file containing the data you want to format.

The Text Import Wizard appears.

Note: *If the Text Import Wizard does not appear, click the* **Data** *tab and then click* **Text to Columns** *in the Data Tools group.*

2 Select **Delimited** (○ changes to ◉).

3 Click **Next**.

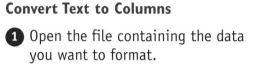

4 Select the delimiter your file uses (☐ changes to ☑).

5 Click **Finish**.

A The file appears on-screen in columnar format. You can widen the columns and, if you want, apply bold formatting to column headings.

Using Flash Fill Formatting

1 Insert a column beside the one you want to format and give it the same name as the one you want to format.

This example inserts column B.

2 Type the first entry from the original column into the inserted column using the format you want.

This example types the contents of cell A2 into cell B2, supplying dashes.

3 Start typing the second entry.

B Once Excel detects the format you want, it applies the formatting of the entry above to the current entry.

Note: *You might need to type a few entries for Excel to detect the format.*

C Excel suggests the same formatting for all other entries in the column.

4 Press **Enter** to accept the formatting into the column.

5 When you finish formatting columns, you can delete the original columns.

simplify it

How do I know which delimiter to select?
When you see your data separated in the Data Preview box at the bottom of the second Text Import Wizard dialog box, you know you have selected the delimiter you need.

How do I get the Flash Fill feature to insert leading zeros in a ZIP or postal code?
By default, Excel formats columns containing numbers as numbers and therefore does not display an initial zero in a ZIP or postal code that begins with a zero.

Before formatting using Flash Fill, format the column you insert as a Text column; click the **Home** tab and, in the Number group, click the dialog box launcher (⌐). In the Format Cells dialog box, click **Text** and then click **OK**.

Add a Worksheet

By default, when you create a new blank workbook in Excel, it contains one worksheet, which may be adequate. In some cases, however, your workbook might require additional worksheets in which to enter more data. For example, if your workbook contains data about products your company sells, you might want to add worksheets for each product category. You can easily add worksheets to a workbook.

When you add a new worksheet, Excel gives it a default name. To help you better keep track of your data, you can rename your new worksheet. For more information, see the next section, "Name a Worksheet."

Add a Worksheet

1 Click the **Insert Worksheet** button (⊕).

You can also right-click a worksheet tab and click **Insert** to open the Insert dialog box, where you can choose to insert a worksheet.

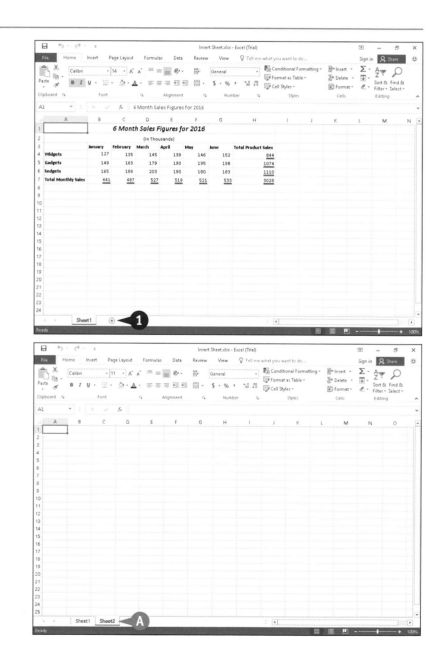

A Excel adds a new blank worksheet and gives it a default worksheet name.

Name a Worksheet

When you create a new workbook, Excel assigns default names to each worksheet in the workbook. Likewise, Excel assigns a default name to each worksheet you add to an existing workbook. To help you identify their content, you can change the names of your Excel worksheets to something more descriptive. For example, if your workbook contains four worksheets, each detailing a different sales quarter, then you can give each worksheet a unique name, such as Quarter 1, Quarter 2, and so on.

Name a Worksheet

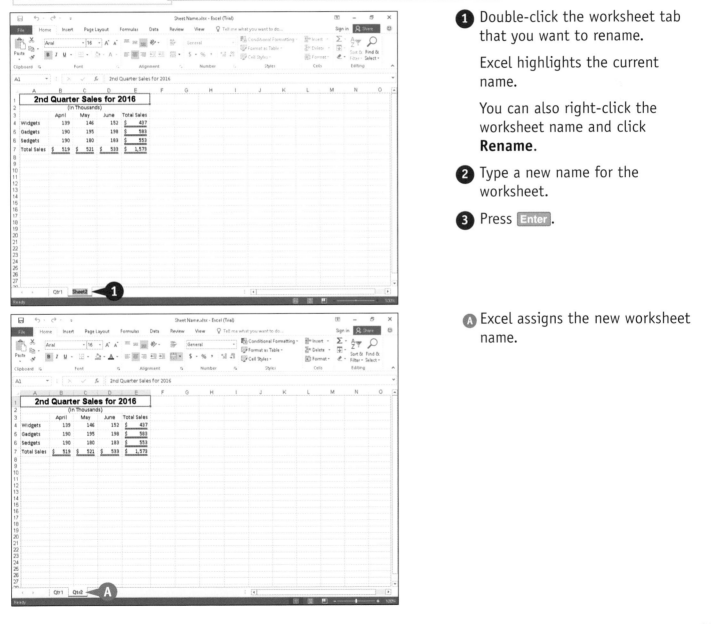

1 Double-click the worksheet tab that you want to rename.

Excel highlights the current name.

You can also right-click the worksheet name and click **Rename**.

2 Type a new name for the worksheet.

3 Press **Enter**.

A Excel assigns the new worksheet name.

Change Page Setup Options

You can change worksheet settings related to page orientation, margins, paper size, and more. For example, suppose that you want to print a worksheet that has a few more columns than will fit on a page in Portrait orientation. (Portrait orientation accommodates fewer columns but more rows on the page and is the default page orientation that Excel assigns.) You can change the orientation of the worksheet to Landscape, which accommodates more columns but fewer rows on a page.

You can also use Excel's page setup settings to establish margins and insert page breaks to control the placement of data on a printed page.

Change Page Setup Options

Change the Page Orientation

Ⓐ Dotted lines identify page breaks that Excel inserts.

① Click the **Page Layout** tab.

② Click **Orientation**.

③ Click **Portrait** or **Landscape**.

Note: *Portrait is the default orientation.*

Excel applies the new orientation. This example applies Landscape.

Ⓑ Excel moves the page break indicator based on the new orientation.

Ⓒ You can click the **Margins** button to set up page margins.

Insert a Page Break

1 Select the row above which you want to insert a page break.

2 Click the **Page Layout** tab.

3 Click **Breaks**.

4 Click **Insert Page Break**.

D Excel inserts a solid line representing a user-inserted page break.

How do I print just part of a worksheet?

To print only a part of a worksheet, select the cells that you want to print, click the **Page Layout** tab on the Ribbon, click the **Print Area** button, and then click **Set Print Area**. Then print as usual.

Can I set different margins for different pages that I print?

Yes. Excel assigns the same margins to all pages of a worksheet. If you need different margins for different sections that you plan to print, place each section for which you need different margins on separate worksheets and set each worksheet's margins accordingly.

Move and Copy Worksheets

You can move or copy a worksheet to a new location within the same workbook, or to an entirely different workbook. For example, moving a worksheet is helpful if you insert a new worksheet and the worksheet tab names appear out of order. Or, you might want to move a worksheet that tracks sales for the year to a new workbook so that you can start tracking for a new year.

In addition to moving worksheets, you can copy them. Copying a worksheet is helpful when you plan to make major changes to the worksheet.

Move and Copy Worksheets

① If you plan to move a worksheet to a different workbook, open both workbooks and select the one containing the worksheet you want to move.

② Click the tab of the worksheet you want to move or copy to make it the active worksheet.

③ Click the **Home** tab.

④ Click **Format**.

⑤ Click **Move or Copy Sheet**.

The Move or Copy dialog box appears.

Ⓐ You can click ⌄ to select a workbook for the worksheet.

⑥ Click the location where you want to place the worksheet that you are moving.

Note: *Excel moves or copies sheets in front of the sheet you select.*

Ⓑ You can copy a worksheet by selecting **Create a copy** (☐ changes to ☑).

⑦ Click **OK**.

Excel moves or copies the worksheet to the new location.

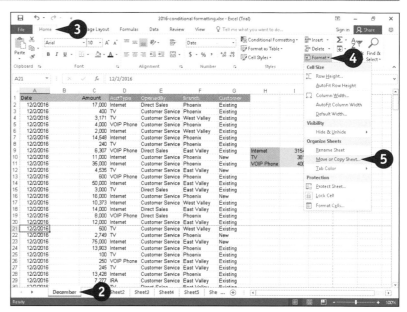

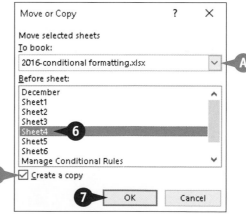

Delete a Worksheet

You can delete a worksheet that you no longer need in your workbook. For example, you might delete a worksheet that contains outdated data or information about a product that your company no longer sells.

When you delete a worksheet, Excel prompts you to confirm the deletion unless the worksheet is blank, in which case it simply deletes the worksheet. As soon as you delete a worksheet, Excel permanently removes it from the workbook file and displays the worksheet behind the one you deleted unless you deleted the last worksheet. In that case, Excel displays the worksheet preceding the one you deleted.

Delete a Worksheet

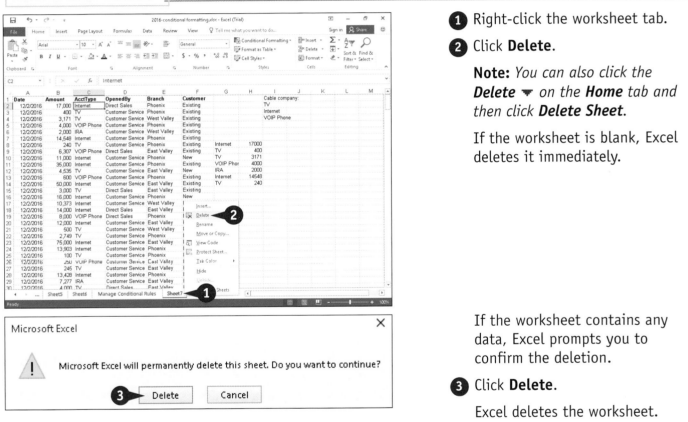

1 Right-click the worksheet tab.

2 Click **Delete**.

Note: *You can also click the* **Delete** ▼ *on the* **Home** *tab and then click* **Delete Sheet**.

If the worksheet is blank, Excel deletes it immediately.

If the worksheet contains any data, Excel prompts you to confirm the deletion.

3 Click **Delete**.

Excel deletes the worksheet.

Find and Replace Data

You can search for information in your worksheet and replace it with other information. For example, suppose that you discover that Northwest Valley was entered repeatedly as West Valley. You can search for West Valley and replace it with Northwest Valley. Be aware that Excel finds all occurrences of information as you search to replace it, so be careful when

replacing all occurrences at once. You can search and then skip occurrences that you do not want to replace.

You can search an entire worksheet or you can limit the search to a range of cells that you select before you begin the search.

Find and Replace Data

1 Click the **Home** tab.

2 Click **Find & Select**.

3 Click **Replace**.

Ⓐ To simply search for information, click **Find**.

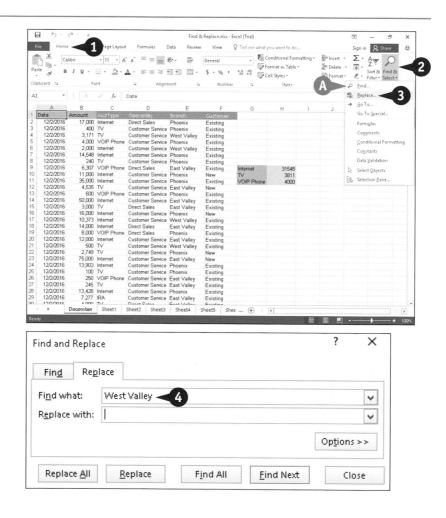

Excel displays the Replace tab of the Find and Replace dialog box.

4 Type the information for which you want to search here.

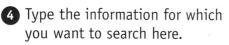

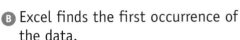

5 Type the information that you want Excel to use to replace the information you typed in Step **4**.

6 Click **Find Next**.

B Excel finds the first occurrence of the data.

7 Click **Replace**.

Excel replaces the information in the cell.

C Excel finds the next occurrence automatically.

8 Repeat Step **7** until you replace all appropriate occurrences.

Note: *You can click **Replace All** if you do not want to review each occurrence before Excel replaces it.*

Excel displays a message when it cannot find any more occurrences.

9 Click **OK** and then click **Close** in the Find and Replace dialog box.

---

simplify it

Where can I find detailed search options?
Click the **Options** button in the Find and Replace dialog box. For example, you can search the entire workbook or the selected worksheet, by rows or columns, and more. You can also search for specific formatting or special characters using Format options.

How can I search for and delete data?
In the Find and Replace dialog box, type the text you want to delete in the **Find what** box; leave the **Replace with** box empty. When you click **Replace**, Excel looks for the data and deletes it without adding new data to the worksheet.

Create a Table

You can create a table from any rectangular range of related data in a worksheet. A *table* is a collection of related information. Table rows — called *records* — contain information about one element, and table columns divide the element into *fields*. In a table containing name and address information, a record would contain all the information about one person, and all first names, last names, addresses, and so on would appear in separate columns.

When you create a table, Excel identifies the information in the range as a table and simultaneously formats the table and adds AutoFilter arrows to each column.

Create a Table

1 Set up a range in a worksheet that contains similar information for each row.

2 Click anywhere in the range.

3 Click the **Insert** tab.

4 Click **Table**.

The Create Table dialog box appears, displaying a suggested range for the table.

A You can deselect this option (☑ changes to ☐) if labels for each column do *not* appear in Row 1.

B You can click the **Range selector** button (▣) to select a new range for the table boundaries by dragging in the worksheet.

5 Click **OK**.

Excel creates a table and applies a table style to it.

C The Table Tools Design tab appears on the Ribbon.

D ▼ appears in each column title.

E Excel assigns the table a generic name.

---

simplify it

When should I use a table?
If you need to identify common information, such as the largest value in a range, or you need to select records that match a criterion, use a table. Tables make ranges easy to navigate. When you press **Tab** with the cell pointer in a table, the cell pointer stays in the table, moving directly to the next cell and to the next table row when you tab from the last column. When you scroll down a table so that the header row disappears, Excel replaces the column letters with the labels that appear in the header row.

Filter or Sort Table Information

When you create a table, Excel automatically adds AutoFilter arrows to each column; you can use these arrows to quickly and easily filter and sort the information in the table.

When you filter a table, you display only those rows that meet conditions you specify, and you specify

those conditions by making selections from the AutoFilter lists. You can also use the AutoFilter arrows to sort information in a variety of ways. Excel recognizes the type of data stored in table columns and offers you sorting choices that are appropriate for the type of data.

Filter or Sort Table Information

Filter a Table

1 Click ▼ next to the column heading you want to use for filtering.

A Excel displays a list of possible filters for the selected column.

2 Select a filter choice (☑ changes to ☐ or ☐ changes to ☑).

3 Repeat Step **2** until you have selected all the filters you want to use.

4 Click **OK**.

B Excel displays only the data meeting the criteria you selected in Step **2**.

C The AutoFilter ▼ changes to ▼ to indicate the data in the column is filtered.

Sort a Table

1 Click ▼ next to the column heading you want to use for sorting.

Ⓓ Excel displays a list of possible sort orders.

2 Click a sort order.

This example sorts from smallest to largest.

Ⓔ Excel reorders the information.

Ⓕ ▼ changes to ⬇ to indicate the data in the column is sorted.

How does the Sort by Color option work?
If you apply font colors, cell colors, or both to some cells in the table, you can then sort the table information by the colors you assigned. You can manually assign colors or you can assign colors using conditional formatting; see Chapter 9 for details on using conditional formatting.

I do not see the AutoFilter down arrow beside my table headings. What should I do?
Click the **Data** tab and then click the **Filter** button. This button toggles on and off the appearance of the AutoFilter ▼ in a table.

Analyze Data Quickly

You can easily analyze data in a variety of ways using the Quick Analysis button. You can apply various types of conditional formatting, create different types of charts, including line and column charts, or add miniature graphs called sparklines (see Chapter 12 for details on sparkline charts). You can also sum, average, and count occurrences of data as well as calculate percent of total and running total values. In addition, you can apply a table style and create a variety of different PivotTables.

The choices displayed in each analysis category are not always the same; the ones you see depend on the type of data you select.

Analyze Data Quickly

1 Select a range of data to analyze.

A The Quick Analysis button (⊞) appears.

2 Click the **Quick Analysis** button (⊞).

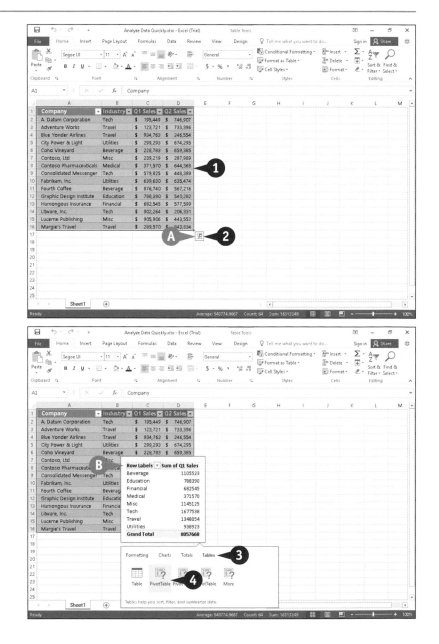

Quick Analysis categories appear.

3 Click each category heading to view the options for that category.

4 Point the mouse (⬚) at a choice under a category.

B A preview of that analysis choice appears.

Note: *For an explanation of the Quick Analysis choices, see the next section, "Understanding Data Analysis Choices."*

5 When you find the analysis choice you want to use, click it and Excel creates it.

Understanding Data Analysis Choices

The Quick Analysis button (■) offers a variety of ways to analyze selected data. This section provides an overview of the analysis categories and the choices offered in each category.

Formatting

Use formatting to highlight parts of your data. With formatting, you can add data bars, color scales, and icon sets. You can also highlight values that exceed a specified number and cells that contain specified text.

Charts

Pictures often get your point across better than raw numbers. You can quickly chart your data; Excel recommends different chart types, based on the data you select. If you do not see the chart type you want to create, you can click **More**.

Totals

Using the options in the Totals category, you can easily calculate sums — of both rows and columns — as well as averages, percent of total, and the number of occurrences of the values in the range. You can also insert a running total that grows as you add items to your data.

Tables

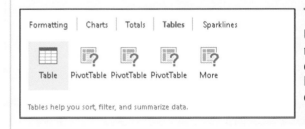

Using the choices under the Tables category, you can convert a range to a table, making it easy to filter and sort your data. You can also quickly and easily create a variety of PivotTables — Excel suggests PivotTables you might want to consider and then creates any you might choose.

Sparklines

Sparklines are tiny charts that you can display beside your data that provide trend information for selected data. See Chapter 12 for more information on sparkline charts.

CHAPTER 10

Track and Review Worksheet Changes

If you share your Excel workbooks with others, you can use the program's Track Changes feature to help you keep track of the edits others have made. As you set up tracking options, you can identify the changes you want Excel to monitor. When tracking changes, Excel adds comments that summarize the type of change made.

When you review changes to a workbook, you can specify the edits you want to review. Excel automatically locates and highlights each edit in a worksheet so that you can accept or reject it. When you finish reviewing, you can turn off tracking.

Track and Review Worksheet Changes

Turn On Tracking

1 Click the **Review** tab.

2 Click **Track Changes**.

3 Click **Highlight Changes**.

The Highlight Changes dialog box appears.

4 Select **Track changes while editing** (☐ changes to ☑).

Ⓐ You can select options to determine when, by whom, or where Excel tracks changes.

Ⓑ You can leave this option selected to display changes on-screen.

5 Click **OK**.

6 Excel prompts you to save the workbook; type a filename and click **Save**.

Excel shares the workbook and begins tracking changes to it.

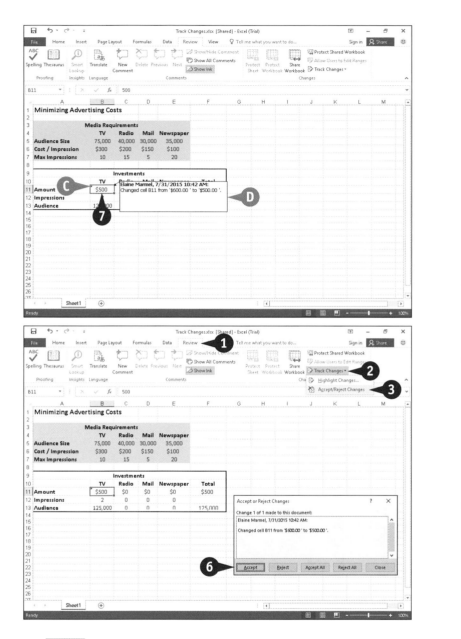

7 Edit your worksheet.

C Excel places a dark-green box around changed cells, and a small blue triangle appears in the upper left corner of the changed cell.

D To view details about a change, position the mouse (⇖) over the highlighted cell.

Review Changes

1 Click the **Review** tab.

2 Click **Track Changes**.

3 Click **Accept/Reject Changes**.

4 Excel prompts you to save the file; click **OK**.

5 The Select Changes to Accept or Reject dialog box appears, which resembles the Highlight Changes dialog box; use it to identify changes to review and click **OK**.

The Accept or Reject Changes dialog box appears.

6 Specify an action for each edit. You can click **Accept** to add the change to the final worksheet, **Reject** to reject the change, or one of these options to accept or reject all the changes at the same time.

How can I stop tracking changes?
To turn off Track Changes, follow these steps: Click the **Review** tab, click the **Track Changes** button, and click **Highlight Changes**. In the Highlight Changes dialog box that appears, deselect **Track changes while editing** (☑ changes to ☐) (**A**). Click **OK**. A message appears, explaining the consequences of no longer sharing the workbook; click **Yes**.

Insert a Comment

You can add comments to your worksheets. You might add a comment to make a note to yourself about a particular cell's contents, or you might include a comment as a note for other users to see. For example, if you share your workbooks with other users, you can use comments to leave feedback about the data without typing directly in the worksheet.

When you add a comment to a cell, Excel displays a small red triangle in the upper right corner of the cell until you choose to view it. Comments you add are identified with your username.

Insert a Comment

Add a Comment

1 Click the cell to which you want to add a comment.

2 Click the **Review** tab on the Ribbon.

3 Click the **New Comment** button.

You can also right-click the cell and choose **Insert Comment**.

A comment balloon appears.

4 Type your comment text.

⑤ Click anywhere outside the comment balloon to deselect the comment.

Ⓐ Cells that contain comments display a tiny red triangle in the corner.

View a Comment

① Position the mouse (⌖) over a cell containing a comment.

Ⓑ The comment balloon appears, displaying the comment.

How do I view all the comments in a worksheet?
If a worksheet contains several comments, you can view them one after another by clicking the **Next** button in the Review tab's Comments area. To view a comment you have already seen, click the **Previous** button. Alternatively, display all comments simultaneously by clicking the **Show All Comments** button.

How do I remove a comment?
To remove a comment, right-click the cell containing the comment and choose **Delete Comment** from the shortcut menu that appears. Alternatively, click the cell containing the comment and click the **Delete** button in the Review tab's Comments group.

Understanding Formulas

You can use formulas, which you build using mathematical operators, values, and cell references, to perform all kinds of calculations on your Excel data. For example, you can add the contents of a column of monthly sales totals to determine the cumulative sales total.

If you are new to writing formulas, this section explains the basics of building your own formulas in Excel. You learn about the correct way to structure formulas in Excel, how to reference cell data in your formulas, which mathematical operators are available for your use, and more.

Formula Structure

Ordinarily, when you write a mathematical formula, you write the values and the operators, followed by an equal sign, such as 2+2=. In Excel, formula structure works a bit differently. All Excel formulas begin with an equal sign (=), such as =2+2. The equal sign tells Excel to recognize any subsequent characters you enter as a formula rather than as a regular cell entry.

Reference a Cell

Every cell in a worksheet has a unique address, composed of the cell's column letter and row number, and that address appears in the Name box to the left of the Formula bar. Cell B3, for example, identifies the third cell down in column B. Although you can enter specific values in your Excel formulas, you can make your formulas more versatile if you include — that is, *reference* — a cell address rather than the value in that cell. Then, if the data in the cell changes but the formula remains the same, Excel automatically updates the result of the formula.

Cell Ranges

A group of related cells in a worksheet is called a *range*. You specify a range using the cells in the upper left and lower right corners of the range, separated by a colon. For example, range A1:B3 includes cells A1, A2, A3, B1, B2, and B3. You can also assign names to ranges to make it easier to identify their contents. Range names must start with a letter, underscore, or backslash, and can include uppercase and lowercase letters. Spaces are not allowed.

Mathematical Operators

You use mathematical operators in Excel to build formulas. Basic operators include the following:

Operator	Operation
+	Addition
-	Subtraction
*	Multiplication
/	Division
%	Percentage
^	Exponentiation
=	Equal to
<	Less than
<=	Less than or equal to
>	Greater than
>=	Greater than or equal to
<>	Not equal to

Operator Precedence

Excel performs operations in a formula from left to right, but gives some operators precedence over others, following the rules you learned in high school math:

Order	Operation
First	All operations enclosed in parentheses
Second	Exponential operations
Third	Multiplication and division
Fourth	Addition and subtraction

When you are creating equations, the order of operations determines the results. For example, suppose you want to determine the average of values in cells A2, B2, and C2. If you enter the equation =A2+B2+C2/3, Excel first divides the value in cell C2 by 3, and then adds that result to A2+B2 — producing the wrong answer. The correct way to write the formula is =(A2+B2+C2)/3. By enclosing the values in parentheses, you are telling Excel to perform the addition operations in the parentheses before dividing the sum by 3.

Reference Operators

You can use Excel's reference operators to control how a formula groups cells and ranges to perform calculations. For example, if your formula needs to include the cell range D2:D10 and cell E10, you can instruct Excel to evaluate all the data contained in these cells using a reference operator. Your formula might look like this: =SUM(D2:D10,E10).

Operator	Example	Operation
:	=SUM(D3:E12)	Range operator. Evaluates the reference as a single reference, including all the cells in the range from both corners of the reference.
,	=SUM(D3:E12,F3)	Union operator. Evaluates the two references as a single reference.
[space]	=SUM(D3:D20 D10:E15)	Intersect operator. Evaluates the cells common to both references.
[space]	=SUM(Totals Sales)	Intersect operator. Evaluates the intersecting cell or cells of the column labeled Totals and the row labeled Sales.

Create a Formula

You can write a formula to perform a calculation on data in your worksheet. In Excel, all formulas begin with an equal sign (=) and contain the values or references to the cells that contain the relevant values. For example, the formula for adding the contents of cells C3 and C4 together is =C3+C4.

Formulas appear in the Formula bar; formula results appear in the cell to which you assign a formula.

Note that, in addition to referring to cells in the current worksheet, you can also build formulas that refer to cells in other worksheets.

Create a Formula

1 Click the cell where you want to place a formula.

2 Type =.

A Excel displays the formula in the Formula bar and in the active cell.

3 Click the first cell that you want to include in the formula.

B Excel inserts the cell reference into the formula.

4 Type an operator for the formula.

5 Click the next cell that you want to include in the formula.

C Excel inserts the cell reference into the formula.

6 Repeat Steps **4** and **5** until all the necessary cells and operators have been added.

7 Press Enter.

D You can also click the **Enter** button (✓) on the Formula bar to accept the formula.

E You can click the **Cancel** button (✗) to cancel the formula.

F The result of the formula appears in the cell.

G The formula appears in the Formula bar; you can view it by clicking the cell containing the formula.

Note: *If you change a value in a cell referenced in your formula, Excel automatically updates the formula result to reflect the change.*

How do I edit a formula?
To edit a formula, click in the cell containing the formula and make any corrections in the Formula bar. Alternatively, double-click in the cell to make edits to the formula from within the cell. When finished, press Enter or click the **Enter** button (✓) on the Formula bar.

How do I reference cells in other worksheets?
To reference a cell in another worksheet, specify the worksheet name followed by an exclamation mark and then the cell address (for example, Sheet2!D12 or Sales!D12). If the worksheet name includes spaces, enclose the sheet name in single quote marks, as in 'Sales Totals'!D12.

Apply Absolute and Relative Cell References

By default, Excel uses relative cell referencing. If you copy a formula containing a relative cell reference to a new location, Excel adjusts the cell addresses in that formula to refer to the cells at the formula's new location. In cell B8, if you enter the formula =B5+B6 and then copy that formula to cell C8, Excel adjusts the formula to =C5+C6.

When a formula must always refer to the value in a particular cell, use an absolute cell reference. Absolute references are preceded with dollar signs. If your formula must always refer to the value in cell D2, enter $D$2 in the formula.

Apply Absolute and Relative Cell References

Copy Relative References

1. Enter the formula.

2. Click the cell containing the formula you want to copy.

   A In the Formula bar, the formula appears with a relative cell reference.

3. Click the **Home** tab.

4. Click the **Copy** button (⧉).

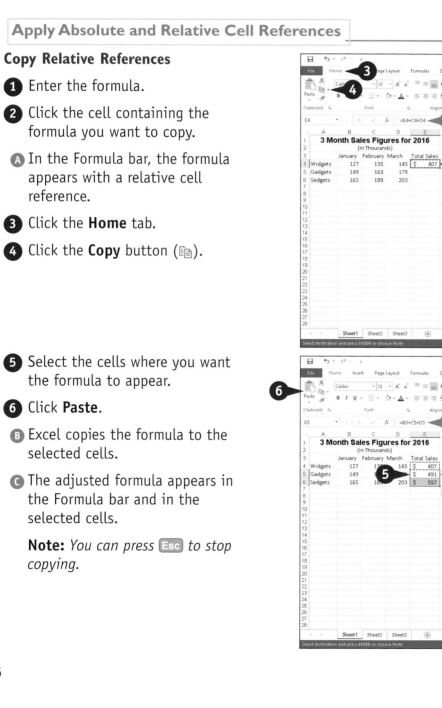

5. Select the cells where you want the formula to appear.

6. Click **Paste**.

   B Excel copies the formula to the selected cells.

   C The adjusted formula appears in the Formula bar and in the selected cells.

   Note: *You can press* Esc *to stop copying.*

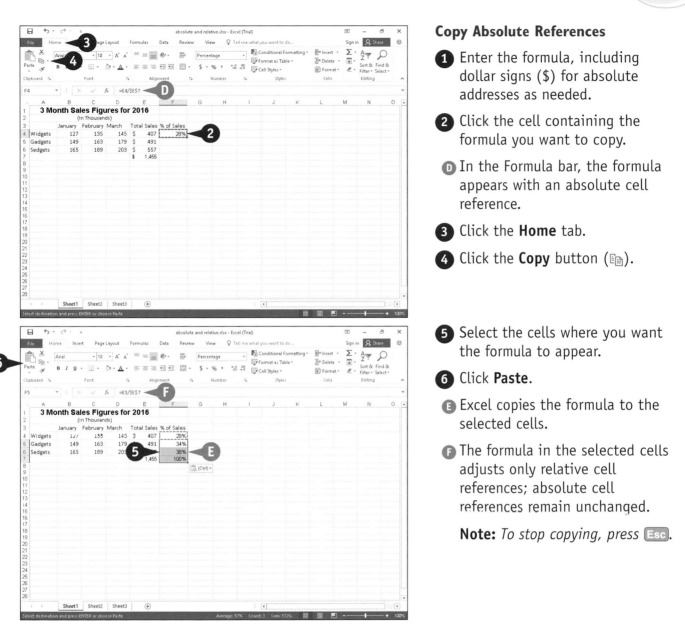

Copy Absolute References

1 Enter the formula, including dollar signs ($) for absolute addresses as needed.

2 Click the cell containing the formula you want to copy.

D In the Formula bar, the formula appears with an absolute cell reference.

3 Click the **Home** tab.

4 Click the **Copy** button (🗐).

5 Select the cells where you want the formula to appear.

6 Click **Paste**.

E Excel copies the formula to the selected cells.

F The formula in the selected cells adjusts only relative cell references; absolute cell references remain unchanged.

Note: *To stop copying, press* Esc.

---

simplify it

When would I use absolute cell referencing?

Use absolute cell referencing to always refer to the same cell in a worksheet. For example, suppose your worksheet contains pricing information that refers to a discount rate in cell G10. When you create a formula that involves the discount rate, that formula must always reference cell G10, even if you move or copy the formula to another cell. In this case, use $G$10. You can also combine absolute and relative references, creating *mixed references* that allow either the row or column to change while the other remains static if you copy the formula.

Understanding Functions

If you are looking for a speedier way to enter formulas, you can use any one of a wide variety of functions. *Functions* are ready-made formulas that perform a series of operations on a specified range of values. Excel offers more than 400 functions, grouped into 13 categories, that you can use to perform various types of calculations.

Functions use arguments to identify the cells that contain the data you want to use in your calculations. Functions can refer to individual cells or to ranges of cells. This section explains the basics of working with functions.

Function Elements

All functions must start with an equal sign (=). Functions are distinct in that each one has a name. For example, the function that adds values is called SUM, and the function for averaging values is called AVERAGE. You can create functions by typing them directly into your worksheet cells or the Formula bar; alternatively, you can use the Insert Function dialog box to select and apply functions to your data.

Construct an Argument

Functions use *arguments* to indicate which cells contain the values you want to calculate. Arguments are enclosed in parentheses. When applying a function to individual cells in a worksheet, you can use a comma to separate the cell addresses, as in =AVERAGE(A5,C5,F5). When applying a function to a range of cells, you can use a colon to designate the first and last cells in the range, as in =AVERAGE(B4:G4). If your range has a name, you can insert the name, as in =AVERAGE(Sales).

Types of Functions

Excel groups functions into 13 categories, not including functions installed with Excel add-in programs:

Category	Description
Financial	Includes functions for calculating loans, principal, interest, yield, and depreciation.
Date & Time	Includes functions for calculating dates, times, and minutes.
Math & Trig	Includes a wide variety of functions for calculations of all types.
Statistical	Includes functions for calculating averages, probabilities, rankings, trends, and more.
Lookup & Reference	Includes functions that enable you to locate references or specific values in your worksheets.
Database	Includes functions for counting, adding, and filtering database items.
Text	Includes text-based functions to search and replace data and other text tasks.
Logical	Includes functions for logical conjectures, such as if-then statements.
Information	Includes functions for testing your data.
Engineering	Offers many kinds of functions for engineering calculations.
Cube	Enables Excel to fetch data from SQL Server Analysis Services, such as members, sets, aggregated values, properties, and key performance indicators (KPIs).
Compatibility	Use these functions to keep your workbook compatible with earlier versions of Excel.
Web	Use these functions when you work with web pages, services, or XML content.

Common Functions

The following table lists some of the more popular Excel functions that you might use with your own spreadsheet work.

Function	Category	Description	Syntax
SUM	Math & Trig	Adds values	=SUM(number1,number2,. . .)
ROUND	Math & Trig	Rounds a number to a specified number of digits	=ROUND(number,number_digits)
ROUNDDOWN	Math & Trig	Rounds a number down	=ROUNDDOWN (number,number_digits)
INT	Math & Trig	Rounds down to the nearest integer	=INT(number)
COUNT	Statistical	Counts the number of cells in a range that contain data	=COUNT(value1,value2,. . .)
AVERAGE	Statistical	Averages a series of arguments	=AVERAGE(number1,number2,. . .)
MIN	Statistical	Returns the smallest value in a series	=MIN(number1,number2,. . .)
MAX	Statistical	Returns the largest value in a series	=MAX(number1,number2,. . .)
MEDIAN	Statistical	Returns the middle value in a series	=MEDIAN(number1,number2,. . .)
PMT	Financial	Finds the periodic payment for a fixed loan	=PMT(interest_rate,number_of_ periods,present_value,future_value,type)
RATE	Financial	Returns an interest rate	=RATE(number_of_periods,payment,present_ value,future_value,type,guess)
TODAY	Date & Time	Returns the current date	=TODAY()
IF	Logical	Returns one of two results that you specify based on whether the value is true or false	=IF(logical_text,value_if_true,value_if_false)
AND	Logical	Returns true if all the arguments are true, and false if any argument is false	=AND(logical1,logical2,. . .)
OR	Logical	Returns true if any argument is true, and false if all arguments are false	=OR(logical1,logical2,. . .)

Apply a Function

You can use functions to speed up your Excel calculations. *Functions* are ready-made formulas that perform a series of operations on a specified range of values.

You use the Insert Function dialog box, which acts like a wizard, to look for a particular function from among Excel's 400-plus available functions and to

guide you through successfully entering the function. After you select your function, the Function Arguments dialog box opens to help you build the formula by describing the arguments you need for the function you chose. Functions use arguments to identify the cells that contain the data you want to use in your calculation.

Apply a Function

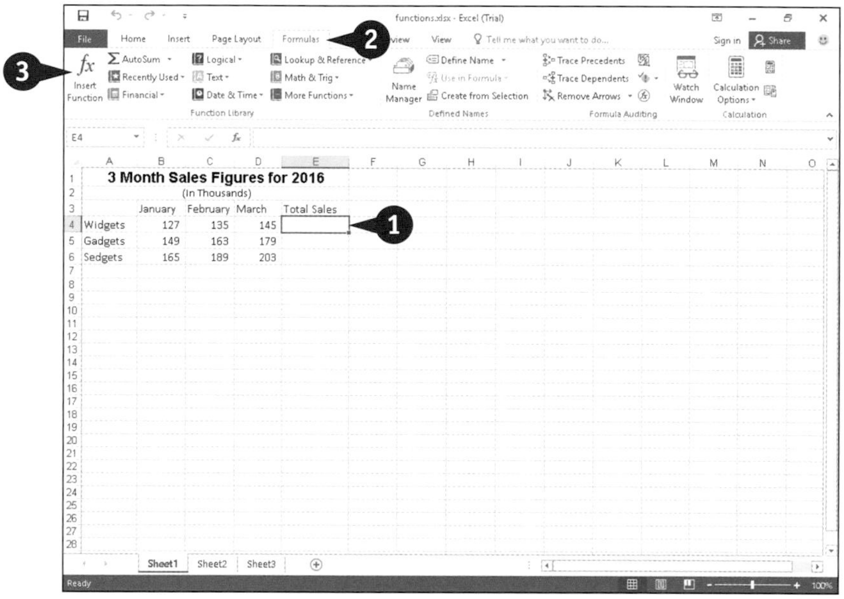

1 Click the cell in which you want to store the function.

2 Click the **Formulas** tab.

3 Click the **Insert Function** button.

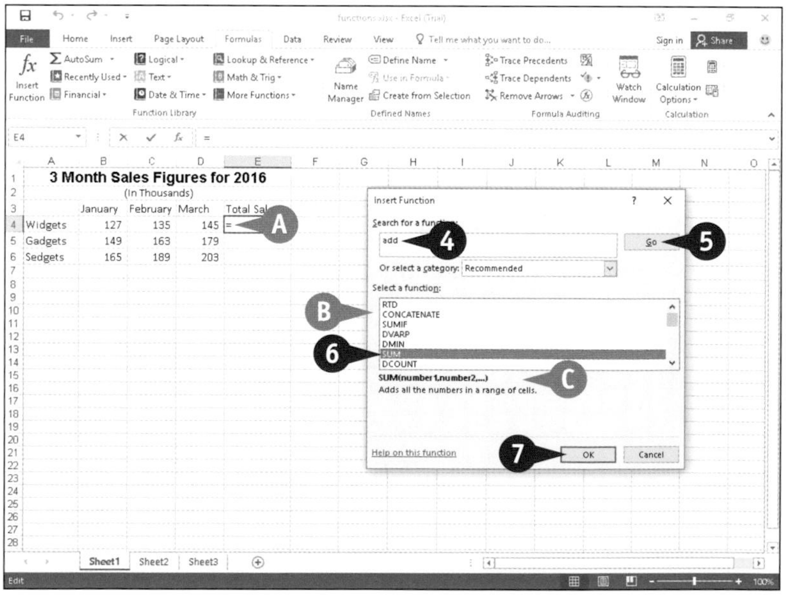

A Excel inserts an equal sign to indicate that a formula follows.

Excel displays the Insert Function dialog box.

4 Type a description of the function you need here.

5 Click **Go**.

B A list of suggested functions appears.

6 Click the function that you want to apply.

C A description of the selected function appears here.

7 Click **OK**.

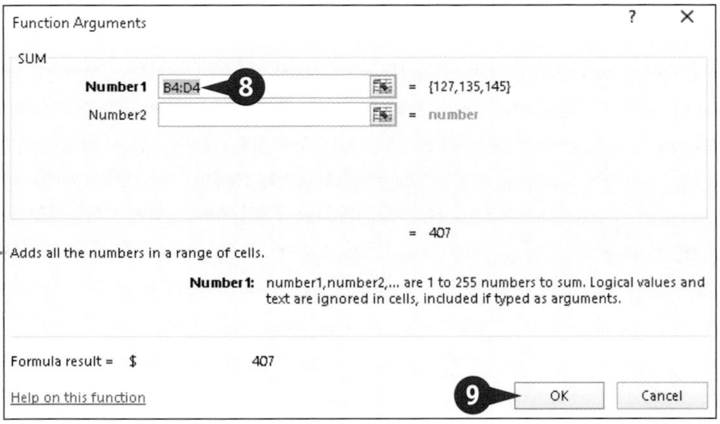

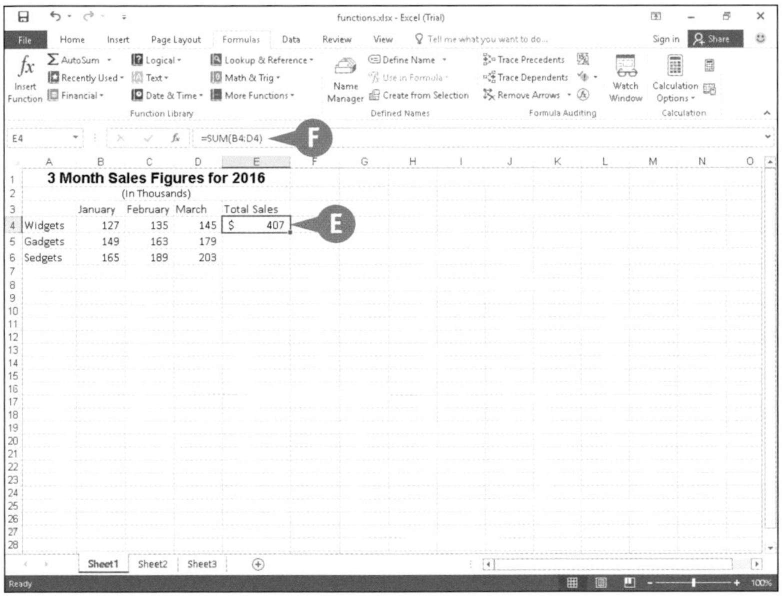

The Function Arguments dialog box appears.

8 Select the cells for each argument required by the function.

In the worksheet, Excel adds the cells as the argument to the function.

D Additional information about the function appears here.

9 When you finish constructing the arguments, click **OK**.

E Excel displays the function results in the cell.

F The function appears in the Formula bar.

---

simplify it

Can I edit a function?
Yes. Click the cell containing the function, click the **Formulas** tab, and then click the **Insert Function** button. Excel displays the function's Function Arguments dialog box, where you can change the cell references or values as needed. You can also edit directly in the cell.

How can I find help with a particular function?
Click the **Help on this function** link in either the Insert Function or Function Arguments dialog box to find out more about the function. The function help includes an example of the function being used and tips about using the function.

Total Cells with AutoSum

One of the most popular Excel functions is the AutoSum function. AutoSum automatically totals the contents of selected cells. For example, you can quickly total a column of sales figures. One way to use AutoSum is to select a cell and let the function guess which surrounding cells you want to total. Alternatively, you can specify exactly which cells to sum.

In addition to using AutoSum to total cells, you can simply select a series of cells in your worksheet; Excel displays the total of the cells' contents in the status bar, along with the number of cells you selected and an average of their values.

Total Cells with AutoSum

Using AutoSum to Total Cells

1 Click the cell in which you want to store a total.

2 Click the **Formulas** tab.

3 Click the **AutoSum** button.

Ⓐ If you click the **AutoSum** ▼, you can select other common functions, such as Average or Max.

You can also click the **AutoSum** button (Σ ·) on the Home tab.

Ⓑ AutoSum generates a formula to total the adjacent cells.

4 Press Enter or click the **Enter** button (✓).

C Excel displays the result in the cell.

D You can click the cell to see the function in the Formula bar.

Total Cells Without Applying a Function

1 Click a group of cells whose values you want to total.

Note: *To sum noncontiguous cells, press and hold* Ctrl *while clicking the cells.*

E Excel adds the contents of the cells, displaying the sum in the status bar along the bottom of the program window.

F Excel also counts the number of cells you have selected.

G Excel also displays an average of the values in the selected cells.

Can I select a different range of cells to sum?
Yes. AutoSum takes its best guess when determining which cells to total. If it guesses wrong, simply click the cells you want to add together before pressing Enter or clicking the **Enter** button (✓).

Why do I see pound signs (#) in a cell that contains a SUM function?
Excel displays pound signs in any cell — not just cells containing formulas or functions — when the cell's column is not wide enough to display the contents of the cell, including the cell's formatting. Resize the column to widen it and correct the problem; see Chapter 9 for details.

Audit a Worksheet for Errors

On occasion, you may see an error message, such as #DIV/0! or #NAME?, in your Excel worksheet. If you do, you should double-check your formula references to ensure that you included the correct cells. Locating the source of an error can be difficult, however, especially in larger worksheets. Fortunately,

if an error occurs in your worksheet, you can use Excel's Formula Auditing tools — namely, Error Checking and Trace Error — to examine and correct formula errors. For more information on types of errors and how to resolve them, see the table in the Simplify It tip.

Audit a Worksheet for Errors

Apply Error Checking

1. Click the **Formulas** tab.

2. Click the **Error Checking** button (✔ ▾).

Ⓐ Excel displays the Error Checking dialog box and highlights the first cell containing an error.

3. To fix the error, click **Edit in Formula Bar**.

Ⓑ To find help with an error, you can click here to open the help files.

Ⓒ To ignore the error, you can click **Ignore Error**.

Ⓓ You can click **Previous** and **Next** to scroll through all the errors on the worksheet.

4. Make edits to the cell references in the Formula bar or in the worksheet.

5. Click **Resume**.

When the error check is complete, a message box appears.

6. Click **OK**.

Trace Errors

1 Click the cell containing the formula or function error that you want to trace.

2 Click the **Formulas** tab.

3 Click ▼ beside the **Error Checking** button (✦ ▾).

4 Click **Trace Error**.

E Excel displays trace lines from the current cell to any cells referenced in the formula.

You can make changes to the cell contents or changes to the formula to correct the error.

F You can click **Remove Arrows** to turn off the trace lines.

simplify it

What kinds of error messages does Excel display for formula errors?
Different types of error values appear in cells when an error occurs:

Error	Problem	Solution
######	The cell is not wide enough to contain the value	Increase the column width.
#DIV/0!	Dividing by zero	Edit the cell reference or value of the denominator.
#N/A	Value is not available	Ensure that the formula references the correct value.
#NAME?	Does not recognize text in a formula	Ensure that the name referenced is correct.
#NULL!	Specifies two areas that do not intersect	Check for an incorrect range operator or correct the intersection problem.
#NUM!	Invalid numeric value	Check the function for an unacceptable argument.
#REF!	Invalid cell reference	Correct cell references.
#VALUE!	Wrong type of argument or operand	Double-check arguments and operands.

Create a Chart

You can quickly convert your spreadsheet data into easy-to-read charts. You can create column, line, pie, bar, area, scatter, stock, surface, doughnut, bubble, and radar charts. Excel even recommends the type of chart that works best for your data. If you do not like Excel's recommendations, you can select the chart of your choice.

You can create charts using the Ribbon or using the Quick Analysis button. After you create a chart, you can use buttons beside the chart or on the Chart Tools tabs to fine-tune the chart to best display and explain the data.

Create a Chart

Using the Ribbon

1. Select the range of data that you want to chart.

   You can include any headings and labels, but do not include subtotals or totals.

2. Click the **Insert** tab.

3. Click **Recommended Charts**.

   The Insert Chart dialog box appears.

   A A preview of your data appears in the selected chart type.

   B If you do not see the chart you want to use, click **All Charts**.

4. Click a chart type.

5. Click **OK**.

   C Excel creates a chart and places it in the worksheet.

   D Whenever you select the chart, Chart Tools tabs appear on the Ribbon.

   E You can use the **Chart Elements** (✚), **Chart Styles** (✎), and **Chart Filters** (▼) buttons to add chart elements such as axis titles, customize the look of your chart, or change the data in the chart.

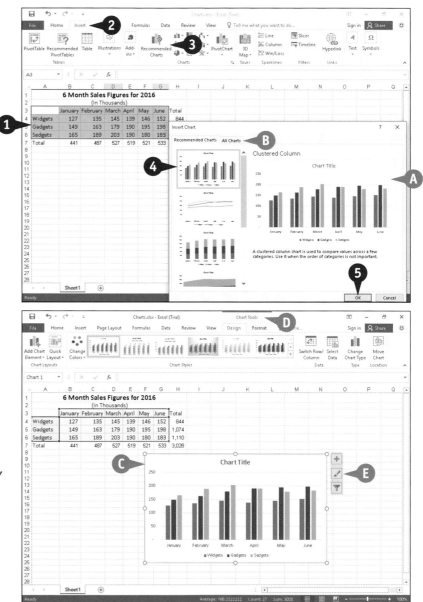

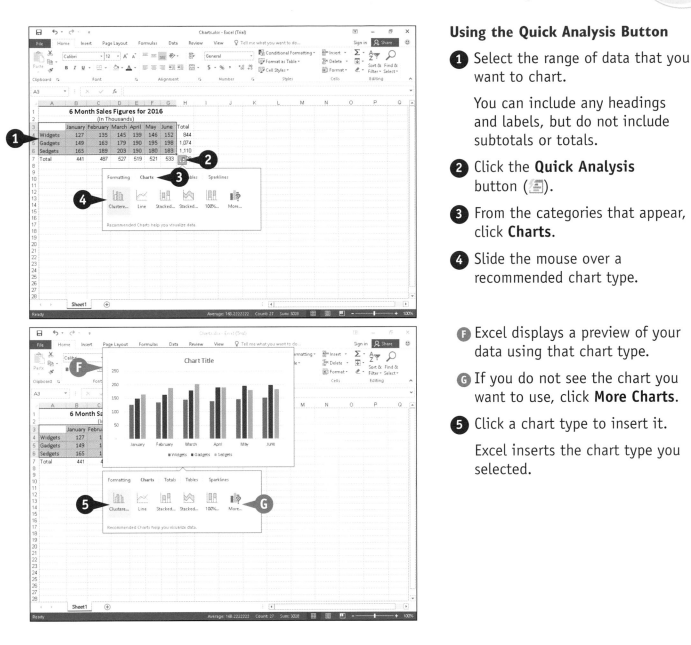

Using the Quick Analysis Button

1 Select the range of data that you want to chart.

You can include any headings and labels, but do not include subtotals or totals.

2 Click the **Quick Analysis** button (📈).

3 From the categories that appear, click **Charts**.

4 Slide the mouse over a recommended chart type.

F Excel displays a preview of your data using that chart type.

G If you do not see the chart you want to use, click **More Charts**.

5 Click a chart type to insert it.

Excel inserts the chart type you selected.

---

simplify it

Can I select noncontiguous data to include in a chart?
Yes. To select noncontiguous cells and ranges, select the first cell or range and then press and hold Ctrl while selecting additional cells and ranges.

In my column chart, I want bars for the elements appearing in the legend; is there an easy way to make that happen?
Yes. The legend displays the row headings in your selected data, whereas the bars represent the column headings. So, you should switch the rows and columns in the chart. Click the chart to select it. Then, click the **Chart Tools Design** tab and, in the Data group, click **Switch Row/Column**.

Move and Resize Charts

After creating a chart, you may decide that it would look better if it were a different size or located elsewhere on the worksheet. For example, you may want to reposition the chart at the bottom of the worksheet or make the chart larger so it is easier to read.

Moving or resizing a chart is like moving or resizing any other type of Office object. When you select a chart, handles appear around that chart; you use these handles to make the chart larger or smaller. Moving the chart is a matter of selecting it and then dragging it to the desired location.

Move and Resize Charts

Resize a Chart

1 Click any edge of the chart.

A Excel selects the chart and surrounds it with handles.

B ⊕ changes to ⬉, ⬍, ⬈, or ⬌.

C ✚, ✐, and ▼ appear.

2 Position the mouse pointer over a handle (⬉ changes to ⬉, ⬍, ⬈, or ⬌).

3 Click and drag a handle to resize the chart.

D A frame appears, representing the chart as you resize it on the worksheet.

E ⬉, ⬍, ⬈, or ⬌ changes to ✚.

4 Release the mouse button.

Excel resizes the chart.

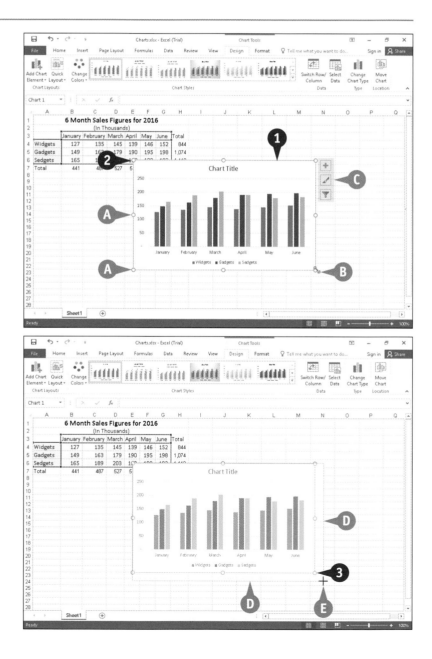

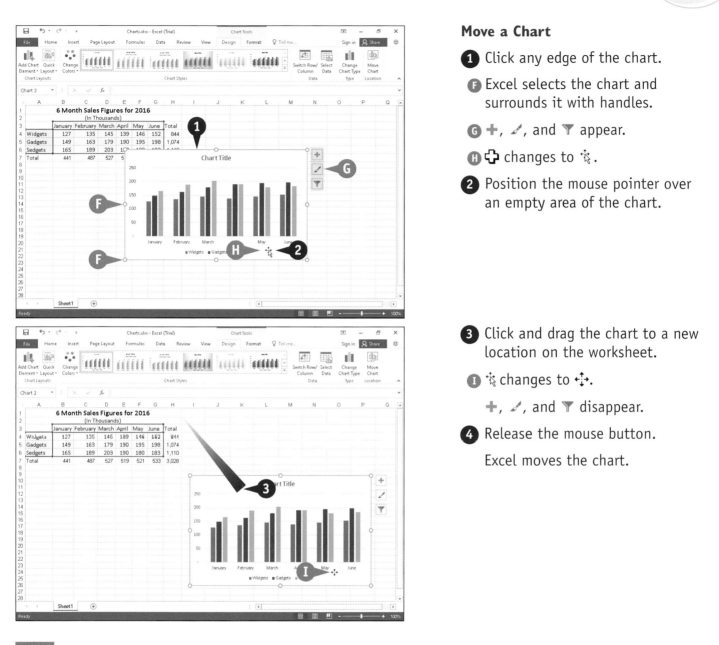

Move a Chart

1 Click any edge of the chart.

F Excel selects the chart and surrounds it with handles.

G ✛, ✎, and ▼ appear.

H ✚ changes to ⌖.

2 Position the mouse pointer over an empty area of the chart.

3 Click and drag the chart to a new location on the worksheet.

I ⌖ changes to ✛.

✛, ✎, and ▼ disappear.

4 Release the mouse button.

Excel moves the chart.

---

simplify it

Can I delete a chart or move it to its own worksheet?

Yes. To delete a chart, click its edge and press `Delete`. To move a chart to its own worksheet, right-click its edge and click **Move Chart** to display the Move Chart dialog box. Select **New sheet** (**A**) (○ changes to ●) and click **OK**. Excel adds a new worksheet called Chart1 to the workbook and places the chart in that worksheet.

Move Chart

Choose where you want the chart to be placed:

A ● New sheet: Chart1

○ Object in: Sheet1

OK   Cancel

Change the Chart Type

Suppose you create a column chart but then realize your data would be better presented in a line chart. Fortunately, Excel makes it easy to change the chart type. Excel recommends chart types that are suitable for your data, but you are not limited to its recommendations.

You select a new chart type using Chart Tools tabs on the Ribbon. To make these tabs available, you select

the chart. You click the edge of the chart to select the entire chart; you can select individual elements of the chart by clicking them. As long as you click anywhere inside the chart, Chart Tools tabs appear on the Ribbon.

Change the Chart Type

1. Click an edge of the chart to select it.

A Handles surround the chart.

2. Click the **Chart Tools Design** tab.

3. Click **Change Chart Type**.

The Change Chart Type dialog box appears.

B To view Excel's recommendations for chart types for your data, click this tab.

4. Click a chart type.

5. Click a chart variation.

C A preview of your chart appears here; point the mouse at the preview to enlarge it.

6. Click **OK**.

D Excel changes the chart to the chart type that you selected.

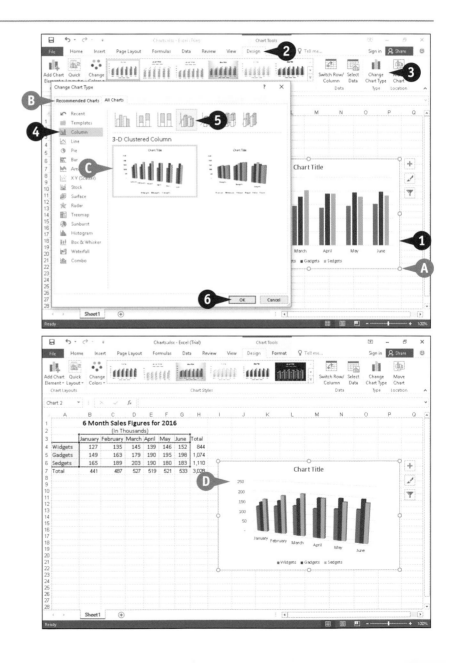

200

Change the Chart Style

You can change the chart style to change the appearance of a chart. You can choose from a wide variety of preset styles to find just the look you want. For example, you might prefer a brighter color scheme for the chart to make it stand out.

You can access various preset chart styles from the Design tab or from the Chart Styles button that appears along the right edge of a selected chart. To select a chart, click along its edge.

Change the Chart Style

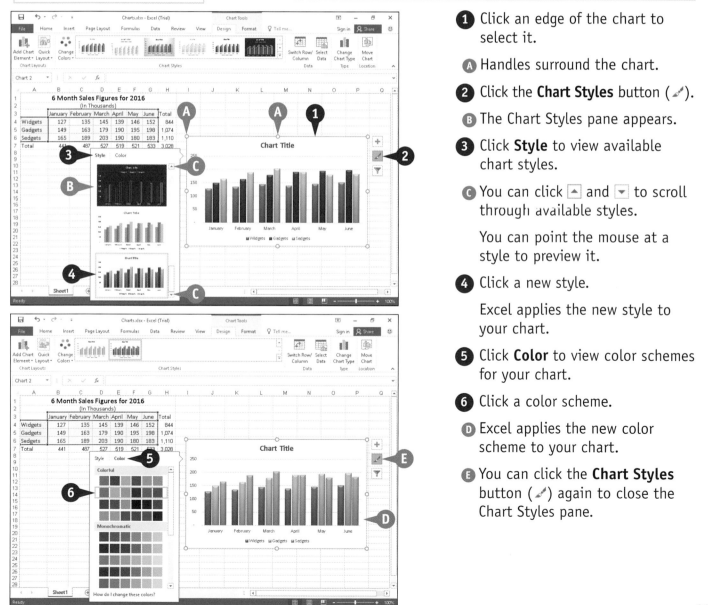

1 Click an edge of the chart to select it.

Ⓐ Handles surround the chart.

2 Click the **Chart Styles** button (🖌).

Ⓑ The Chart Styles pane appears.

3 Click **Style** to view available chart styles.

Ⓒ You can click ▲ and ▼ to scroll through available styles.

You can point the mouse at a style to preview it.

4 Click a new style.

Excel applies the new style to your chart.

5 Click **Color** to view color schemes for your chart.

6 Click a color scheme.

Ⓓ Excel applies the new color scheme to your chart.

Ⓔ You can click the **Chart Styles** button (🖌) again to close the Chart Styles pane.

Change the Chart Layout

You can customize your chart's appearance by using Excel's preset chart layout options to change the chart layout. Changing the chart layout changes how Excel positions chart elements. For example, you may prefer to show a legend on the side of the chart rather than on the bottom. Or, you might want a chart title to appear above the chart rather than

below it. Or, you might not want to display a chart title at all.

The various preset chart layouts are available on the Design tab. To display this tab, select the chart whose layout you want to change by clicking any chart edge.

Change the Chart Layout

① Click an edge of the chart to select it.

Ⓐ Handles surround the chart.

② Click the **Chart Tools Design** tab.

③ Click **Quick Layout**.

Ⓑ A palette of layouts appears.

You can point the mouse at each layout to preview its appearance.

④ Click a layout.

Ⓒ Excel applies the new layout to the existing chart.

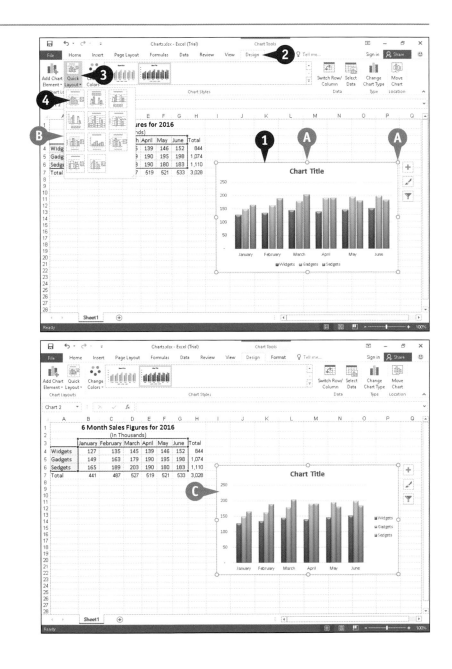

Add Chart Elements

You can add a variety of elements to your chart. For example, you can include or exclude axes, axis titles, a chart title, data labels, a data table, error bars, gridlines, a legend, and a trendline. Remember that displaying too many elements on a chart can make it hard to understand. This section shows you how to add axis titles; you use the same technique to add any chart element.

Add Chart Elements

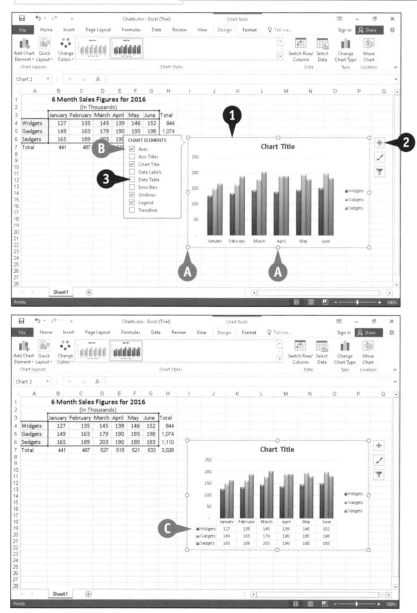

① Click an edge of the chart to select it.

Ⓐ Handles surround the chart.

② Click the **Chart Elements** button (➕).

Ⓑ The Chart Elements pane appears.

You can point the mouse at an element to preview it.

③ Select a new element to add or deselect an element to remove (☐ changes to ☑ or ☑ changes to ☐).

You can click the **Chart Elements** button (➕) again to close the Chart Elements pane.

Ⓒ Excel applies the change to your chart.

Note: *If you add any type of title, Excel inserts dummy text representing the title. You can replace the dummy text by clicking the title box to select it. Click again inside the box and select the dummy text. Then, type your replacement title.*

Format Chart Objects

You can change the formatting of any element, or *object*, in a chart, such as the background pattern for the plot area or the color of a data series. You use the Format pane to apply formatting to selected objects. The pane appears automatically when you format an object.

The available settings in the Format pane change, depending on the object you select. This section shows you how to add a fill color to the chart area, which is the area behind your data in the chart. You can apply these same techniques to format other chart objects.

Format Chart Objects

1 Click the object that you want to format.

To add a fill to the chart area, select the chart by clicking an edge of the chart, as shown in this example.

2 Click the **Chart Tools Format** tab.

3 Click **Format Selection**.

Ⓐ The Format Chart Area pane appears.

Ⓑ You can click ▾ to display other chart elements to format.

Ⓒ You can click these icons to display chart area fill, effects, or size and properties formatting you can apply.

Ⓓ You can click here to apply a variety of text formatting to the chart area.

4 Select the type of formatting that you want to change (○ changes to ◉).

Ⓔ Excel displays the effect.

5 Change any format settings.

6 Click ✕ to close the Format pane.

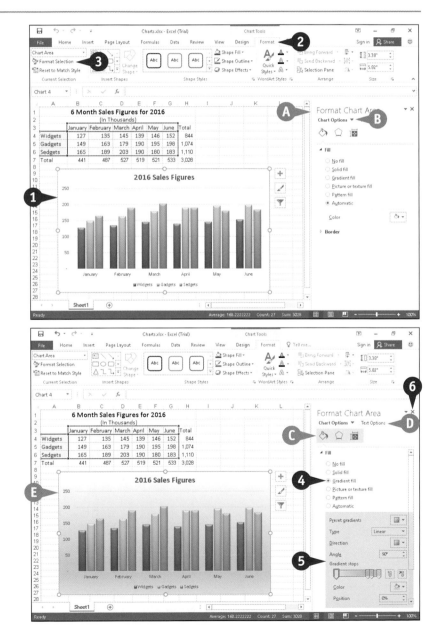

Change the Chart Data

You can quickly and easily filter the information displayed in your chart. Whenever you change data referenced in your chart, Excel automatically updates the chart to reflect your changes. But suppose that your chart shows several months of sales data for several products and you want to focus on one

month only. There is no need to create a new chart; you can simply filter your existing chart. When you are ready, you can easily redisplay all data in your chart.

Change the Chart Data

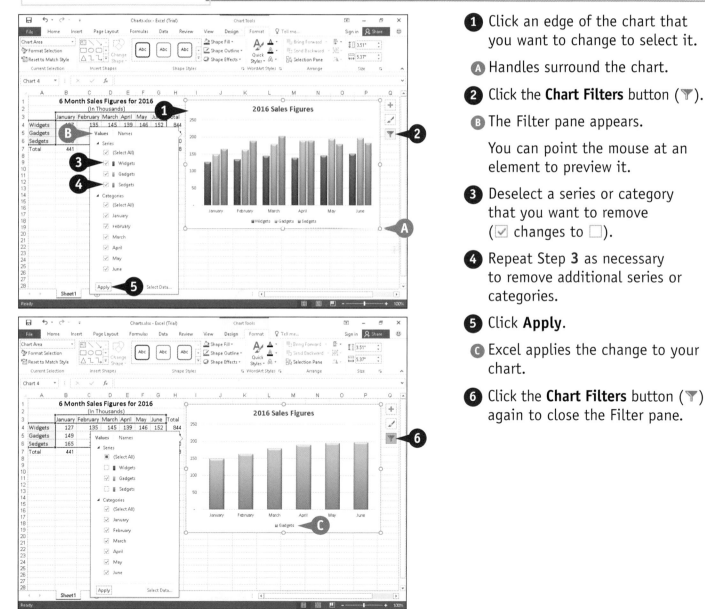

① **Click** an edge of the chart that you want to change to select it.

Ⓐ Handles surround the chart.

② **Click** the **Chart Filters** button (🛦).

Ⓑ The Filter pane appears.

You can point the mouse at an element to preview it.

③ **Deselect** a series or category that you want to remove (☑ changes to ☐).

④ **Repeat Step 3** as necessary to remove additional series or categories.

⑤ **Click Apply**.

Ⓒ Excel applies the change to your chart.

⑥ **Click** the **Chart Filters** button (🛦) again to close the Filter pane.

205

Using Sparklines to View Data Trends

You can place a micro-chart of data in a single cell in your worksheet. Excel refers to these micro-charts as *sparkline* charts.

You can create three types of sparkline charts: line, column, or win/loss. All three show you, at a glance, trend information for a range of data you select.

Excel places a sparkline chart in the cell immediately beside the cells you use to create the chart; if that cell contains data, Excel places the chart on top of the data, obscuring it but not deleting it. You can then move the sparkline chart to any cell you choose.

Using Sparklines to View Data Trends

Insert a Sparkline Chart

Note: *To avoid later moving a sparkline chart, make sure an empty cell appears beside the cells you intend to chart.*

1 Select the cells containing the data you want to include in the sparkline chart.

2 Click the **Quick Analysis** button (⬚) to display Quick Analysis categories.

3 Click **Sparklines**.

4 Click the type of sparkline chart you want to insert.

This example creates a column sparkline chart.

Ⓐ Excel inserts the sparkline chart in the cell immediately next to the selected cells.

Ⓑ The Sparkline Tools tab appears.

Ⓒ Any data in the cell containing the sparkline becomes obscured but remains in the worksheet, as you can see in the Formula bar.

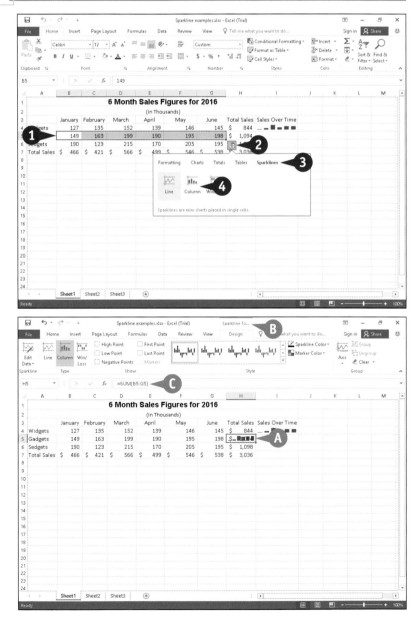

Move a Sparkline Chart

1 Click the cell containing a sparkline chart that you want to move.

2 Click the **Sparkline Tools Design** tab.

3 Click **Edit Data**.

The Edit Sparklines dialog box appears.

4 Select a new location in the worksheet for the sparkline chart(s).

Note: *The number of cells you select at the new location must match the number of sparklines you want to move.*

5 Click **OK**.

D Excel moves the sparkline chart(s).

E Any previously obscured data becomes visible.

Note: *To delete a sparkline chart, right-click it and point to **Sparklines**. Then, click **Clear Selected Sparklines** or **Clear Selected Sparkline Groups**.*

Can I create multiple sparkline charts simultaneously?
Yes. You can select data on multiple rows; Excel creates a sparkline chart for each row and treats the sparkline charts as a group; for example, if you change the chart type of one sparkline, Excel changes the group.

How can I change the type of sparkline chart?
Click the cell containing the sparkline to display the Sparkline Tools Design tab; in the Type group, click a different chart type.

PART IV

PowerPoint

PowerPoint is a presentation program that you can use to create slide shows to present ideas to clients, explain a concept or procedure to employees, or teach a class. In this part, you learn how to create PowerPoint presentation files, add slides to a presentation, rearrange slides within a presentation, and change the layout of a slide. You also can incorporate tables, charts, and even video clips on slides. In this part, you also learn to present slide shows in person and online, and how to package them on a CD-ROM.

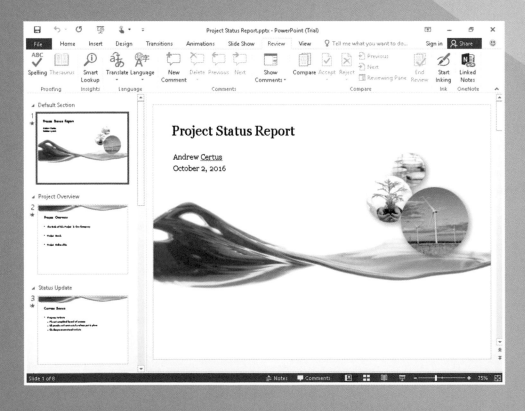

Create a New Presentation

When you first start PowerPoint, the PowerPoint Start screen appears. From it — or, if PowerPoint is open, from Backstage view — you can choose to create a new blank presentation. Or, you can use a presentation template or theme as the foundation of your presentation.

Templates contain themes that make up the design of the slide. *Themes* are groups of coordinated colors,

fonts, and effects such as shadows, reflections, and glows. See Chapter 14 for more information on themes. Templates can contain more than just themes, though. For example, they can contain prompts to help you set up the slides in the presentation for a particular subject.

Create a New Presentation

Create a Blank Presentation

1 Start PowerPoint.

The PowerPoint Start screen appears.

2 Click **Blank Presentation**.

A PowerPoint creates a new presentation with one blank slide.

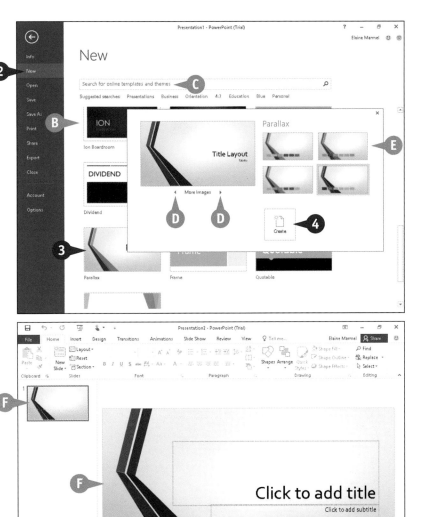

Using a Template

1 With the new presentation from the previous subsection open, click the **File** tab.

Backstage view appears.

2 Click **New**.

B Potential templates appear here.

C If you are signed into Office 365, you can type a search term and click 🔎 or press **Enter**.

Note: *See Chapter 4 for details about signing in to Office 365.*

3 Click a template to display a preview of the template design.

D You can click these arrows (◀ and ▶) to scroll through the slides available by default in the template.

E Many templates offer color variations; you can click to view the variations and select one.

4 Click **Create**.

F PowerPoint creates a new presentation with one blank slide.

What is the default aspect ratio for PowerPoint slides, and can I change it?
The default aspect ratio is 16:9, but you can change the default aspect ratio for your slides to 4:3 by following these steps. Apply the 4:3 aspect ratio to your slides (see the section "Change the Slide Size," later in this chapter). Click the **Design** tab, and click the **More** button (▼) in the Themes group. Click **Save Current Theme**. In the Save Current Theme dialog box, type the name of the theme, and then click **Save**. In the Themes Gallery on the Design tab, right-click the saved theme. Click **Set as Default Theme** from the menu that appears.

Create a Photo Album Presentation

You can quickly turn any collection of digital photos on your computer into a slide show presentation in PowerPoint. For example, you might compile your photos from a recent vacation into a presentation. Alternatively, you might gather your favorite photos of a friend or loved one in a presentation. To liven up the presentation, you can include captions with your photos. You can also vary the layout of slides, including having one (the default), two, three, or more photos per slide. You can then share the presentation with others, or email the file to family and friends.

Create a Photo Album Presentation

1. Click the **Insert** tab.

2. Click **Photo Album**.

   The Photo Album dialog box appears.

3. Click **File/Disk**.

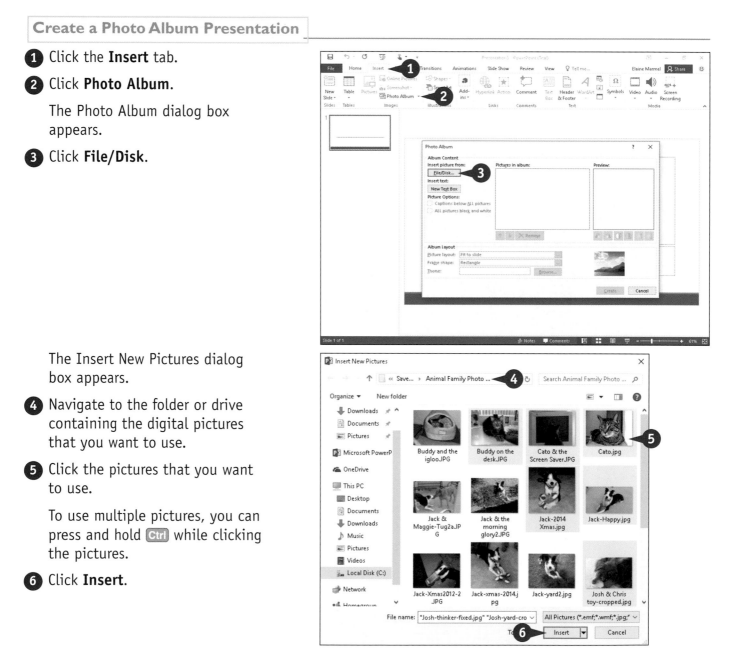

   The Insert New Pictures dialog box appears.

4. Navigate to the folder or drive containing the digital pictures that you want to use.

5. Click the pictures that you want to use.

   To use multiple pictures, you can press and hold **Ctrl** while clicking the pictures.

6. Click **Insert**.

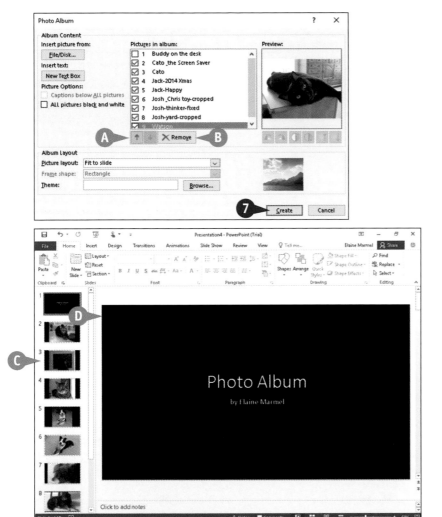

A You can change the picture order using these arrows (⬆ and ⬇).

B To remove a picture, you can select it in the Pictures in Album list (☐ changes to ☑) and then click **Remove**.

7 Click **Create**.

PowerPoint creates the slide show as a new presentation file.

C Each picture appears on its own slide.

D The first slide in the show is a title slide, containing the title "Photo Album" and your username.

simplify it

How do I fit multiple pictures onto a single slide and add captions?

Click the **Insert** tab, and then click ▼ beside **Photo Album** and choose **Edit Photo Album**. In the Edit Photo Album dialog box, click the **Picture layout** ⌄ and choose to display as many as four pictures on a slide, with or without title text (**A**). Select **Captions below All pictures** (☐ changes to ☑) (**B**). If this option is grayed out, choose a different Picture Layout option. Click **Update** (**C**). You can type your captions after closing the Photo Album dialog box.

Change PowerPoint Views

You can use views in PowerPoint to change how your presentation appears on-screen. By default, PowerPoint displays your presentation in Normal view, with thumbnails of each slide showing the order of slides in your presentation. You can click the **View** tab to see your presentation in an outline format, or switch to Slide Sorter view to see all the slides at the same time.

In addition to changing PowerPoint views, you can use the PowerPoint zoom settings to change the magnification of a slide. You can also change the size of the panes in the PowerPoint window, making them larger or smaller as needed.

Change PowerPoint Views

Using Normal View

1 Click the **View** tab.

2 Click **Normal**.

Ⓐ You can also use these buttons to switch views.

Ⓑ Thumbnails of slides appear here.

Ⓒ The currently selected slide appears here; its thumbnail displays an orange border.

Using Outline View

1 Click **View**.

2 Click **Outline View**.

Ⓓ PowerPoint displays the presentation in an outline format.

Ⓔ You can click the outline text to edit it.

Ⓕ You can click a slide icon to view the slide.

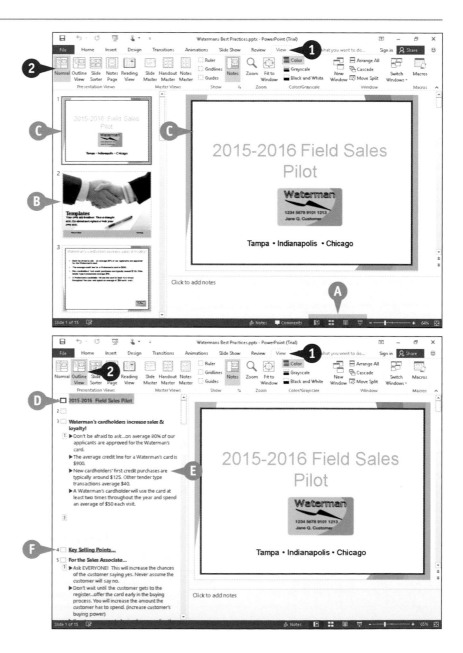

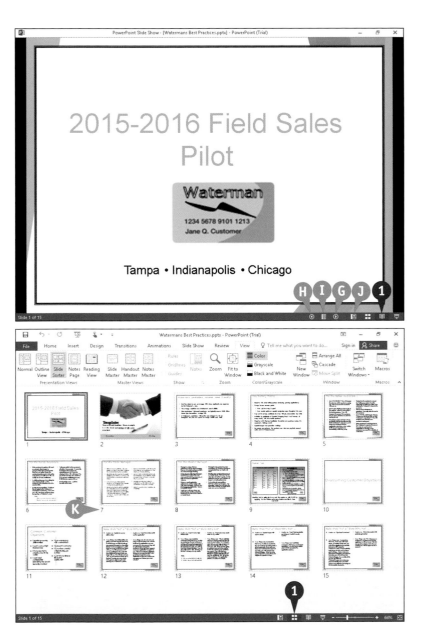

Using Read Mode View

1 Click 📖 to display the document in Read Mode view.

PowerPoint hides the Ribbon and fills the screen with the first slide in the presentation.

G To view the next slide, click the slide or click ▶.

H To view the previous slide, click ◀.

I To display a menu of available options while reading a presentation, click 📖.

J You can click 🖵 to redisplay the presentation in Normal view.

Using Slide Sorter View

1 Click ⊞ to display the document in Slide Sorter view.

PowerPoint displays thumbnails of all slides in the presentation.

K A number appears under each slide representing its position in the presentation.

You can double-click a slide to switch to Normal view and display the slide's content.

---

simplify it

How do I zoom my view of a slide?
You can drag the **Zoom** slider, which appears beside the view buttons on the status bar at the bottom of the PowerPoint window. Or, you can click the **View** tab, click the **Zoom** button, and choose the desired magnification in the Zoom dialog box that opens. Click the **Fit to Window** button on the View tab to return slides to the default size for the current view.

Can I resize the PowerPoint pane?
Yes. Position the mouse over the pane's border. When ⌖ changes to ⤡, ↕, ⤢, or ↔, click and drag inward or outward to resize the pane.

Insert Slides

PowerPoint makes it easy to add more slides to a presentation. To add a slide, you use the New Slide button on the Home tab. Clicking the top half of the New Slide button adds a slide with the same layout as the one you selected in the Slides pane; alternatively, you can click the bottom half of the button and select a different layout.

You can add and remove slides on the Slides tab in Normal view, or you can switch to Slide Sorter view and manage your presentation's slides.

Insert Slides

1 Click the thumbnail of the slide after which you want to insert a new slide.

2 Click the **Home** tab.

3 Click the bottom half of the **New Slide** button.

> **Note:** *Clicking the top half of the New Slide button adds a slide with the same layout as the one you selected in Step 1.*

A A gallery of slide layouts appears.

4 Click a slide layout.

B PowerPoint adds a new slide after the one you selected in Step **1**.

C The new slide uses the layout you selected in Step **4**.

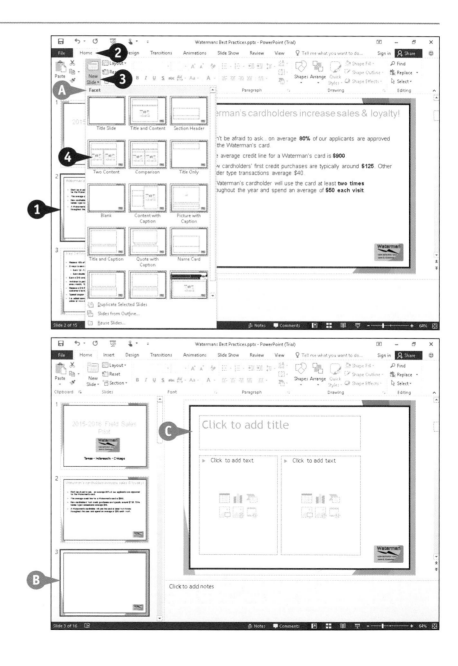

Change the
Slide Layout

PowerPoint includes several predesigned slide layouts that you can apply to your slide. For example, you might apply a layout that includes a title with two content sections or a picture with a caption. For best results, you should assign a new layout before adding content to your slides; otherwise, you may need to make a few adjustments to the content's position and size to fit the new layout.

Change the Slide Layout

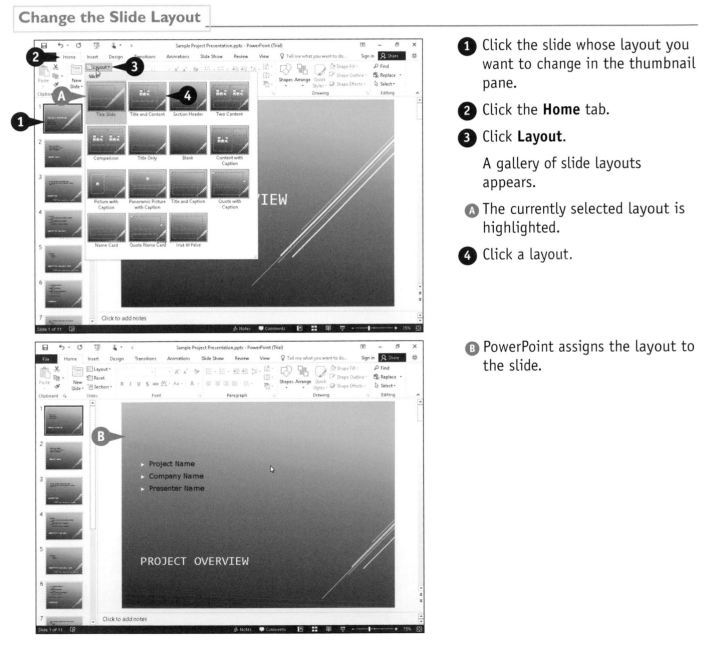

① Click the slide whose layout you want to change in the thumbnail pane.

② Click the **Home** tab.

③ Click **Layout**.

A gallery of slide layouts appears.

Ⓐ The currently selected layout is highlighted.

④ Click a layout.

Ⓑ PowerPoint assigns the layout to the slide.

Change the Slide Size

You can easily change the size of your presentation's slides. In versions of PowerPoint prior to 2013, slides used the 4:3 aspect ratio that was common on televisions. To accommodate widescreen and high-definition formats, PowerPoint 2016's default slide size uses an aspect ratio of 16:9.

If you change the size of a slide that contains content, PowerPoint attempts to automatically scale your content; if it cannot, PowerPoint offers to maximize or ensure the fit of content. If you maximize the content, it is larger but may not fit on the slide. If you apply the Ensure Fit option, your content is smaller but fits on the slide.

Change the Slide Size

1 Open the presentation containing the slides you want to resize.

2 Click the **Design** tab.

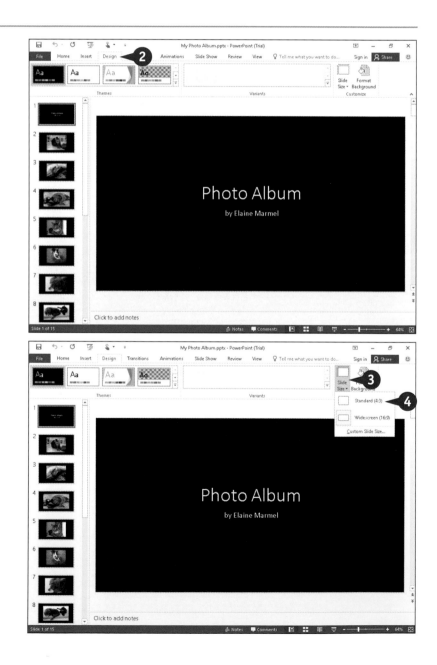

3 Click **Slide Size**.

4 From the drop-down list that appears, click **Standard (4:3)**.

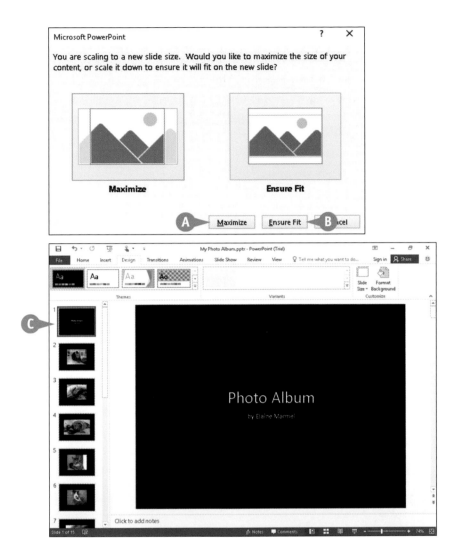

PowerPoint displays a message, asking how you want to handle content on the new slide size.

Ⓐ You can click **Maximize** to increase the size of the slide content when you scale to a larger slide size. Be aware that your content might not fit on the slide.

Ⓑ You can click **Ensure Fit** to decrease the size of your content when you scale to a smaller slide size. Although the slide content might appear smaller, you can see all content on your slide.

Ⓒ PowerPoint resizes all the slides in the presentation.

Note: *You might need to reapply a theme.*

simplify it

Can I establish a size for my slides other than 4:3 or 16:9?
Yes. Complete Steps **1** to **3** and, from the drop-down menu, click **Custom Slide Size**. In the dialog box that appears, use the **Slides sized for** ⌄ (Ⓐ) to select a slide size. You can also specify slide width, height, numbering, and orientation. Click **OK** to apply your changes.

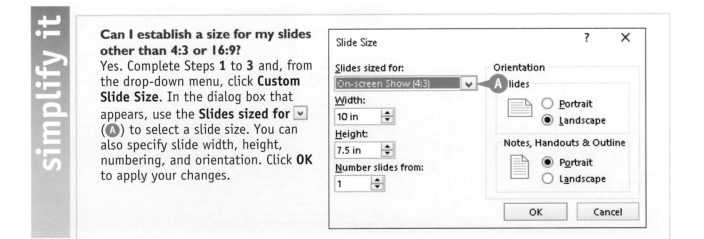

Add and Edit Slide Text

All slide layouts except for the blank slide layout are designed to automatically hold some text. To help you enter text, PowerPoint includes a text box that contains placeholder text, such as "Click to add title," "Click to add subtitle," or "Click to add text."

You can replace the placeholder text with your own text by typing directly in the slide.

After you add your text, you can change its font, size, color, and more, as shown in the next section.

Add and Edit Slide Text

Add Slide Text

1 Click the text box to which you want to add text.

PowerPoint hides the placeholder text and displays an insertion point.

2 Type the text that you want to add.

3 Click anywhere outside the text box to continue working.

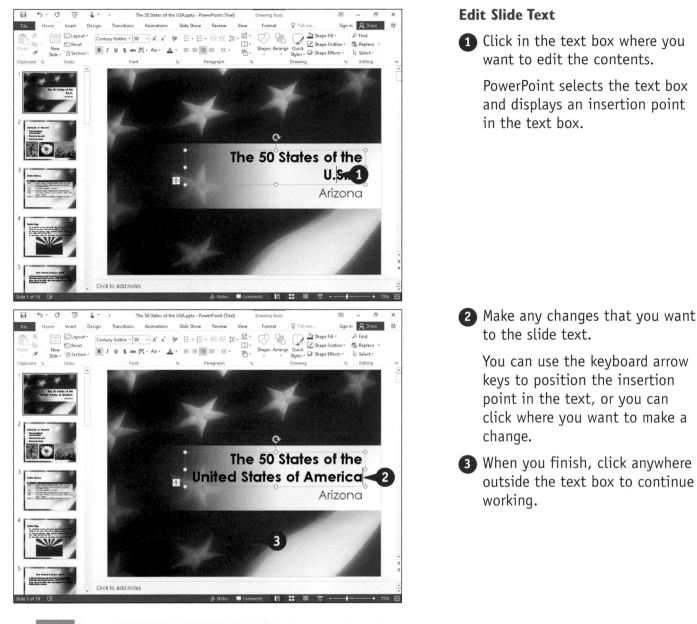

Edit Slide Text

1 Click in the text box where you want to edit the contents.

PowerPoint selects the text box and displays an insertion point in the text box.

2 Make any changes that you want to the slide text.

You can use the keyboard arrow keys to position the insertion point in the text, or you can click where you want to make a change.

3 When you finish, click anywhere outside the text box to continue working.

What should I do if my text does not fit in the text box, or fit the way I want?
You can resize the text, as described in the next section, or you can drag one of the handles of the text box to enlarge it, as shown here. When you position the mouse over a handle, � changes to ⬉, ↕, ⬈, or ↔. When you drag, the mouse changes to + (**A**).

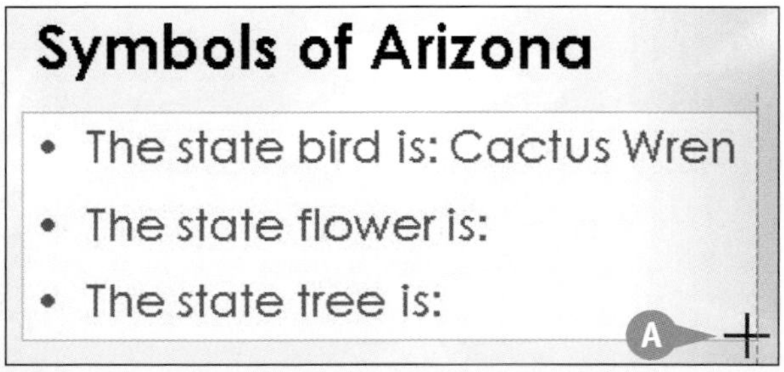

Symbols of Arizona

- The state bird is: Cactus Wren
- The state flower is:
- The state tree is:

Change the Font, Size, and Color

After you add text to a slide (as described in the previous section, "Add and Edit Slide Text"), you can change the text font, size, color, and style to alter its appearance. For example, you might choose to increase the size of a slide's title text to draw attention to it, or change the font of the body text

to match the font used in your company logo. Alternatively, you might change the text's color to make it stand out against the background color. You can also apply formatting to the text, such as bold, italics, underlining, shadow, or strikethrough.

Change the Font, Size, and Color

Change the Font

1. Click inside the text box and select the text that you want to edit.

2. Click the **Home** tab.

3. Click the **Font** ⯆.

4. Click a font.

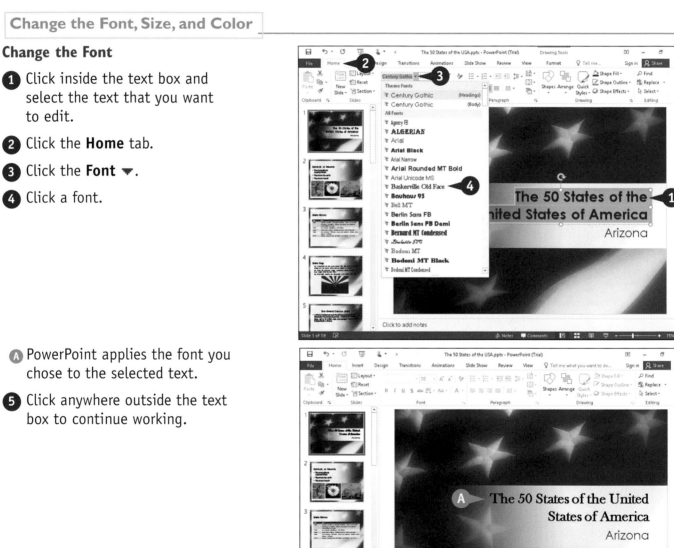

Ⓐ PowerPoint applies the font you chose to the selected text.

5. Click anywhere outside the text box to continue working.

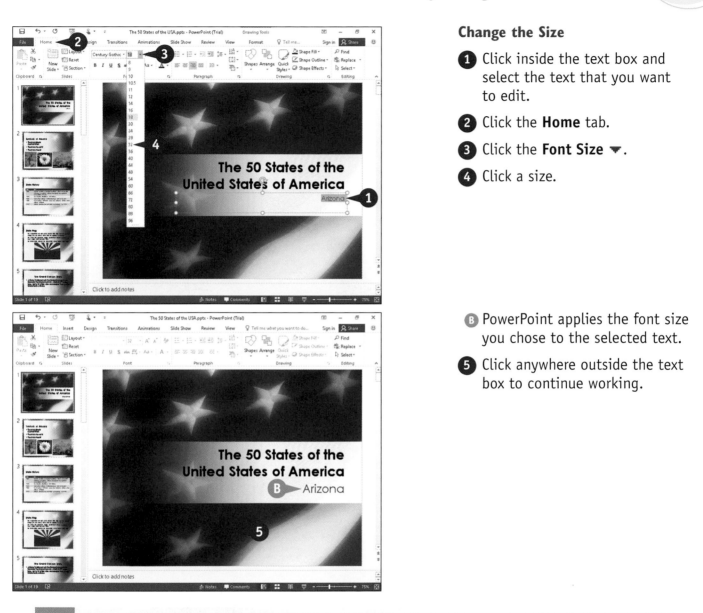

Change the Size

1. Click inside the text box and select the text that you want to edit.

2. Click the **Home** tab.

3. Click the **Font Size** ▼.

4. Click a size.

Ⓑ PowerPoint applies the font size you chose to the selected text.

5. Click anywhere outside the text box to continue working.

Is there a quicker way to change the text size?
Yes. To quickly increase or decrease the font size, you can select the text you want to change and then click the **Increase Font Size** (A˄) or **Decrease Font Size** (A˅) button in the Home tab's Font group as many times as needed until the text is the desired size.

How do I apply text formatting?
Select the text whose format you want to change, and then click the **Bold** button (**B**), the **Italic** button (*I*), the **Underline** button (U̲), the **Text Shadow** button (S), or the **Strikethrough** button (a̶b̶c̶).

continued

Change the Font, Size, and Color *(continued)*

In addition to changing the text's font and size, you can change its color. You might do so to make the text stand out better against the background, or to coordinate with colors used in other slide elements such as photographs.

You can change the text color in a few different ways. For example, you can select a color from the

Font Color button on the Home tab, or you can open the Colors dialog box and select a color from the palette that appears. In addition, you can apply your own custom color to text.

Change the Font, Size, and Color *(continued)*

Choose a Coordinating Color

1 Click in the text box and select the text that you want to edit.

2 Click the **Home** tab.

3 Click ▼ next to the **Font Color** button (**A** ▼).

Ⓐ PowerPoint displays coordinating theme colors designed to go with the current slide design.

4 Click a color.

Ⓑ PowerPoint applies the color you chose to the selected text.

5 Click anywhere outside the text box to continue working.

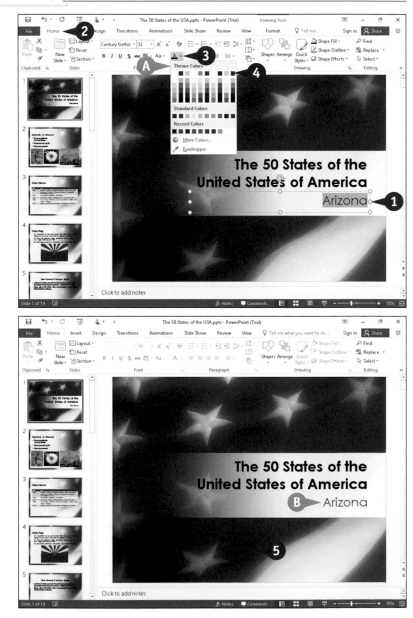

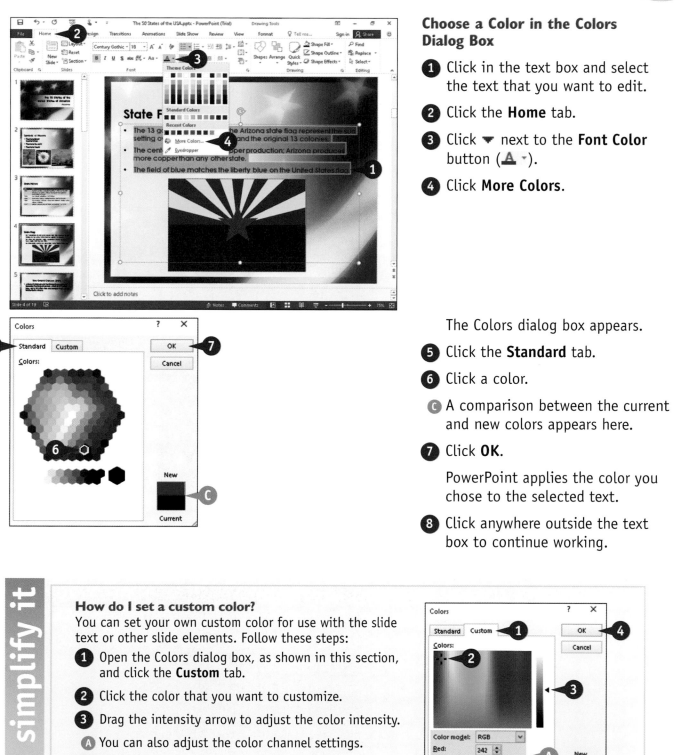

Choose a Color in the Colors Dialog Box

1. Click in the text box and select the text that you want to edit.

2. Click the **Home** tab.

3. Click ▼ next to the **Font Color** button (**A** ▼).

4. Click **More Colors**.

The Colors dialog box appears.

5. Click the **Standard** tab.

6. Click a color.

⊙ A comparison between the current and new colors appears here.

7. Click **OK**.

PowerPoint applies the color you chose to the selected text.

8. Click anywhere outside the text box to continue working.

simplify it

How do I set a custom color?

You can set your own custom color for use with the slide text or other slide elements. Follow these steps:

1. Open the Colors dialog box, as shown in this section, and click the **Custom** tab.

2. Click the color that you want to customize.

3. Drag the intensity arrow to adjust the color intensity.

Ⓐ You can also adjust the color channel settings.

4. Click **OK**.

Apply a Theme

PowerPoint includes a variety of preset designs, called themes. A *theme* is a predesigned set of colors, fonts, backgrounds, and other visual attributes. When you apply a theme to your presentation, you give every slide in your presentation the same look and feel. Alternatively, you can apply a theme to selected slides in your presentation. After you apply the theme, you can use controls in the Design tab to change various aspects of the theme.

Themes are shared among the Office programs; you can use the same theme in your PowerPoint presentations that you have applied to worksheets in Excel or documents in Word.

Apply a Theme

Note: *To apply a theme to selected slides, press and hold* Ctrl *as you click each slide thumbnail in Normal view. To apply a theme to all slides, simply select any slide.*

1 Click the **Design** tab.

Ⓐ In the Themes group, you can click ▲ and ▼ to scroll through the palette of themes.

Ⓑ Alternatively, you can click the **More** button (▼) to view all available themes.

2 Click a theme.

Ⓒ PowerPoint applies the theme. Any slides you add will use the same theme.

Ⓓ You can use these controls to select a color variant of the theme.

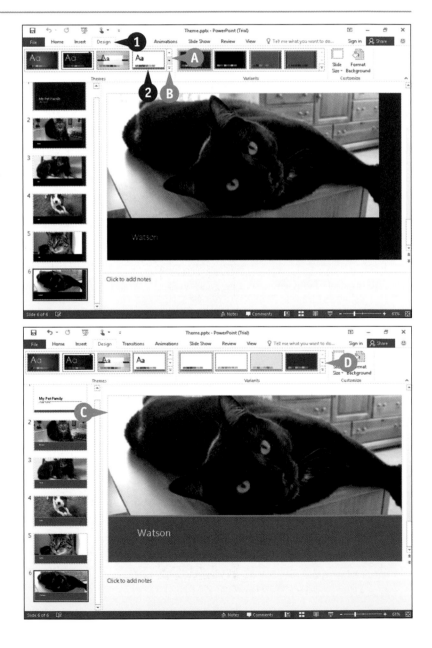

Set Line
Spacing

You can change the line spacing in a PowerPoint slide to create more or less space between lines of text. For example, you can increase line spacing from the 1.0 setting to a larger setting to make the text easier to read. If, after increasing the line spacing, your text does not fit in the text box, you can reduce the line spacing or increase the size of the text box, as described in the Simplify It tip in the section "Add and Edit Slide Text."

Set Line Spacing

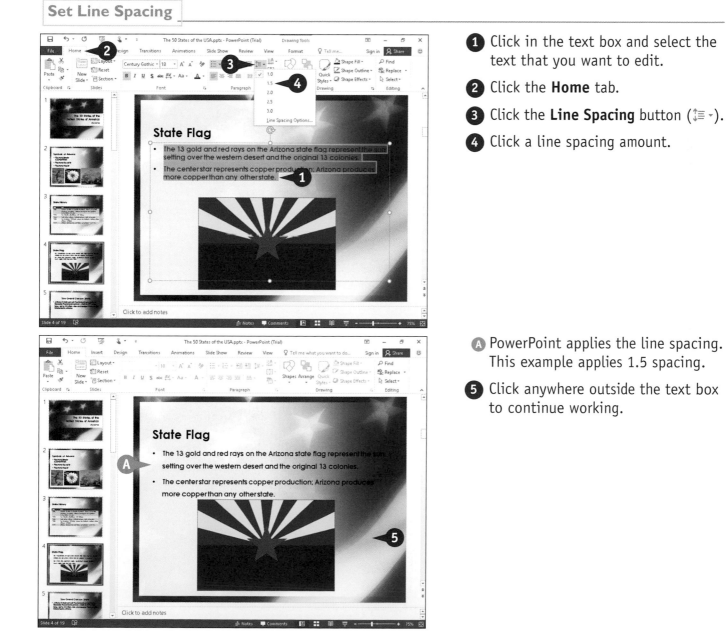

1 Click in the text box and select the text that you want to edit.

2 Click the **Home** tab.

3 Click the **Line Spacing** button (‡≡ ⋅).

4 Click a line spacing amount.

A PowerPoint applies the line spacing. This example applies 1.5 spacing.

5 Click anywhere outside the text box to continue working.

Align Text

By default, PowerPoint centers most text in text boxes (bulleted lists are left-aligned). If you want, you can use PowerPoint's alignment commands, located on the Home tab, to change how text is positioned horizontally in a text box. You can choose to center text in a text box (using the Center command), align text to the right side of the text box (using the Right Align command), or justify text and objects so they line up at both the left and right margins of the text box (using the Justify command).

Align Text

1 Click in the text box containing the text that you want to align.

2 Click the **Home** tab.

3 Click an alignment button:

Click the **Align Left** button (≡) to align the text to the left side of the text box.

Click the **Center** button (≡) to align the text in the center of the text box.

Click the **Align Right** button (≡) to align the text to the right side of the text box.

Click the **Justify** button (≡) to justify text between the left and right margins.

Ⓐ PowerPoint applies the formatting. In this example, the text is centered between the left and right margins of the text box.

4 Click anywhere outside the text box to continue working.

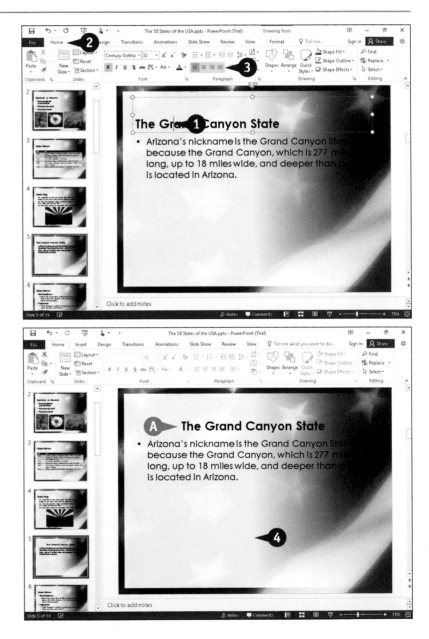

Add a Text Box to a Slide

Typically, you insert slides containing a predefined layout. You can customize the slide layout by adding a *text box*, a receptacle for text in a slide. To add text to a text box, see the section "Add and Edit Slide Text."

When you add a new text box to a slide, you can control the placement and size of the box. (To move and resize text boxes and other slide objects, see the sections "Move a Slide Object" and "Resize a Slide Object," later in this chapter.)

Add a Text Box to a Slide

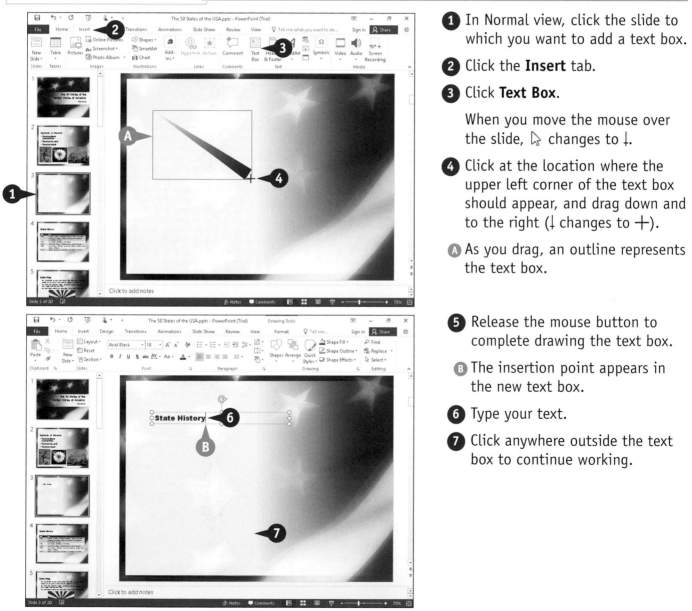

1 In Normal view, click the slide to which you want to add a text box.

2 Click the **Insert** tab.

3 Click **Text Box**.

When you move the mouse over the slide, ⩔ changes to ↧.

4 Click at the location where the upper left corner of the text box should appear, and drag down and to the right (↧ changes to ✛).

A As you drag, an outline represents the text box.

5 Release the mouse button to complete drawing the text box.

B The insertion point appears in the new text box.

6 Type your text.

7 Click anywhere outside the text box to continue working.

Add a Table to a Slide

You can customize the layout of a slide by adding a table to it. You can add tables to your slides to organize data in an orderly fashion. For example, you might use a table to display a list of products or classes. Tables use a column-and-row format to present information.

After you add the table to your slide, you can control the placement and size of the table. (For help moving and resizing tables and other slide objects, see the sections "Move a Slide Object" and "Resize a Slide Object," later in this chapter.)

Add a Table to a Slide

1 Click the slide to which you want to add a table.

Note: *If an Insert Table icon (▦) appears in your slide, click it and skip Steps 2 to 4.*

2 Click the **Insert** tab.

3 Click **Table**.

4 Click **Insert Table**.

The Insert Table dialog box appears.

5 Type the number of columns and rows that you want to appear in the table.

Note: *If you need more rows, just press Tab in the last table cell, and PowerPoint automatically adds a row.*

6 Click **OK**.

Ⓐ PowerPoint inserts the table into the slide.

Ⓑ PowerPoint displays the Table Tools tabs.

Ⓒ You can change the table's appearance by clicking a style in the Table Styles group.

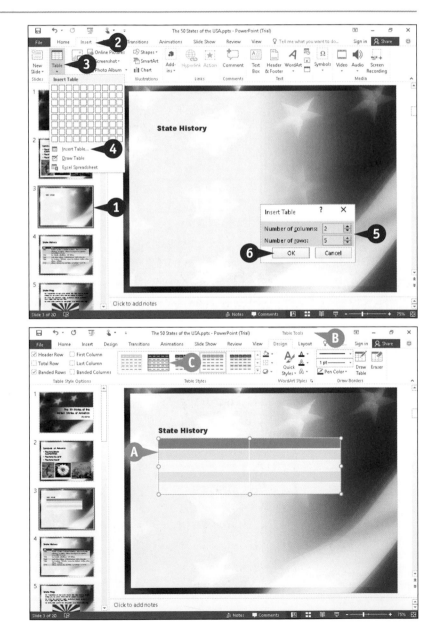

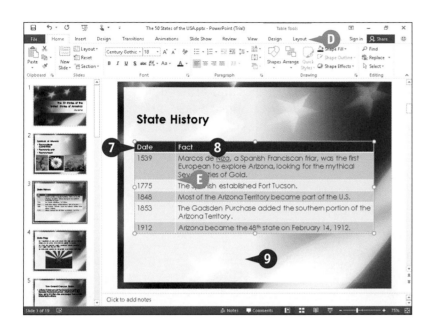

7 Click inside the first table cell and type your data.

You can press **Tab** to move to the next table cell.

8 Continue typing in each cell to fill the table.

D You can use the tools in the Layout tab to merge or split table cells, change alignment, add borders, and more.

E You can resize columns or rows by dragging their borders.

9 When you finish typing table data, click anywhere outside the table to continue working.

simplify it

How do I add a row or column to my table?

To add a row to the bottom of the table, click in the last table cell and press **Tab**. To insert a row in the middle of the table or add a column anywhere in the table, follow these steps:

1 Click in a cell adjacent to where you want to insert a new row or column.

2 Click the **Table Tools Layout** tab.

3 Click one of these buttons.

A PowerPoint inserts a new row or column.

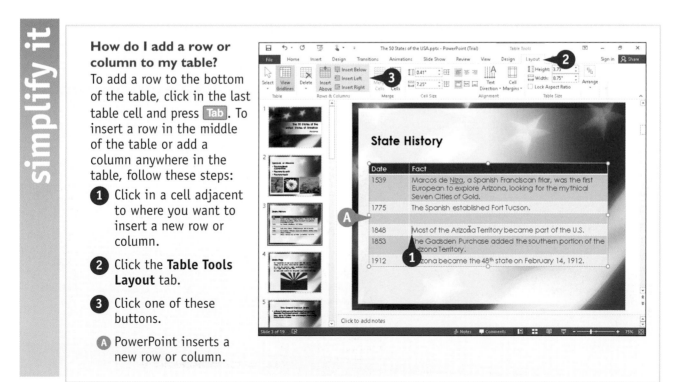

Add a Chart to a Slide

You can customize the layout of a slide by adding a chart to it. You might add a chart to a PowerPoint slide to turn numeric data into a visual element that your audience can quickly interpret and understand. When you add a chart, PowerPoint launches an Excel window, which you use to enter the chart data. After you add a chart to a slide, you can control the placement and size of the chart. (For help moving and resizing charts and other slide objects, see the sections "Move a Slide Object" and "Resize a Slide Object," later in this chapter.)

Add a Chart to a Slide

1. If an Insert Chart icon () appears in your slide, click it.

Ⓐ If an Insert Chart icon does not appear in your slide, click **Chart** on the Insert tab.

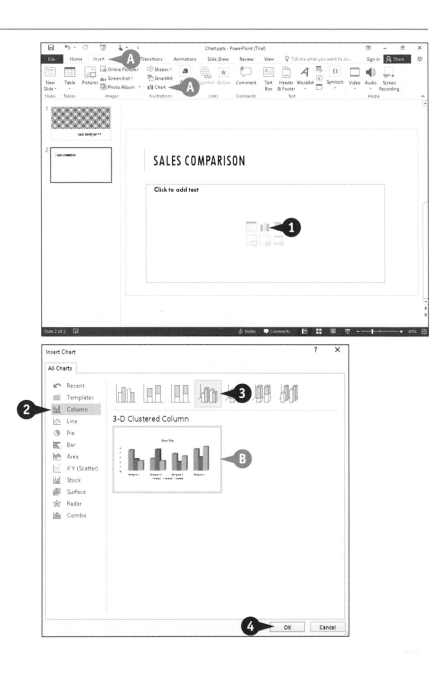

The Insert Chart dialog box appears.

2. Click a chart category.

3. Click a chart type.

Ⓑ A preview of the chart appears here.

4. Click **OK**.

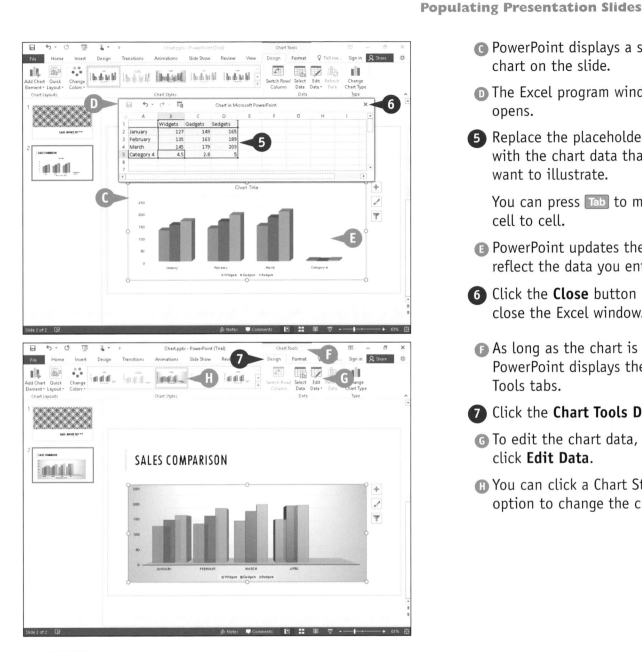

C PowerPoint displays a sample chart on the slide.

D The Excel program window opens.

5 Replace the placeholder data with the chart data that you want to illustrate.

You can press Tab to move from cell to cell.

E PowerPoint updates the chart to reflect the data you enter.

6 Click the **Close** button (✖) to close the Excel window.

F As long as the chart is selected, PowerPoint displays the Chart Tools tabs.

7 Click the **Chart Tools Design** tab.

G To edit the chart data, you can click **Edit Data**.

H You can click a Chart Styles option to change the chart style.

simplify it

Can I insert an existing Excel chart into my PowerPoint slide?
Yes. You can use the Copy and Paste commands to copy an Excel chart and insert it into a PowerPoint slide. To learn more about copying and pasting data between Office programs, see Chapter 2.

How do I make changes to my chart formatting?
When you click a chart in a PowerPoint slide, the Ribbon displays two Chart Tools tabs: **Design**, with options for changing the chart type, layout, data, elements, and style; and **Format**, with tools for changing fill colors and shape styles.

Add a Video Clip to a Slide

You can add video clips to your PowerPoint slides to play during a slide show presentation. For example, when creating a presentation showcasing the latest company product, you might place a video clip of the department head discussing the new item.

After you add a video to a slide, you can control the placement and size of the video. (For help moving

and resizing video clips and other slide objects, see the sections "Move a Slide Object" and "Resize a Slide Object," later in this chapter.) You can also perform certain edits to the video from within PowerPoint.

Add a Video Clip to a Slide

1 If an Insert Media Clip icon (⊞) appears in your slide, click it.

A If an Insert Media Clip icon does not appear in your slide, click **Video** on the Insert tab and choose **Online Video** or **Video on My PC**.

The Insert Video window appears.

Note: *You can browse for videos on your computer or on YouTube, or you can supply an embed code for a video stored on a website. If you sign in using a Microsoft account, you can browse your OneDrive, Facebook, and other sites. This example browses your computer.*

2 Click a location containing the video clip.

234

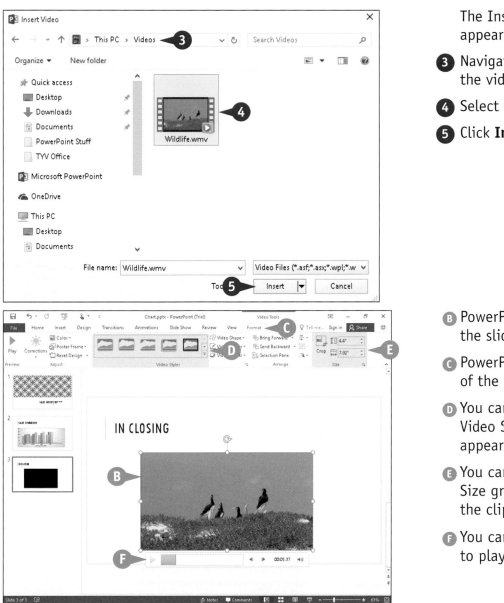

The Insert Video dialog box appears.

3 Navigate to the folder containing the video file.

4 Select the video.

5 Click **Insert**.

B PowerPoint inserts the clip into the slide.

C PowerPoint displays the Format tab of the Video Tools tabs.

D You can click an option in the Video Styles group to change the appearance of the video.

E You can use the options in the Size group to adjust the size of the clip on the slide.

F You can click the **Play** button (▶) to play the clip.

simplify it

What tools appear on the Playback tab?

You can use the settings in the Video Options group to specify options such as when the clip should start playing, whether it should be looped, and how loudly it should play. You can edit your video using the tools in the Editing group; using the **Fade In** and **Fade Out** boxes, you can set up the clip to fade in and fade out. You can also click the **Trim Video** button to open the Trim Video dialog box, where you can change the duration of the video by trimming frames from the beginning or end of the clip.

Move a Slide Object

You can move any element on a slide — a text box, table, chart, picture, video clip, or graphic — to reposition it. These slide elements are often referred to as objects. For example, you might move a text box to make room for a video clip or reposition a picture to improve the overall appearance of the slide.

You can move a slide object using the standard Office Cut and Paste buttons, discussed in Chapter 2. Or, you can drag and drop the object, as discussed in this section.

Move a Slide Object

1 Click the slide containing the object that you want to move.

2 Select the slide object by clicking it (⟍ changes to ⊹).

Note: *To select a table or a chart, click anywhere in the object; then, slide the mouse (⟍) along any of the object's edges. Click when you see the mouse (⊹).*

3 Drag the object to a new location on the slide. As you drag, ⊹ changes to ✛.

4 Release the mouse button.

Ⓐ PowerPoint repositions the object.

5 Click anywhere outside the slide object to continue working.

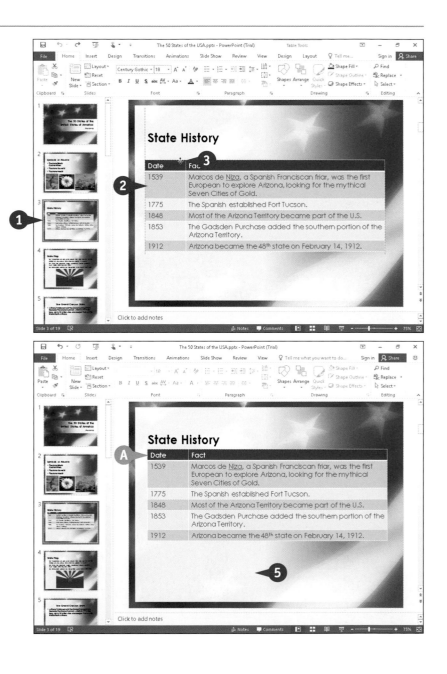

Resize a Slide Object

After you insert a slide object — a text box, table, chart, picture, video clip, or graphic — you may find that you need to make it larger or smaller to achieve the desired effect. For example, you might want to resize a text box to make room for more text or resize a picture object to enlarge the artwork. Fortunately, PowerPoint makes it easy to change the size of a slide object.

Resize a Slide Object

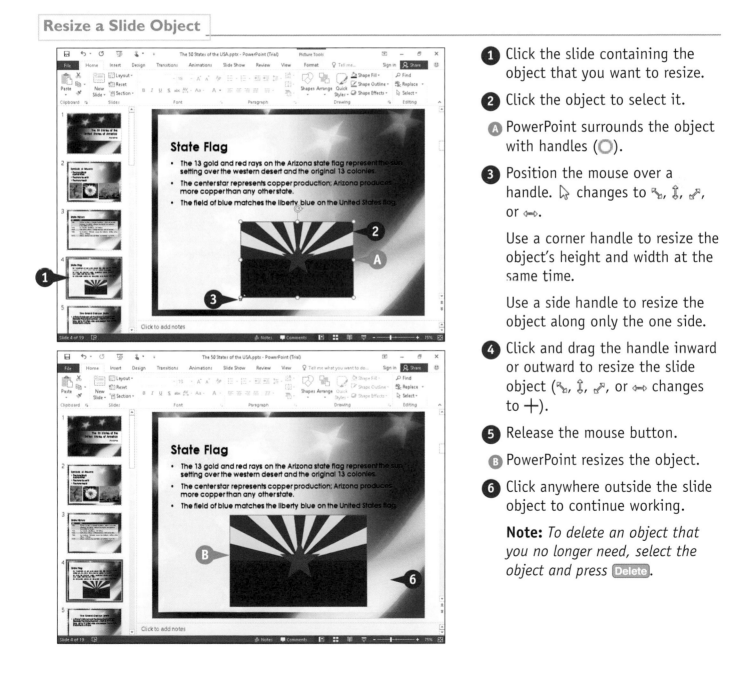

1 Click the slide containing the object that you want to resize.

2 Click the object to select it.

Ⓐ PowerPoint surrounds the object with handles (○).

3 Position the mouse over a handle. ▷ changes to ↖, ↕, ↗, or ↔.

Use a corner handle to resize the object's height and width at the same time.

Use a side handle to resize the object along only the one side.

4 Click and drag the handle inward or outward to resize the slide object (↖, ↕, ↗, or ↔ changes to ╋).

5 Release the mouse button.

Ⓑ PowerPoint resizes the object.

6 Click anywhere outside the slide object to continue working.

Note: *To delete an object that you no longer need, select the object and press* Delete.

Reorganize Slides

You can change the order of the slides in your presentation. For example, you might want to move a slide to appear later in the presentation, or swap the order of two adjacent slides. You can move individual slides, or move multiple slides simultaneously.

You can change the slide order in Slide Sorter view or in Normal view; choose the view based on the

distance from the original position to the new position. If you need to move a slide only a few positions, use Normal view. Slide Sorter view works best when you need to move a slide to a new position several slides away.

Reorganize Slides

Move Slides in Normal View

1 Click  to switch to Normal view.

2 Click to select the slide you want to move.

Note: *To move multiple slides, select them by pressing and holding* Ctrl *as you click each slide.*

3 Drag the slide to a new position.

Ⓐ As you drag, ⬇ changes to ⬇.

4 Release the mouse button.

Ⓑ PowerPoint moves the slide.

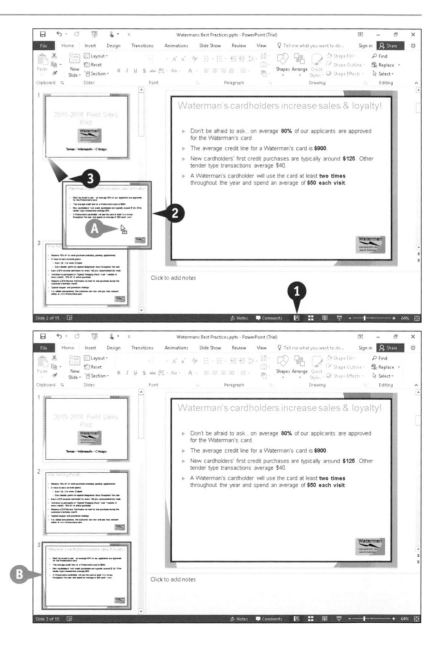

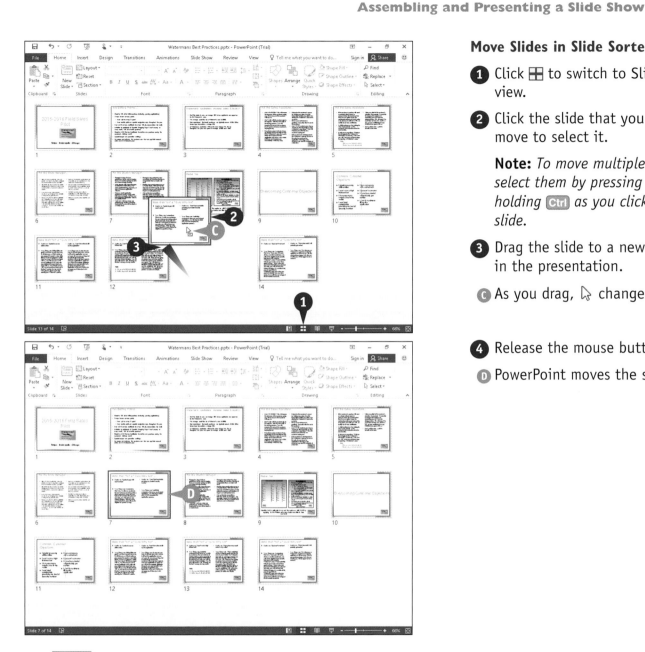

Move Slides in Slide Sorter View

1 Click ▦ to switch to Slide Sorter view.

2 Click the slide that you want to move to select it.

Note: *To move multiple slides, select them by pressing and holding* Ctrl *as you click each slide.*

3 Drag the slide to a new location in the presentation.

C As you drag, ⬚ changes to ⬚.

4 Release the mouse button.

D PowerPoint moves the slide.

---

simplify it

How do I hide a slide?
Suppose you frequently give the same presentation, but your next audience does not require the information in one of the presentation slides. In that case, you can hide the slide. Click the slide, click the **Slide Show** tab, and then click the **Hide Slide** button. PowerPoint crosses out the slide. To unhide the slide, repeat these steps.

How do I delete a slide?
To delete a slide, click the slide and then click the **Cut** button (✂) on the **Home** tab, or right-click the slide and choose **Delete Slide** from the menu that appears.

239

Reuse a Slide

Suppose you are creating a new PowerPoint presentation, but you want to reuse a slide from an existing one. Assuming the presentation containing the slide you want to reuse has been saved on your hard drive or is accessible to you via a network connection, you can easily do so. You can choose the slide you want to reuse in the Reuse Slides pane.

When you reuse a slide, PowerPoint updates the slide to match the formatting used in the new presentation. You can reuse a single slide from a presentation, multiple slides from a presentation, or all the slides in a presentation.

Reuse a Slide

1 Click the slide that you want to appear before the new slide.

2 Click the **Home** tab.

3 Click the bottom half of the **New Slide** button.

4 Click **Reuse Slides**.

Ⓐ The Reuse Slides pane opens.

5 Click **Browse**.

6 Click **Browse File**.

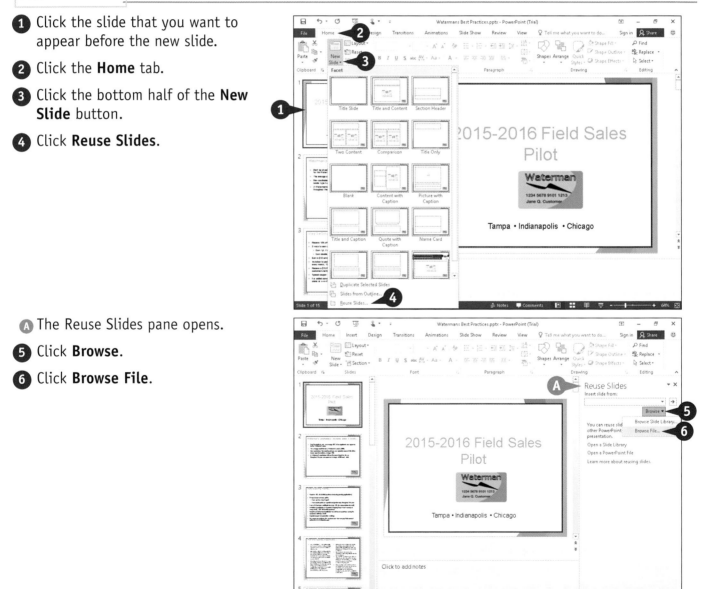

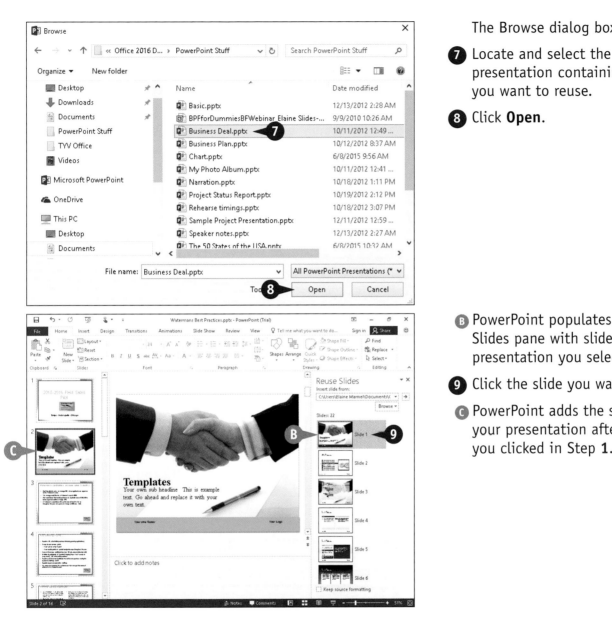

The Browse dialog box opens.

7 Locate and select the presentation containing the slide you want to reuse.

8 Click **Open**.

B PowerPoint populates the Reuse Slides pane with slides from the presentation you selected.

9 Click the slide you want to reuse.

C PowerPoint adds the slide to your presentation after the slide you clicked in Step **1**.

Can I retain the reused slide's original formatting?

Yes. To retain the reused slide's original formatting, select **Keep source formatting** (☐ changes to ☑) in the Reuse Slides pane. To change all the slides in the new presentation to match the reused slide, right-click the reused slide in the Reuse Slides pane and choose **Apply Theme to All Slides**.

How do I reuse all the slides in a presentation?

To reuse all the slides in a presentation, right-click any slide in the Reuse Slides pane and choose **Insert All Slides**. PowerPoint inserts all the slides from the existing presentation into the new presentation.

Define Slide Transitions

You can add transition effects, such as fades, dissolves, and wipes, to your slides to control how one slide segues to the next. You can control the speed with which the transition appears. You can also specify how PowerPoint advances the slides, either manually using a mouse click or automatically after a time you specify passes. In addition to adding visual transition effects between your slides, you can add sound effects to serve as transitions.

Use good judgment when assigning transitions. Using too many different types of transitions might distract your audience from your presentation.

Define Slide Transitions

1 Click ⊞ to switch to Slide Sorter view.

2 Click the slide to which you want to apply a transition.

3 Click the **Transitions** tab.

Ⓐ Available transition effects appear in the Transition to This Slide group. You can click ▲ or ▼ to scroll through them or click the **More** button (▼) to view the gallery of transition effects.

4 Click a transition.

Ⓑ PowerPoint demonstrates the animation as it applies it and adds an animation indicator below the slide's lower right corner.

Ⓒ You can click **Preview** to display a preview of the transition effect.

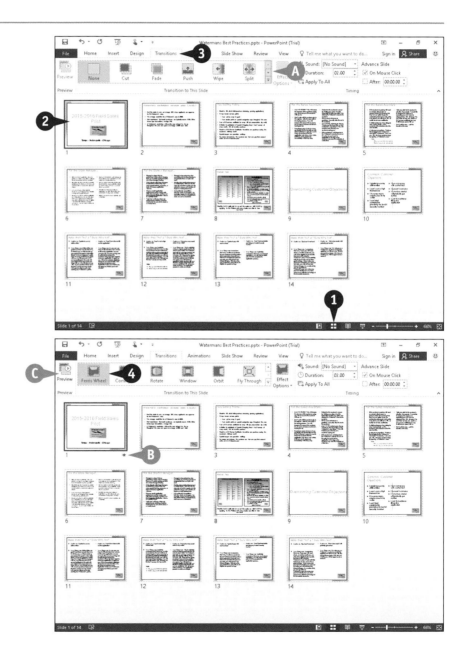

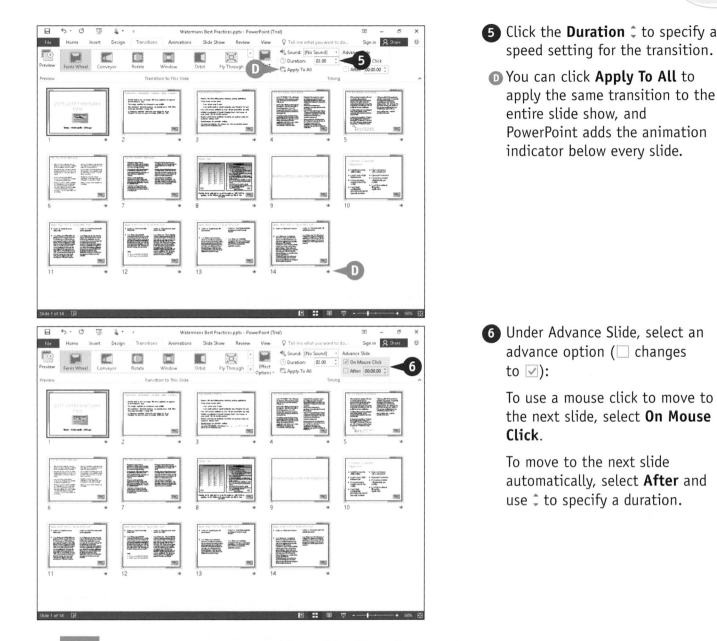

5 Click the **Duration** ↕ to specify a speed setting for the transition.

D You can click **Apply To All** to apply the same transition to the entire slide show, and PowerPoint adds the animation indicator below every slide.

6 Under Advance Slide, select an advance option (☐ changes to ☑):

To use a mouse click to move to the next slide, select **On Mouse Click**.

To move to the next slide automatically, select **After** and use ↕ to specify a duration.

How do I remove a transition effect?
To remove all transitions, press Ctrl+A in Slide Sorter view to select all slides; otherwise, select the slide containing the transition that you want to remove. Then click the **Transitions** tab and click the **None** option in the Transition to This Slide group.

How do I assign a sound as a transition effect?
To assign a transition sound, click the **Sound** ▼ in the Timing group on the Transitions tab and select a sound. For example, you might assign the Applause sound effect for the first or last slide in a presentation.

Add Animation Effects

You can use PowerPoint's animation effects to add visual interest to your presentation. For example, if you want your audience to notice a company logo on a slide, you might apply an animation effect to that logo.

You can use four different types of animation effects: entrance effects, emphasis effects, exit effects, and

motion paths. You can add any of these effects to any slide object. You can also change the direction of your animations. To avoid overwhelming your audience, limit animations to slides in which the effects will make the most impact.

Add Animation Effects

Add an Animation Effect

1 Click 🖫 to display the presentation in Normal view.

2 Click the slide containing the object to which you want to apply an effect.

3 Click the object.

You can assign an animation to any object on a slide, including text boxes, shapes, and pictures.

4 Click the **Animations** tab.

Ⓐ You can click ▲ and ▼ to scroll through the available animation effects or click the **More** button (▼) to view the gallery of animation effects.

5 Click an animation effect.

Ⓑ PowerPoint demonstrates the effect as it applies it and displays a numeric indicator for the effect.

Ⓒ You can click **Preview** to preview the effect.

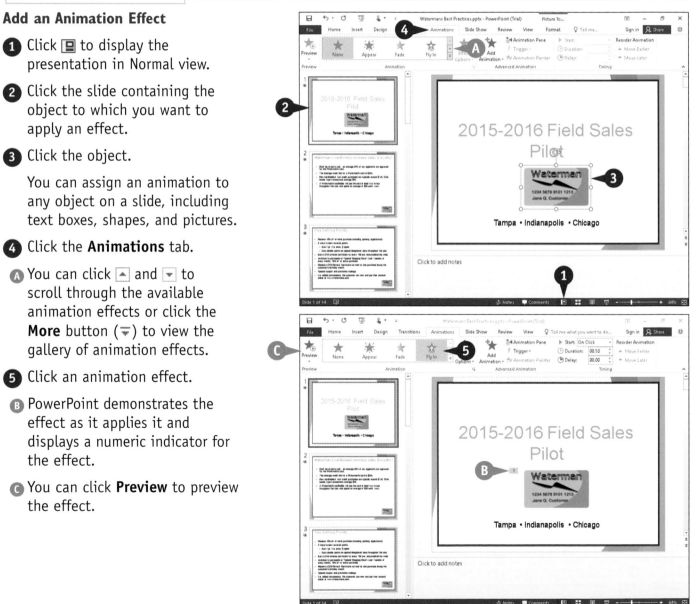

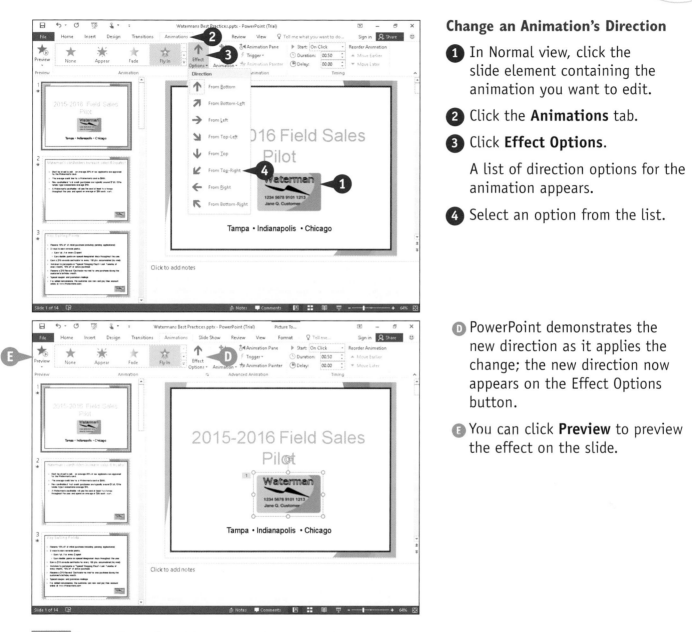

Change an Animation's Direction

1 In Normal view, click the slide element containing the animation you want to edit.

2 Click the **Animations** tab.

3 Click **Effect Options**.

A list of direction options for the animation appears.

4 Select an option from the list.

D PowerPoint demonstrates the new direction as it applies the change; the new direction now appears on the Effect Options button.

E You can click **Preview** to preview the effect on the slide.

Can I copy an animation effect to another slide object?
Yes. PowerPoint's Animation Painter feature enables you to copy an animation effect applied to one slide object to another slide object. To copy an animation effect, select the slide object whose effect you want to copy; then, in the Animations tab's Advanced Animation group, click the **Animation Painter** button. Next, click the slide containing the object to which you want to apply the effect; then click the object. PowerPoint copies the animation effect to the slide object.

Record Narration

Most presentations benefit from narration. You can speak as you present, or you can use PowerPoint's Record Narration feature to record a narration track to go along with the show. That way, you do not need to be present for your audience to receive the full impact of your presentation.

To record narration for a presentation, your computer must be equipped with a microphone. When you finish recording, an audio icon appears at the bottom of each slide for which you have recorded narration. When you save the presentation, PowerPoint saves the recorded narration along with the presentation file.

Record Narration

① Click the **Slide Show** tab.

② Click **Record Slide Show**.

The Record Slide Show dialog box appears.

Ⓐ Make sure that **Narrations, ink, and laser pointer** is selected (☑).

③ Click **Start Recording** to start the slide show.

④ Speak into the computer's microphone.

Ⓑ Click ➡ to move to the next slide in the show and continue recording.

Ⓒ Click ❚❚ to pause the recording. To continue recording, click **Resume Recording** in the window that appears.

Ⓓ Click ↩ to start over on the current slide.

When you finish, right-click the last slide and click **End Show**.

An audio indicator appears in the lower right corner on each slide for which you record narration. You can click the indicator to hear that slide's narration.

Note: *You do not need to record all narration at one time. If you end the show and later want to complete the narration, select the first slide that needs narration. Then, click the **Slide Show** tab, click the bottom of the **Record Slide Show** button, and click **From Current Slide**.*

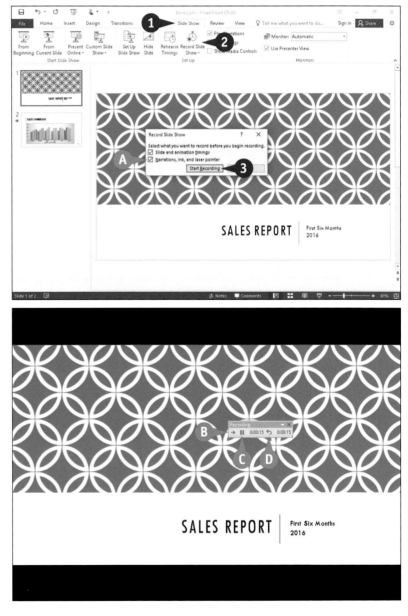

Insert a Background Song

You can insert a song that plays repeatedly in the background during your presentation. Playing a background song can be most effective in setting a mood for your presentation with no narration. PowerPoint can play AIFF Audio (.aif), AU Audio (.au), MIDI (.mid or .midi), MP3 (.mp3), Advanced Audio Coding - MPEG-4 (.m4a, .mp4), Windows Audio (.wav), and Windows Media Audio (.wma) files, among others.

You can download music from the Internet for your presentation, but you must first download it to your computer's hard drive.

Insert a Background Song

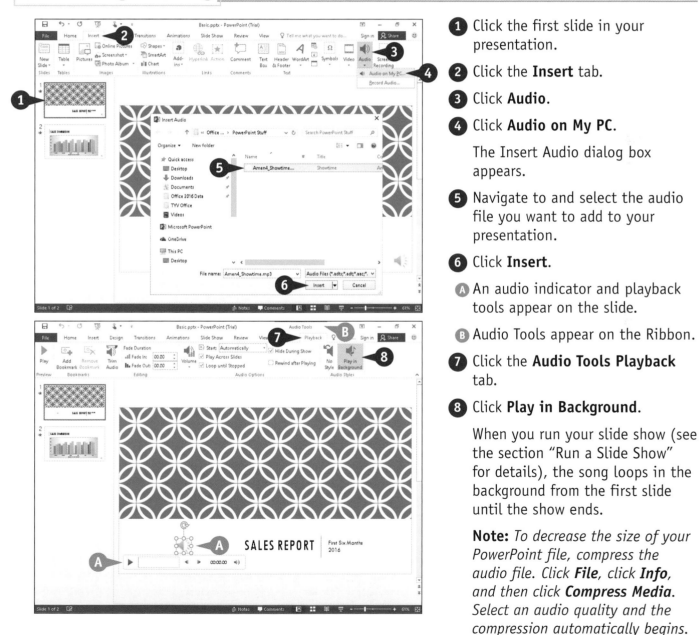

1 Click the first slide in your presentation.

2 Click the **Insert** tab.

3 Click **Audio**.

4 Click **Audio on My PC**.

The Insert Audio dialog box appears.

5 Navigate to and select the audio file you want to add to your presentation.

6 Click **Insert**.

Ⓐ An audio indicator and playback tools appear on the slide.

Ⓑ Audio Tools appear on the Ribbon.

7 Click the **Audio Tools Playback** tab.

8 Click **Play in Background**.

When you run your slide show (see the section "Run a Slide Show" for details), the song loops in the background from the first slide until the show ends.

Note: *To decrease the size of your PowerPoint file, compress the audio file. Click **File**, click **Info**, and then click **Compress Media**. Select an audio quality and the compression automatically begins.*

Create Speaker Notes

You can create speaker notes for your presentation. Speaker notes, also called notes pages, are notations that you add to a slide and that you can print out and use to help you give a presentation. You can also use speaker notes as handouts for your presentation. When creating notes pages, PowerPoint includes any note text that you add, as well as a small picture of the actual slide. You can add speaker notes in the Notes pane or on the Notes page.

You can print your speaker notes along with their associated slides. For details, see the Simplify It tip.

Create Speaker Notes

Using the Notes Pane

1. Click ▣ to switch to Normal view.

2. Click a slide to which you want to add notes.

3. Click here to display the Notes pane.

   Note: *The Notes pane button acts as a toggle; each click displays or hides the Notes pane.*

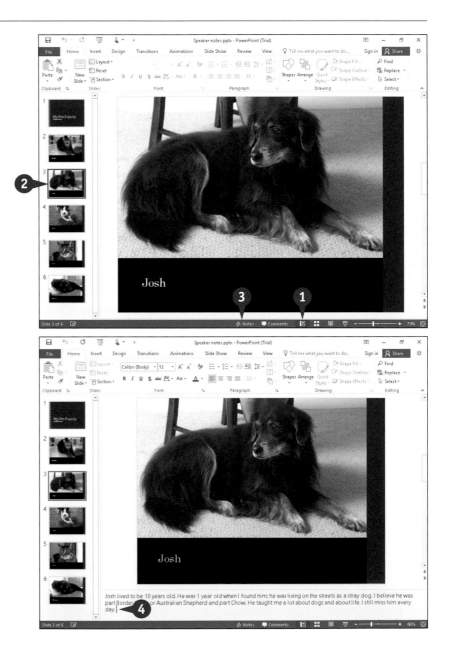

4. Click in the Notes pane and type any notes about the current slide that you want to include.

   Note: *You can enlarge the Notes pane. Position the mouse (⬚) over the line separating the Notes pane from the slide (⬚ changes to ⬍) and drag up.*

   You can repeat Steps **2** to **4** for other slides to which you want to add notes.

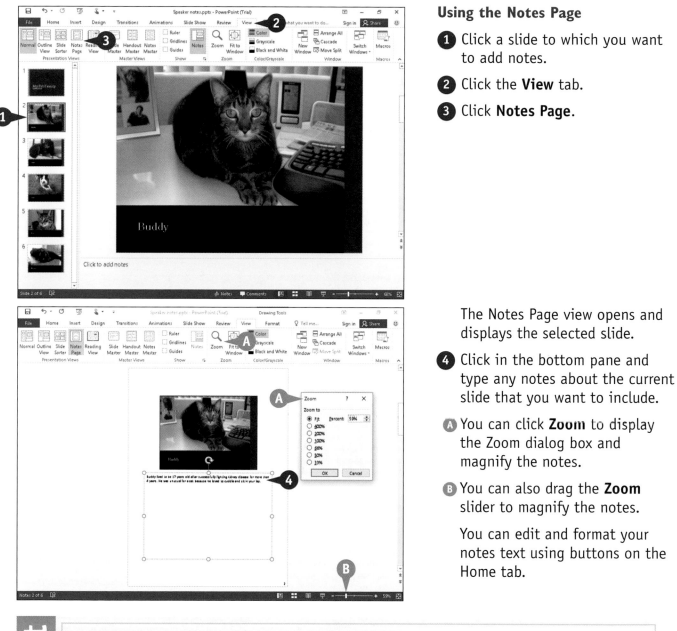

Using the Notes Page

1 Click a slide to which you want to add notes.

2 Click the **View** tab.

3 Click **Notes Page**.

The Notes Page view opens and displays the selected slide.

4 Click in the bottom pane and type any notes about the current slide that you want to include.

Ⓐ You can click **Zoom** to display the Zoom dialog box and magnify the notes.

Ⓑ You can also drag the **Zoom** slider to magnify the notes.

You can edit and format your notes text using buttons on the Home tab.

How do I print my notes with my slides?
Follow these steps: Click the **File** tab, and then click **Print.** Click to select your printer. In the Settings section, click ▼ for the second setting (Ⓐ) and click **Notes Pages** (Ⓑ). Click **Print.**

Print Layout

Full Page Slides

Notes Pages Ⓑ

Outline

Handouts

Full Page Slides
Print 1 slide per page Ⓐ

Rehearse a Slide Show

You can determine exactly how long PowerPoint displays each slide during a presentation using PowerPoint's Rehearse Timings feature. When you use Rehearse Timings, PowerPoint switches to Slide Show mode, displaying your slides in order; you control when PowerPoint advances to the next slide in the show.

When recording how long PowerPoint displays each slide, you should rehearse what you want to say during each slide as well as allow the audience time to read the entire content of each slide. After you record the timings, PowerPoint saves them for use when you present the slide show to your audience.

Rehearse a Slide Show

1 Click to switch to Slide Sorter view.

2 Click the **Slide Show** tab.

3 Click **Rehearse Timings**.

PowerPoint switches to Slide Show view and displays the first slide.

Ⓐ PowerPoint displays the Record Slide Show toolbar and starts a timer.

4 Rehearse what you want to say.

Ⓑ Click ❚❚ to pause the timer. To restart the timer, click **Resume Recording** in the window that appears.

Ⓒ To cancel the timer on a slide and start timing that slide again, click ↩.

5 When you finish timing the first slide, click ➡ to proceed to the next slide.

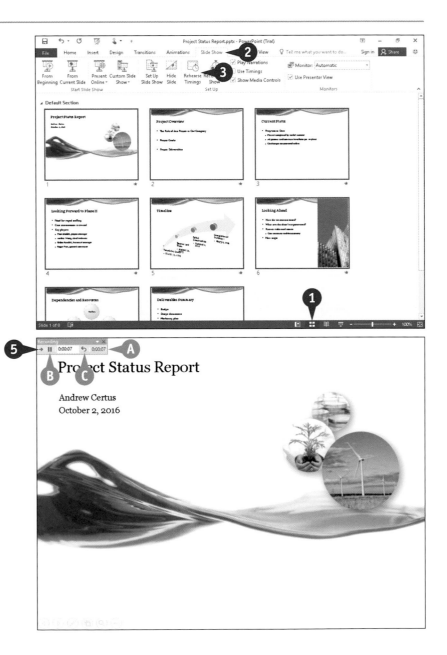

Microsoft PowerPoint ✕

ⓘ The total time for your slide show was 0:00:43. Do you want to save the new slide timings?

⑦ ─→ Yes   No

PowerPoint displays the next slide.

⑥ Repeat Steps **4** and **5** for each slide in your presentation.

When the slide show finishes, a dialog box appears and displays the total time for the slide show.

⑦ Click **Yes**.

Ⓓ PowerPoint saves the timings and displays them below each slide.

How do I create handouts for my audience?
Follow these steps:

① Click **File**.

② Click **Print**.

③ Select your printer.

④ In the Settings section, click ▼ for the second setting.

⑤ In the Handouts section, select a handout layout.

⑥ Click **Print**.

Print Layout

Full Page Slides   Notes Pages   Outline

Handouts

⑤ → 1 Slide   2 Slides   3 Slides

4 Slides Horizontal   6 Slides Horizontal   9 Slides Horizontal

4 Slides Vertical   6 Slides Vertical   9 Slides Vertical

Frame Slides

Scale to Fit Paper

High Quality

Print Comments and Ink Markup

Full Page Slides
Print 1 slide per page   ▼ ─④

Run a Slide Show

You can run a presentation using PowerPoint's Slide Show view, which displays full-screen images of your slides. Slides advance in order, but you can, if necessary, view thumbnails of all your slides so that you can display a particular slide out of order.

To enrich the experience for your audience, you can use PowerPoint's pointer options to draw directly on

the screen using the mouse (⌖). You can choose from several pen tools and colors, and you can present your slide show using a single monitor or two monitors.

Run a Slide Show

Run a Presentation

1 Click the **Slide Show** tab.

2 Click **From Beginning**.

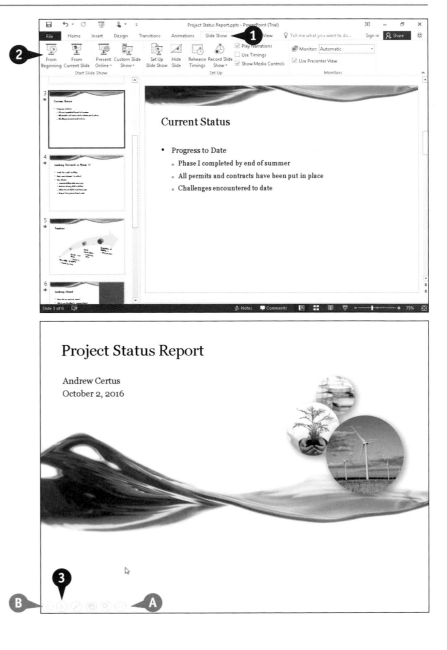

PowerPoint switches to Slide Show mode and displays the first slide.

Ⓐ When you move the mouse (⌖) to the bottom left corner, faint slide show control buttons appear.

3 Click anywhere in the slide to advance to the next slide or click the **Next** button.

Ⓑ To redisplay the previous slide, you can click the **Previous** button.

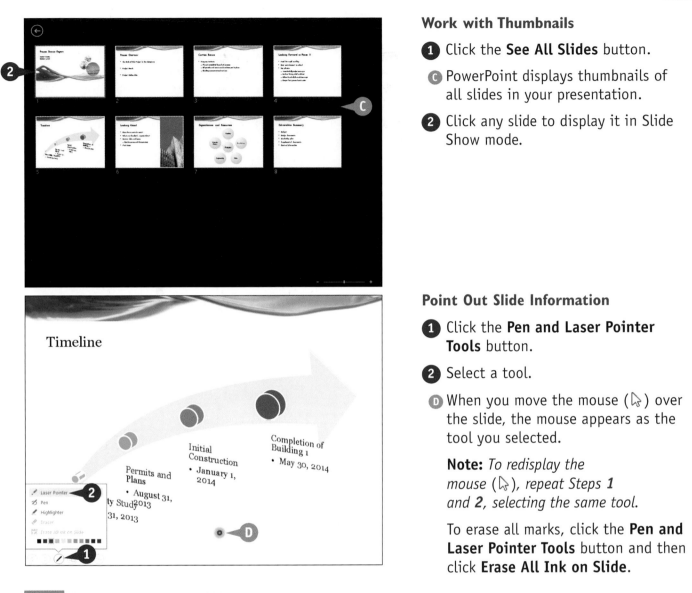

Work with Thumbnails

1 Click the **See All Slides** button.

C PowerPoint displays thumbnails of all slides in your presentation.

2 Click any slide to display it in Slide Show mode.

Point Out Slide Information

1 Click the **Pen and Laser Pointer Tools** button.

2 Select a tool.

D When you move the mouse (⬚) over the slide, the mouse appears as the tool you selected.

Note: *To redisplay the mouse (⬚), repeat Steps 1 and 2, selecting the same tool.*

To erase all marks, click the **Pen and Laser Pointer Tools** button and then click **Erase All Ink on Slide**.

---

simplify it

Can I change the color of the ink I use for pen and laser pointer tools?
Yes. Follow the steps in the subsection "Point Out Slide Information" once to select a pointing tool and once again to select the tool's color. The order in which you make these selections does not matter.

Can I hide a slide while I talk?
Yes. You can do this by changing the screen color to black or white. Click the **Menu** button and point the mouse (⬚) at **Screen**. Then click **Black Screen** or **White Screen**. Presenter view contains a shortcut **Black Screen** button (▨). To redisplay the slide, click anywhere on-screen.

continued

Run a Slide
Show *(continued)*

In addition to using pen and laser pointer tools, you can call the audience's attention to objects by zooming in on them. This approach can be particularly useful if you display a slide for a lengthy time; zooming in can recapture your audience's attention.

Many people like to work in PowerPoint's Presenter view, which displays your notes as you present, but your audience sees only your slides. If you present on two monitors, PowerPoint automatically uses Presenter view to display notes and slides on separate monitors. Using only one monitor, you can still set up your presentation to use Presenter view.

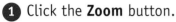

Run a Slide Show *(continued)*

Zoom an Object

1 Click the **Zoom** button.

Ⓐ PowerPoint grays the slide background and displays a lighted square that you can use to focus on an object.

2 Slide 🔍 over the object you want to enlarge and click.

Ⓑ PowerPoint zooms in on the object.

To redisplay the original size of the slide, press ⎋.

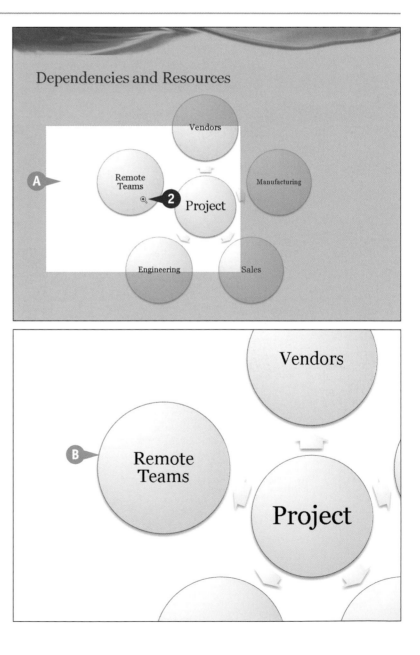

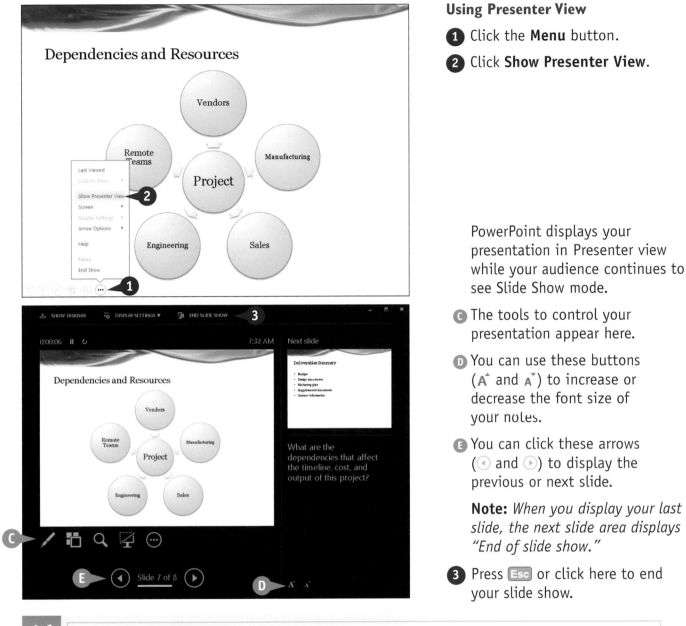

Using Presenter View

1 Click the **Menu** button.

2 Click **Show Presenter View**.

PowerPoint displays your presentation in Presenter view while your audience continues to see Slide Show mode.

C The tools to control your presentation appear here.

D You can use these buttons ($A^\wedge$ and $A^\vee$) to increase or decrease the font size of your notes.

E You can click these arrows ($\odot$ and $\odot$) to display the previous or next slide.

Note: *When you display your last slide, the next slide area displays "End of slide show."*

3 Press Esc or click here to end your slide show.

simplify it

Can I display the Windows taskbar so that I can switch to another program if necessary?
Yes. When working with a single monitor, click the **Menu** button (**A**), click **Screen**, and then click **Show Taskbar** (**B**). From Presenter view, you can click **Show Taskbar** at the top of the screen.

Review a Presentation

You can use comments to review a presentation and provide feedback. Comments appear in a pane along the right side of the PowerPoint window. Small balloons appear on the slide to indicate that a comment exists, and you can click a balloon to view that comment.

PowerPoint displays comment information in the Comments pane along the right side of the

PowerPoint window. In the Comments pane, you can click the **New** button to add another comment to the same slide, and you can view the next and previous comments using the Next and Previous buttons.

Review a Presentation

Insert a Comment

1 Click 📖 to display the presentation in Normal view.

2 Click the slide on which you want to comment.

Note: *To add a general comment about the slide, skip Step 3.*

3 Click the text or object on which you want to comment.

4 Click the **Review** tab.

5 Click **New Comment**.

Ⓐ The Comments pane appears, containing a new comment block.

Ⓑ A comment balloon appears on the slide.

6 Type your comment here.

7 When you finish typing your comment, click outside the comment block or press **Tab**.

Ⓒ You can add another comment to the same slide by clicking **New**.

Ⓓ You can click ✕ to close the Comments pane.

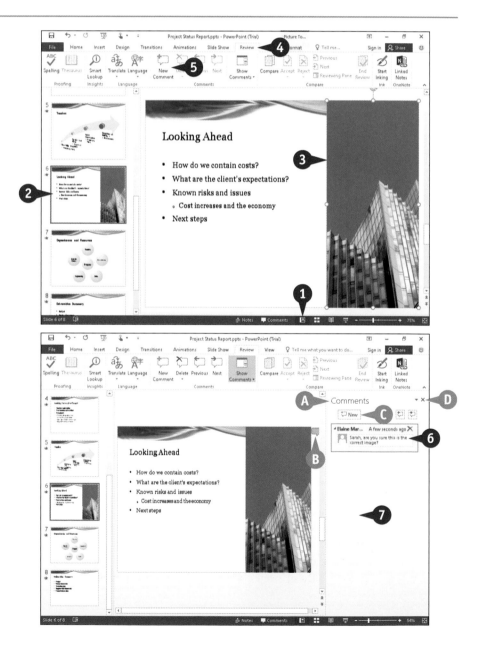

POWERPOINT

CHAPTER

Assembling and Presenting a Slide Show

Reply to a Comment

1 Click the **Review** tab.

2 Click **Show Comments**.

The Comments pane appears.

3 Click in the **Reply** box of the comment you want to answer.

4 Type your reply.

5 Press **Tab** or click outside the Reply box.

Ⓔ PowerPoint stores the reply and adds another Reply box.

Ⓕ PowerPoint adds another comment balloon almost on top of the original comment balloon.

Ⓖ To read the previous or next comment, click 🗩 or 🗩.

simplify it

How can I edit or delete a comment?
To edit a comment, click the text of the comment that you want to edit to open a text box containing the comment. Make your changes and then click outside the comment box. To delete a comment, right-click it on the slide and then click **Delete Comment**. You can also delete it from the Comments pane. Slide the mouse (↳) over the comment or reply until ✕ appears (Ⓐ). Then, click ✕. Deleting a comment also deletes its replies.

257

Package Your Presentation on a CD

To share your PowerPoint presentation with others, you can save it to a CD. With the Package for CD feature, PowerPoint bundles the presentation along with all the necessary clip art, multimedia elements, and other items needed to run your show, including any linked files contained in your presentation. The CD even includes a PowerPoint Viewer with the file in case the recipient does not have PowerPoint installed on his or her computer.

If you prefer, you can save your presentation as a WMV movie file that includes any narration and timings you record.

Package Your Presentation on a CD

1. Click the **File** tab.

2. Click **Export**.

3. Click **Package Presentation for CD**.

4. Click **Package for CD**.

The Package for CD dialog box appears.

5. Type a name no longer than 16 characters for the CD.

6. Click **Options**.

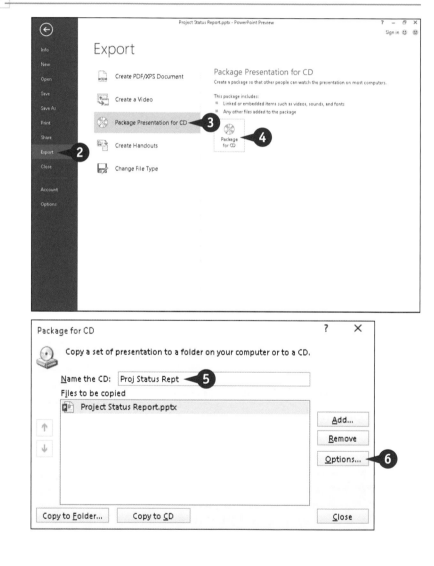

Options

Include these files

(These files will not display in the Files to be copied list)

☑ Linked files
☑ Embedded TrueType fonts ◀ A

Enhance security and privacy

Password to open each presentation: _____

Password to modify each presentation: _____ ◀ B

☐ Inspect presentation for inappropriate or private information

7 ▶ OK   Cancel

Package for CD

Copy a set of presentation to a folder on your computer or to a CD.

Name the CD: | Proj Status Rept

Files to be copied

▣ Project Status Report.pptx

Add...
Remove
Options...

Copy to Folder...   Copy to CD **8**   Close **10**

A You can use these options to determine the files that will be included with the packaged presentation.

B You can use these options to password-protect the presentation and to inspect the presentation for private information.

7 Click **OK**.

The Package for CD dialog box reappears.

8 Click **Copy to CD**.

Note: *PowerPoint prompts you to insert a blank CD; do so and click **Retry**.*

PowerPoint copies the presentation files. The size of the presentation determines how long copying takes.

When PowerPoint finishes copying the presentation, a dialog box appears, indicating that the files were copied successfully and asking if you want to create another CD.

9 Click **No**.

10 Click **Close** to close the Package for CD dialog box.

---

simplify it

How do I save my presentation as a video?

To save your presentation as a video, follow these steps: Click the **File** tab and then click **Export**. Click **Create a Video**. Click ▼ and choose a quality level (**A**). Click ▼ and specify whether PowerPoint should use recorded narration and timings (**B**). Click **Create Video** (**C**). In the Save As dialog box, specify the filename, file type, and folder in which PowerPoint should save the video. Click the **Save** button. PowerPoint saves the presentation as a video in the folder you specified.

Create a Video

Save your presentation as a video that you can burn to a disc, upload to the web, or email

▪ Incorporates all recorded timings, narrations, and laser pointer gestures
▪ Preserves animations, transitions, and media

? Get help burning your slide show video to DVD or uploading it to the web

Presentation Quality
Largest file size and highest quality (1440 x 1080)   ◀ A

Use Recorded Timings and Narrations
Slides without timings will use the default duration (set below). This option in...   ◀ B

Seconds spent on each slide: 05.00 ⬍

Create Video   ◀ C

Present Online

You can deliver your PowerPoint presentation online at no cost to you by taking advantage of the free Office Presentation Service that Microsoft offers.

When you present online, members of your audience view your presentation in their web browsers. They use a link that you provide to connect to your presentation. They do not need to set up anything; they need only their browser and the link you provide either via email or at a location where members of your audience can click it. You make a presentation online the same way you present a slide show; see the section "Run a Slide Show" for details.

Present Online

1 Open only the presentation you want to share.

2 Click the **Slide Show** tab.

3 Click the ▼ on the **Present Online** button.

4 Click **Office Presentation Service**.

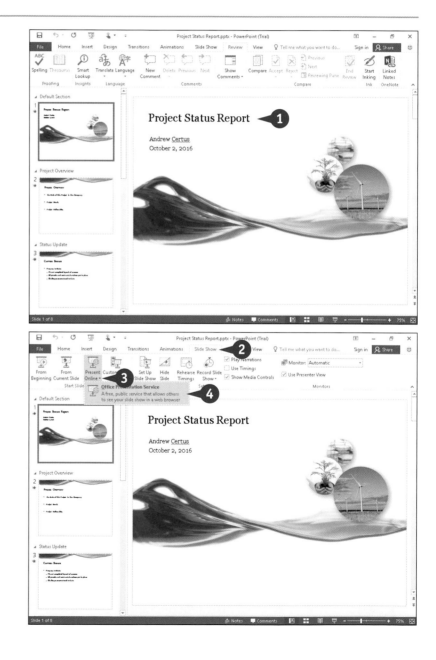

Present Online

Office Presentation Service

The Office Presentation Service is a free, public service that comes with Microsoft Office. You can use this service to present to people who can watch in a web browser and download the content. You will need a Microsoft account to start the online presentation.

More Information

☐ Enable remote viewers to download the presentation

By clicking Connect, you agree to the following terms:

Service Agreement

⑤ CONNECT   CANCEL

The Present Online dialog box appears, explaining how the Office Presentation Service works.

⑤ Click **Connect**.

Present Online

Connecting to Office Presentation Service

Preparing presentation...

CANCEL

The Present Online dialog box indicates that PowerPoint is connecting to the Office Presentation Service and eventually connects.

What happens after I connect to the presentation service?
Click an invitation option. You can click **Copy Link** to paste a link to your presentation where others can access it. Or, you can click **Send in Email** to send the link via email to presentation recipients. A Present Online tab appears in your presentation; on it, click **Start Presentation**. PowerPoint switches to Slide Show mode. When your presentation concludes, press Esc to return to Normal view in PowerPoint. Then, click the **Present Online** tab and click **End Online Presentation**.

PART V

Access

Access is a robust database program that you can use to store and manage large quantities of data related to anything from a home inventory to a giant warehouse of products. Although you might be tempted to use Excel, Access gives you far more control over the use and management of your data. Access organizes your information into tables, speeds up data entry with forms, and performs powerful analysis using filters and queries. In this part, you learn how to build and maintain a database file, add tables, create forms, and analyze your data using filters, sorting, and queries.

Understanding Database Basics

Access is a popular database program that you can use to catalog and manage large amounts of data. You can use Access to manage anything from a simple table of data to large, multifaceted lists of information. For example, you might use Access to maintain a list of your clients or a catalog of products you sell.

If you are new to Access, you should take a moment and familiarize yourself with the basic terms associated with the program, such as *database*, *table*, *record*, *field*, *form*, *report*, and *query*. This section contains definitions of all these key terms.

Databases

Simply defined, a *database* is a collection of related information. You may not be aware, but you use databases every day. Common databases include telephone directories or television program schedules. Your own database examples might include a list of contacts that contains addresses and phone numbers. Other examples of real-world databases include product inventories, client invoices, and employee payroll lists.

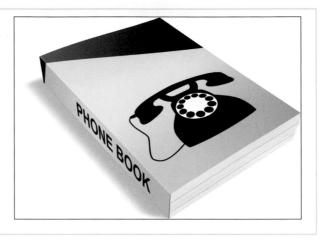

Tables

ID	First Name	Last Name	State
1	Karen	Arnold	VA
2	Thomas	Barnhart	VA
3	Paul	Bonner	VA
4	Camilla	Cox	MD

The heart of any Access database is a table. A table is a list of information organized into columns and rows. In the example of a client contact database, the table might list the names, addresses, phone numbers, company names, titles, and email addresses of your clients. You can have numerous tables in your Access database. For example, you might have one table listing client information and another table listing your company's products.

Records and Fields

Every entry that you make in an Access table is called a *record*. Records always appear as rows in a database table. Every record consists of *fields*,

First Name	Last Name	Company	Address	State
Donald	Wulf	Perform Tech	99 New York Avenue	VA

which are the separate pieces of information that make up each record. Each field of a record appears in a separate column. For example, in a client contact list, each record (row) might include fields (columns) for first name, last name, company name, title, address, city, ZIP code, phone number, and email address. Field names appear at the top of each column.

Forms

You can enter your database records directly into an Access table or you can simplify the process by using a *form*. Access forms present your table fields in an easy-to-read, fill-in-the-blank format. Forms enable you to enter records one at a time. Forms are a great way to ensure consistent data entry, particularly if other users are adding information to your database list.

General	
First Name	Karen
Last Name	Arnold
Company	UNITECH Consulting ▽
Job Title	▽

CONTACTS

Karen Arnold	**Dynatech Consulting**
Centreville, VA 20101	**1870 Taskey Parkway**
Phone	
(703) 655-1212	

Thomas Barnhart	**Management Partners Inc.**
Alexandria, VA 22311	**8522 Montegue St.**
Phone	
(703) 671-6600	

Reports and Queries

You can use the report feature to summarize data in your tables and generate printouts of pertinent information, such as your top ten salespeople and your top-selling products. You can use queries to sort and filter your data. For example, you can choose to view only a few of your table fields and filter them to match certain criteria.

Plan a Database

The first step to building an Access database is deciding what sort of data you want it to contain. What sorts of actions do you want to perform on your data? How do you want to organize it? How many tables of data do you need? What types of fields do you need for your records? What sort of reports and queries do you hope to create? Consider sketching out on paper how you want to group the information into tables and how the tables will relate to each other. Planning your database in advance can save you time when you build the database file.

Tables I need:
   Contacts
Fields I need in the Contacts table:
   Name
   State
   Phone
Reports I need:
   Report that lists all fields
   Report that lists just name and phone
Forms I need:
   Contact list that shows all information for all entries
   Contact details that lists all information for one entry

Create a Database Based on a Template

You can build web apps — a kind of database designed with Access and published online — or desktop databases based on any of the predefined Access templates. For example, you can create databases to track contact lists, assets, and task management. You can also search Office.com to find new, featured templates. This book focuses on building desktop databases.

When you create a new database using a template, the database includes prebuilt tables and forms, which you populate with your own data. You control the structure of your database by modifying or eliminating preset tables and fields and adding database content such as tables, forms, and reports.

Create a Database Based on a Template

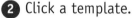

① Start Access.

Note: *You can also create a new database from within Access; click the **File** tab and then click **New**.*

Ⓐ On the Access Start screen or the New screen, templates appear.

Ⓑ You can search for additional templates online by typing keywords here.

② Click a template.

Note: *To build a database, select a template that contains "Desktop" as the first word in its name. Web app template names do not contain the word "Desktop."*

A window appears, displaying the template information.

Ⓒ To view the previous or next template, click these arrows (◁ and ▷).

③ Type a new name in the **File Name** field.

④ To change the folder in which you store the database file, click the **Open file** button (📁).

Note: *If you are satisfied with the folder Access suggests, skip to Step **7**.*

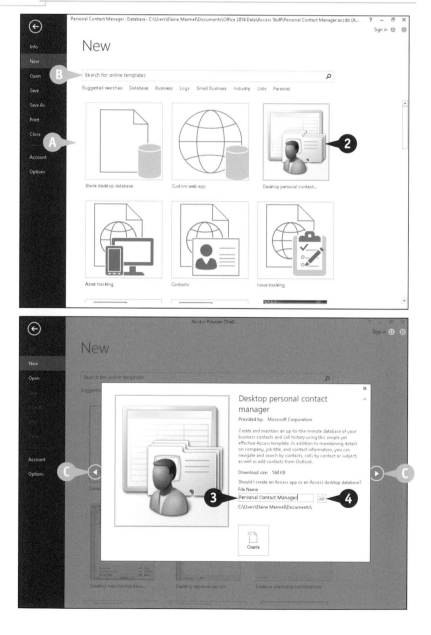

The File New Database dialog box appears.

⑤ Locate and select the folder in which you want to store the database file.

⑥ Click **OK**.

⑦ Click **Create**.

ⓓ Access downloads the template and creates a new, blank database, ready for data.

⑧ A security warning appears; to hide the warning and enable the macros in this template, click **Enable Content**.

---

simplify it

How do I know what fields to keep in or remove from my table?
To determine the fields you need in your database, decide the kinds of information you want to track in your database and the types of reports and queries you want to generate to view your data. For best results, use the suggested fields; you can always remove or hide fields that you do not use at a later time. (For help removing or hiding fields from a table, see the sections "Delete a Field from a Table" and "Hide a Field in a Table," later in this chapter.)

Create a Blank Database

Access includes many predefined database templates, including templates for creating contact lists, assets, project management, task management, and more. You can also find additional downloadable templates online.

If you determine that none of these predesigned Access templates suits your purposes, you can create a new, blank database and then decide on the tables, fields, forms, and other objects your database will include.

Create a Blank Database

1 Start Access.

Note: *You can also create a new database from within Access; click the **File** tab and then click **New**.*

Ⓐ On the Access Start screen or the New screen, templates appear.

2 Click **Blank desktop database**.

A window appears, displaying the template information.

Ⓑ To view the previous or next template, click these arrows (◂ and ▸).

3 Type a new name in the **File Name** field.

4 To change the folder in which you store the database file, click the **Open file** button (📁).

Note: *If you are satisfied with the folder Access suggests, skip to Step **7**.*

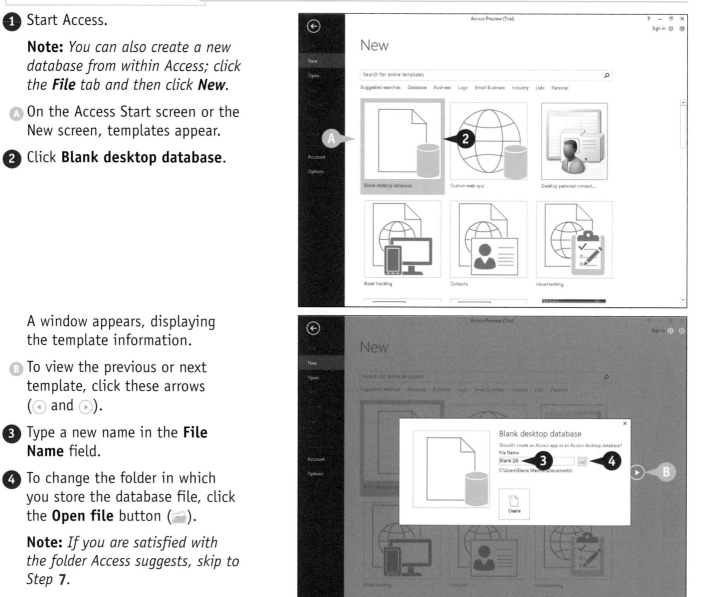

The File New Database dialog box appears.

5 Locate and select the folder in which you want to store the database file.

6 Click **OK**.

7 Click **Create**.

© Access creates a new, blank database and opens a new table, ready for data.

What is the pane on the left?
This is the Navigation pane, which you can use to open various database objects. Click the **Shutter Bar Open/Close** button (≪) to collapse the pane; click the button again (≫) to expand the pane.

How do I open an existing database?
Click the **File** tab, click **Open**, click **Recent**, and then click the database in the Recent Databases list that appears. If the database is not listed in the Recent Databases list, click the **File** tab, click **Computer** or your OneDrive, and then click **Browse** to display an Open dialog box. Locate and select the database file, and click **Open**.

Create a New Table

Access databases store all data in tables. A *table* is a list of information organized into columns and rows. A table might list the names, addresses, phone numbers, company names, titles, and email addresses of your clients. Each row in a table is considered a *record*. You use columns to hold *fields*, which are the individual units of information contained within a record.

If you need to add a table to a database, you can easily do so. All table objects that you create appear listed in the Navigation pane; simply double-click a table object to open it.

Create a New Table

1 With your database open in Access, click the **Create** tab.

2 Click **Table**.

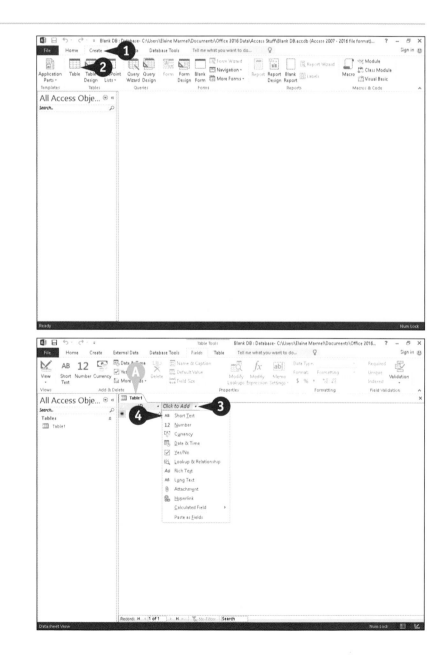

A Access creates a new table and displays it in Datasheet view.

Note: *See the next section, "Change Table Views," to learn more about Datasheet view.*

3 To name a field, click the **Click to Add** link at the top of the field column.

4 Click the type of field you want to add.

In this example, a Short Text field is added.

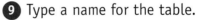

5. Type a name for the field and press **Enter**.

6. Repeat Steps **3** to **5** to create more fields for the table.

7. When you are finished adding fields, close the table by clicking the **Close** button (✕).

Access prompts you to save the table changes.

8. Click **Yes**.

The Save As dialog box appears.

9. Type a name for the table.

10. Click **OK**.

Access lists the table among the database objects in the Navigation pane.

Note: *After you save a table, you can reopen it by double-clicking it in the Navigation pane.*

simplify it

Can I rename table fields?
Yes. To do so, just double-click the field label and type a new name. When you finish, press **Enter**.

How do I remove a table that I no longer want?
Before attempting to remove a table, ensure that it does not contain any important data that you need, because deleting a table also deletes the data in the table. To delete the table, select it in the Navigation pane and press **Delete**. Access asks you to confirm the deletion before permanently removing the table, along with any data that it contains.

Change Table Views

You can view your table data using two different view modes: Datasheet view and Design view. In Datasheet view, the table appears as an ordinary grid of intersecting columns and rows where you can enter data. In Design view, you can view the skeletal structure of your fields and their properties and modify the design of the table.

In either view, you can add fields by typing new field names in the Field Name column, or change the field names. In Design view, you can also change the type of data allowed within a field, such as text or number data.

Change Table Views

Switch to Design View

1 Open any table by double-clicking it in the Navigation pane.

A Access displays the table in the default Datasheet view.

2 Click the **Home** tab.

3 Click the bottom half of the **View** button.

4 Click **Design View**.

Note: *You can quickly switch from Datasheet view to Design view by clicking the top half of the **View** button.*

B Access displays the table in Design view.

C The bottom of the view displays the properties of the field you select in the top of the view.

D Access displays the Table Tools Design tab.

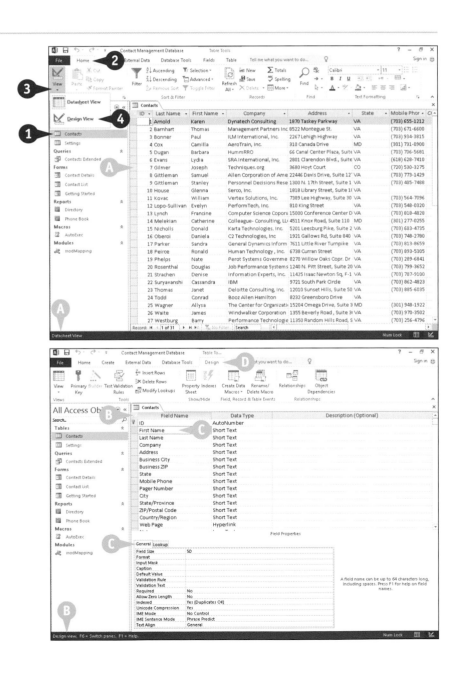

Switch to Datasheet View

1 Click the **Home** tab.

2 Click the bottom half of the **View** button.

3 Click **Datasheet View**.

Note: *You can quickly switch from Design view to Datasheet view by clicking the top half of the **View** button.*

E Access displays the default Datasheet view of the table.

Do all Access objects have the same views?
No. All Access objects have a Design view, but other available views depend on the object you select in the Navigation pane. For example, in addition to a Design view, reports have a Report view, a Print Preview, and a Layout view, and forms have a Form view and a Layout view.

What is the purpose of the Field Properties area in Design view?
The Field Properties area enables you to change the design of the field, specifying how many characters the field can contain, whether fields can be left blank, and other properties.

simplify it

Add a Field to a Table

You can add fields to your table to include more information in your records. For example, you may need to add a separate field to a Contacts table for mobile phone numbers. Or, you may need to add a field to a table that contains a catalog of products to track each product's availability.

After you add a field, you can name it whatever you want. To name a field, double-click the field label in Datasheet view, type a new name, and press Enter. Alternatively, you can change the field name in Design view.

Add a Field to a Table

① Double-click to open the table to which you want to add a field in Datasheet view.

② Click the column heading to the left of where you want to insert a new field.

Note: *Access adds the column for the new field to the right of the column you select.*

③ Click the **Fields** tab.

④ In the Add & Delete group, click the button for the type of field you want to add.

In this example, a Short Text field is added.

Ⓐ Access adds the new field to the right of the column you selected in Step **2**.

Note: *You can rename the field by typing a new name and pressing* Enter.

Delete a Field from a Table

You can delete a field that you no longer need in a table. For example, if your employee contact information database contains a Pager Number field, you might opt to delete that field.

When you remove a field, Access permanently removes any data contained within the field for every record in the table. If you do not want to delete the information in the field, you might choose to hide the field. For information, see the next section, "Hide a Field in a Table."

Delete a Field from a Table

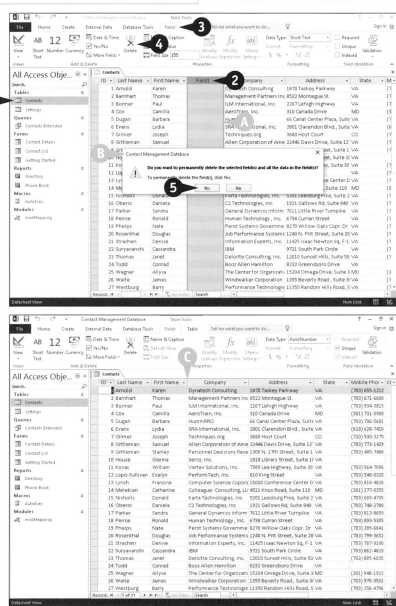

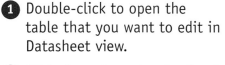

1 Double-click to open the table that you want to edit in Datasheet view.

2 Click the column header for the field you want to remove.

Ⓐ Access selects the entire column.

3 Click the **Fields** tab.

4 Click **Delete**.

Ⓑ Access prompts you to confirm the deletion.

5 Click **Yes**.

Note: *You might also see a message warning you that deleting the field will also delete an index; click **Yes**.*

Ⓒ Access removes the field and any record content for the field from the table.

Hide a Field in a Table

Suppose your table contains fields that you do not want to view on a regular basis, but that you do not want to delete from the table. For example, a table containing a catalog of products might include a field indicating the country in which the product was manufactured — information that you might not need to view on a regular basis but still need occasionally. You also might hide a field to prevent another user on your computer from seeing the field. Whatever the reason, you can hide the field. When you are ready to view the field again, you can easily unhide it.

Hide a Field in a Table

1 Double-click the table that you want to edit to open it in Datasheet view.

2 Right-click the column heading of the field you want to hide.

3 Click **Hide Fields**.

A Access hides the field.

Note: *To view the field again, right-click any column heading and click **Unhide Fields**. In the Unhide Columns dialog box that appears, select the column that you want to display again (☐ changes to ☑) and click **Close**. Access displays the hidden field as the last column in the table.*

Move a Field in a Table

You can change the order of fields in a table. Moving fields is particularly useful if you built your database from a predesigned template, because you may find that the order in which fields appear in the table does not suit your needs.

It is important to understand that moving a field changes its position in Datasheet view but does not change the order of the fields in the table design. If you create a form after reordering fields, the form fields appear in their original position.

Move a Field in a Table

① **Double-click the table that you want to edit to open it in Datasheet view.**

② **Click the column heading of the field you want to move.**

Ⓐ **Access selects the entire column.**

③ **Drag the column to a new position in the table (⬚ changes to ⬚).**

Ⓑ **A bold vertical line marks the new location of the column as you drag.**

④ **Release the mouse button.**

Ⓒ **Access moves the field to the new location.**

Create a Form

Although you can enter data into your database by typing it directly into an Access table, you can simplify data entry, especially if someone else will be entering the data, by creating a form based on your table. Forms present your table fields in an easy-to-read, fill-in-the-blank format. When you create a form based on a table, Access inserts fields into the form for each field in the table.

Using forms is a great way to help ensure accurate data entry, particularly if other users are adding information to your database.

Create a Form

1. Double-click the table that you want to edit to open it in Datasheet view.

2. Click the **Create** tab.

3. Click **Form**.

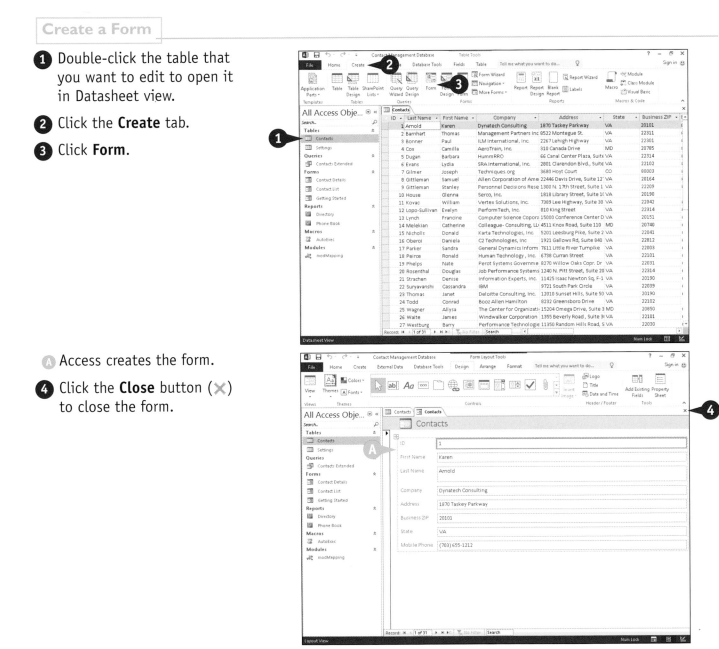

A. Access creates the form.

4. Click the **Close** button (✖) to close the form.

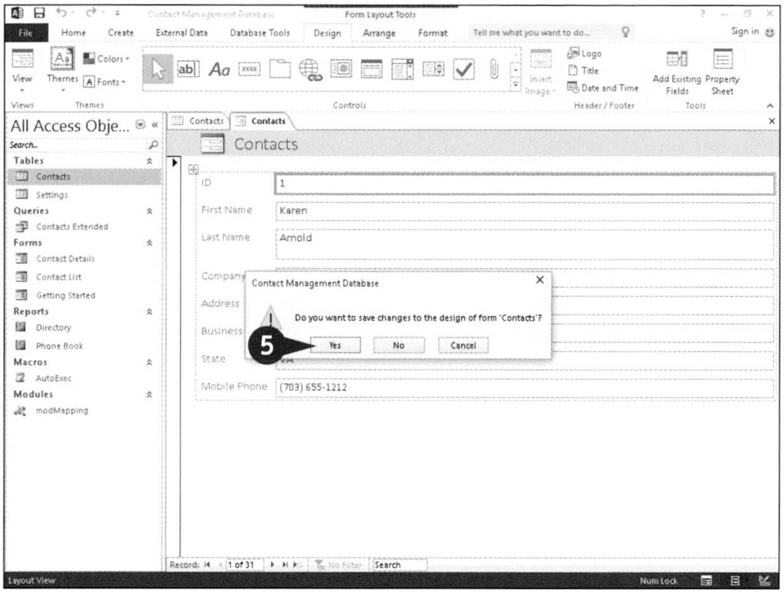

Access prompts you to save your changes.

5 Click **Yes**.

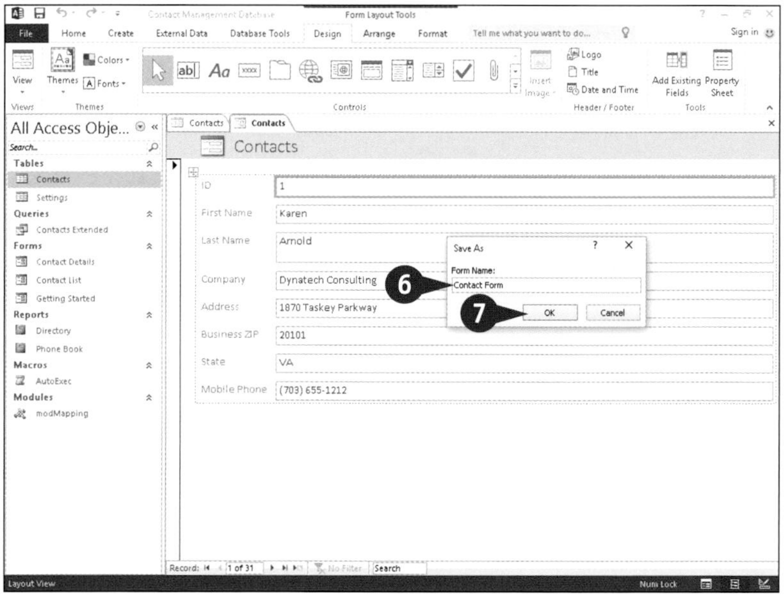

The Save As dialog box appears.

6 Type a name for the form.

7 Click **OK**.

Access lists the form among the database objects in the Navigation pane.

Note: *After you save a form, you can reopen it by double-clicking it in the Navigation pane.*

---

simplify it

How do I delete a form that I no longer need?
To delete a form, click it in the Navigation pane, and then press Delete or click the **Delete** button on the Home tab. Access asks you to confirm the deletion; click **Yes**.

Can I create a blank form?
Yes. Click the **Blank Form** button on the Create tab to open a blank form. A field list appears, containing all the fields from all the tables in the database. To add a field to the form, drag it from the list onto the form. You can populate the form with as many fields as you need.

Change Form Views

You can view your form using three form views: Form view, Design view, and Layout view. Form view is the default; in this view, you can simply enter data. In Design view, each form object appears as a separate, editable element. For example, in Design view, you can edit both the box that contains the data and the

label that identifies the data. In Layout view, you can rearrange the form controls and adjust their sizes directly on the form. Access makes it easy to switch from Form view to Design view to Layout view and back.

Change Form Views

Switch to Design View

1 Double-click the form that you want to edit to open it in Form view.

2 Click the **Home** tab.

3 Click the bottom half of the **View** button.

4 Click **Design View**.

Ⓐ Access displays the form in Design view.

Switch to Layout View

1 Click the **Home** tab.

2 Click the bottom half of the **View** button.

3 Click **Layout View**.

Ⓑ Access displays the form in Layout view.

To return to Form view, you can click the bottom half of the **View** button and then click **Form View**.

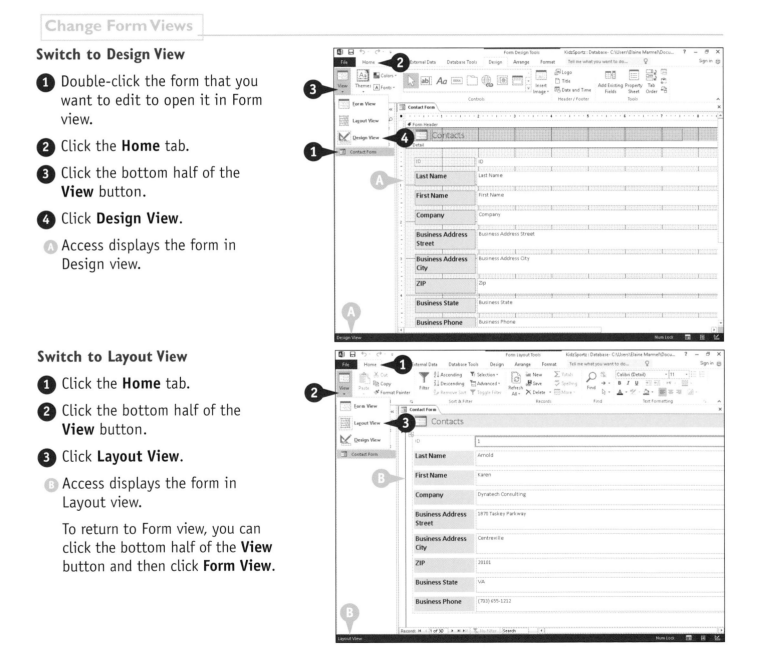

Move a Field in a Form

You can move a field to another location on your form. For example, you might move a field to accommodate the order in which data is entered in the form. To easily move both a field label and the field contents, select both at the same time.

Although you can move a field in either Design view or Layout view, you might find it easier to make changes to your form in Layout view.

Move a Field in a Form

1 Double-click the form that you want to edit to open it in Form view.

2 Switch to Layout view (see the previous section, "Change Form Views," for details).

3 Click the label of the field that you want to move.

A ☐ changes to ☐.

4 Press and hold **Ctrl** as you click the contents of the field.

5 Click and drag the field label and contents to the new location on the form.

B This symbol (a pink line) identifies the proposed position of the field label and contents.

C When you release the mouse button, Access repositions the field.

6 Click anywhere outside the field label and contents to deselect them.

Delete a Field in a Form

You can delete a field that you no longer need in a form. When you remove a field, you need to remove both the data box and the field label. Although you can delete a field in Design view or in Layout view, you might find it easier to do this in Layout view.

Note that removing a form field does not remove the field from the table upon which the form is originally based or any of the data within that field; it simply removes the field from the form.

Delete a Field in a Form

① Double-click the form that you want to edit to open it in Form view.

② Switch to Layout view (see the section "Change Form Views" for details).

③ Click the label of the field that you want to delete.

Ⓐ ⍔ changes to ⍔.

④ Press and hold Ctrl as you click the contents of the field.

⑤ Press Delete, or click the **Home** tab and then click **Delete**.

Ⓑ Access removes the field and label from the form.

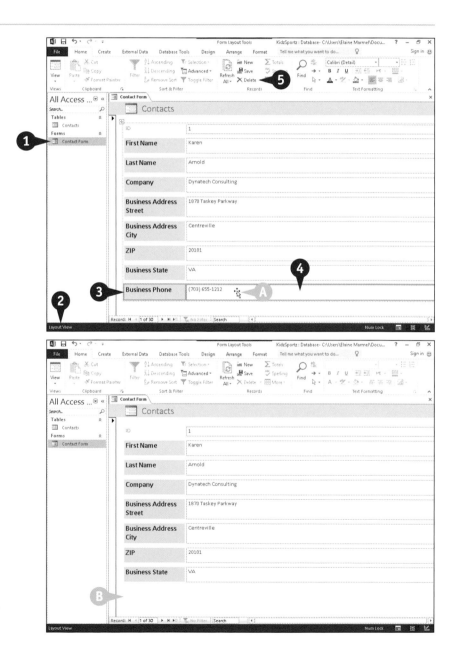

Apply a Database Theme

A *theme* is a predesigned set of color schemes, fonts, and other visual attributes. Applying a theme to an Access database adds polish to it and makes it more visually appealing. When you apply a theme to an Access database, that same theme is applied to all forms and tables in your database.

Themes are shared among the Office programs; you can use the same theme in your Access database that you have applied to worksheets in Excel, documents in Word, slides in PowerPoint, or publications in Publisher.

Apply a Database Theme

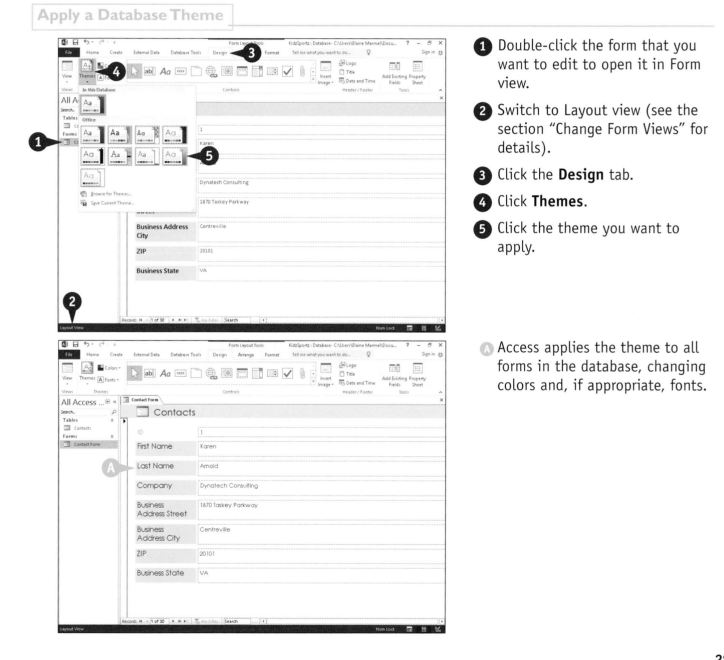

1 Double-click the form that you want to edit to open it in Form view.

2 Switch to Layout view (see the section "Change Form Views" for details).

3 Click the **Design** tab.

4 Click **Themes**.

5 Click the theme you want to apply.

Ⓐ Access applies the theme to all forms in the database, changing colors and, if appropriate, fonts.

Add a Record to a Table

You build a database by adding records to a table in the database. Any new records that you add appear at the end of the table. You add records to a table in Datasheet view. As your table grows longer, you can use the navigation buttons on your keyboard to navigate it. You can press Tab to move from cell to cell, or you can press the keyboard arrow keys. To move backward to a previous cell, press Shift + Tab.

After you enter a record in a database table, you can edit it if necessary. You edit records in a table in Datasheet view.

Add a Record to a Table

① In the Navigation pane, double-click the table to which you want to add a record.

Ⓐ Access opens the table, placing the cell pointer in the first cell of the first row.

Ⓑ By default, the first field in each table is a unique ID number for the record. Access sets this value automatically as you create a record.

② Click in the second cell of the first empty row.

③ Type the desired data in the selected cell.

④ Press Tab.

Access fills in the ID number to add the new record.

⑤ Repeat Steps 3 and 4 until you have filled the entire row.

⑥ Press Enter or press Tab to move to the next row or record.

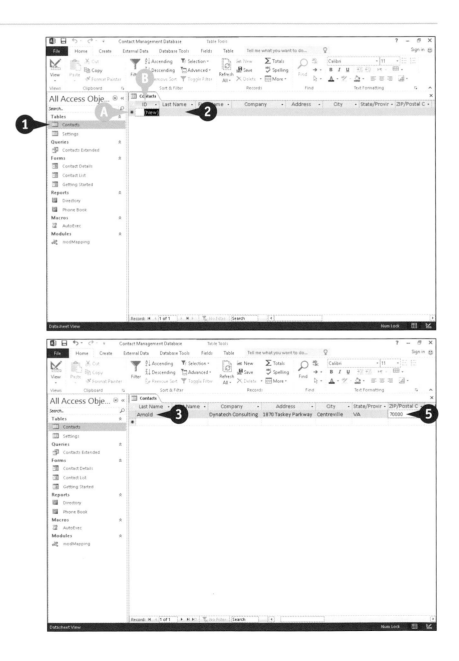

284

C The new record appears here.

D Access moves the cell pointer to the first cell in the next row.

7 Repeat Steps **3** to **6** to add more records to the table.

Access adds your records.

E You can resize a column by dragging the column border left or right.

F You can use the scroll bars to view different parts of the table.

What is a primary key?

A *primary key* uniquely identifies each record in a table. For many tables, the primary key is the ID field by default. The ID field, which Access creates automatically, stores a unique number for each record entered into the database. If you want, however, you can designate another field (or even multiple fields) as a primary key. To do so, switch the table to Design view, select the field that you want to set as the primary key, and click the **Primary key** button on the Design tab.

Add a Record to a Form

You can use forms to quickly add records to your Access databases. Forms present your record fields in an easy-to-read format. When you use a form to add records, the form presents each field in your table as a labeled box that you can use to enter data.

After you enter a record in a form, you can edit it if necessary. (See the second Simplify It tip for more information.) For help locating a particular record in the form window in order to edit it, see the next section, "Navigate Records in a Form."

Add a Record to a Form

① In the Navigation pane, double-click the form to which you want to add a record.

Ⓐ Access opens the form.

② Click the **Home** tab.

③ Click **New** in the Records group.

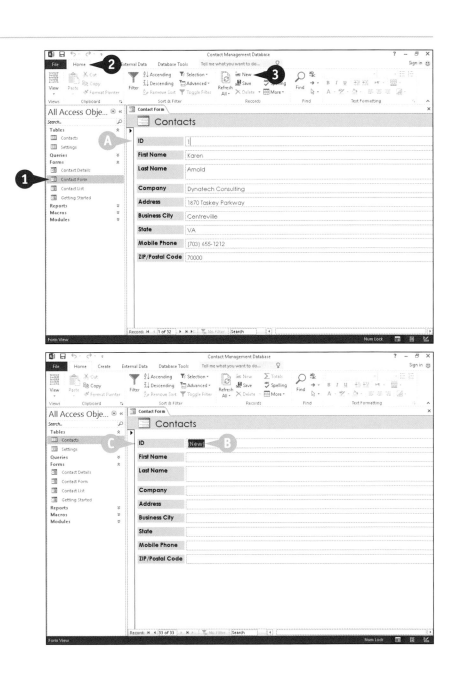

Ⓑ Access displays a blank form, placing the insertion point in the first field.

Ⓒ By default, the first field in the table associated with this form is a unique ID number for the record. Access sets this value automatically.

④ Press Tab .

Access assigns an ID number and moves the insertion point to the next field in the form.

5 Type the desired data in the selected field.

6 Repeat Steps **4** and **5** until you have filled the entire form.

7 Click **Save** or press Enter and press Tab.

Access saves the record and displays another blank form, ready for data.

Ⓓ To close the form window, you can click the **Close** button (✕).

Are there other ways to insert a new record?
Yes. You can click the **New (Blank) Record** button (▶︎) on the form window's Navigation bar, located along the bottom of the form.

How do I edit a record in a form?
You can reopen the form, navigate to the record that you want to change, and make your edits directly to the form data. When you save your changes, Access automatically updates the data in your table. To learn how to display a particular record in a form, see the next section, "Navigate Records in a Form."

Navigate Records in a Form

You may find it easier to read a record using a form instead of reading it from a large table containing other records. Similarly, editing a record in a form may be easier than editing a record in a table. You can locate records you want to view or edit using the Navigation bar that appears along the bottom of the

form window. The Navigation bar contains buttons for locating and viewing different records in your database. The Navigation bar also contains a search box for locating a specific record. (You learn how to search for a record in a form in the next section.)

Navigate Records in a Form

1 In the Navigation pane, double-click the form whose records you want to navigate.

Ⓐ Access displays the form.

Ⓑ The Current Record box indicates which record you are viewing.

2 Click the **Previous Record** button (◀) or **Next Record** button (▶) to move back or forward by one record.

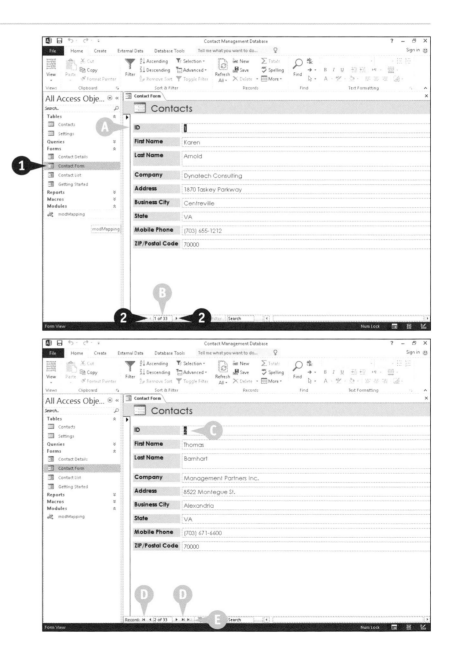

Ⓒ Access displays the previous or next record in the database.

Ⓓ You can click the **First Record** button (◀◀) or **Last Record** button (▶▶) to navigate to the first or last record in the table.

Ⓔ You can click the **New (Blank) Record** button (▶※) to start a new, blank record.

Search for a Record Using a Form

You may find it easier to read and edit records in a form than in a large table containing other records. As described in the previous section, you can locate records by using the various buttons in the Navigation bar. However, that method can become time consuming if the table associated with the form contains many records. This section describes how to search for specific text in a record — an easier approach to finding a record while using a form. You search using the form's Navigation bar.

Search for a Record Using a Form

① In the Navigation pane, double-click the form containing the record you want to find.

Ⓐ Access displays the form.

② Click in the search box.

③ Type a keyword that relates to the record you want to find.

Ⓑ As you type, Access displays the first record containing any field that matches your search.

④ After you finish typing your keyword, press Enter to display the next match, if any.

Delete a Record from a Table

You can remove a record from your database if it holds data that you no longer need. Removing old records can reduce the overall file size of your database and make it easier to manage. When you delete a record, all the data within its fields is permanently removed.

You can remove a record from a database by deleting it from a table or by deleting it from a form. This section shows you how to delete a record from a table. (For help deleting a record from a form, see the next section, "Delete a Record Using a Form.")

Delete a Record from a Table

1. In the Navigation pane, double-click the table that contains the record you want to delete.

A. Access opens the table.

2. Position your mouse over the gray box to the left of the record that you want to delete (⇦ changes to ➡) and click.

B. Access selects the record.

3. Click the **Home** tab.

4. Click **Delete**.

   Note: *You can also right-click the record, and then click **Delete Record**.*

   Access asks you to confirm the deletion.

5. Click **Yes**.

C. Access permanently removes the row containing the record from the table.

Delete a Record Using a Form

In addition to removing records directly from a table, as described in the previous section, you can remove records that you no longer need by using a form. Removing old records can reduce the overall file size of your database and make it easier to manage. When you delete a record, whether from a table or a form,

Access permanently removes all the data within its fields.

The first step is to locate the record you want to delete; refer to the sections "Navigate Records in a Form" and "Search for a Record Using a Form" for help locating the record.

Delete a Record Using a Form

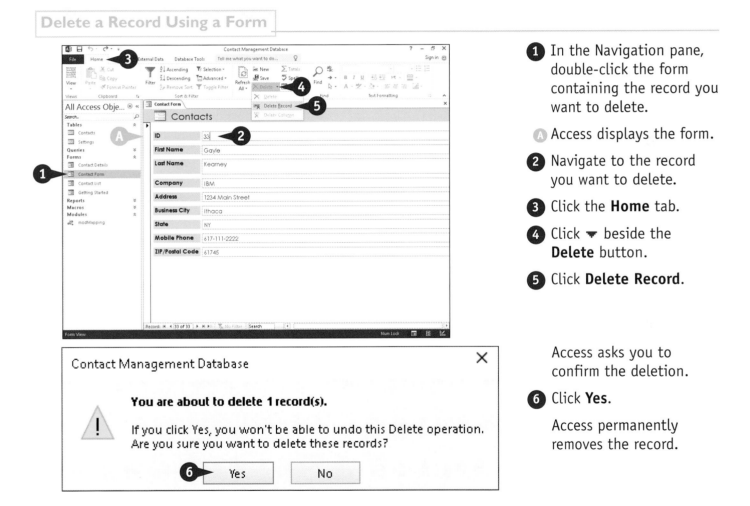

1. In the Navigation pane, double-click the form containing the record you want to delete.

   Ⓐ Access displays the form.

2. Navigate to the record you want to delete.

3. Click the **Home** tab.

4. Click ▼ beside the **Delete** button.

5. Click **Delete Record**.

   Access asks you to confirm the deletion.

6. Click **Yes**.

   Access permanently removes the record.

Sort Records

Sorting enables you to arrange your database records in a logical order to match any criteria that you specify. By default, Access sorts records in ID order. However, you may want to sort the records alphabetically or based on the ZIP code. You can sort in ascending order or descending order.

You can sort records in a table, or you can use a form to sort records. Sorting records in a table has no effect on the order in which records appear in an associated form; similarly, sorting in a form has no effect on the records in an associated table.

Sort Records

Sort a Table

1. In the Navigation pane, double-click the table you want to sort.

2. Position your mouse over the column heading for the field by which you want to sort (changes to ↓) and click to select the column.

3. Click the **Home** tab.

4. Click a sort button:

   Click **Ascending** to sort the records in ascending order.

   Click **Descending** to sort the records in descending order.

   Access sorts the table records based on the field you choose.

   Ⓐ In this example, Access sorts the records alphabetically by company name in ascending order.

5. Click ✕ to close the table.

   Ⓑ In the dialog box that appears, you can click **Yes** to make the sort permanent or **No** to leave the original order intact.

292

Sort Using a Form

1 In the Navigation pane, double-click the form you want to use to sort records.

2 Click in the field by which you want to sort.

3 Click the **Home** tab.

4 Click a sort button:

Click **Ascending** to sort the records in ascending order.

Click **Descending** to sort the records in descending order.

Access sorts the table records based on the field you chose.

C In this example, Access sorts the records alphabetically by company name in ascending order.

D You can use the navigation buttons (▶, ◀, I◀, and ▶I) to navigate through the sorted records.

---

simplify it

How are empty records sorted?
If you sort using a field for which some records are missing data, those records are included in the sort; they appear first in an ascending sort, or last in a descending sort.

How do I remove a sort order?
With the sorted table or form open, click the **Remove Sort** button in the Sort & Filter group on the Home tab. This returns the table to its original sort order. You can also use this technique to remove a sort from a query or report. (Queries and reports are covered later in this chapter.)

Filter Records

You can use an Access filter to view only specific records that meet criteria you set. For example, you may want to view all clients buying a particular product, anyone in a contacts database who has a birthday in June, or all products within a particular category. You can also filter by exclusion — that is,

filter out records that do not contain the search criteria that you specify.

You can apply a simple filter on one field in your database using the Selection tool, or you can filter several fields using the Filter by Form command.

Filter Records

Apply a Simple Filter

1 In the Navigation pane, double-click the form you want to use to filter records.

2 Click in the field by which you want to filter.

3 Click the **Home** tab.

4 Click **Selection**.

5 Click a criterion.

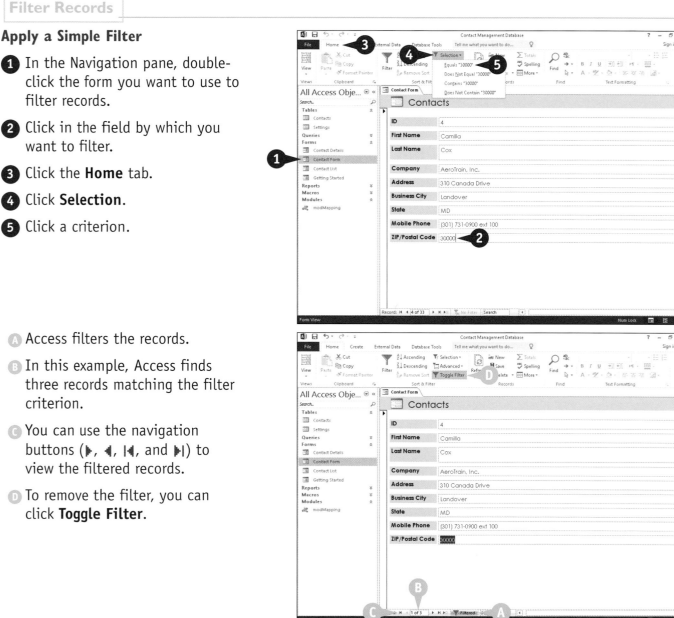

A Access filters the records.

B In this example, Access finds three records matching the filter criterion.

C You can use the navigation buttons (▶, ◀, ◀, and ▶|) to view the filtered records.

D To remove the filter, you can click **Toggle Filter**.

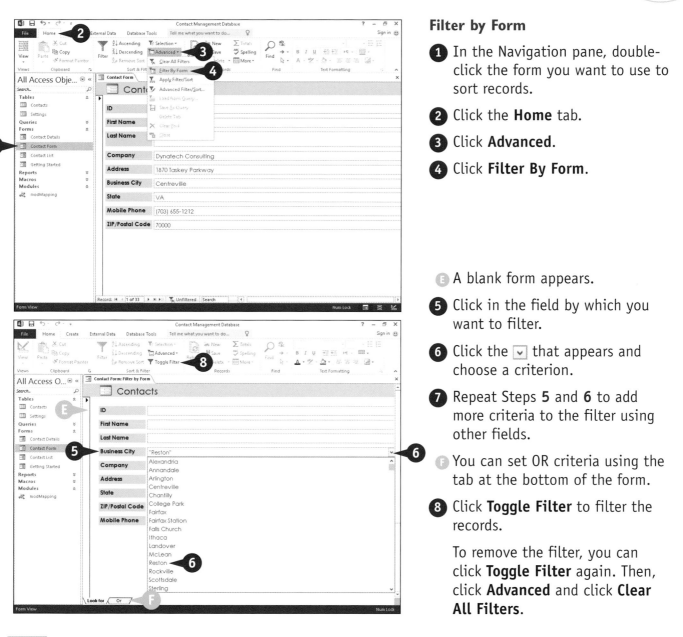

Filter by Form

1. In the Navigation pane, double-click the form you want to use to sort records.

2. Click the **Home** tab.

3. Click **Advanced**.

4. Click **Filter By Form**.

Ⓔ A blank form appears.

5. Click in the field by which you want to filter.

6. Click the ⌄ that appears and choose a criterion.

7. Repeat Steps **5** and **6** to add more criteria to the filter using other fields.

Ⓕ You can set OR criteria using the tab at the bottom of the form.

8. Click **Toggle Filter** to filter the records.

   To remove the filter, you can click **Toggle Filter** again. Then, click **Advanced** and click **Clear All Filters**.

How do I filter by exclusion?
Click in the field that you want to filter in the form, click the **Selection** button on the Home tab, and then click an exclusion option.

What are OR criteria?
Setting OR criteria enables you to display records that match one set of criteria or another. For example, you might set up your filter to display only those records with the value 46989 OR 46555 in the ZIP field. After you set a criterion, Access adds an OR tab. If you set an OR criterion using that tab, Access adds another OR tab, and so on.

Apply Conditional Formatting

You can use Access's Conditional Formatting tool to apply certain formatting attributes, such as bold text or a fill color, to data in a form when the data meets a specified condition. For example, if your database tracks weekly sales, you might set up the Conditional Formatting feature to alert you if sales figures fall below what is required for you to break even.

You apply conditional formatting by creating a rule that specifies the criteria that the value in a field must meet. Access formats values that meet the criteria using settings you specify.

Apply Conditional Formatting

1 In the Navigation pane, double-click the form to which you want to apply conditional formatting.

2 Switch to Layout view.

Note: *For details on changing form views, see Chapter 16.*

3 Click the field to which you want to apply conditional formatting.

4 Click the **Format** tab.

5 Click **Conditional Formatting**.

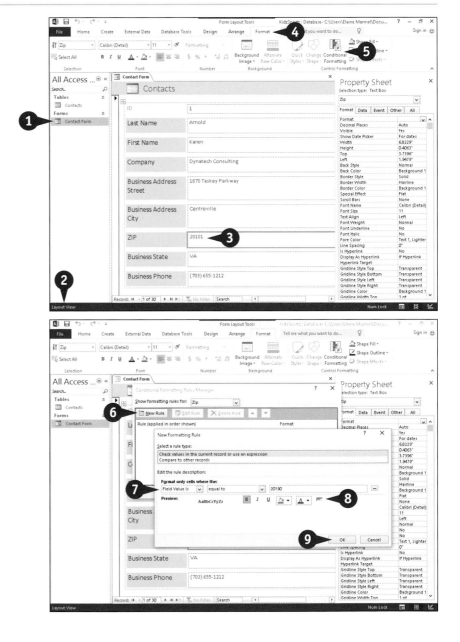

The Conditional Formatting Rules Manager dialog box opens.

6 Click **New Rule**.

The New Formatting Rule dialog box opens.

7 Set the criteria you want to use to apply conditional formatting.

8 Specify how values that meet your criteria should be formatted.

9 Click **OK**.

Conditional Formatting Rules Manager

Show formatting rules for: Zip

New Rule   Edit Rule   Delete Rule

Rule (applied in order shown)   Format

Value = 20190   AaBbCcYyZz

OK   Cancel   Apply

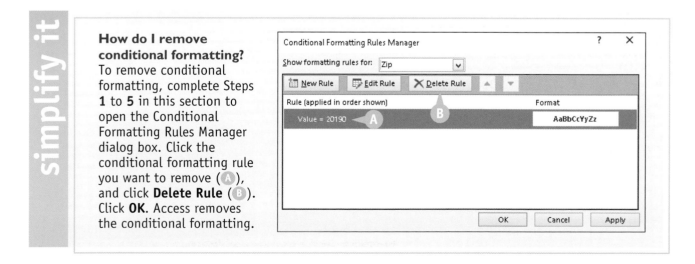

A Access creates a rule based on the criteria you set.

10 Click **OK**.

B Access applies the conditional formatting.

How do I remove conditional formatting?

To remove conditional formatting, complete Steps **1** to **5** in this section to open the Conditional Formatting Rules Manager dialog box. Click the conditional formatting rule you want to remove (**A**), and click **Delete Rule** (**B**). Click **OK**. Access removes the conditional formatting.

Conditional Formatting Rules Manager

Show formatting rules for: Zip

New Rule   Edit Rule   Delete Rule

Rule (applied in order shown)   Format

Value = 20190 **A**   **B**   AaBbCcYyZz

OK   Cancel   Apply

Perform a Simple Query

You can use a query to extract information that you want to view in a database. Queries are similar to filters, but offer you greater control. You can use the Query Wizard to help you select the fields you want to include in the analysis. There are several types of query wizards. This section covers using the Simple Query Wizard.

Although beyond the scope of this book, queries also can help you collect information from multiple tables that you can then use to perform a mail merge; see *Teach Yourself VISUALLY Word 2016* for details on using Word's Mail Merge feature.

Perform a Simple Query

Create a Query

1. In the Navigation pane, double-click the table for which you want to create a simple query.

2. Click the **Create** tab.

3. Click **Query Wizard**.

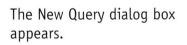

The New Query dialog box appears.

4. Click **Simple Query Wizard**.

5. Click **OK**.

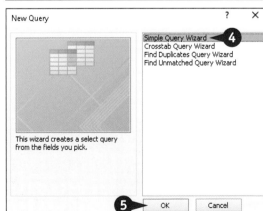

The Simple Query Wizard opens.

6 Click the **Tables/Queries** 🔽 and choose the table containing the fields on which you want to base the query.

7 In the Available Fields list, click a field that you want to include in the query.

8 Click the **Add** button (⊳).

Ⓐ The field appears in the Selected Fields list.

9 Repeat Steps **7** and **8** to add more fields to your query.

You can repeat Step **6** to choose another table from which to add fields.

Note: *When using fields from two or more tables, the tables must have a relationship.*

10 Click **Next**.

What is a table relationship?

A table relationship enables you to combine related information for analysis. For example, you might define a relationship between one table containing customer contact information and another table containing customer orders. With that table relationship defined, you can then perform a query to, for example, identify the addresses of all customers who have ordered the same product. To access tools for defining table relationships, click the **Database Tools** tab on the Ribbon and then click **Relationships**. If you created your database from a template, then certain table relationships are predefined.

continued ▶

Perform a Simple Query *(continued)*

During the process of creating a new query, the Query Wizard asks you to give the query a unique name so that you can open and use the query later. All queries that you create appear in the Navigation pane; you can double-click a query in the Navigation pane to perform it again.

If, after creating and performing a query, you determine that you need to add more criteria to it, you can easily do so. For example, you may realize that the query needs to include an additional table from your database or additional criteria to expand or limit the scope of the query.

Perform a Simple Query *(continued)*

11 Type a name for the query.

12 Select **Open the query to view information** (○ changes to ◉).

13 Click **Finish**.

A A query datasheet appears, listing the fields.

B The query appears in the Navigation pane.

Add Criteria to the Query

1 If necessary, open the query that you want to modify by double-clicking it in the Navigation pane.

2 Click the **Home** tab.

3 Click the bottom half of the **View** button.

4 Click **Design View**.

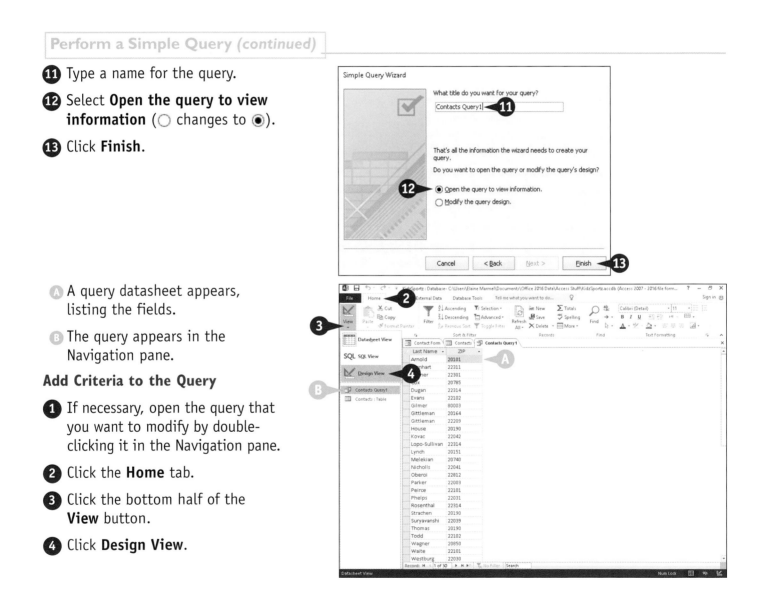

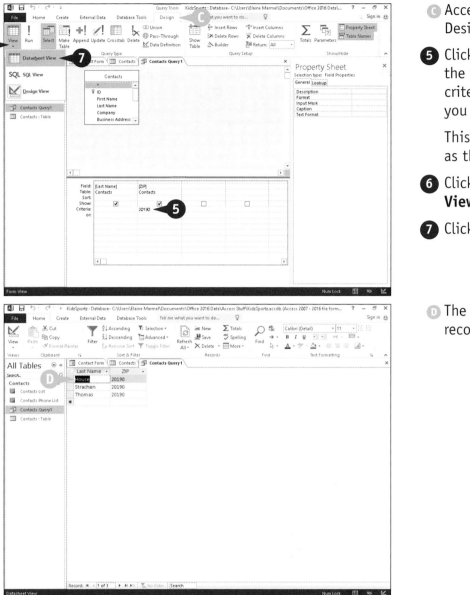

C Access displays the Query Tools Design tab.

5 Click in the **Criteria** box for the field you want to use as a criterion and type the data that you want to view.

This example specifies a ZIP code as the criterion.

6 Click the bottom half of the **View** button.

7 Click **Datasheet View**.

D The table now shows only the records matching the criteria.

<table>
<tr><td rowspan="2">simplify it</td><td>

How do I add another table to my query?
Switch to Design view, click the **Design** tab on the Ribbon, and then click the **Show Table** button to open the Show Table dialog box, where you can add another table to the query.

</td><td>

What kinds of queries do the other wizards in the New Query dialog box create?
The Crosstab Query Wizard's query displays information in a spreadsheet-like format, the Find Duplicates Query Wizard's query finds records with duplicate field values, and the Find Unmatched Query Wizard's query finds records in one table with no related records in another table.

</td></tr>
</table>

Create a Report

You can use Access to create a report based on one or more database tables. You can create a simple report, which contains all the fields in a single table, or a custom report, which can contain data from multiple tables in a database. Note that to use fields from two or more tables, the tables must have a relationship. Refer to the Simplify It tip "What is a table relationship?" in the previous section, "Perform a Simple Query."

To create a custom report, you can use the Report Wizard; it guides you through the steps to turn database data into an easy-to-read report.

Create a Report

1 In the Navigation pane, double-click the table for which you want to create a simple report.

2 Click the **Create** tab.

3 Click **Report Wizard**.

The Report Wizard opens.

4 Click the **Tables/Queries** and choose the table containing the fields on which you want to base the report.

5 In the Available Fields list, click a field that you want to include in the report.

6 Click the **Add** button (>).

Ⓐ The field appears in the Selected Fields list.

7 Repeat Steps **5** and **6** to add more fields to your report.

8 Click **Next**.

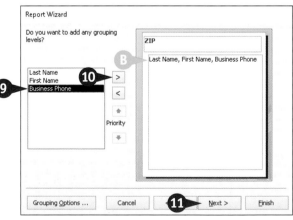

9 Optionally, click the field you want to use to group the data.

10 Click the **Add** button (>).

Ⓑ A preview of the grouping appears here.

11 Click **Next**.

Report Wizard

How would you like to lay out your report?

Layout
- ○ Stepped
- ⑫ ● Block
- ○ Outline

Orientation
- ● Portrait ← C
- ○ Landscape

☑ Adjust the field width so all fields fit on a page.

Cancel   ⑬ < Next >   Finish

Contacts Phone List

ZIP	Last Name	First Name	Business Phone
20101	Arnold	Karen	(703) 655-1212
20151	Lynch	Francine	(703) 818-4828
20164	Gittleman	Samuel	(703) 773-1429
20190	House	Glenna	
	Strachen	Denise	(703) 787-9100 ext 37
	Thomas	Janet	(703) 885-6035
20226	Wulf	Donald	(202) 648-8460
20740	Melekian	Catherine	(301) 277-0255
20785	Cox	Camilla	(301) 731-0900 ext 100
20850	Wagner	Allysa	(301) 948-1922 ext 249
22003	Parker	Barbara	(703) 813-8659
22030	Westburg	Barry	(703) 256-4796 Ext 6125
22031	Phelps	Nate	(703) 289-6841
22039	Suryavanshi	Cassandra	(703) 862-4823
22041	Nicholls	Donald	(703) 683-4735
22042	Kovac	William	(703) 564-7096
22101	Peirce	Ronald	(703) 893-5305 Ext 200
	Waite	James	(703) 970-3502
22102	Evans	Lydia	(618) 628-7410

Note: *You can use the dialog box that appears to establish a sort order for your data. Click the first* ⌄ *and click the field by which you want to sort. You can add more sort fields as needed. Fields are sorted in ascending order by default. Click the* **Ascending** *button to toggle to descending order. Click* **Next**.

⑫ Select a layout option (○ changes to ●).

C You can set the page orientation for a report here (○ changes to ●).

⑬ Click **Next**.

Note: *In the dialog box that appears, type a name for the report and select* **Preview the report** (○ *changes to* ●). *Then click* **Finish**.

D Access creates and displays the report.

E The report appears in the Navigation pane.

---

simplify it

How do I create a simple report?
Follow these steps: In the Navigation pane, double-click the table for which you want to create a simple report. Then click the **Create** tab and click the **Report** button. Access creates a simple report based on the table you selected. When you click ✕ to close the report, Access prompts you to save the report. Click **Yes**, and, in the dialog box that appears, supply a report name and click **OK**. The report appears in the Navigation pane.

PART VI

Outlook

Outlook is an email program and a personal information manager for the computer desktop. You can use Outlook to send and receive email messages and send attachments, including files and pictures, with an email. You also can reduce the amount of junk mail you receive. To keep you organized, use Outlook to schedule calendar appointments, keep track of contacts, organize lists of things to do, and add notes that might otherwise fall through the cracks. In this part, you learn how to put Outlook to work for you using each of its major components to manage everyday tasks.

Navigate in Outlook

Outlook functions as a personal organizer, with Mail, Calendar, People, Tasks, and Notes components. You switch between these components using the Navigation bar.

The Outlook Mail component appears by default when you open Outlook, and enables you to send and receive email messages. The Outlook Calendar component enables you to keep track of appointments. The Outlook People component enables you to maintain a database of your contacts and include those contacts in email messages you send and appointments you schedule. The Outlook Tasks component enables you to keep a to-do list.

Navigate in Outlook

Note: *When Outlook opens, the Mail component (✉) appears by default. You can read more about using the Mail component in Chapter 19.*

1 Click **Calendar** (▦) in the Navigation bar.

Note: *As you hover the mouse (▷) over Calendar (▦), Outlook displays a preview of upcoming appointments.*

Outlook displays the Month view of the Calendar component.

A Today's date appears selected in the main calendar and in the navigational calendars.

2 Click **People** (👥) in the Navigation bar.

Note: *As you hover the mouse (▷) over People (👥), Outlook displays a search box so you can easily find a contact.*

Note: *In earlier versions of Outlook, People was called Contacts, and the two terms are often used interchangeably.*

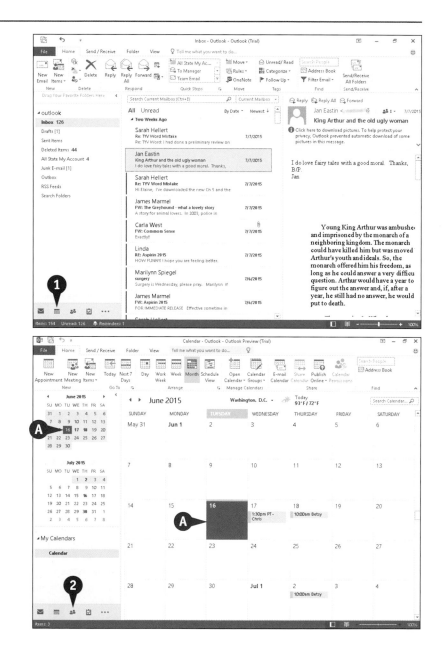

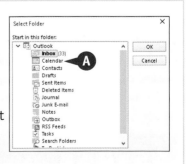

Outlook displays the People component.

③ Click **Tasks** (📋) in the Navigation bar.

Note: *As you hover the mouse (👆) over Tasks (📋), Outlook displays a preview of upcoming tasks.*

Ⓑ Outlook displays the To-Do List of the Tasks component.

simplify it

How do I change which component opens by default when I start Outlook?

To start with a different Mail folder or another component, such as Calendar (📅), click the **File** tab, and click **Options** to display the Outlook Options dialog box. On the left, click **Advanced**. In the Outlook Start and Exit section, click the **Browse** button to display the Select Folder dialog box. Click the component or Mail folder that you want to set as the default component (Ⓐ). Click **OK** twice to close both dialog boxes.

Schedule an Appointment

You can use Outlook's Calendar component to keep track of your schedule. When adding new appointments to the Calendar, you fill out appointment details, such as the name of the person with whom you are meeting, the location and date, and the start and end times. You can also enter notes about the appointment, as well as set up Outlook to remind you of the appointment in advance.

If your appointment occurs regularly, such as a weekly department meeting, you can set it as a recurring appointment. Outlook adds recurring appointments to each day, week, or month as you require.

Schedule an Appointment

① Click **Calendar** (▦) in the Navigation bar.

② Click the date for which you want to set an appointment.

Ⓐ You can click these arrows (◀ and ▶) to navigate to a different month.

Ⓑ You can click these buttons to select a different calendar view, such as a daily or weekly view.

③ Click **New Appointment** to display the Appointment window.

④ Type a name for the appointment.

Ⓒ You can type the appointment location here.

⑤ Click the **Start time** ▼ and set a start time.

Note: *In the Month view, Outlook allots 30 minutes for an appointment. You can click the* **End time** ▼ *and change the end time.*

Ⓓ You can type notes about the appointment here.

Ⓔ Outlook automatically sets a reminder that you can change by clicking ▼.

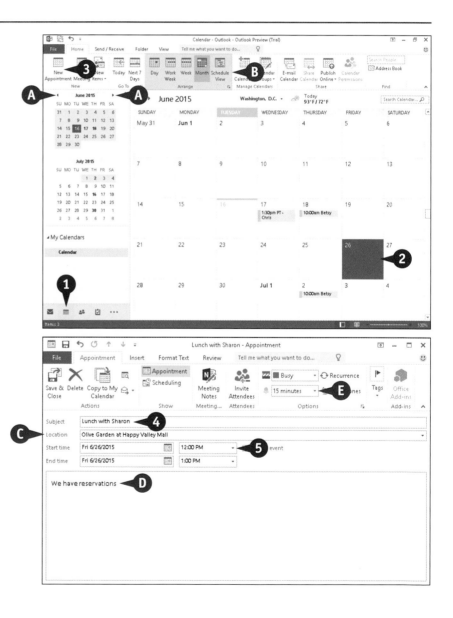

6 If your appointment occurs regularly, click **Recurrence**. Otherwise, skip to Step **9**.

Note: *If the Appointment window does not display* **Recurrence** *or a reminder time, click* **Options**.

The Appointment Recurrence dialog box appears.

7 Select the recurrence pattern.

F In the Range of Recurrence section, you can limit the appointments if they continue only for a specified time.

8 Click **OK**.

G Outlook marks the appointment as a recurring appointment.

9 Click **Save & Close**.

Outlook displays the appointment in the Calendar. To view the appointment details or make changes, double-click the appointment. To delete an appointment, right-click it and click **Delete**.

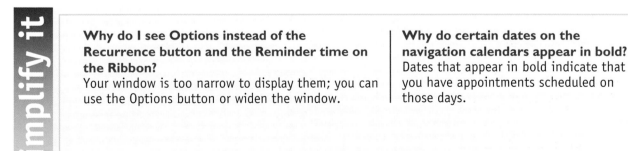

Why do I see Options instead of the Recurrence button and the Reminder time on the Ribbon?
Your window is too narrow to display them; you can use the Options button or widen the window.

Why do certain dates on the navigation calendars appear in bold?
Dates that appear in bold indicate that you have appointments scheduled on those days.

Create a New Contact

You can use Outlook's People component to maintain a list of contact information. You can track information such as your contacts' home and business addresses; email addresses; instant message addresses; company information; home, work, fax, and mobile phone numbers; and social media updates. You can also enter notes about a contact.

By default, Outlook displays contact information using the People view; you can edit contact information and interact with your contacts from the People view. You can also switch to other views such as the Business Card or List view.

Create a New Contact

Create a Contact

1 Click **People** (☺☺) in the Navigation bar.

2 Click **New Contact**.

Outlook opens a Contact window.

3 Fill in the contact's information.

You can press `Tab` to move from field to field.

A You can click **Show** and then click **Details** to fill in additional information about the contact.

4 Click **Save & Close**.

B Outlook saves the information and displays the contact in the People component.

C You can click the **More** button (⤓) to see and switch to available views.

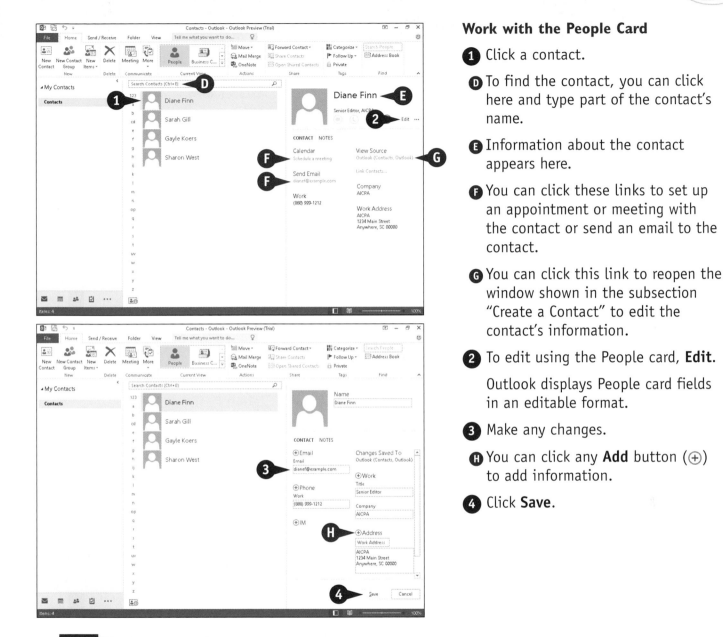

Work with the People Card

1 Click a contact.

D To find the contact, you can click here and type part of the contact's name.

E Information about the contact appears here.

F You can click these links to set up an appointment or meeting with the contact or send an email to the contact.

G You can click this link to reopen the window shown in the subsection "Create a Contact" to edit the contact's information.

2 To edit using the People card, **Edit**.

Outlook displays People card fields in an editable format.

3 Make any changes.

H You can click any **Add** button (⊕) to add information.

4 Click **Save**.

Is there an easy way to set up an appointment or email one of my contacts if I am using Business Card view?

Yes. Right-click the contact and click **Create**. Click **Email** or **Meeting** (**A**). If you click **Email**, Outlook opens a Message window containing the contact's email address in the To field; see Chapter 19 for details on completing the message. If you click **Meeting**, a Meeting window appears, where you can enter appointment details and email a meeting request to the contact.

Create a New Task

You can use Outlook's Tasks component to keep track of things that you need to do; for example, you can create tasks for a daily list of activities or project steps that you need to complete. You can assign a due date to each task, prioritize and categorize tasks, and set a reminder date and time. You can set up a recurring task and even assign tasks to other people.

When you finish a task, you can mark it as complete. Depending on the current view, completed tasks may appear with a strikethrough on the Tasks list or they may not appear at all.

Create a New Task

1 Click **Tasks** (☑) in the Navigation bar to open the Tasks component.

2 Click **New Task**.

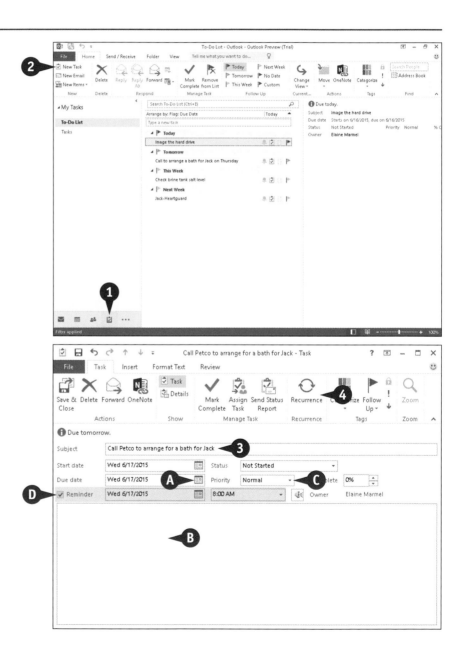

Outlook displays a Task window.

3 Type a subject for the task.

Ⓐ You can click the calendar icon (▦) to enter a due date.

Ⓑ You can type notes or details about the task here.

Ⓒ You can set a priority for the task using the **Priority** ▼.

Ⓓ You can select **Reminder** (☐ changes to ☑) and then set a reminder date and time.

4 If your task occurs regularly, click **Recurrence**; otherwise, skip to Step **7**.

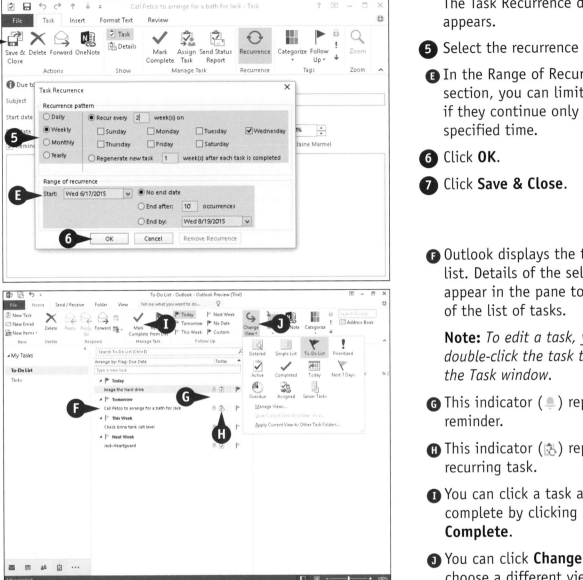

The Task Recurrence dialog box appears.

⑤ Select the recurrence pattern.

Ⓔ In the Range of Recurrence section, you can limit the tasks if they continue only for a specified time.

⑥ Click **OK**.

⑦ Click **Save & Close**.

Ⓕ Outlook displays the task in the list. Details of the selected task appear in the pane to the right of the list of tasks.

Note: *To edit a task, you can double-click the task to reopen the Task window.*

Ⓖ This indicator (🔔) represents a reminder.

Ⓗ This indicator (🔄) represents a recurring task.

Ⓘ You can click a task and mark it complete by clicking **Mark Complete**.

Ⓙ You can click **Change View** and choose a different view of tasks.

What happens if I click Tasks on the left side of the Tasks component?
You see an alternative view of the items in the To-Do List. From the To-Do List view (shown throughout this section), you see only outstanding tasks you have not yet completed. From the Tasks view, you see all your tasks; the ones you have completed (Ⓐ) appear with a strikethrough line and a check mark to indicate they are complete.

🗋	☑	SUBJECT
		Click here to add a new Task
☑	☑	~~Image the hard drive~~ ← Ⓐ
🔄	☐	Call Petco to arrange for a bath for Jack
☑	☐	Check brine tank salt level
☑	☐	Jack-Heartguard

Add a Note

Outlook includes a Notes component, which you can use to create notes for yourself. Much like an electronic version of yellow sticky notes, Outlook's Notes component enables you to quickly and easily jot down your ideas and thoughts. You can attach Outlook Notes to other items in Outlook, as well as drag them from the Outlook window onto the Windows desktop for easy viewing.

Add a Note

1 Click the **More** button (•••) to display a pop-up menu.

2 Click **Notes** to open the Notes component.

Ⓐ Notes appear in Icon view.

3 Click **New Note**.

Ⓑ Outlook displays a yellow note.

4 Type your note text.

5 When you finish, click the note's **Close** button (✖).

Ⓒ Outlook adds the note.

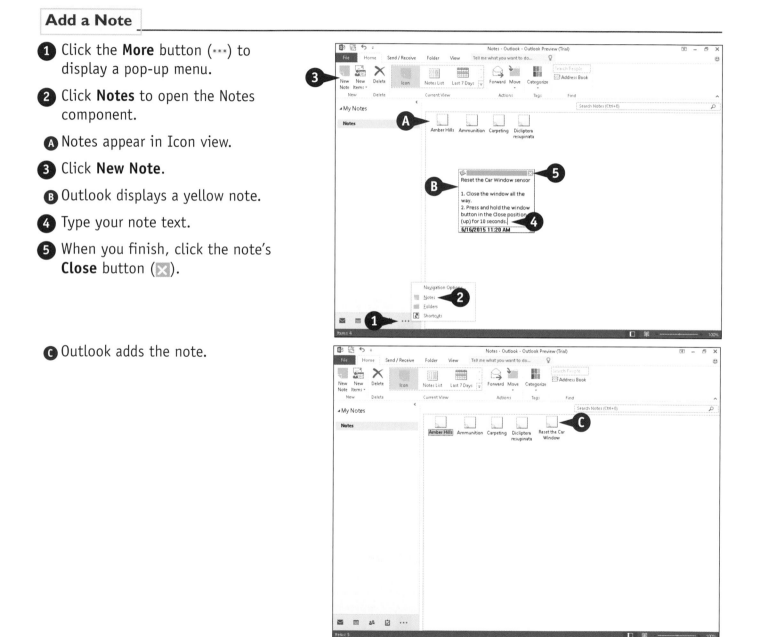

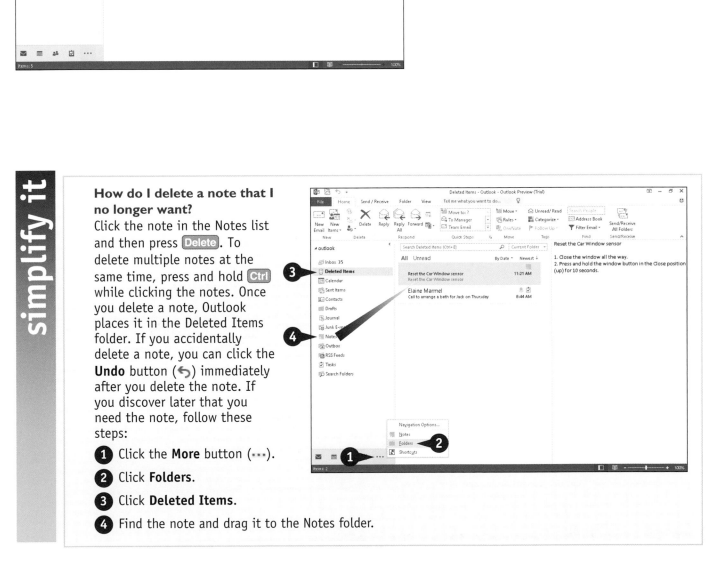

To view the note again or to make changes, you can double-click it.

D To change your view of notes, you can click an option in the Current View group.

This example displays the Notes List view.

simplify it

How do I delete a note that I no longer want?

Click the note in the Notes list and then press `Delete`. To delete multiple notes at the same time, press and hold `Ctrl` while clicking the notes. Once you delete a note, Outlook places it in the Deleted Items folder. If you accidentally delete a note, you can click the **Undo** button (↺) immediately after you delete the note. If you discover later that you need the note, follow these steps:

1 Click the **More** button (•••).

2 Click **Folders**.

3 Click **Deleted Items**.

4 Find the note and drag it to the Notes folder.

Customize the Navigation Bar

You can control the appearance of the Navigation bar, displaying fewer items or more items to suit your needs. For example, suppose that you use the Notes component regularly. You can save mouse clicks if you display the Notes component as part of the Navigation bar.

In addition to determining which components appear on the Navigation bar, you can control the order in which they appear. You can also control the size of the Navigation bar by choosing to display buttons that represent each component instead of displaying the component name.

Customize the Navigation Bar

1. From any Outlook component, click the **More** button (•••).

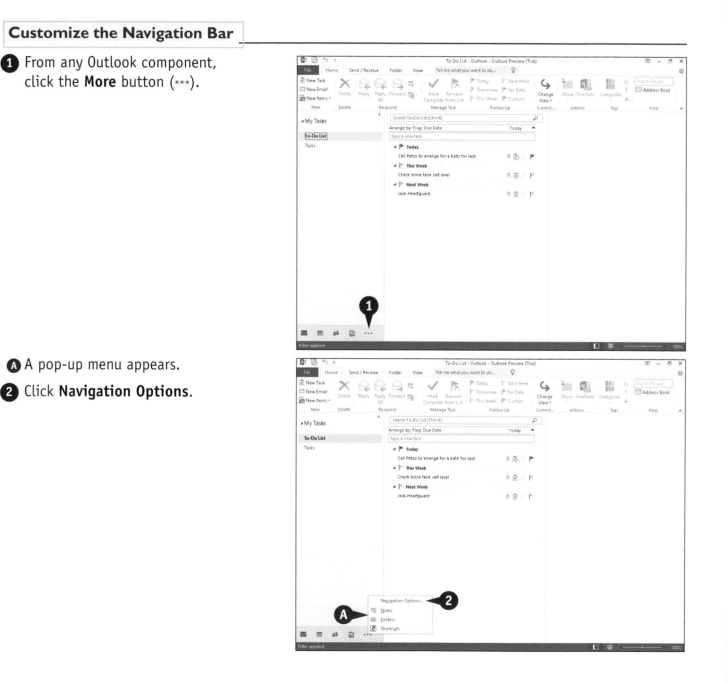

A. A pop-up menu appears.

2. Click **Navigation Options**.

The Navigation Options dialog box appears.

3 Click $\updownarrow$ to specify the number of items you want visible on the Navigation bar.

4 To reorder the Navigation bar entries, click an item and then click **Move Up** or **Move Down**.

B You can click **Reset** if you want to return the Navigation bar to its original state.

5 Click **OK**.

C The Navigation bar appears with your changes.

Note: *You might need to widen the left pane in Outlook to see all the Navigation buttons. Slide the mouse over the pane divider ($\triangleright$ changes to $\leftrightarrow$) and drag the pane divider to the right.*

simplify it

Can I display labels rather than icons in the Navigation bar?
Yes. Complete Steps **1** and **2** to display the Navigation Options dialog box shown earlier in this section. Then, select **Compact Navigation** ($\checkmark$ changes to $\square$). Click **OK**, and labels for each Outlook module replace the buttons on the Navigation bar (**A**).

Mail   Calendar   People   Tasks   Notes   ···   **A**

Filter applied

Peek at Appointments and Tasks

From any Outlook component, you can take a peek at today's appointments and at your task list. You do not need to select the Calendar component or the Tasks component to view appointments or tasks.

If you also unpin the Folder pane, which is pinned by default, you hide the leftmost pane in each

component view and give more real estate to each component. When you hide the Folder pane, you can peek at appointments and tasks, and you also can pin the peeked view so that it remains visible for as long as you need to see it.

Peek at Appointments and Tasks

① To hide the Folder pane, click the **Collapse Folder** button (◄).

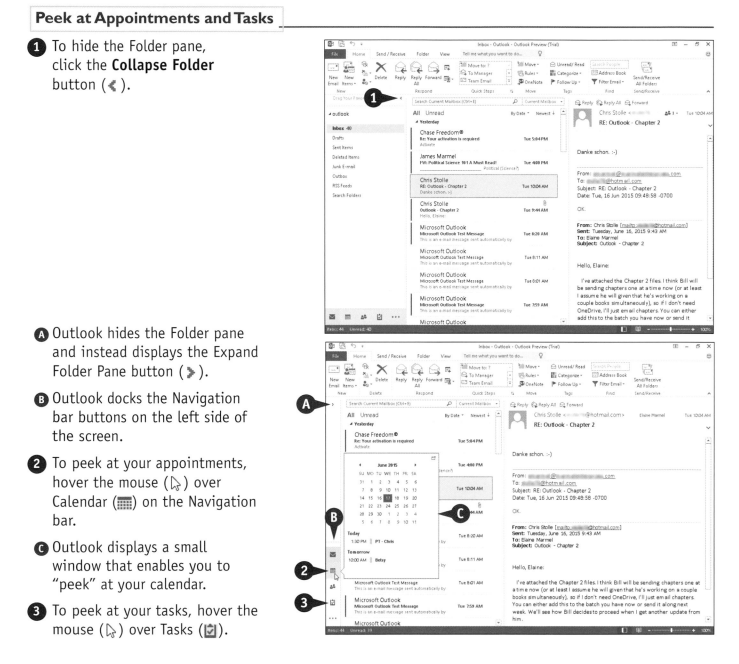

Ⓐ Outlook hides the Folder pane and instead displays the Expand Folder Pane button (❯).

Ⓑ Outlook docks the Navigation bar buttons on the left side of the screen.

② To peek at your appointments, hover the mouse ( ) over Calendar ( ) on the Navigation bar.

Ⓒ Outlook displays a small window that enables you to "peek" at your calendar.

③ To peek at your tasks, hover the mouse ( ) over Tasks ( ).

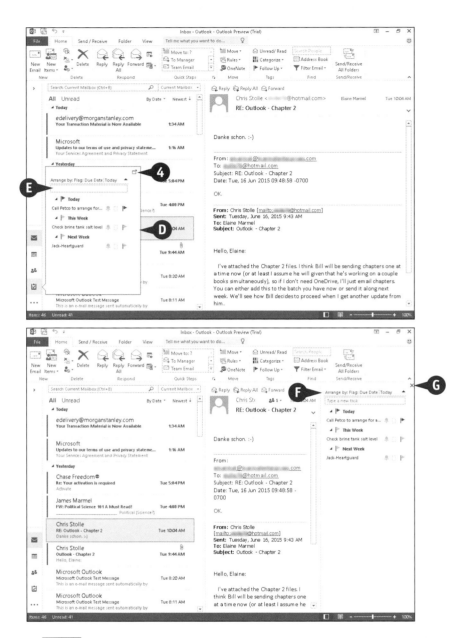

D Outlook displays a list of your tasks.

E You can click here and type a name to add a new task.

Note: *When you press* Enter *to add the task, Outlook adds the task to your list as a task for today. See the section "Create a New Task" for details on editing the task.*

4 To pin a peek view so that it is permanently visible, click the docking button (⬚).

F Outlook pins the tasks or appointments to the right side of the current component's window.

Note: *The pinned peek view appears only in the component you were viewing when you pinned it.*

G You can click the **Close** button (✕) to unpin the peek view.

Can I peek at the calendar or my tasks without collapsing the Folder pane?
Yes, but you cannot pin a peeked view unless you collapse the Folder pane. Just perform all steps in this section except Step **1**.

How do I redisplay the Folder pane?
First, unpin any peek views you pinned. Then, click the **Expand Folder Pane** button (❯). In the upper right corner of the Folder pane that appears, click the pushpin icon (📌) to pin the Folder pane back in place.

Search for Outlook Items

Suppose you need to locate an Outlook item, such as an email message about a project you are working on, an item on your to-do list that you need to review, or the contact record for a co-worker that you need to call. Instead of sifting through your Outlook folders to locate it, you can use Outlook's Search tool to quickly find it. Each component includes a search box; you simply enter a keyword or phrase, and Outlook searches for a match. You can search a single Outlook component or all of Outlook.

Search for Outlook Items

Perform a Basic Search

1 Click the Outlook component you want to search.

> **Note:** This example uses the Tasks component.

2 Click in the search box.

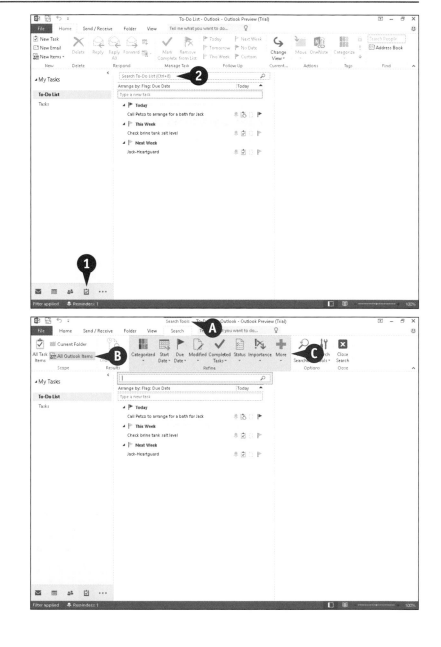

A Outlook displays the Search Tools Search tab, with several search-specific tools.

B You can click **All Outlook Items** to search all Outlook folders rather than just the current component's folder.

C These tools change, depending on the component you selected in Step **1**.

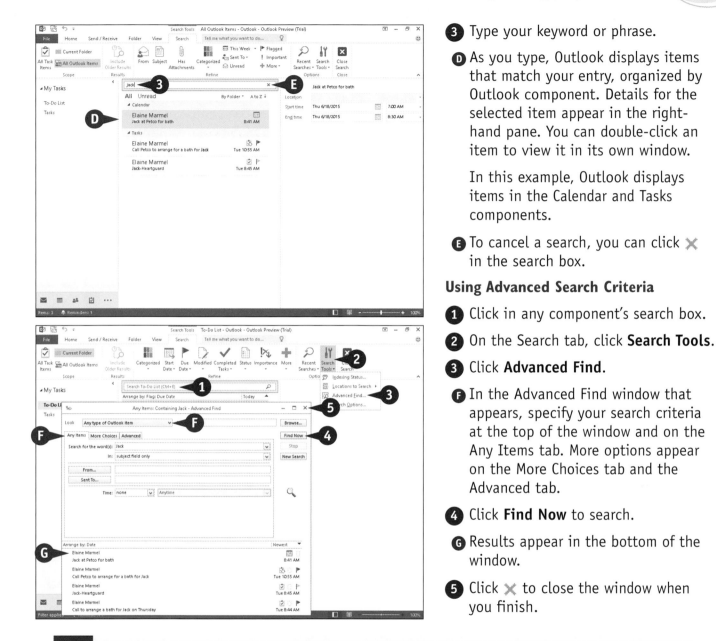

3 Type your keyword or phrase.

D As you type, Outlook displays items that match your entry, organized by Outlook component. Details for the selected item appear in the right-hand pane. You can double-click an item to view it in its own window.

In this example, Outlook displays items in the Calendar and Tasks components.

E To cancel a search, you can click ✕ in the search box.

Using Advanced Search Criteria

1 Click in any component's search box.

2 On the Search tab, click **Search Tools**.

3 Click **Advanced Find**.

F In the Advanced Find window that appears, specify your search criteria at the top of the window and on the Any Items tab. More options appear on the More Choices tab and the Advanced tab.

4 Click **Find Now** to search.

G Results appear in the bottom of the window.

5 Click ✕ to close the window when you finish.

Can I control search options?
Yes. Perform Steps **1** and **2** in the subsection "Using Advanced Search Criteria." Then, click **Search Options** to display the search options available in the Outlook Options dialog box. You can, for example, improve search speed by limiting the number of results Outlook displays, and you can control the color Outlook uses to highlight terms in the list of search results that match your search criteria. Make any necessary changes and click **OK**.

Work with the To-Do Bar

Outlook's To-Do Bar can display three elements: a small monthly calendar and appointments for today or the day you select, your favorite contacts, or your tasks. The To-Do Bar appears along the right side of the Outlook window and closely resembles a docked peek view (see the section "Peek at Appointments and Tasks," earlier in this chapter).

To-Do Bar elements can appear in any Outlook component. Although displaying To-Do Bar elements in one Outlook component does not display them in any other Outlook component, you can display To-Do Bar elements individually in each Outlook component so that they appear in all Outlook components.

Work with the To-Do Bar

1 In the Navigation bar, click the Outlook component in which you want to display To-Do Bar elements.

2 Click the **View** tab.

3 Click **To-Do Bar**.

4 Click the To-Do Bar element you want to display.

In this example, Outlook displays the calendar.

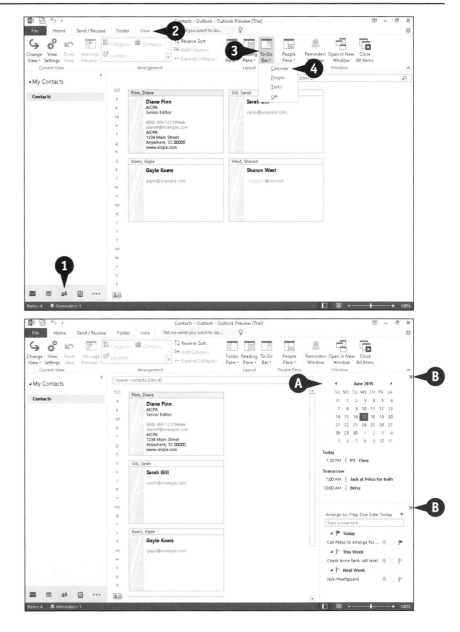

Ⓐ The To-Do Bar appears along the right side of the Outlook window, displaying the element you selected in Step **4**.

5 Repeat Steps **3** and **4** to display another To-Do Bar element.

6 Repeat Steps **1** to **5** to display To-Do Bar elements in another Outlook component.

Ⓑ To hide an individual To-Do Bar element, you can click ✕ for the element.

Note: *To hide the entire To-Do Bar in a particular Outlook component, repeat Steps **2** and **3** and then click **Off**.*

Link
Contacts

You can link two contacts so that, in the People view of your contacts, you can see all information for the linked contacts on one card.

For example, suppose that you set up two cards for one contact because you want to be able to easily email that person at two different email addresses. If you link the two cards, you can still email to whichever address you want, but you have the added benefit of viewing all the person's contact information on one card in the People view.

Link Contacts

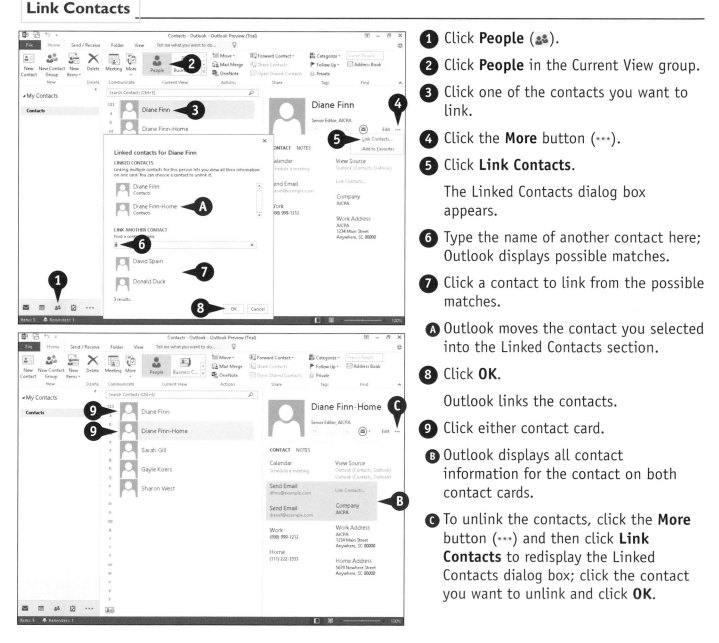

1 Click **People** (👥).

2 Click **People** in the Current View group.

3 Click one of the contacts you want to link.

4 Click the **More** button (•••).

5 Click **Link Contacts**.

The Linked Contacts dialog box appears.

6 Type the name of another contact here; Outlook displays possible matches.

7 Click a contact to link from the possible matches.

Ⓐ Outlook moves the contact you selected into the Linked Contacts section.

8 Click **OK**.

Outlook links the contacts.

9 Click either contact card.

Ⓑ Outlook displays all contact information for the contact on both contact cards.

Ⓒ To unlink the contacts, click the **More** button (•••) and then click **Link Contacts** to redisplay the Linked Contacts dialog box; click the contact you want to unlink and click **OK**.

Compose and Send a Message

You can use Outlook to compose and send email messages. When you compose a message in Outlook, you designate the email address of the message recipient (or recipients) and type your message text. You can also give the message a subject title to identify the content of the message for recipients.

You can compose a message offline, but you must be working online to send it. If you do not have time to finish composing your message during your current work session, you can save the message as a draft and come back at a later time to finish it.

Compose and Send a Message

1 In the Navigation bar, click **Mail** (✉) to display the Mail component.

2 Click the **Home** tab.

3 Click **New Email**.

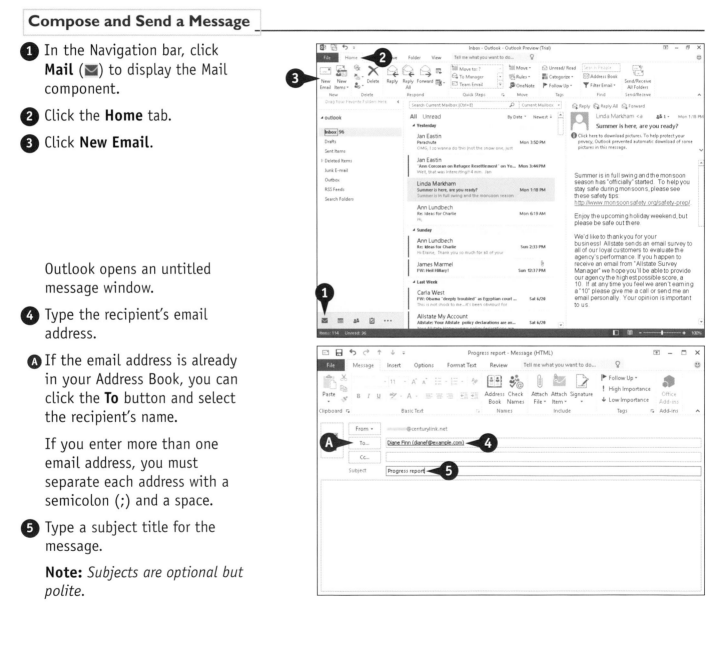

Outlook opens an untitled message window.

4 Type the recipient's email address.

Ⓐ If the email address is already in your Address Book, you can click the **To** button and select the recipient's name.

If you enter more than one email address, you must separate each address with a semicolon (;) and a space.

5 Type a subject title for the message.

Note: *Subjects are optional but polite.*

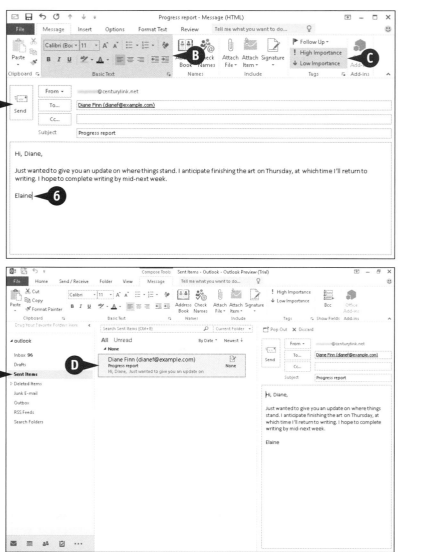

6 Type the message text.

B You can use the formatting buttons to change the appearance of your message text.

C To set a priority level for the message, you can click **High Importance** or **Low Importance**.

Note: *By default, the message priority level is Normal.*

7 Click **Send**.

Outlook places the message in your Outbox.

Note: *You might need to press* F9 *or click the* **Send/Receive** *tab and click* **Send All** *or* **Send/Receive All Folders** *to send the message.*

8 Click the **Sent Items** folder.

D The message you sent appears in the list; Outlook stores a copy of all messages you send in the Sent Items folder.

simplify it

How do I save a message as a draft?
Click the message window's ✖ and click **Yes** when prompted to save the message. Outlook saves the message in the Drafts folder. When you are ready to continue composing your message, click the **Drafts** folder and double-click the saved message to open it.

How do I send a copy of my message to someone?
To copy or blind copy the message to another recipient, either type the recipient's email address directly in the field or click the **Cc** or **Bcc** button to select the address from your contacts.

Send a File Attachment

You can send files stored on your computer to other email recipients. For example, you might send an Excel worksheet or Word document to a work colleague, or send a digital photo of your child's birthday to a relative. Assuming that the recipient's computer has the necessary software installed, that person can open and view the file on his or her own system.

Note that some email systems are not set up to handle large file attachments. If you are sending a large attachment, check with the recipient to see if his or her system can handle it.

Send a File Attachment

① Create a new email message as described in the previous section, "Compose and Send a Message."

② Click the **Message** tab.

③ Click **Attach File**.

The Recent Items list appears, showing attachments you have sent recently.

④ Click the file you want to send.

Ⓐ If the file does not appear in the Recent Items list, click **Browse This PC**, navigate to the folder containing the file, and select it.

Ⓑ Outlook adds the file attachment to the message, displaying the filename and file size.

⑤ Click **Send**.

Outlook sends the email message and attachment.

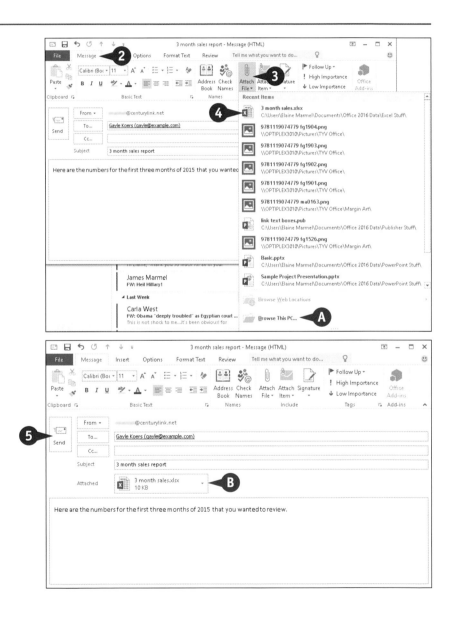

Read an Incoming Message

You can use Outlook's Mail feature to retrieve new email messages that others have sent you and view them on-screen. You can view a message in a separate message window or in the Reading pane, as described in this section. By default, the Reading pane appears beside the list of messages, but you can place it below the message list.

Note that you must be connected to the Internet to receive email messages.

Read an Incoming Message

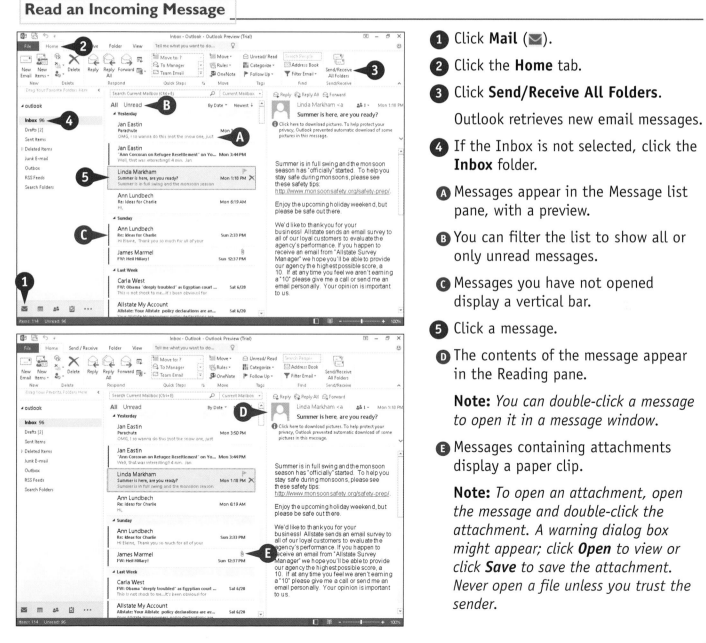

1. Click **Mail** (✉).

2. Click the **Home** tab.

3. Click **Send/Receive All Folders**.

    Outlook retrieves new email messages.

4. If the Inbox is not selected, click the **Inbox** folder.

A. Messages appear in the Message list pane, with a preview.

B. You can filter the list to show all or only unread messages.

C. Messages you have not opened display a vertical bar.

5. Click a message.

D. The contents of the message appear in the Reading pane.

    Note: *You can double-click a message to open it in a message window.*

E. Messages containing attachments display a paper clip.

    Note: *To open an attachment, open the message and double-click the attachment. A warning dialog box might appear; click **Open** to view or click **Save** to save the attachment. Never open a file unless you trust the sender.*

Reply To or Forward a Message

You can reply to an email message by sending a return message to the original sender. For example, if you receive an email message containing a question, you can reply to that email with your answer. When you reply to an email, the original sender's name is added to the To field in the message.

You can also forward the message to another recipient. For example, you might forward a message that you receive from one co-worker to another co-worker who will find its contents useful. Note that you must be connected to the Internet in order to send replies or forward email messages.

Reply To or Forward a Message

Reply To a Message

1. Click **Mail** (✉).

2. In the Message list pane, click the message to which you want to reply.

3. In the Reading pane, click **Reply** to reply to the original sender.

Ⓐ To reply to the sender as well as to everyone else who received the original message, you can click **Reply All**.

Ⓑ The original sender's address appears in the To field.

Ⓒ You can click **Pop Out** to open your reply in its own message window.

4. Type your reply.

Ⓓ If you change your mind and do not want to reply to the message, you can click **Discard**.

5. Click **Send**.

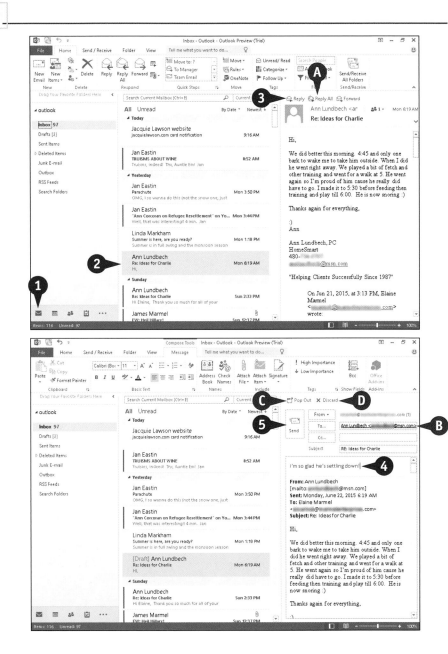

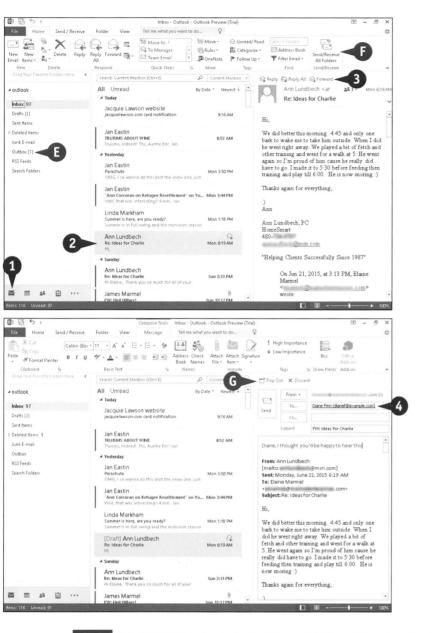

E Outlook places the email message in the Outbox.

F Outlook sends the message at its next automatically scheduled send/receive action; to send the message, click **Send/Receive All Folders** on the Home tab.

Forward a Message

1 Click **Mail** (✉).

2 In the Message list pane, click the message you want to forward.

3 In the Reading pane, click **Forward**.

4 Type the recipient's email address in the **To** field.

G You can click **Pop Out** to open your message in its own window.

5 Perform Steps **4** and **5** in the previous subsection, "Reply To a Message."

simplify it

How do I look up an email address when forwarding a message?
Perform Steps **1** to **3** in the subsection "Forward a Message." Click the **To** button to display a list of your contacts. Type a few letters to identify the contact. Outlook highlights the first contact that matches what you typed. If necessary, use the arrow keys to highlight the correct contact. Press Enter to display the contact in the To field. Click **OK** and Outlook places the contact name in the To field of your message.

Add a Sender to Your Outlook Contacts

Suppose you receive an email message from someone with whom you expect to correspond regularly, but you do not have a record for that individual in Outlook contacts. You can easily add the contact information of the sender of any message you receive to your Outlook contacts, directly from the message.

If, at a later time, you want to send a new message to that person, you can click the **To** button and in the Message window choose his or her name from the Select Names: Contacts dialog box.

Add a Sender to Your Outlook Contacts

1 Click **Mail** (✉).

2 In the Message list pane, click the message from the sender you want to add as a contact.

3 In the Reading pane, right-click the sender's name.

4 Click **Add to Outlook Contacts**.

A A window opens with the sender's email address already filled in.

5 Type a name for the contact.

B You can click any **Add** button (⊕) to add additional information.

6 Click **Save**.

Outlook saves the contact information and displays a page you can use to schedule a meeting, send an email, link contacts, and more. You can click ✕ to close the window.

Delete a Message

As you receive email messages, you can eliminate clutter and keep things manageable if you delete messages you no longer need from your Inbox and other Outlook folders.

Note that when you delete a message from your Inbox or any other Outlook folder, Outlook does not remove it from your system. Rather, it moves it to the Deleted Items folder. To permanently remove deleted messages from your system, thereby maximizing your computer's storage capacity, you should empty the Deleted Items folder on a regular basis.

Delete a Message

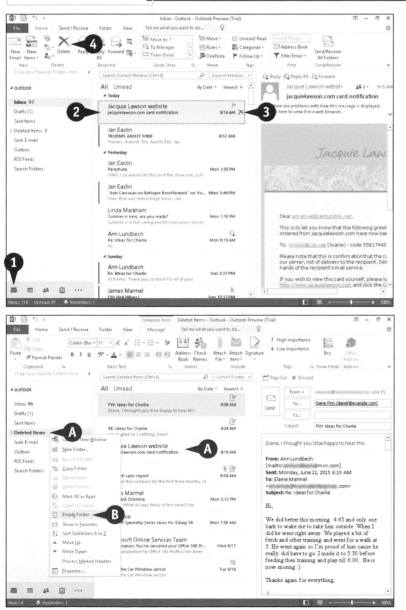

1 Click **Mail** (✉).

2 In the Message list pane, click the message you want to delete.

3 Make sure the mouse (🔓) remains over the message you clicked in Step **2**.

The Delete button (✕) appears.

4 Press Delete, or click the **Delete** button (✕) in the Message list pane, or click **Delete** on the Home tab.

Outlook deletes the message from the Inbox and the Message list pane and adds it to the Deleted Items folder.

A You can click the **Deleted Items** folder to view the message that you deleted.

B To empty the Deleted Items folder, right-click it and click **Empty Folder**.

Work with Conversations

You can view your email messages as conversations in Outlook. In Conversation view, Outlook groups related messages that are part of the same *thread* — the electronic term for a conversation — in the Message list pane.

Using Conversation view, you might find the Message list pane easier to navigate because all related messages, including messages that you have sent as replies or forwarded to others, appear under a single heading — typically the subject of the message. By default, Outlook does not display all messages in Conversation view, but you can change this behavior.

Work with Conversations

View a Conversation

1. Click **Mail** (✉).

2. Click the **View** tab.

3. Click **Show as Conversations** (☐ changes to ☑).

4. In the Message list pane, click a conversation entry.

   Note: *You can identify a conversation because ▷ appears on the left side of the entry.*

A The number of unread messages in the conversation appears here.

5. Click ▷ to expand the conversation.

B Outlook expands the conversation, displaying all the related messages (▷ changes to ◢).

C Outlook displays the conversation using the subject as a heading.

6. Click ◢ to close the conversation (◢ changes to ▷).

   Outlook closes the conversation, displaying a single entry for the conversation as it appeared before you opened the conversation.

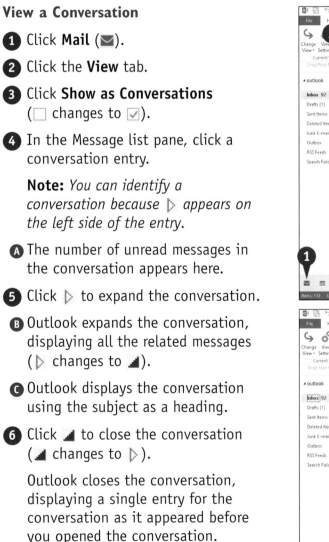

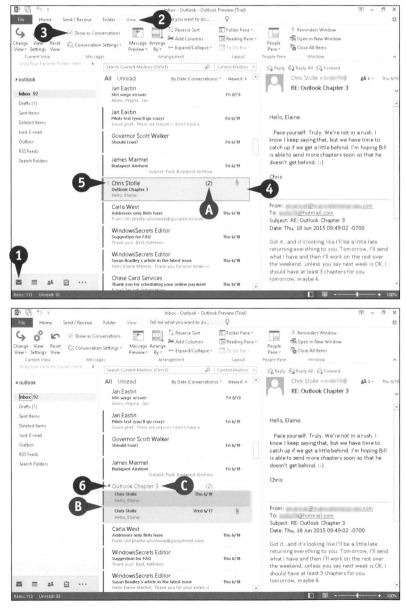

Clean Up a Conversation

1 Perform Steps **1** to **3** in the previous subsection, "View a Conversation."

2 Click a message in the conversation you want to clean up and note the number of messages it contains; this example contains six messages.

3 Click the **Home** tab.

4 Click the **Clean Up** button (🗑-) in the Delete group.

5 Click **Clean Up Conversation**.

The Clean Up Conversation dialog box opens.

6 Click **Clean Up**.

Outlook displays a message explaining that the action will apply to all items in the selected conversation; click **OK**.

Ⓓ Outlook removes redundant messages from the conversation, and the number of messages in the conversation changes.

Ⓔ Outlook places the removed messages in the Deleted Items folder.

Note: *To permanently remove the messages, right-click the **Deleted Items** folder and click **Empty Folder**.*

Is there a way to ignore conversations where I am included but that are not relevant to me?
Yes. Perform Steps **1** to **4** in the subsection "View a Conversation." Then, click the **Home** tab and click the **Ignore** button (🗑). In the message box that appears, click **OK**. Outlook removes the conversation and places it in the Deleted Items folder. If you realize you have ignored a conversation in error, you can stop ignoring it. Click the **Deleted Items** folder, repeat Steps **1** to **4** in the subsection "Clean Up a Conversation," and then, on the **Home** tab, click the **Ignore** button (🗑) and click **Stop Ignoring Conversation** in the dialog box that appears.

Screen Junk Email

Junk email, also called *spam*, is overly abundant on the Internet and often finds its way into your Inbox. You can safeguard against wasting time viewing unsolicited messages by setting up Outlook's Junk Email feature. This feature enables you to make sure that Outlook bypasses email from specific web domains and instead deposits those messages into the Outlook Junk E-mail folder.

Note that Outlook might erroneously place email that is *not* spam in the Junk E-mail folder. For this reason, you should periodically scan the contents of this folder to ensure that it does not contain any messages you want to read.

Screen Junk Email

View Junk Email Options

1 Click **Mail** (✉).

2 Click the **Home** tab.

3 Click the **Junk** button (⊗ ▾).

4 Click **Junk E-mail Options**.

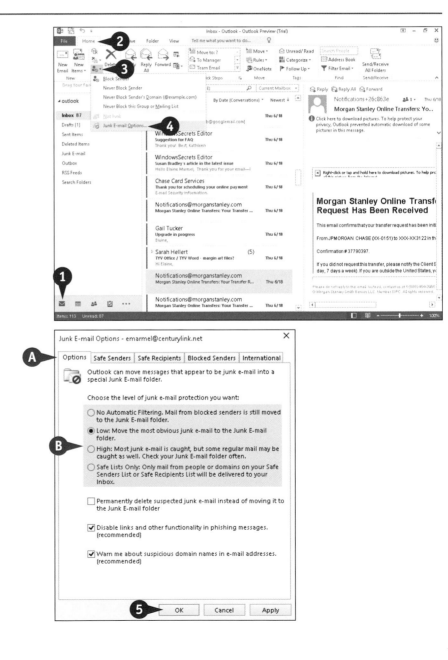

The Junk E-mail Options dialog box appears.

Ⓐ You can use the various tabs to view and change junk email settings, blocked domains, and safe senders.

Ⓑ You can click one of these options to control the level of junk email filtering that Outlook applies.

5 Click **OK**.

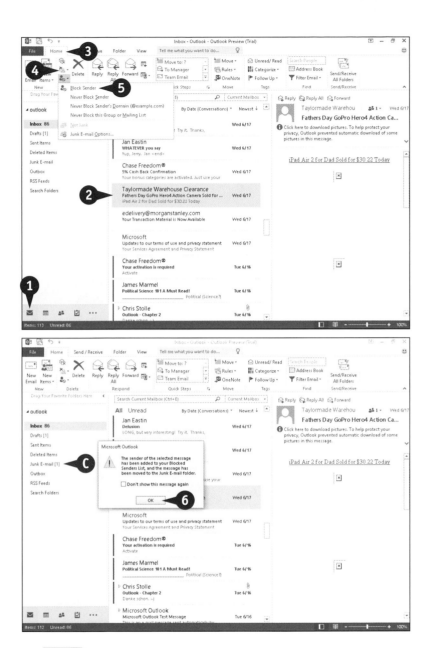

Designate a Message as Junk

1 Click **Mail** (✉).

2 Click the message in the Message list pane.

3 Click the **Home** tab.

4 Click the **Junk** button (✍-).

5 Click **Block Sender**.

A dialog box appears.

6 Click **OK**.

© Outlook adds the sender's email address to the list of filtered addresses and moves the message to the Junk E-mail folder.

simplify it

How can I restore a junk email to my safe list?
Right-click the message in the Junk E-mail folder and, from the menu that appears, point at **Junk** and click **Not Junk**. Outlook alerts you that it will move the message back to its original location and gives you the option of removing the sender from the filter list; click **OK**.

Does Outlook empty the Junk E-mail folder?
No. To empty the folder, right-click it and click the **Empty Folder** button. Outlook permanently removes all items in the Junk E-mail folder.

PART VII

Publisher

You can use Publisher to design and produce a variety of publications. Publisher installs with a large selection of predesigned publications that you can use as templates to build your own desktop publishing projects; additional templates are available from Office.com. In this part, you learn how to build and fine-tune publications, tapping into Publisher's formatting features to make each document suit your own design and needs. With Publisher features, you can, for example, add text boxes to publications and change font, size, color, and alignment. You also can and pictures and control the way Publisher wraps text around pictures.

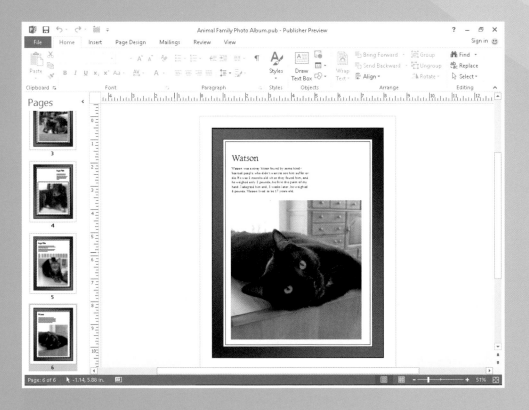

Create a Publication

You can use Publisher to create all kinds of publications, such as brochures, flyers, newsletters, and letterhead stationery. Publisher installs with a wide variety of publication design templates, including templates that control the layout and formatting of the publication. In addition, you can search for templates on the Internet.

If none of Publisher's predesigned publication templates suits your needs, you can create a blank publication, populate it with your own text boxes, and design your own layout. For example, you might want to create your own brochure or invitation and customize it.

Create a Publication

1 Open Publisher.

The Publisher Start screen appears.

Note: *If Publisher is already open, click the **File** tab and then click **New**.*

2 Click these arrows (and ▾) to scroll through the available publication templates.

3 Click a publication design to preview it.

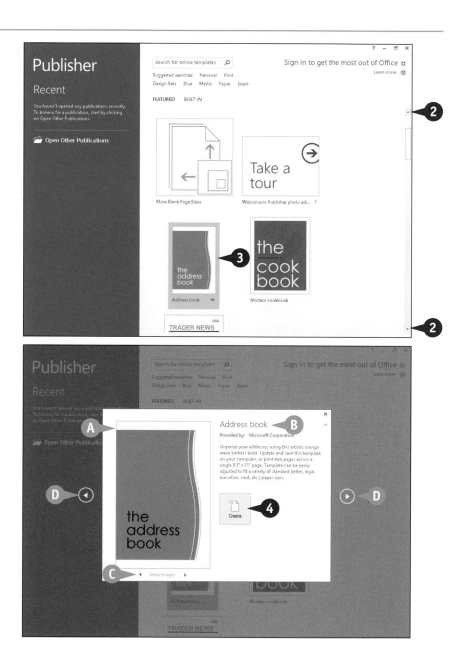

Ⓐ Publisher displays a preview of the selected design template.

Ⓑ A description of the template appears here.

Ⓒ You can click these arrows (◂ and ▸) to view more images of the template.

Ⓓ You can click these arrows (◀ and ▶) to preview the next or previous template design.

4 Click **Create**.

Publisher creates the publication.

 Thumbnail images of each page of the publication appear here.

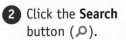

How can I search for additional templates?
Follow these steps:

1 In the search box at the top of the Publisher Start screen or the New screen, type a keyword that describes the type of publication template you want to find.

Note: *Click **File** and then click **New** to display the New screen.*

2 Click the **Search** button ($\mathcal{P}$).

A You can now filter the search results by clicking a category. Each category you click reduces the search results further.

B If nothing appeals to you, click **Home** and then click a blank template.

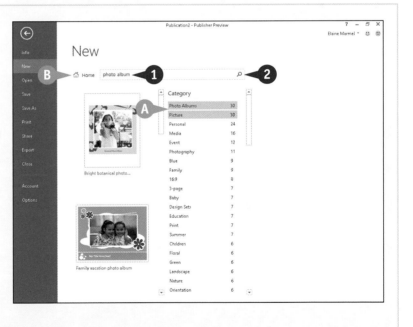

Zoom
In and Out

You can use Publisher's Zoom feature to control the on-screen magnification of your publication. By default, Publisher displays your document in a zoomed-out view so that you can see all the elements on a page. When you begin adding text and formatting, you can zoom in to better see what you are doing.

There are a few ways to zoom in and out of your publication. One is to use the Zoom settings on the View tab. Another is to use the Zoom buttons. A third is to use your keyboard. You learn how to use all three of these techniques in this section.

Zoom In and Out

Specify a Magnification

1 Click a page in the publication.

2 Click the **View** tab.

3 Click the **Zoom** ▼.

4 Click a percentage.

A You can also type a value in the **Zoom** field.

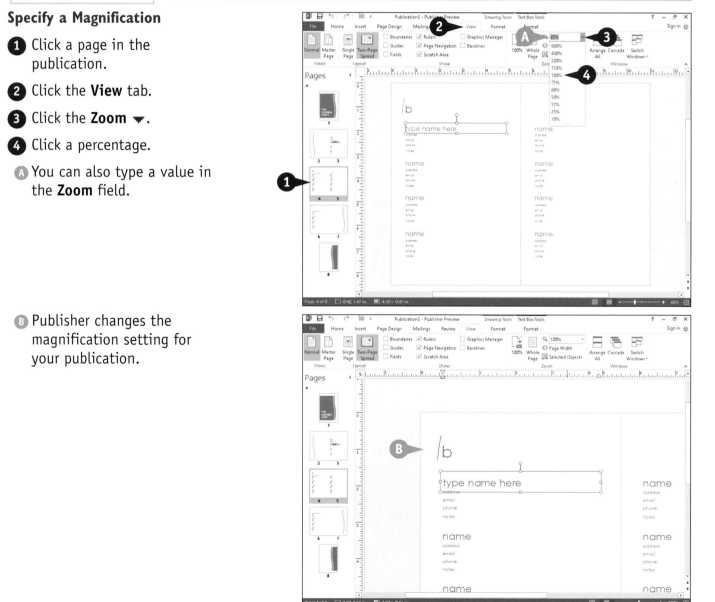

B Publisher changes the magnification setting for your publication.

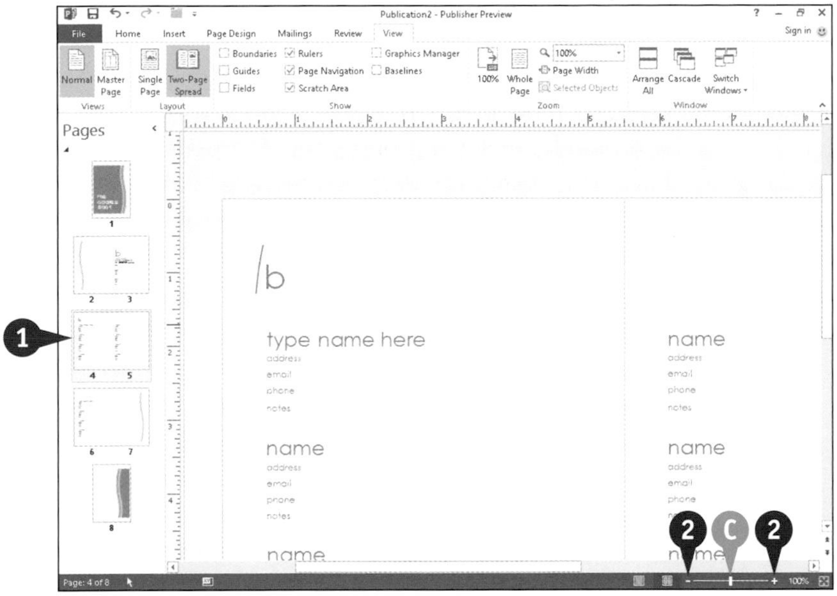

Using Zoom Buttons

❶ Click a page in a publication.

❷ Click a Zoom button to magnify the view.

You can click the Zoom buttons multiple times to change the level of magnification.

Ⓒ You can also click and drag the slider to change the level of magnification.

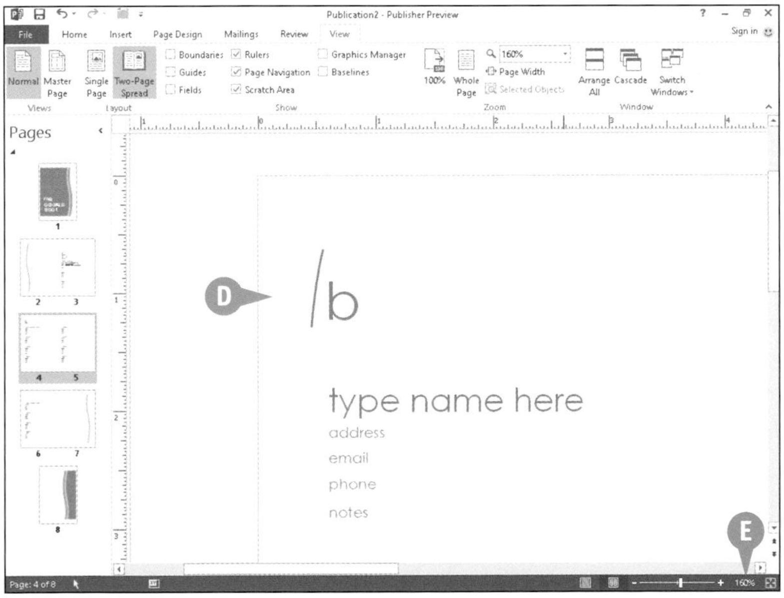

Ⓓ Publisher changes the magnification setting for your publication.

Ⓔ You can see the current magnification level here.

simplify it

Are there other ways to zoom my publication?

Yes, there are several shortcuts you can use to quickly zoom a publication. For example, you can press F9 on the keyboard to quickly zoom in and out of a publication. To quickly zoom to 100 percent, you can click the **View** tab and, in the Zoom group, click the **100%** button. To quickly view the whole page, click the **Whole Page** button in the same Zoom group. You can click the **Page Width** button in the Zoom group to match the width of the page to the width of the Publisher window.

Add
Text

When you create a new publication based on a design, Publisher inserts a layout for the text and displays placeholder text in the text boxes, also called *objects* or *frames*. The placeholder text gives you an idea of the text formatting that the design applies and what sort of text you might place in the text box.

As you build your publication, you replace the placeholder text with your own text. After you add your text, you can apply formatting to it, as well as move and resize it. For help formatting, moving, and resizing text in Publisher, see Chapter 21.

Add Text

1 Click the text object that you want to edit.

You may need to zoom in first to see the text object; see the previous section, "Zoom In and Out," for details.

A Publisher surrounds the selected object with selection handles (○ and □).

2 Select the placeholder text within the object.

Note: *The Mini Toolbar might appear. You can ignore it for this section.*

3 Type your own text.

Publisher replaces any placeholder text with the new text that you type.

Note: *To apply formatting to text and to move and resize text box objects, see Chapter 21.*

4 Click anywhere outside the text object to deselect the text box.

To edit the text at any time, you can click the text box and make your changes.

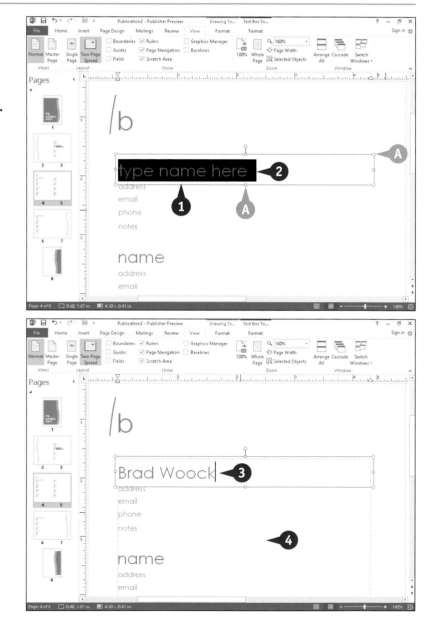

Add a New Text Box

CHAPTER 20

You can add new text boxes to a publication and type your own text. For example, you might need to add a new text box to an empty area in your layout to include additional information, or you might need to add new text boxes to a blank publication.

When you add a text box to a publication, Publisher does not supply any placeholder text. After you enter text, you can format it or move and resize it, as described in Chapter 21.

Add a New Text Box

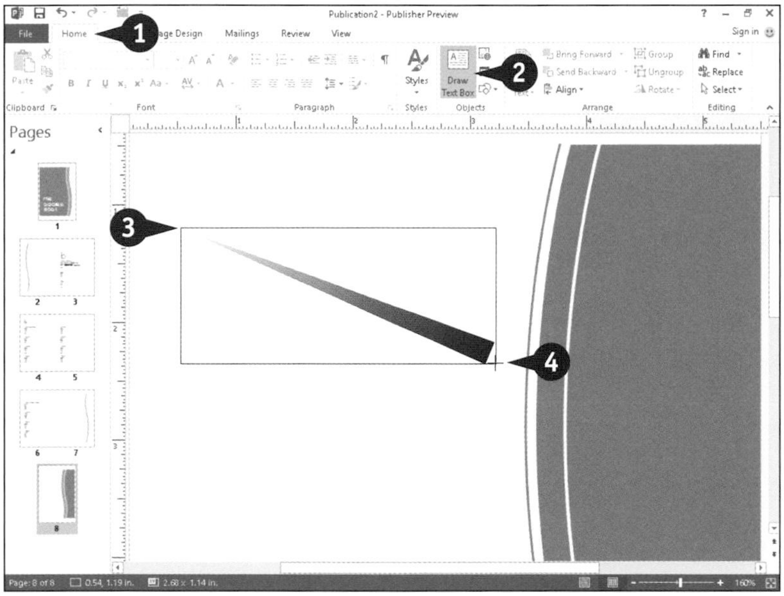

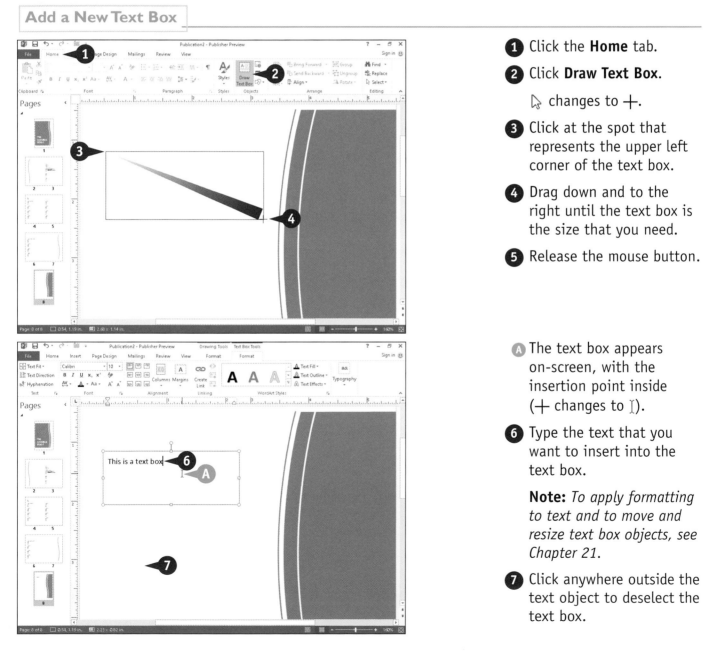

1. Click the **Home** tab.
2. Click **Draw Text Box**.

   changes to +.

3. Click at the spot that represents the upper left corner of the text box.
4. Drag down and to the right until the text box is the size that you need.
5. Release the mouse button.

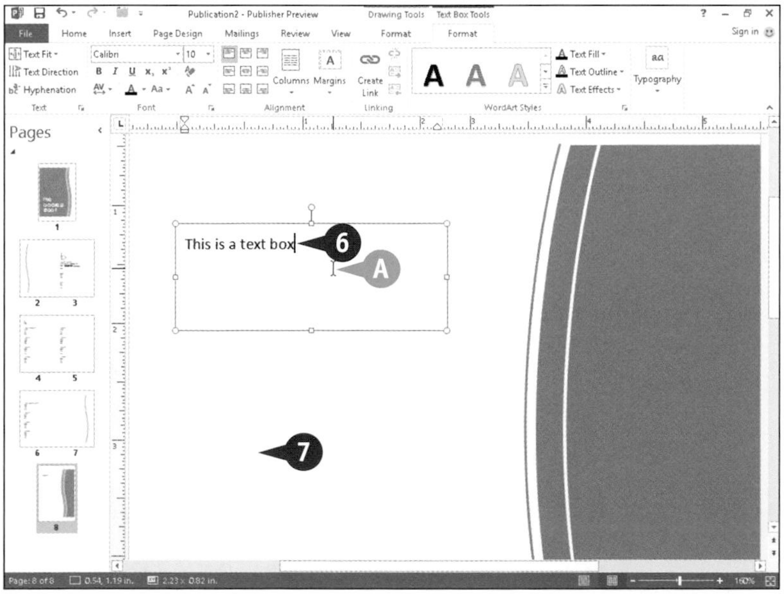

A The text box appears on-screen, with the insertion point inside (+ changes to I).

6. Type the text that you want to insert into the text box.

   Note: *To apply formatting to text and to move and resize text box objects, see Chapter 21.*

7. Click anywhere outside the text object to deselect the text box.

Swap Pictures

You can add pictures to your publication — pictures stored on your hard drive or pictures you download from the Internet — as described in Chapter 3. But you might not know what photo you want at a particular spot in your publication.

Publisher's Swap Pictures feature enables you to insert several pictures simultaneously into the *scratch*

area, a space outside the publication page. Then, you can swap a picture in your publication for a picture in the scratch area. You can continue substituting different pictures until you find the right one for your publication.

Swap Pictures

Note: *This section assumes that you already have inserted one picture, as described in Chapter 3.*

1 Click the **Insert** tab.

2 Click **Pictures**.

The Insert Picture dialog box appears.

3 Navigate to and select the pictures you want to consider.

You can select multiple pictures by holding Ctrl as you click each one.

4 Click **Insert**.

Ⓐ The pictures appear in the scratch area outside your publication page.

Note: *Publisher surrounds each picture with selection handles (○ and □) to indicate they are all selected.*

5 Click anywhere in the scratch area outside the pictures so that none is selected.

6 Click a picture you want to place on the publication page.

Ⓑ A button containing an image of a mountain (⛰) appears in the center of the selected picture.

7 Drag to place the picture from the scratch area on top of the image that is already on the publication page.

C The picture disappears from the scratch area as you drag it to the publication page.

8 Release the mouse button when a pink outline appears.

D Publisher swaps the original picture for the new one.

simplify it

To swap pictures, do they have to be in the scratch area?
No. You can swap two pictures on a publication page. Just follow the steps in this section, dragging on one picture on top of the other picture. The two pictures exchange places on the page. The scratch area is useful when you want to choose between multiple pictures for a page or when you want to add pictures to several pages. The pictures can temporarily reside in the scratch area while you make your decisions. When you no longer need a picture in the scratch area, click it to select it and then press Delete.

Save a Publication for Photo Center Printing

Publisher enables you to save each page of a publication as an image that you can print as a photo using any photo printing method. Publisher saves each page of the publication as a JPEG or TIFF image — using the best possible resolution for photo printing — in a folder on your hard drive, and Publisher names the folder using the name of your publication.

You can print photos from your own printer, take a CD or DVD of photos to a photo printing location like Costco or Walgreens, or upload photos to commercial websites that will prepare printouts of your images.

Save a Publication for Photo Center Printing

① Open the publication containing the pictures you want to save for photo center printing.

Note: *Publisher saves each page of the publication as a separate image.*

② Click the **File** tab.

Backstage view appears.

③ Click **Export**.

④ Click **Save for Photo Printing**.

⑤ Click ▼ and choose whether you want to create JPEG images or TIFF images.

⑥ Click **Save Image Set**.

346

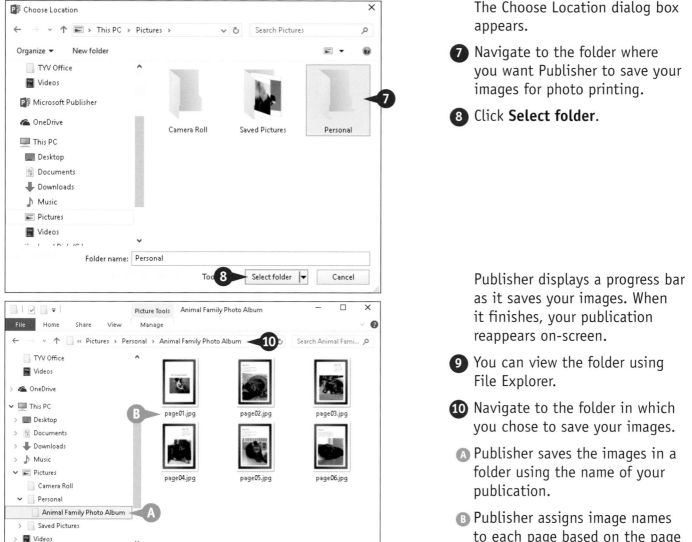

The Choose Location dialog box appears.

7 Navigate to the folder where you want Publisher to save your images for photo printing.

8 Click **Select folder**.

Publisher displays a progress bar as it saves your images. When it finishes, your publication reappears on-screen.

9 You can view the folder using File Explorer.

10 Navigate to the folder in which you chose to save your images.

Ⓐ Publisher saves the images in a folder using the name of your publication.

Ⓑ Publisher assigns image names to each page based on the page number in the publication.

simplify it

Can I change the names that Publisher assigns to each image?
Yes. You can change them in File Explorer after Publisher creates them, or you can change them in Publisher before creating them by performing the steps that follow: In the Pages pane on the left side of the Publisher window, right-click a page. From the menu that appears, click **Rename**. In the Rename Page dialog box, type the name you want to use for the photo image (Ⓐ) and click **OK**. Repeat these steps for each page in the publication. When you create photos for printing, Publisher names the photos using the page names you provided.

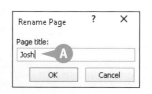

Change the Font, Size, and Color

You can control the font, size, and color of the text in your publication. By default, when you assign a publication design, Publisher uses a predefined set of formatting for the text, including a specific font, size, and color. You may need to change the font or increase the size to suit your publication's needs.

For example, you might change the font, size, and color of the publication's title text to emphasize it. In addition, you can use Publisher's basic formatting commands — Bold, Italic, Underline, Subscript, and Superscript — to quickly add formatting to your text.

Change the Font, Size, and Color

Change the Font

1. Select the text that you want to format.

2. Click the **Home** tab.

3. Click the **Font** ▼.

4. Click a font.

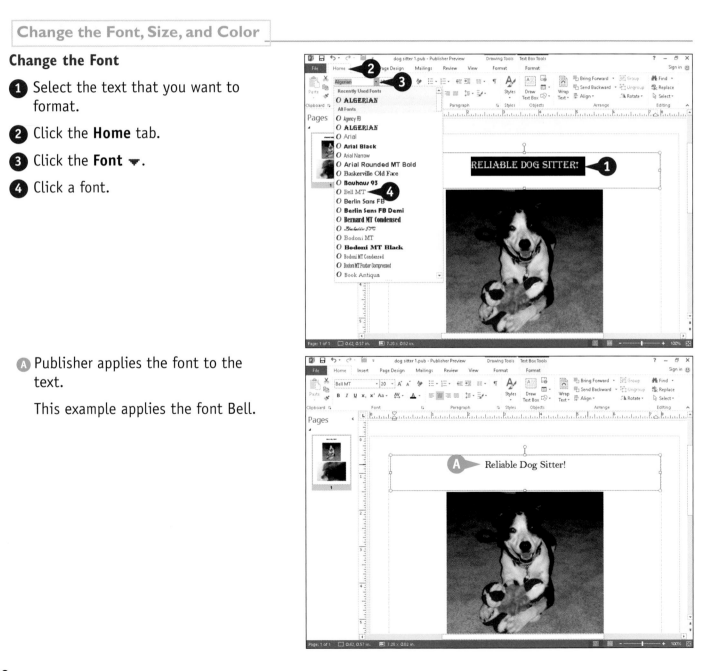

Ⓐ Publisher applies the font to the text.

This example applies the font Bell.

Change the Font Size

1 Select the text that you want to format.

2 Click the **Home** tab.

3 Click the **Font Size** ▼.

4 Click a size.

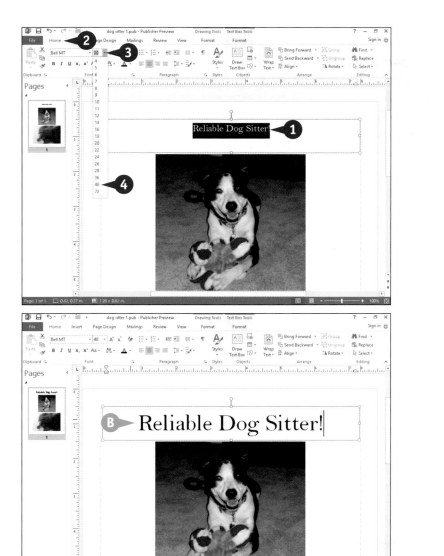

Ⓑ Publisher applies the font size to the text.

This example applies a 48-point font size.

Note: *You can also change the font size by clicking the **Grow Font** and **Shrink Font** buttons (A˄ and A˅) on the Home tab. Publisher increases or decreases the font size with each click of the button.*

simplify it

How do I apply formatting to my text?
Select the text you want to format, click the **Home** tab, and click the **Bold** (**B**), **Italic** (*I*), **Underline** (**U**), **Subscript** (**x₂**), or **Superscript** (**x²**) buttons.

What is the toolbar that appears when I select text?
When you select text, the Mini Toolbar appears, giving you quick access to common formatting commands. You can also right-click selected text to display the toolbar. If you want to use any of the tools on the toolbar, simply click the desired tool; otherwise, continue working, and the toolbar disappears.

 continued

Change the Font, Size, and Color *(continued)*

Changing the text color can go a long way toward emphasizing it in your publication. For example, if you are creating an invitation, you might make the description of the event a different color to stand out from the other details. Likewise, if you are creating a newsletter, you might make the title of the newsletter a different color from the information contained in the newsletter or even color-code certain data in the newsletter. Obviously, when selecting text colors, you should avoid choosing colors that make your text difficult to read.

Change the Font, Size, and Color *(continued)*

Change the Color

1 Select the text that you want to format.

2 Click the **Home** tab on the Ribbon.

3 Click ▼ next to the **Font Color** button (**A** ▼).

Ⓐ In the color palette that appears, you can click a color to apply to the selected text and skip the rest of these steps.

4 Click **More Colors**.

The Colors dialog box opens.

5 Click the **Custom** tab.

6 Click a color in the Colors field.

7 Click a shade to refine your selection.

8 Click **OK**.

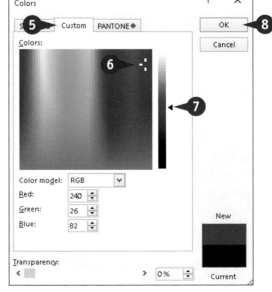

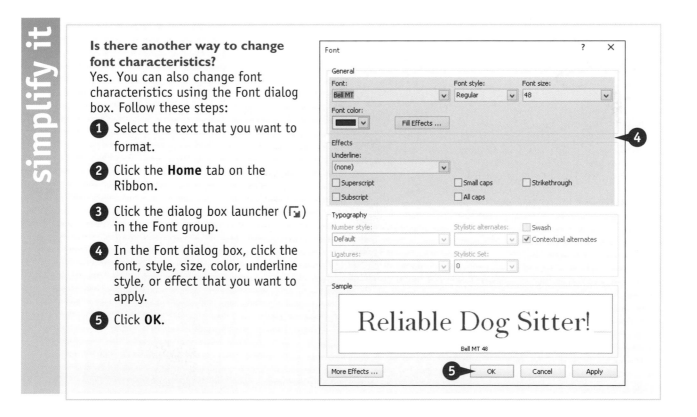

B Publisher applies the color to the text.

This example applies a red color.

Is there another way to change font characteristics?

Yes. You can also change font characteristics using the Font dialog box. Follow these steps:

1 Select the text that you want to format.

2 Click the **Home** tab on the Ribbon.

3 Click the dialog box launcher (⌐▪) in the Font group.

4 In the Font dialog box, click the font, style, size, color, underline style, or effect that you want to apply.

5 Click **OK**.

Apply a Text Effect

In addition to changing the font, size, and color of text in your publication, you can also apply text effects. These include a shadow effect, a reflection effect, a glow effect, and a bevel effect. Text effects can go a long way toward making your newsletter, brochure, postcard, or other type of publication appear more professional.

You apply text effects from the Format tab, under Text Box Tools. This tab appears on the Ribbon when you click in a text box or select text in your publication.

Apply a Text Effect

1 Select the text that you want to format.

2 Click the **Text Box Tools Format** tab.

3 Click **Text Effects**.

4 Point at the type of effect you want to apply to view a gallery of choices.

This example shows shadow effects.

5 Click an effect.

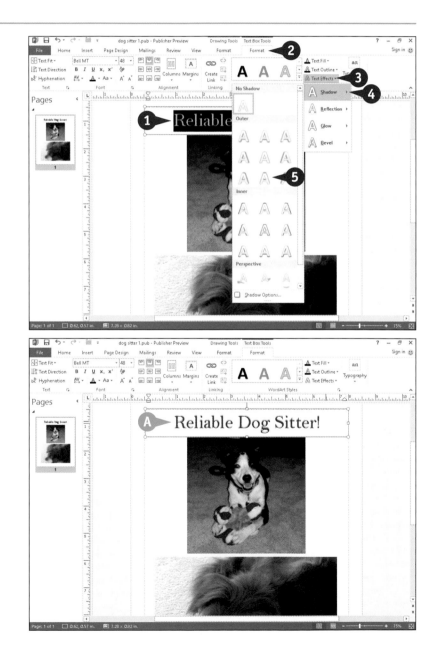

Ⓐ Publisher applies the text effect.

Change Text Alignment

Although each publication design automatically establishes an alignment to best suit the design, you can change the alignment to suit your own needs. You can use Publisher's alignment commands to change the way in which text is positioned both horizontally and vertically in a text object box. For example, you might choose to align text in the bottom right corner of the text object box. There are nine alignment options.

Change Text Alignment

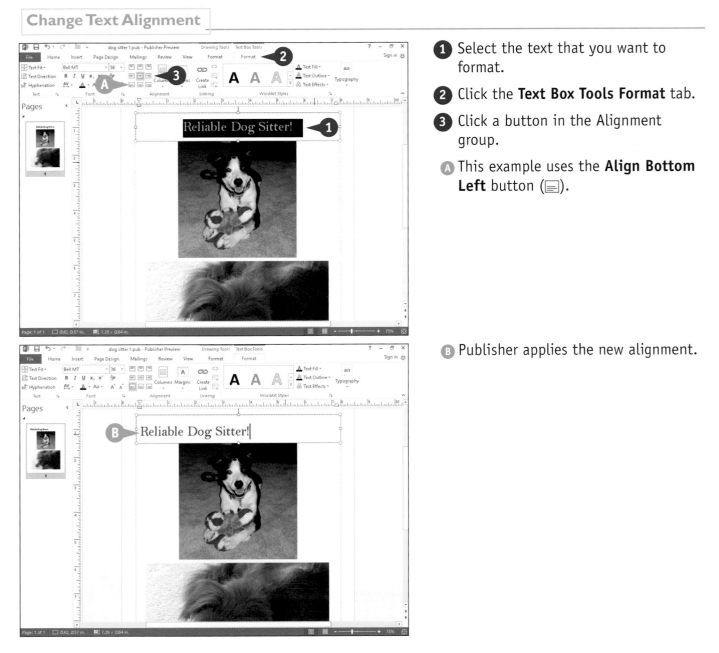

1 Select the text that you want to format.

2 Click the **Text Box Tools Format** tab.

3 Click a button in the Alignment group.

Ⓐ This example uses the **Align Bottom Left** button (▤).

Ⓑ Publisher applies the new alignment.

353

Add a Border

You can add a border to any object in a publication, including text boxes, clip art, and pictures, to add emphasis or make the publication more aesthetically appealing. Publisher comes with several predesigned border effects that you can apply to your publication.

These include borders of various colors, shapes, and thicknesses, with or without background shading. If none of these suits you, you can create your own custom borders — for example, making each border line a different color or thickness.

Add a Border

1 Select the text or object to which you want to apply a border.

2 Click the **Drawing Tools Format** tab.

3 Click a border style.

Ⓐ You can click the **More** button ($\overline{\ast}$) to display a gallery of borders from which to choose.

Ⓑ You can click **Shape Outline** to make selections from available line styles, colors, and weights.

Ⓒ Publisher applies the border to the object.

Ⓓ You can click **Change Shape** to view available shapes for the border.

Control Text Wrap

To add visual interest, many publications include text as well as objects, such as photographs, clip art images, tables, charts, or other visual elements. You can control the way in which text wraps around a picture, table, chart, or any other object in a publication. For example, you may want a column of text to wrap tightly around an object, to appear above and below the object but not on the sides, and so on.

Control Text Wrap

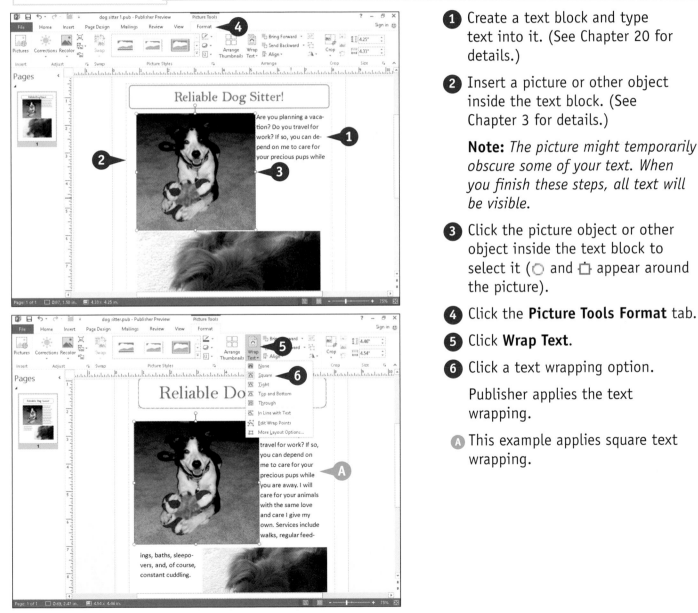

1 Create a text block and type text into it. (See Chapter 20 for details.)

2 Insert a picture or other object inside the text block. (See Chapter 3 for details.)

Note: *The picture might temporarily obscure some of your text. When you finish these steps, all text will be visible.*

3 Click the picture object or other object inside the text block to select it (○ and ⊕ appear around the picture).

4 Click the **Picture Tools Format** tab.

5 Click **Wrap Text**.

6 Click a text wrapping option.

Publisher applies the text wrapping.

Ⓐ This example applies square text wrapping.

Link Text Boxes

When you add too much text to a text object, any text that does not fit in the text box is called *overflow*. In some cases, Publisher attempts to correct this problem with its AutoFit feature, which reduces the size of your text to make it fit. Alternatively, you can correct the problem of overflow text by creating a new text box adjacent to the existing one, linking the two text boxes, and flowing the extra text into the new text box. You use the Linking tools on the Text Box Tools Format tab to navigate and connect text boxes in a publication.

Link Text Boxes

1. Create a text block and type text into it. (See Chapter 20 for details.)

   Note: *Type all the text you need, even though you cannot see all of it.*

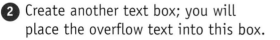

2. Create another text box; you will place the overflow text into this box.

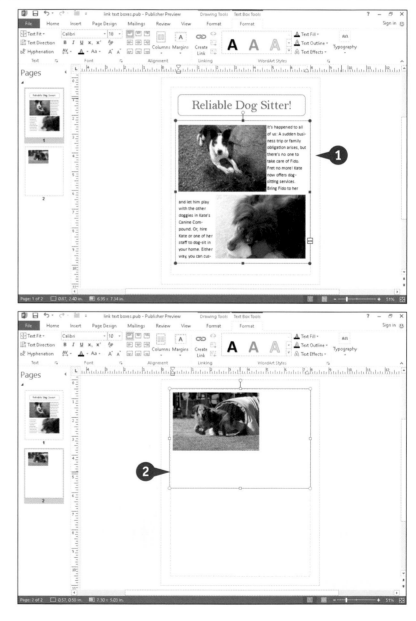

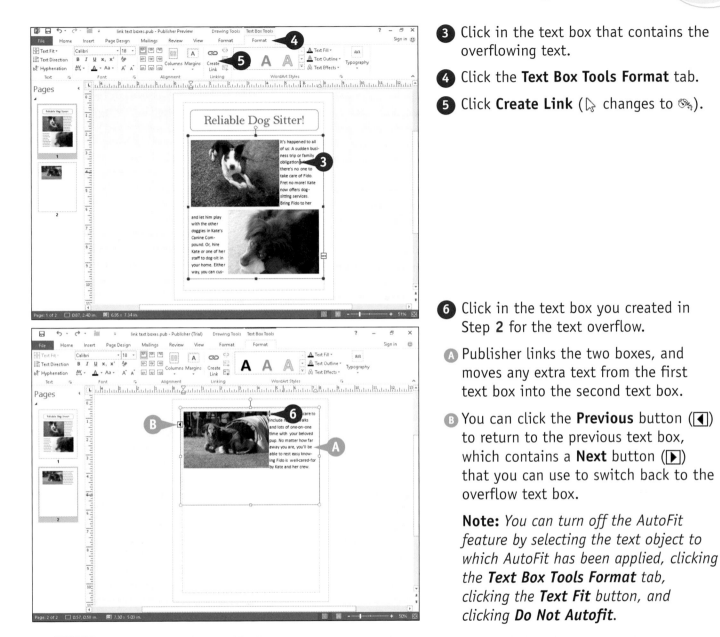

③ Click in the text box that contains the overflowing text.

④ Click the **Text Box Tools Format** tab.

⑤ Click **Create Link** (⟍ changes to ⟍).

⑥ Click in the text box you created in Step **2** for the text overflow.

Ⓐ Publisher links the two boxes, and moves any extra text from the first text box into the second text box.

Ⓑ You can click the **Previous** button (◀) to return to the previous text box, which contains a **Next** button (▶) that you can use to switch back to the overflow text box.

Note: *You can turn off the AutoFit feature by selecting the text object to which AutoFit has been applied, clicking the **Text Box Tools Format** tab, clicking the **Text Fit** button, and clicking **Do Not Autofit**.*

How do I break a link?
Click in the first linked text box, click the **Text Box Tools Format** tab, and then click the **Break** button (⟍).

Are there other ways to handle overflow?
Yes. You can also use Publisher's Text Fit tools to auto-fit your text into the text box. Click the text box to select it, click the **Text Box Tools Format** tab, click the **Text Fit** button, and choose **Best Fit**.

Edit the Background

You can add visual interest to your publication by changing the background. Clicking the Background button in the Page Design tab enables you to quickly choose from among several solid backgrounds and gradient backgrounds; alternatively, you can choose from a variety of textures, patterns, and tints, or even add one of your own photographs. If you decide you no longer want a background, you can quickly remove it.

You can change the background of your publication page by assigning a new background color, gradient effect, or texture.

Edit the Background

Apply a Background

1 Click the **Page Design** tab.

2 Click **Background**.

3 Click the background that you want to apply.

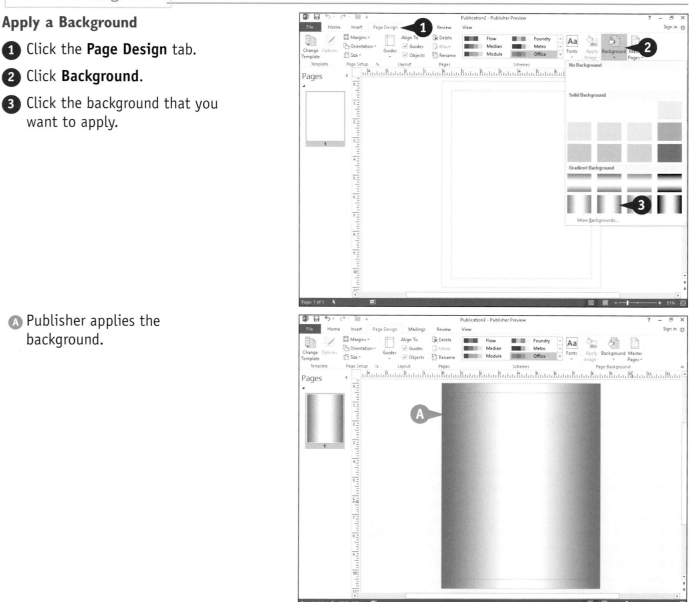

A Publisher applies the background.

Create a Picture Background

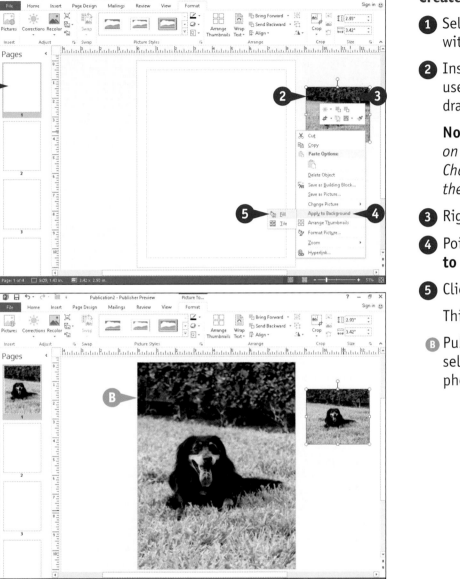

1. Select the page you want to fill with a background picture.

2. Insert the picture you want to use into your publication and drag it to the scratch area.

   Note: *See Chapter 3 for details on inserting a picture, and Chapter 20 for details on using the scratch area to swap pictures.*

3. Right-click the picture.

4. Point the mouse (⊳) at **Apply to Background**.

5. Click either **Fill** or **Tile**.

   This example uses Fill.

Ⓑ Publisher fills the page you selected in Step **1** with the photo or tiles of the photo.

simplify it

How do I remove a background?
Click the **Page Design** tab, click the **Background** button, and click at the left edge of the gallery under **No Background**. The option for no background is white and fades into the gallery, but as you move the mouse (⊳), the white square becomes visible.

Can I apply a custom background?
Yes. You can assign a one-color or two-color gradient background using colors you choose. You can also apply a texture, a pattern, or your own custom tint. You access these options from the Format Background dialog box. To open this dialog box, click the **Page Design** tab, click the **Background** button, and choose **More Backgrounds**.

PART VIII

OneNote

OneNote acts like a digital notebook; you can think of OneNote as a digital way to create yellow sticky notes. OneNote enables you to jot down ideas, sketch out plans, brainstorm business strategies, and compile scraps of information in one searchable, shareable, easy-to-access location. You might use OneNote to take notes during meetings and lectures, collect research materials from the web, and gather information about an upcoming trip. Within a notebook, you can create multiple pages and organize your notes by including related pages in a section. You also can have multiple OneNote notebooks and multiple sections within a notebook.

Navigate OneNote

You can digitally use OneNote the same way that you use physical binders, with the added improvement of being able to easily search and share your notes.

In OneNote, you can create notebooks in which you jot down ideas; sketch out plans; compile scraps of information; type, write, and draw your ideas; create tables; and paste in digital images such as a

screenshot of a web page or a photograph. You can divide notebooks into sections — represented as tabs — to organize them, and you can group sections containing related information together, as described in Chapter 23. This section introduces you to navigation in OneNote.

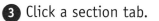

Navigate OneNote

① Click the **Show Notebook** ▼ to display a list of notebooks that you can open.

② Click the notebook you want to open.

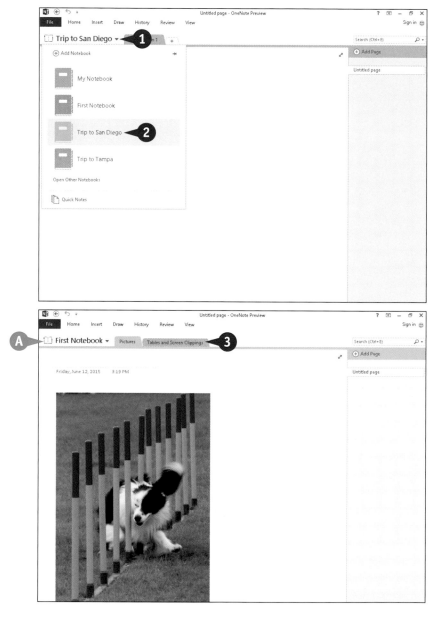

Ⓐ OneNote opens the notebook you clicked and displays the first section tab.

③ Click a section tab.

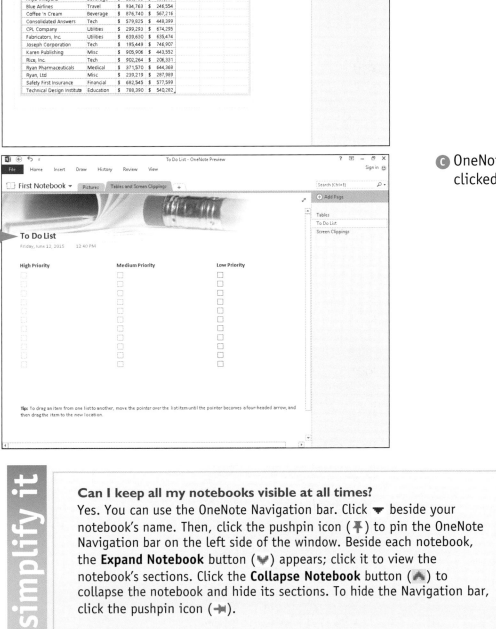

B OneNote displays the section tab you clicked.

4 Click a page in the tab.

C OneNote displays the page you clicked.

simplify it

Can I keep all my notebooks visible at all times?
Yes. You can use the OneNote Navigation bar. Click ▼ beside your notebook's name. Then, click the pushpin icon (📌) to pin the OneNote Navigation bar on the left side of the window. Beside each notebook, the **Expand Notebook** button (▼) appears; click it to view the notebook's sections. Click the **Collapse Notebook** button (▲) to collapse the notebook and hide its sections. To hide the Navigation bar, click the pushpin icon (📌).

Type and Draw Notes

You can jot down ideas in OneNote in a few ways. For example, you can type them using your keyboard. You can then format your text as desired, changing the font, size, and color; applying bold, italics, underline, subscript, or superscript formatting; and more.

Alternatively, you can use OneNote's drawing tools to sketch drawings, such as a map. And, on touch devices, you can use drawing tools to handwrite notes and then convert them to typewritten notes. Regardless of the method you use, you can move the notes you create around on the page as desired.

Type and Draw Notes

Type Notes

1 Click a section and a page on which you want to type a note.

2 Click the **Draw** tab.

3 Click **Type**.

4 Click the spot on the page where you want to type.

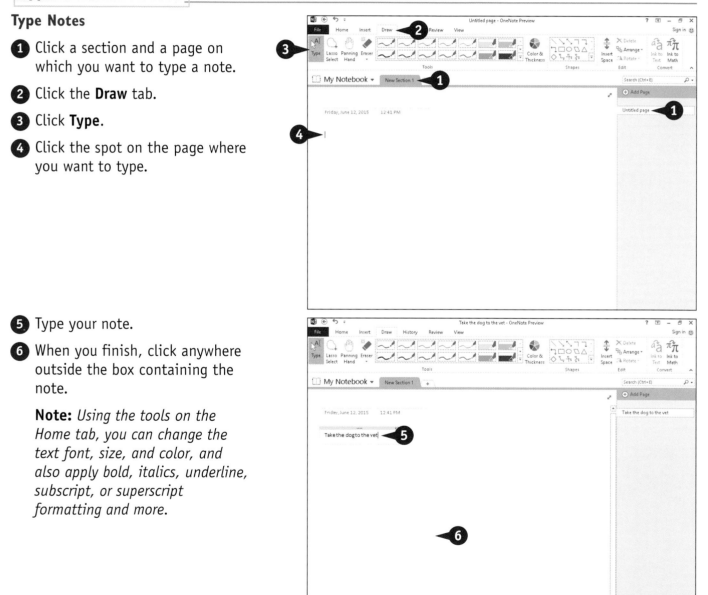

5 Type your note.

6 When you finish, click anywhere outside the box containing the note.

Note: *Using the tools on the Home tab, you can change the text font, size, and color, and also apply bold, italics, underline, subscript, or superscript formatting and more.*

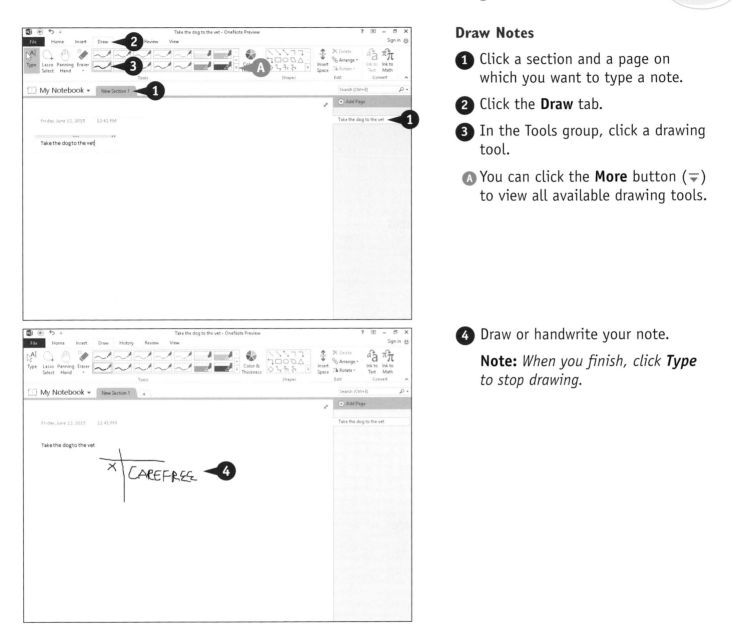

Draw Notes

1. Click a section and a page on which you want to type a note.

2. Click the **Draw** tab.

3. In the Tools group, click a drawing tool.

Ⓐ You can click the **More** button (▾) to view all available drawing tools.

4. Draw or handwrite your note.

Note: *When you finish, click* **Type** *to stop drawing.*

How do I move a note?

To move a typed note, position the mouse over the text; the note container appears. Position the mouse over the container's top; when I changes to ✥, click and drag the container to the desired location. To move a drawing, click the **Lasso Select** button on the Draw tab and draw a box around the drawing. Then click **Type** and move the mouse over the drawing (I changes to ✥); drag the drawing.

Can I convert handwriting to typing?

Yes. Click **Type**, drag the mouse (⟍) over the handwriting to select it, and click **Ink to Text**.

Insert and Format a Table

You can create sophisticated-looking tables in your notes. In addition to inserting and deleting rows in tables as needed, OneNote supports formatting options for cells, including shading them and hiding their borders. You can also align cell information to the left or right edge of the cell or center it within the cell. In addition, you can sort data in your table so you can organize and display information the way you want. You can also convert a table in OneNote to an Excel spreadsheet if you need to perform detailed analysis on the table data.

Insert and Format a Table

Insert a Table

1. Click in the notebook where you want the table to appear.

2. Click the **Insert** tab.

3. Click **Table** to display a table grid.

4. Slide the mouse (↖) across the squares that represent the number of rows and columns you want in your table.

5. Click the square representing the lower right corner of your table.

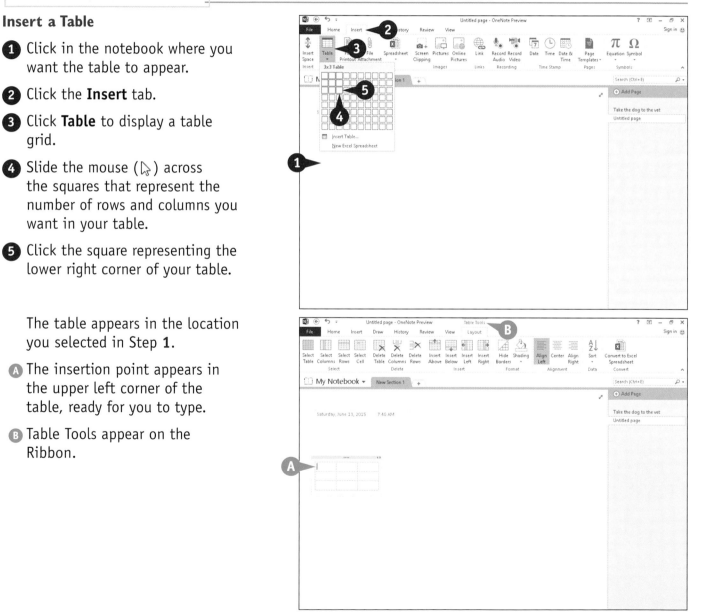

The table appears in the location you selected in Step **1**.

Ⓐ The insertion point appears in the upper left corner of the table, ready for you to type.

Ⓑ Table Tools appear on the Ribbon.

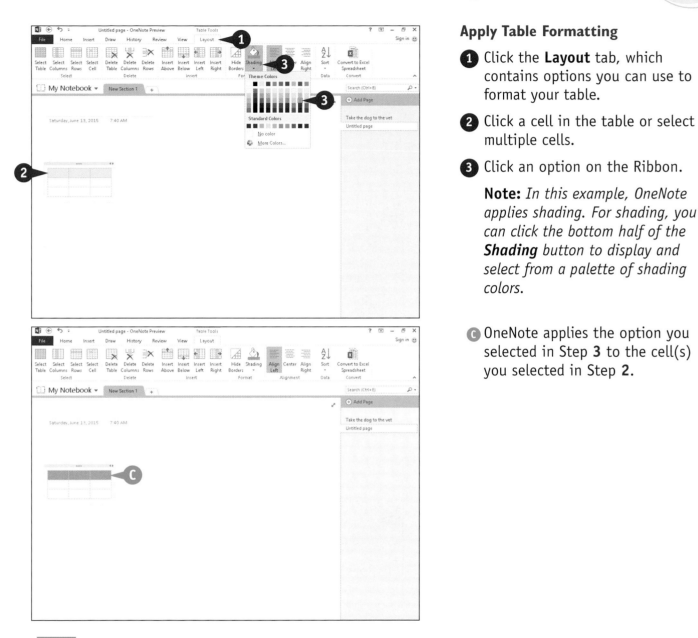

Apply Table Formatting

1 Click the **Layout** tab, which contains options you can use to format your table.

2 Click a cell in the table or select multiple cells.

3 Click an option on the Ribbon.

Note: *In this example, OneNote applies shading. For shading, you can click the bottom half of the* **Shading** *button to display and select from a palette of shading colors.*

C OneNote applies the option you selected in Step **3** to the cell(s) you selected in Step **2**.

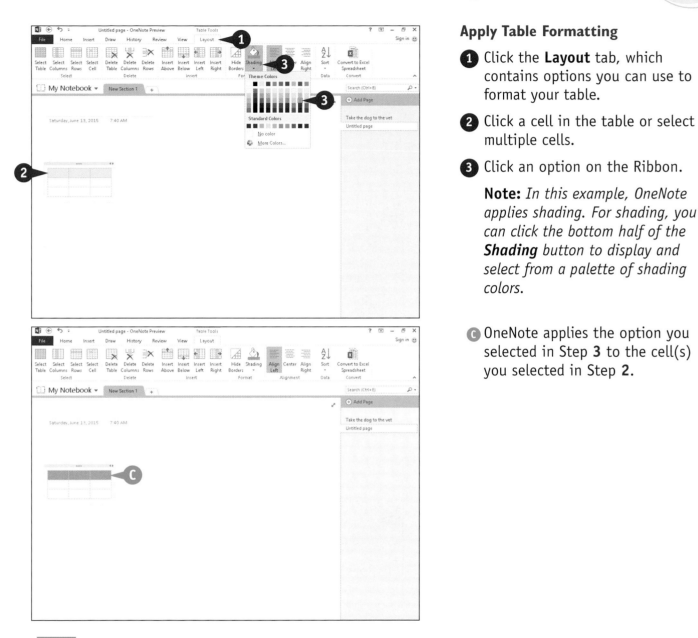

simplify it

How do I select more than one cell?
Selecting multiple cells is useful when you want to apply the same option to several table cells. Click in the first cell you want to select and drag either across or down to select adjacent cells. You can select nonadjacent sets of cells if you press and hold Ctrl + Shift as you drag across each cell you want to select.

How do I delete a table?
Click in the table, click **Layout** on the Ribbon, and then click the **Delete Table** button.

Attach Files to Notes

Sometimes it is helpful to attach a document or other file to a page in OneNote. For example, suppose you have created a spreadsheet for expense account transactions in Microsoft Excel; you can attach that spreadsheet to a OneNote page devoted to work. Likewise, you could attach a PowerPoint presentation to a OneNote page devoted to a business meeting that you plan to attend.

When you attach a file to a note in a OneNote notebook, an icon for that file appears on the note; you can double-click the icon to open the file.

Attach Files to Notes

1 Click a section and a page on which you want to attach a file.

2 Click the place on the page where you want the file attachment to appear.

3 Click the **Insert** tab.

4 Click **File Attachment**.

The Choose a File or a Set of Files to Insert dialog box opens.

5 Locate and select the file you want to insert.

6 Click **Insert**.

OneNote displays the Insert File window.

7 Click **Attach File**.

A OneNote inserts an icon for the file.

You can move the shortcut icon as needed by dragging it.

You can double-click the icon to open the program associated with it and work with the file.

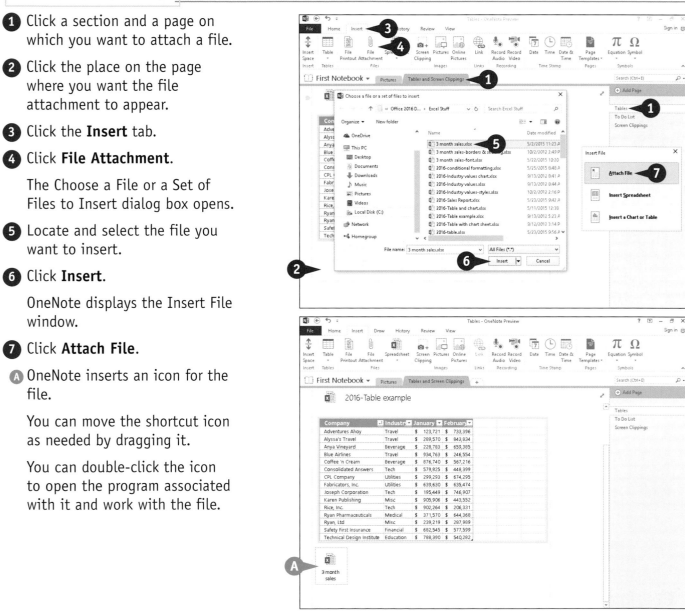

Create a Quick Note

Even if OneNote is not open, you can create a Quick Note to quickly jot down information. You can position Quick Notes anywhere on your screen and leave them there for as long as you need to refer to them. When you no longer need a particular Quick

Note, you can close its window. As soon as you create a Quick Note, OneNote saves it to your OneNote notebook, so you can view it again from OneNote.

Create a Quick Note

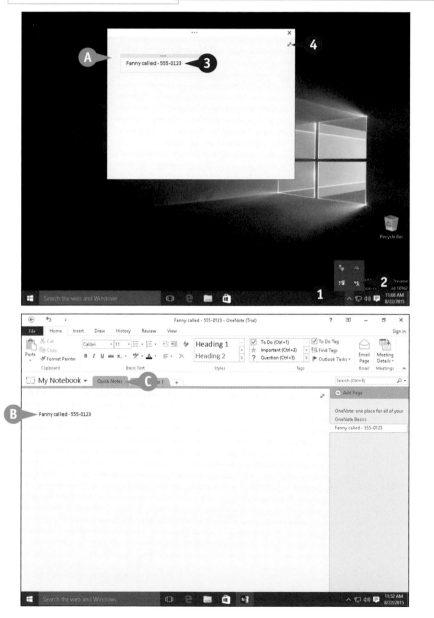

1 In the Windows system tray area, click the **Show Hidden Icons** button (⌃).

2 Click the **Send to OneNote** button (⧉).

A A Quick Note window appears.

3 Type your note.

Note: *To format note text, select it and use the commands on the Mini Toolbar.*

4 Click the **Normal View** button (⤢).

B One Note opens and displays the Quick Note.

C The Quick Note appears with your other Quick Notes on the Quick Notes section in OneNote.

Insert a Screen Clipping

You can use OneNote's Screen Clipping tool to capture parts of anything you can view on-screen — including program interfaces, documents and web pages — and paste them into OneNote. Suppose that you compose a letter in Word or create a worksheet in Excel. You can send a copy of your work in a OneNote notebook.

Think of using the OneNote Screen Clipping tool as a quick and easy way to copy and paste information. If you have multiple documents open in multiple programs, the OneNote Clipping tool assumes you want to copy information from the document on-screen.

Insert a Screen Clipping

1 Open any document in any Office program.

This example uses a letter in Word.

2 In the Windows system tray area, click the **Show Hidden Icons** button ().

3 Right-click the **Send to OneNote** button (🗒).

4 Click **Take screen clipping**.

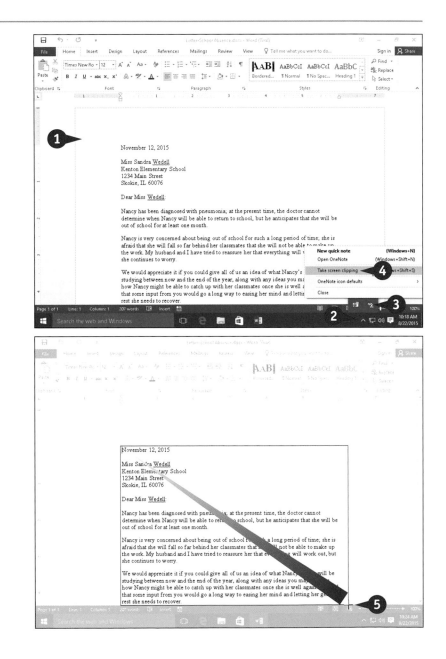

The OneNote Screen Clipping tool prompts you to select the content you want to place in OneNote.

5 Drag to select content.

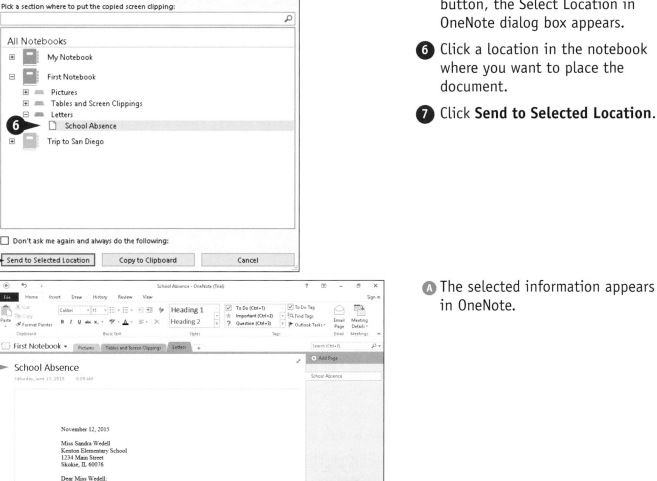

When you release the mouse button, the Select Location in OneNote dialog box appears.

6 Click a location in the notebook where you want to place the document.

7 Click **Send to Selected Location**.

Ⓐ The selected information appears in OneNote.

simplify it

What does the prompt mentioned after Step 4 look like, and what should I do with it?
It is a Windows 10 prompt with no action required other than to do what it suggests. If you want, you can click ✕ to close it; if you ignore the prompt, it hides itself after a few moments.

> **Microsoft OneNote 2016**
> Select a region of the screen to create a screen clipping, or click anywhere to cancel.

Record an Audio Note

If you are attending a significant meeting or participating in an important conference call, you can use OneNote to record it and store the recording as part of your notes. As you record, you can type notes into OneNote; when you do, OneNote links the note to the recording, displaying a small icon

alongside it. You can then click this icon to listen to the audio that was recorded at the time you typed the note.

To record audio, you must have a microphone. Most laptop and tablet PCs come with microphones built in. Ask permission before recording someone.

Record an Audio Note

1 With the page to which you want to attach a file open in OneNote, click the **Insert** tab.

2 Click **Record Audio** and begin speaking.

OneNote begins recording.

Ⓐ A shortcut icon for the audio file appears.

Ⓑ The Audio & Video Recording tab appears, displaying playback controls.

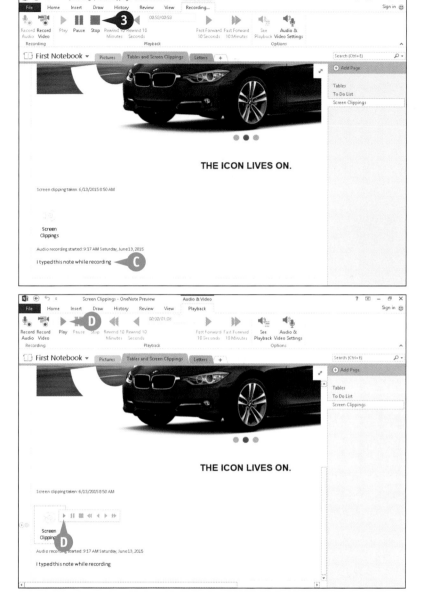

C You can type a note as you record, and OneNote links the note to the recording.

3 To stop recording, click **Stop**.

OneNote stops recording.

D To listen to the recording, click the audio recording icon and then click ▶. Or, click **Play** on the Ribbon.

Can I record video notes?
Yes, if your computer features a webcam. Click the **Record Video** button on the Insert tab. OneNote displays the Audio & Video Recording tab and launches a video screen in which you can view the footage as it is recorded. To stop recording, click the **Stop** button on the Ribbon.

What kind of audio settings can I control?
You can select an audio device, a *codec* — which is the program that encodes and decodes digital data — and a format, which controls the speed of the recording and often determines the quality of the recording.

Create a New Notebook

You can create as many notebooks as you want. For example, you might create a notebook to hold notes for a trip you are planning or a notebook to hold information relating to a home project.

New notebooks contain one section and one page by default; you can add more sections and pages

as needed. See the sections "Create a New Section" and "Create a New Page" for details. When you create a new notebook, you specify where the notebook should be stored — on the web, on a network, or on your computer.

Create a New Notebook

1 Click the **File** tab.

2 Click **New**.

3 Choose a place to store the notebook.

In this example, OneNote saves the notebook to the computer's hard drive.

4 Type a name for the notebook.

Ⓐ To save the notebook somewhere other than the default folder, click **Create in a different folder** and select the folder in which to save the notebook.

5 Click **Create Notebook**.

Ⓑ OneNote creates a new notebook.

Ⓒ The new notebook contains one section.

Ⓓ The section contains one page.

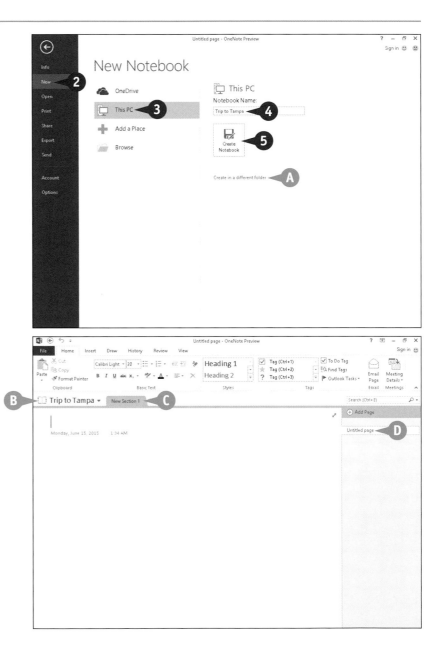

Create a New Section

You can use sections in notebooks to help you organize information. For example, if you are planning a trip to multiple cities, you might want to create new sections for each city.

You can easily add new sections to notebooks. OneNote names each new section as New Section 1, New Section 2, and so on, by default, but you can also rename the sections. For help renaming sections, see the section "Rename a Section or Page."

Create a New Section

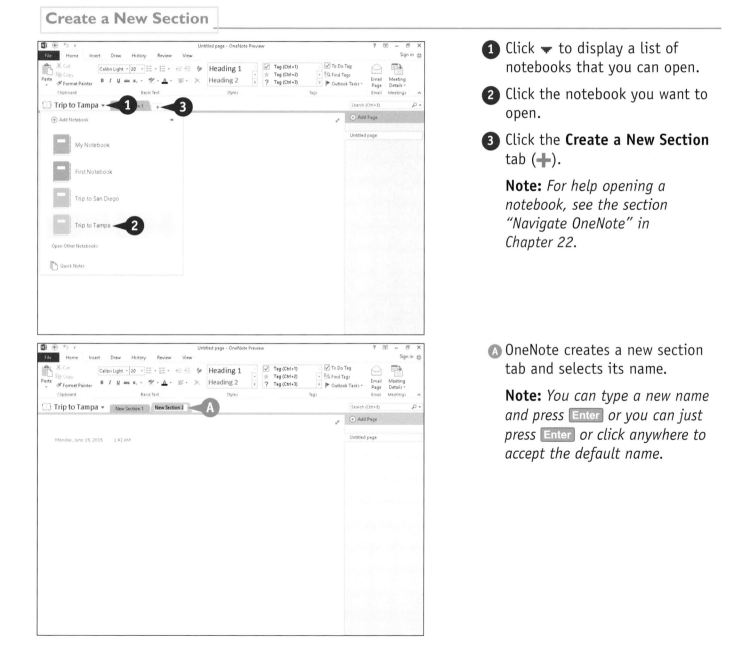

① Click ▼ to display a list of notebooks that you can open.

② Click the notebook you want to open.

③ Click the **Create a New Section** tab (➕).

Note: *For help opening a notebook, see the section "Navigate OneNote" in Chapter 22.*

Ⓐ OneNote creates a new section tab and selects its name.

Note: *You can type a new name and press* Enter *or you can just press* Enter *or click anywhere to accept the default name.*

Create a New Page

You can easily add new pages to a notebook section. For example, if you are using OneNote to plan a vacation, you might create a notebook with one page for each phase of the trip or for travel arrangements, hotel arrangements, and sites to visit. Or if you are using OneNote to plan a meeting, you might create a notebook with one page for each topic the meeting will cover.

When you create a new page, you can opt to create a blank page, or you can create a page using a template — for example, to create a to-do list.

Create a New Page

1 Click the **Insert** tab.

2 Click **Page Templates**.

Ⓐ The Templates pane appears.

3 Click the name of a category to reveal templates available in that category.

4 Click a template.

Ⓑ OneNote creates a new page based on the template you selected.

Ⓒ The page title appears here.

Ⓓ To close the Templates pane, click ✖.

Ⓔ To create a blank, untitled page, you can click the **Add Page** button (⊕).

Note: *To move a page to a different section or notebook, right-click the page title and choose **Move or Copy**. In the Move or Copy Pages dialog box, click beside the notebook in which you want to store the page, click the desired section, and then click **Move** or **Copy**.*

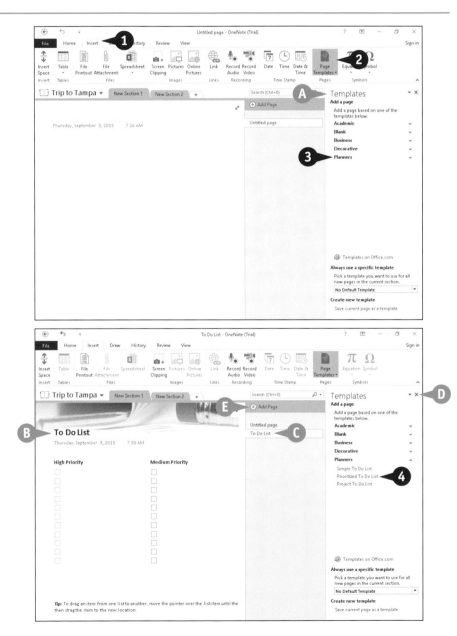

Rename a Section or Page

OneNote assigns new section names, such as New Section 1, New Section 2, and so on, by default. OneNote also assigns default names to pages.

You can assign your sections and pages more descriptive names to keep better track of where you have stored various pieces of information. For example, if your notebook relates to a project, you might create sections for each phase of the project and assign section names accordingly.

Rename a Section or Page

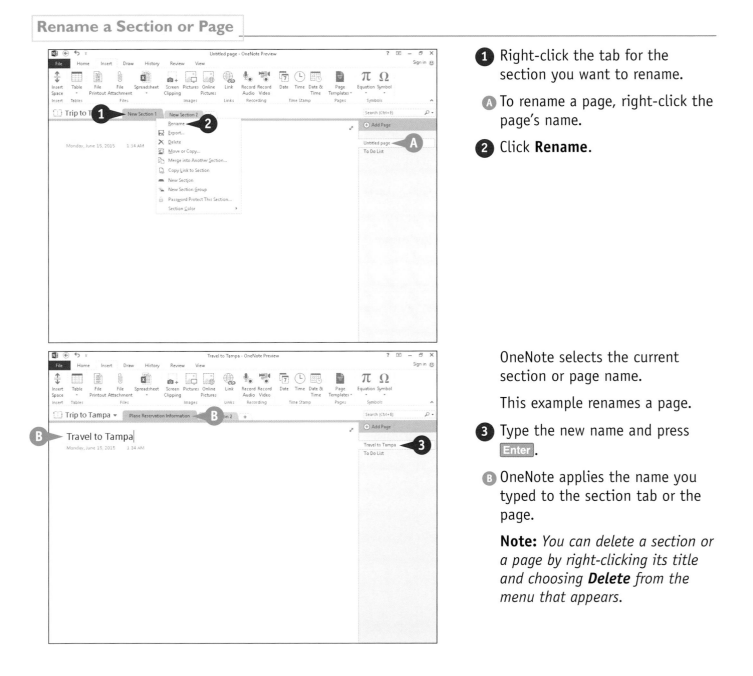

1 Right-click the tab for the section you want to rename.

A To rename a page, right-click the page's name.

2 Click **Rename**.

OneNote selects the current section or page name.

This example renames a page.

3 Type the new name and press **Enter**.

B OneNote applies the name you typed to the section tab or the page.

Note: *You can delete a section or a page by right-clicking its title and choosing **Delete** from the menu that appears.*

Group Sections

If your notebook contains several related sections, you can gather those sections into a group to make it easier to locate the section you need. For example, suppose that you are planning a vacation and have created a OneNote notebook to keep track of your research. You might gather the notebook's transportation-related sections — one with flight information, one for rental cars, one for hotel information, and so on — into a group. Or if you are using OneNote to jot down ideas for your business, you might gather all the sections that pertain to a particular project in one group.

Group Sections

1 Right-click any section.

2 Click **New Section Group**.

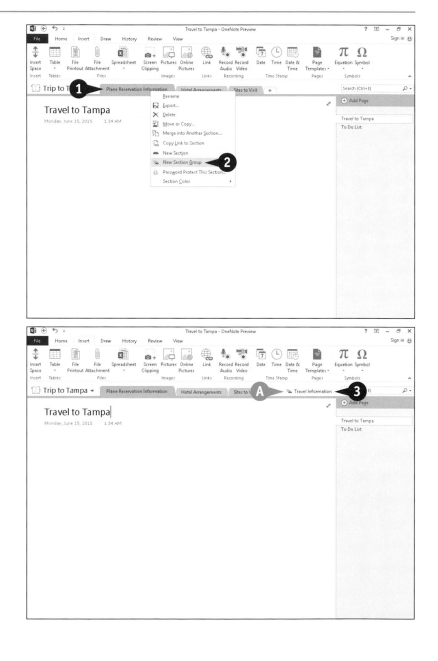

OneNote creates a new section group.

Ⓐ 🗁 appears on section group tabs.

3 Type a name for the section group and press Enter.

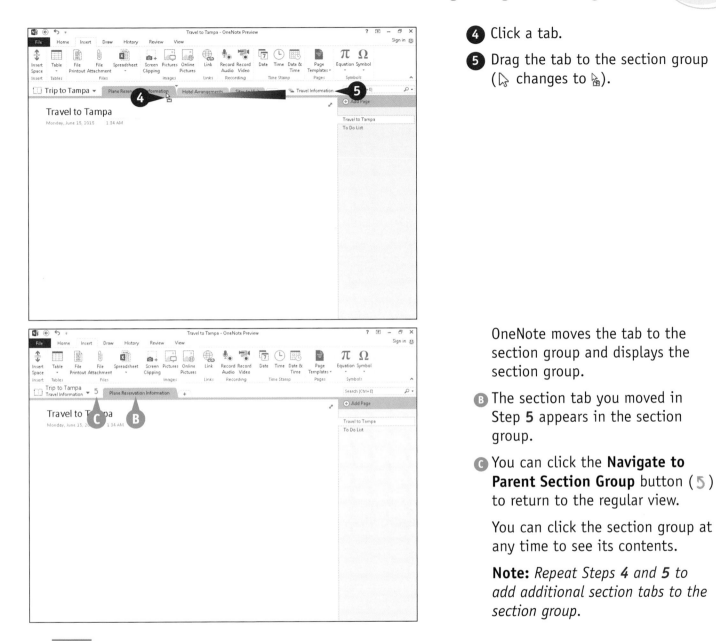

④ Click a tab.

⑤ Drag the tab to the section group (◻ changes to ◻).

OneNote moves the tab to the section group and displays the section group.

Ⓑ The section tab you moved in Step **5** appears in the section group.

Ⓒ You can click the **Navigate to Parent Section Group** button (5) to return to the regular view.

You can click the section group at any time to see its contents.

Note: *Repeat Steps 4 and 5 to add additional section tabs to the section group.*

---

simplify it

Can I remove a section tab from a group?
Yes. Click the section group, click the tab you want to move, and drag it to the **Navigate to Parent Section Group** button (5).

Can I change the order in which sections appear?
Yes. Click the tab for the section you want to move, drag the tab to the desired position among the sections, and release the mouse button. You can also change the order of pages in a section; to do so, click the page title and drag it up or down to the desired position among the pages.

Search
Notes

As you enter more notes into OneNote, you may find it difficult to locate the information you need. Fortunately, OneNote offers a robust search function. Using it, you can locate any text in your OneNote notebooks — even text found in graphics. You can limit your search to a particular notebook or section or search all notebooks and sections. If you have enabled OneNote's Audio Search feature, you can also search audio and video for spoken words. Note that in order to search audio and video, you must enable the Audio Search function. For help, see the Simplify It tip.

Search Notes

Set the Search Scope

1 Click the **Search** ▼.

A A list of OneNote elements that you can search appears.

2 From the list, click the OneNote element you want to search.

This example uses All Notebooks.

Conduct a Search

1 Click in the OneNote search box.

B A drop-down list appears, displaying previous search results.

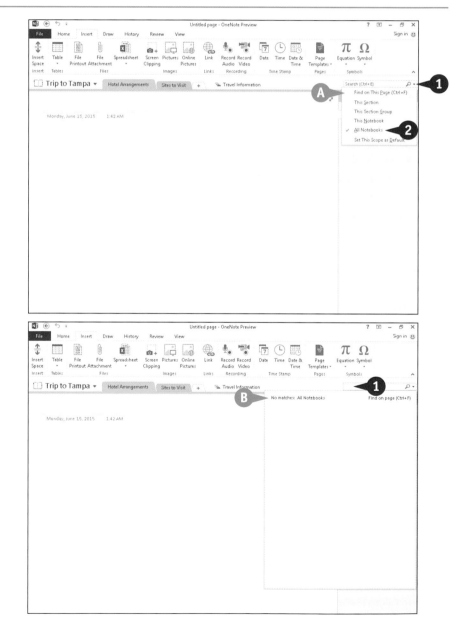

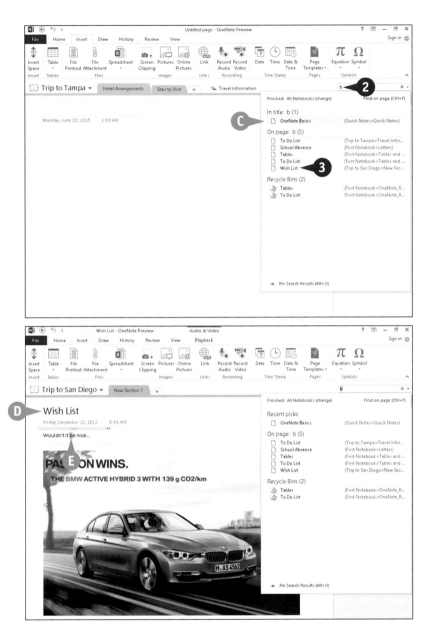

2 Type your search text.

C As you type, potential matches to your search criteria appear.

3 Click a match to view the page.

D OneNote displays the page you selected in Step **3**.

E OneNote highlights the search text.

How do I search audio and video?
To search audio and video, you must enable OneNote's Audio Search function. To do so, click the **File** tab and choose **Options**. In the OneNote Options dialog box that appears, click **Audio & Video** and select **Enable searching audio and video recordings for words** (☐ changes to ☑). The Audio Search dialog box appears; click the **Enable Audio Search** button. Finally, click **OK** to close the OneNote Options dialog box.

Search for Recent Edits

You can search for recent changes that you have made in OneNote. Suppose that you made a change to your notebook that you want to view, but you cannot remember exactly where in your notebook you made the change. You can search the current notebook, section, section group, or all notebooks.

You can search for any change you might have made today, since yesterday, within the last 7, 14, or 30 days, within the last 3 months, or within the last 6 months. Or, you can search for changes made to all pages sorted by date.

Search for Recent Edits

1 Click the **History** tab.

2 Click **Recent Edits**.

3 Click a timeframe.

Ⓐ OneNote opens the Search Results pane and displays pages in the current notebook that you have edited in the timeframe you selected in Step **3**.

You can click any page in the list to view that page; edits appear highlighted in yellow.

Ⓑ You can click ▼ to change the elements OneNote searches.

Ⓒ You can click ▼ to control the order in which the search results appear.

4 Click ✕ to close the Search Results pane.

Set Synchronization Options

OneNote enables you to store your notebooks in the cloud, and, when you do, OneNote keeps them synchronized and up to date by default. You can access them using the OneNote web app on any computer running Windows 7 or later, and many mobile devices.

But there may be times when you want or need to synchronize changes manually. For example, suppose that you want to synchronize notebook changes to the cloud before you shut down your computer. OneNote enables you to check sync status as well as synchronize your changes manually.

Set Synchronization Options

1 Click the **File** tab.

2 Click **Info**.

3 Click **View Sync Status**.

OneNote displays the Shared Notebook Synchronization window.

4 Select a synchronization method (○ changes to ⦿).

This example uses the **Sync manually** option.

5 Click the **Sync All** button or an individual notebook's **Sync Now** button.

OneNote synchronizes changes to the cloud.

Note: *To continue automatic synchronization, click* **Sync automatically whenever there are changes**.

6 Click **Close**.

Share Notes with People Who Do Not Have OneNote

You can share pages in your OneNote notebooks with others who do not have OneNote by emailing the pages or by converting them to PDF or XPS files. When you email pages from OneNote, it starts your email program, creates a new message containing the OneNote page in HTML, and applies the page's title to the message's Subject line. You enter the recipient's address and additional text and send the message.

You can also convert note pages, sections, or entire notebooks into PDF or XPS format so that you can distribute them to others who do not have OneNote.

Share Notes with People Who Do Not Have OneNote

Email a Note Page

① Display the page you want to email in OneNote.

② Click the **Home** tab.

③ Click **Email Page**.

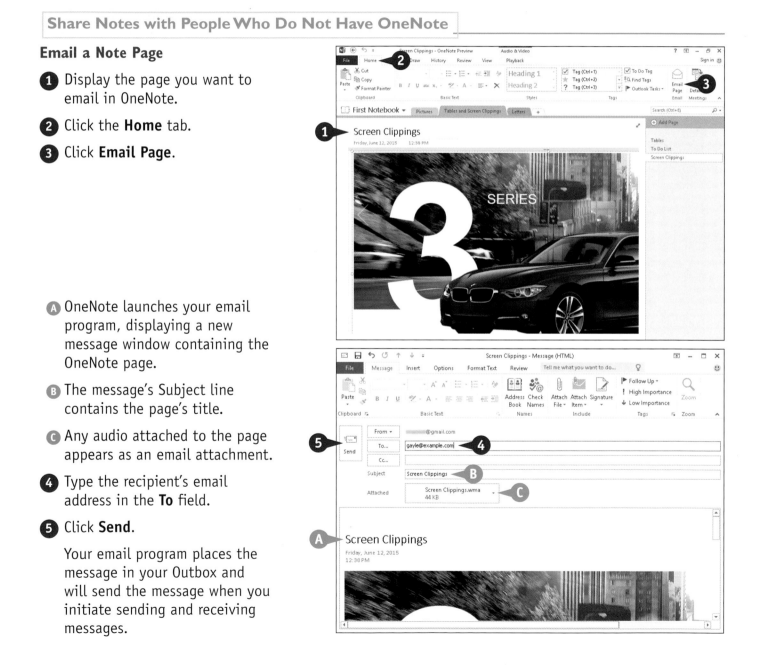

Ⓐ OneNote launches your email program, displaying a new message window containing the OneNote page.

Ⓑ The message's Subject line contains the page's title.

Ⓒ Any audio attached to the page appears as an email attachment.

④ Type the recipient's email address in the **To** field.

⑤ Click **Send**.

Your email program places the message in your Outbox and will send the message when you initiate sending and receiving messages.

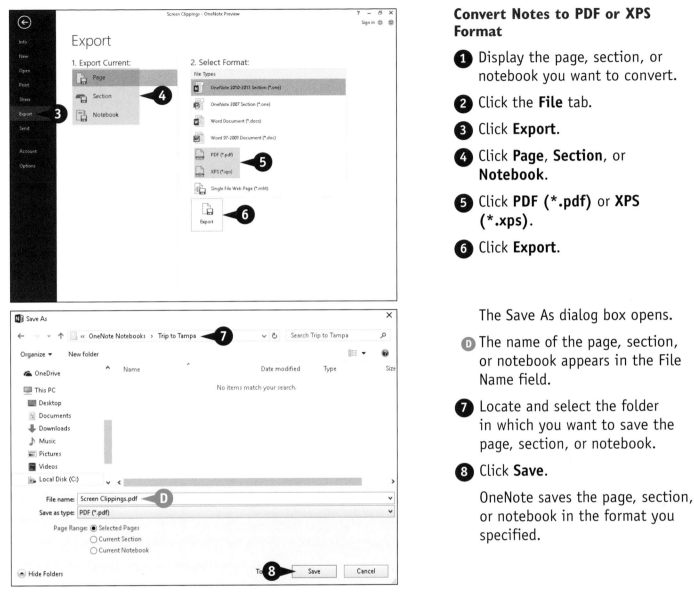

Convert Notes to PDF or XPS Format

1 Display the page, section, or notebook you want to convert.

2 Click the **File** tab.

3 Click **Export**.

4 Click **Page**, **Section**, or **Notebook**.

5 Click **PDF (*.pdf)** or **XPS (*.xps)**.

6 Click **Export**.

The Save As dialog box opens.

D The name of the page, section, or notebook appears in the File Name field.

7 Locate and select the folder in which you want to save the page, section, or notebook.

8 Click **Save**.

OneNote saves the page, section, or notebook in the format you specified.

simplify it

Can I send a OneNote page as a PDF attachment to an email message?
Yes. Display the page. Click the **File** tab, click **Send**, and click **Send as PDF**. Your email program opens and displays a message with the OneNote page attached as a PDF file, and the page name appears in the Subject line, or, if the page is untitled, One Note Notes appears in the Subject line. Type a recipient name and send the message.

Index